MADE IN MEXICO

MADE IN MEXICO

Regions, Nation, and the State
in the Rise of Mexican Industrialism,
1920s–1940s

Susan M. Gauss

The Pennsylvania State University Press
University Park, Pennsylvania

Library of Congress Cataloging-in-Publication Data

Gauss, Susan M., 1968–
Made in Mexico : regions, nation, and the state in the rise of Mexican industrialism, 1920s–1940s / Susan M. Gauss.
    p. cm.
Includes bibliographical references and index.
Summary: "Traces conflicts in Mexico over regional authority and labor-employer relations between the state and competing industrialist and labor groups in Guadalajara, Mexico City, Monterrey, and Puebla from the 1920s to the 1950s"—Provided by publisher.
ISBN 978-0-271-03759-2 (cloth : alk. paper)
ISBN 978-0-271-03760-8 (pbk. : alk. paper)
    1. Industries—Mexico—History.
    2. Mexico—Economic policy.
    I. Title.

HC135.G348 2011
338.097209′041—dc22
2010036084

Copyright © 2010 The Pennsylvania State University
All rights reserved
Printed in the United States of America
Published by The Pennsylvania State University Press,
University Park, PA 16802-1003

The Pennsylvania State University Press is a member of the Association of American University Presses.

It is the policy of The Pennsylvania State University Press to use acid-free paper. Publications on uncoated stock satisfy the minimum requirements of American National Standard for Information Sciences—Permanence of Paper for Printed Library Material, ANSI Z39.48-1992.

Contents

Acknowledgments vii

Abbreviations xi

Introduction 1

1
The Politics of State Economic Intervention from the Revolution to the Great Depression 24

2
"Jalisco, Open Your Arms to Industry":
Industrialism and Regional Authority in Guadalajara in the 1930s and 1940s 53

3
The Passion and Rationalization of Mexican Industrialism:
Rival Visions of State and Society in the Early 1940s 94

4
Sowing Exclusion:
Machinery, Labor, and Industrialist Authority in Puebla in the 1940s 131

5
The Politics of Nationalist Development in Postwar Mexico City 169

6
Recentering the Nation: Industrial Liberty in Postrevolutionary Monterrey 205

Conclusion 241

Bibliography 249

Index 276

Acknowledgments

I can think of no better way to begin these acknowledgments than by expressing my deep appreciation to the individuals and institutions in Mexico that work to preserve the documents that I used in researching this book. Without them, the past would be hidden, perhaps irretrievably, and the field of historical research greatly impoverished. I want to thank the Cámara de la Industria Textil de Puebla y Tlaxcala, where so many people went out of their way to supply me with the assistance and space to complete my research. The kind family of lawyer and PAN founder Manuel Gómez Morin gave me access to his papers. I particularly wish to acknowledge the late Don Mauricio and his wife Doña Elena, as well as their daughter Alejandra, and archive director Angélica Oliver for their warm welcome and delightful conversation. The archivists at the state and municipal archives in both Guadalajara and Monterrey shared their knowledge about and enthusiasm for regional research with me, and they were indispensable for the development of this project. I am also grateful to Leticia Fuentes Aquino at the Biblioteca Miguel Lerdo de Tejada for her tireless searches and friendly discussions. Additionally, I owe thanks to the archivists at the Archivo General de la Nación, whose professionalism and interest propelled my research along. At critical moments in its earliest stages, Leticia Gamboa Ojeda at the Universidad Autónoma de Puebla, and Javier Garciadiego, the late Víctor Urquidi, Carlos Marichal, and Blanca Torres at El Colegio de México offered insights, institutional support, and key contacts that facilitated this project.

The generous support of both a Fulbright-García Robles Grant and an American Philosophical Society Franklin Research Grant provided the resources to complete long stretches of archival work in Mexico. Financial assistance in the form of a Stony Brook Graduate Fellowship Award in the Humanities and Social Sciences also helped. Finally, both the University at Albany and United University Professions funded research trips and, most importantly, time off from teaching to complete the writing of this manuscript.

I owe many, many thanks to Paul Gootenberg. His incisive critiques, enthusiasm for historical political economy, generosity, and warm friendship helped to carry this project from its earliest conception through its incarnation as a book. I had the inestimable fortune to work with Barbara Weinstein and Temma Kaplan during the course of this project. They have inspired me, educated me, and befriended me, and I will always be grateful for that. Ted Beatty graciously and with great forbearance read and critiqued many versions of this manuscript. His insights and enthusiasm are imprinted on this book. Also, I thank Richard Warren for his keen questions and comments, and Peter Winn, who exposed me to a world of Latin American literature that I may never have discovered without him. I am also deeply indebted to Liz Dore, who shared her knowledge and passion about Latin America with me during my undergraduate days. If not for her, this book would most likely instead be about Kenya. I am grateful to María Teresa Fernández Aceves, Julio Moreno, Andrew Paxman, and Rick Weiner, each of whom read and commented on substantial sections of the manuscript. Each sparked new and valuable lines of thinking, as well as rescued me from many errors; the errors that remain are wholly my own. Tere Fernández also helped me with archival research in Guadalajara, giving me information and access that I likely never would have gained without her. I presented various iterations of this project at the New York State Latin American History Workshop, at the New York City Workshop on Latin American History, and at the Latin American History Workshop at the University of Chicago. I benefited immeasurably from these discussions, and I want to thank Karin Rosemblatt, in particular, for her thoughtful commentary. I also want to thank my colleagues in the Department of History and the Department of Latin American, Caribbean, and U.S. Latino Studies at the University at Albany, SUNY, whose conviviality and zeal for scholarship created a wonderful setting to write this book. Edna Acosta-Belén, Iris Berger, Glyne Griffith, Richard Hamm, Amy Murrell Taylor, and Patricia Pinho, in particular, each contributed to this project in unique ways. Finally, I want to thank the two external readers at Penn State University Press, including Alan Knight, who provided incisive, extensive, and provocative critiques. They helped to improve the manuscript dramatically, along with the people at Penn State University Press, including the eminently professional and supportive Sandy Thatcher, as well as the meticulous copyeditor Patricia Rosas.

It is hard for me to separate the process of writing this book from the friends who have accompanied me along the way. Stephanie Smith and Patricia Vassos both appeared at a particularly important moment in my life during graduate school, and they have remained dear friends ever since.

While I was in Mexico and beyond, Elizabeth Bayley, Ted Beatty, Dina Berger, Sarah Buck, Steve Bunker, Alec Dawson, Tere Fernández, Emilio Kourí, Michael Krysko, Heather McCrea, Jolie Olcott, Stephen Patnode, Andrew Paxman, Nikki Sanders, and Katy Stewart shared camaraderie and laughter. I'd also like to thank Gene Lebovics for sharing his garden, food, wine, and *bonhomie* while I was writing the early drafts of this work.

My family sustained me through the long process of completing this book. My parents, Eugene and Marlene, gave me the greatest gifts, which were their confidence and joy in all that I did. I dedicate this book to my father and to the memory of my mother. My brother Gene and sister Christine and their families gave me love and encouragement. My sister, in particular, showed unwavering faith and interest in the project. Even more, she and my father provided invaluable technical expertise about textile manufacturing and steel production, respectively. Most importantly, I want to thank Eduardo González, my best friend, ardent advocate, and inspiration for things to come. His intelligence, humor, and integrity have helped to create a warm home in all of the places we have lived. To him, as well as to our delightful son Luca, I will always be grateful.

Abbreviations

ABM	Asociación de Banqueros de México
	Mexican Bankers Association
AETPT	Asociación de Empresarios Textiles de Puebla y Tlaxcala
	Association of Textile Entrepreneurs of Puebla and Tlaxcala
CANACINTRA	Cámara Nacional de la Industria de Transformación
	National Chamber of Manufacturing Industry
CAOLJ	Confederación de Agrupaciones Obreras Libertarias de Jalisco
	Confederation of Libertarian Workers Groups of Jalisco
CEIMSA	Compañía Exportadora e Importadora Mexicana, S.A.
	Mexican Export and Import Company
CGT	Confederación General de Trabajadores
	General Confederation of Workers
CIM	Centro Industrial Mexicano
	Mexican Industrial Center
COJ	Confederación Obrera de Jalisco
	Labor Confederation of Jalisco
CONCAMIN	Confederación de Cámaras Industriales
	Confederation of Industrial Chambers
CONCANACO	Confederación de Cámaras Nacionales de Comercio
	Confederation of National Chambers of Commerce
CONCANACOMIN	Confederación de Cámaras Nacionales de Comercio y de Industria
	Confederation of National Chambers of Commerce and Industry
COPARMEX	Confederación Patronal de la República Mexicana
	Mexican Employers Association

CPN	Confederación Proletaria Nacional
	National Proletarian Confederation
CROM	Confederación Regional Obrera Mexicana
	Regional Confederation of Mexican Workers
CTM	Confederación de Trabajadores de México
	Confederation of Mexican Workers
ECLA	Economic Commission for Latin America
FROC	Federación Regional de Obreros y Campesinos
	Regional Workers and Campesinos Federation
ISI	Import Substitution Industrialization
JCCA	Junta Central de Conciliación y Arbitraje
	Central Board of Conciliation and Arbitration
NAFINSA	Nacional Financiera, S.A.
	National Finance Bank
OIE	Departamento (or Oficina) de Investigaciones Económicas
	Office of Economic Research
OII	Oficina de Investigaciones Industriales
	Office of Industrial Research
PAN	Partido Acción Nacional
	National Action Party
PCM	Partido Comunista Mexicano
	Mexican Communist Party
PNR	Partido Nacional Revolucionario
	National Revolutionary Party
PRI	Partido Revolucionario Institucional
	Institutional Revolutionary Party
PRM	Partido de la Revolución Mexicana
	Party of the Mexican Revolution
SEN	Secretaría de la Economía Nacional
	Secretariat of the National Economy
SHCP	Secretaría de Hacienda y Crédito Público
	Secretariat of the Treasury and Public Credit
SICT	Secretaría de Industria, Comercio, y Trabajo
	Secretariat of Industry, Commerce, and Labor
STPS	Secretaría del Trabajo y Previsión Social
	Secretariat of Labor and Social Welfare
UNAM	Universidad Nacional Autónoma de México
	National Autonomous University of Mexico

INTRODUCTION

On October 21, 1952, President Miguel Alemán (1946–52) enacted a decree mandating that all clothing manufactured for domestic consumption carry a label stating "Hecho en México" and giving the product's region and factory of origin.[1] The provenance of the "Hecho en México" decree dated to 1927, when officials and producers perceived a crisis of consumer confidence in domestic goods.[2] Officials in 1952 cited quality and consistency problems when explaining consumer preference for imported goods. However, industrialists offered other explanations. Leaders of the National Chamber of Manufacturing Industry (Cámara Nacional de la Industria de Transformación, CANACINTRA), dominated by consumer manufacturers in Mexico City, instead pointed to cultural and psychological causes. In particular, they condemned the "Malinche complex," arguing that it led Mexican consumers to scorn nationally made goods in favor of foreign manufactures, even when they were of equal price and quality. Even more shameful, they complained, were the mercenary merchants who profited from this national affliction by actively encouraging the consumption of imported goods. CANACINTRA spokesmen concluded that the solution lay not in changes to prices or quality, but in the cultivation of a "national mystique that would convince consumers that whatever immediate sacrifice they would have to make by consuming nationally produced goods, even in terms of lower quality or higher prices, would soon bring economic independence and a considerable improvement in standards of living for

1. Secretaría de Economía, Secretaría Particular del Presidente Alemán, and manufacturers, correspondence, October 1952–January 1953, Fondo Dirección General de Industrias (DGI)/Archivo General de la Nación (AGN), v. 27, 391/300 (03)/-1–16, letra N.
2. Jefe, Departamento de Industrias, Secretaría de Industria, Comercio, y Trabajo (SICT) to Oficial Mayor, February 1927, Fondo Departamento del Trabajo (DT)/AGN, c. 1211, exp. 7.

all Mexicans."³ Although increased consumption of Mexican-made goods certainly would bring these manufacturers greater profits, their goal was to convince people that industrial development would eventually benefit all Mexicans.

The Alemán administration censured producers, especially textile manufacturers, for concealing the origins of their wares in an effort to raise prices on low-quality goods.⁴ The 1952 decree, as well as its predecessors, included provisions for fines and even imprisonment for producers who failed to label their goods as products of Mexico.⁵ Many scholars portray the Alemán administration as the highpoint of an alliance between the state and the national bourgeoisie that underpinned Mexico's "miracle" of midcentury economic growth and state power. Therefore, the 1952 decree is revealing because it shows that ruling-party officials still viewed industrialists as a threat to their project for statist industrialization.

Perceptions of this threat were not chimerical. They can be traced to postrevolutionary conflicts over regional variants of industrial development that arose between the state and industrialist and labor groups in Guadalajara, Mexico City, Monterrey, and Puebla. These competing industrial visions often lay bare regional industrialists' preoccupation with preserving aspects of local political power and managerial authority over labor-employer relations in the face of an increasingly interventionist state. This book traces these conflicts and visions in order to explore how mid-twentieth-century statist industrialism evolved as a fairly flexible, nationalist political project that encompassed the state's distinct relationships with regional industrialists based on accommodation, collaboration, and exclusion. These relationships, in turn, contributed to the consolidation of a stable ruling party during much of the rest of the century.

In this light, the 1952 decree appears as part of a broader crusade by the ruling party to unite producers and consumers behind the party's goals for statist development. After World War II, President Alemán initiated the Campaign for Economic Recovery (Campaña de Recuperación Económica), a widely supported campaign for economic development whose key

3. Colín, *Requisitos fundamentales*, 26, 35–36, 40–41; Lavín, "Dos conferencias," 13–16. Businessman and Secretary of the Economy Antonio Ruiz Galindo (1946–48) agreed that the "Malinche complex" was largely to blame for consumer preference for foreign goods. Ruiz Galindo to Alemán, September 10, 1947, Fondo Miguel Alemán Valdés (MAV)/AGN, exp. 433/133; Ruiz Galindo to Alemán, December 16, 1950, MAV/AGN, exp. 411/13044.

4. Warren Dean identified a similar problem in late nineteenth- and early twentieth-century Brazil, when merchants engaged in "reverse contraband" by disguising the origin of domestically produced goods in order to sell them at higher prices. Dean, *Industrialization of São Paulo*, 11.

5. Junta de la Directiva, Asociación de Empresarios Textiles de Puebla y Tlaxcala (AETPT), meeting minutes, March 17, 1943, Archivo de la Cámara de la Industria Textil de Puebla y Tlaxcala (CITPT), F-VI/LAJD-3; Moreno, *Yankee Don't Go Home!* 29–32.

missions were independence and collective welfare. These could be accomplished, President Alemán argued, by improving the quality of nationally manufactured goods in order to supplant the high-quality, low-priced imports flooding into Mexico and eating up its postwar monetary reserves.[6] To encourage support for the campaign, President Alemán linked it to the postrevolutionary cultural project of *mexicanidad* (mexicanness). Originally, mexicanidad had been framed to address the political and social turmoil that attended the reconstruction of the state and society after the violence of the Revolution. Its architects had sought to foster unity built upon conceptions of a national character defined by a common psychological and spiritual condition and located in Mexico's rural, agrarian roots.[7] Unlike earlier versions of mexicanidad, however, pride in national production and consumption of modern manufactured goods became the essence of President Alemán's definition. The campaign therefore proposed "to incorporate fifteen million Mexicans into the economic life of the nation" and to instruct them on the virtues of savings and responsible consumption. It also condemned the immoral and rapacious behavior of some merchants and industrialists whose actions betrayed the nation.[8] By tapping into the revolutionary and nationalist genealogy of mexicanidad, President Alemán promoted the potential of statist industrialism to achieve social justice and collective welfare. He concurrently affirmed the legitimacy of the claims by the ruling Institutional Revolutionary Party (Partido Revolucionario Institucional, PRI) that it was leading the moral and material regeneration of the Mexican nation.[9]

President Alemán's conception of mexicanidad, as with all assertions of national identity, divulged more about its proponents' aspirations than about

6. "Acotaciones al primer mensaje del Presidente Lic. Alemán," *Actividad*, December 15, 1946; various letters to Alemán, early 1947, MAV/AGN, exp. 708.1/5 and exp. 708.1/5-8; Secretaría de la Economía Nacional (SEN), memorandum, early 1947, MAV/AGN, exp. 708.1/5; Jesús Leal Carrillo, "Se cristalizan los deseos del C. Presidente de la República al establecerse una nueva industria en la Baja California," December 7, 1947, DGI/AGN, v. 25, 391/300 (03)/-1-9, letra H; Secretaría de Economía, "El esfuerzo económico de México," December 8, 1947, MAV/AGN, exp. 523/1; Secretario General de Gobierno de Jalisco Carlos G. Guzmán to municipal presidents, circular, March 22, 1947, Archivo Municipal de Guadalajara Salvador Gómez García (MGSGG), correspondencia, 1-02-48.

7. Schmidt, *Roots of "Lo Mexicano,"* xi–xii; Vaughan, *State, Education, and Social Class*, 239–66; Brandenburg, *Making of Modern Mexico*, 8–10; Glade, "Revolution and Economic Development," 28–32.

8. Antonio Ruiz Galindo to Héctor Martínez D'Meza (Banco de México), "Informe sobre la situación actual de las diversas industrias de transformación de México, política nacional al respecto, problemas más importantes y los medios empleados o que se intenta emplear para resolverlos," September 8, 1947, DGI/AGN, v. 26, 391/300 (03)/-1-11, letra J, p. 27, SEN, memorandum, early 1947, MAV/AGN, exp. 708.1/5.

9. PRI, *Programa de acción para 1947*, 16–17; "Enfáticamente lo anunció al ser investido como Presidente," *Excélsior*, December 2, 1946.

any sort of genuine national character or affinities. It ascribed a stability and uniformity to the Mexican industrial experience based on abstract ideas about economic independence, national regeneration, and collective welfare. Yet, the rival visions of political authority and modern social relations that influenced debates about industrialization among industrialists, labor, and the state between the 1920s and the early 1950s belied this official version of midcentury industrialism. Mexicanidad therefore helped to mask the fact that statist industrialism, although a nationalist project, was hardly a national one.

President Alemán was able to cast mexicanidad as a project for national economic recovery and moral regeneration because of the endorsement for protected industrialization he received from CANACINTRA and the Confederation of Mexican Workers (Confederación de Trabajadores de México, CTM). The leaders of CANACINTRA and the CTM supported President Alemán in part because they believed in the power of the state to resolve a looming postwar economic crisis and repress labor radicalism. They also viewed an alliance with the PRI as a means to secure official sanction for their influence over national industry and labor. In return, the alliance provided the ruling party with critical backing as it struggled to contain challenges from an array of labor and industrialist groups. It also enabled the state to pursue types of protected development that justified state economic intervention on a scale never before seen in Mexico's national history. In the process, the alliance helped to portray as a national phenomenon a version of statist industrialism largely derived from the urban industrial experience in the capital.[10]

After the Revolution, the political and ideological bankruptcy of late nineteenth-century economic liberalism and, by the 1950s, the rising influence of structuralists across Latin America secured the nationalist credentials of this pro-protectionist alliance.[11] It was also sustained by the apparent limits of postrevolutionary agrarianism as a project for political pacification and economic growth. Betraying those limits were persistent poverty, social

---

10. Similarly, see Hudson, "Introduction," in Hudson, *Regions and Industries*, 3.

11. The ECLA group used the term "structuralism" because of its focus on "structures, blockages, and imbalances." Its doctrine of unequal exchange argued that higher rates of technological innovation and higher wages in industrial "center" countries would lead to higher export prices and "oligopol[ies] in markets for manufactured goods" that would foster a deterioration in the terms of trade for dependent, peripheral, agriculture-exporting countries. Accordingly, protected industrialization was the only way to challenge inequality and underdevelopment. Love, "Rise and Fall of Economic Structuralism," 101–2.

unrest, rural-to-urban migration, and electoral fraud that outlasted the 1930s *cardenista* reforms. In this climate, industrialization appeared to be a way to free Mexico from revolutionary turbulence, economic backwardness, paternalism, and Catholic provincialism, which many technocrats and politicians believed were continuing to burden the country. Protectionist policies, including trade controls and tariffs, therefore became more than simply a means to enhance revenue or develop industry. They became the cornerstone of ruling-party efforts to forge political unity, achieve economic independence from the United States, and improve national standards of living. Protected industrialization, in turn, helped to spur the dramatic social, cultural, and economic transitions of mid-twentieth-century Mexico. As industry emerged as a motor of the Mexican economy, agriculture declined in relative importance. Mexico consequently changed from a predominantly rural, agrarian country to one that by the 1970s was largely urban, literate, and industrial. With these social and cultural transformations in mind, in this book "industrialism" does not denote solely the economic changes and transformations in the material basis of production that constituted the historical process of "industrialization." The use of "industrialism" here seeks also to capture and highlight the intellectual culture and popular mentalities that underpinned the different forms of political rule and modernizing social changes that also constituted industrialization.[12] Additionally, the dramatic expansion of the regulatory aims of the Mexican state after the Revolution, and especially beginning in the late 1940s, marked a departure from prior levels of state economic intervention, even if the state's capacity or will to direct industrialization remained uneven. Therefore, although the state has always influenced industrialization in some measure, this study refers to "statist" industrialism to emphasize this rupture and to underscore its political and social character.

For many social scientists, the domestic political and social influences behind the rise of Import Substitution Industrialization (ISI) are less significant than the global forces that they argue compelled much of Latin America to protect industry more aggressively in the middle of the twentieth century.[13] Most have mapped the rise of ISI as coming out of the ashes of the Great Depression or World War II. Some have portrayed it as a "healthy" or "natural" stage of modernizing development or the result of

---

12. Similarly, see Farnsworth-Alvear, *Dulcinea in the Factory*, 4.
13. ISI is a type of forced industrialization aimed at replacing imports and characterized by the use of protection to encourage the domestic production of manufactured goods.

cumulative shocks, dwindling trade options, missed opportunities, monetary concerns, or structural distortions and rigidities that prevented Latin American economies from responding to market cues.[14] For example, Enrique Cárdenas emphasized the Great Depression as being the first major shock to the export-oriented model of growth that had dominated in Latin America since the nineteenth century. According to Cárdenas, however, World War II provided the impetus for a maturation of Depression-era "spontaneous" import substitution into a conscious project to develop industry that would replace imports.[15] For others, World War II itself was the tipping point. Some called attention to a postwar "export pessimism" sparked by concerns about the devastation of former primary product markets in Europe and influenced by the writings of the Economic Commission for Latin America (ECLA) about the secular decline of Latin America's terms of trade.[16] Others, such as Rosemary Thorp, agreed that World War II caused a global disturbance in trade that exposed the vulnerability of export-led growth. Thorp added, however, that the difficulty of obtaining needed imports during the war was also a key factor spurring ISI.[17] By contrast, although others agreed that the Great Depression significantly influenced banking and commerce and prompted more state intervention, they found its impact on the rise of ISI across Latin America to be on a par with other factors reaching back to the nineteenth century.[18]

Together these varied accounts have evinced the broader economic determinants that have driven ISI as a historical process in Latin America. Structuralists from ECLA also noted these similarities, for example, by stressing the critical role of foreign-exchange constraints in encouraging ISI. However, as a developmental model to counteract midcentury economic crises, ISI has not been particularly agile when accounting for the distinct political and social trajectories attending protected industrialization across Latin America.[19] By emphasizing Mexico's relatively open economy and its unique postrevolutionary state, some scholars have already pinpointed the

14. Thorp, "Reappraisal"; Hirschman, "Political Economy of Import-Substituting Industrialization"; Fishlow, "Origins and Consequences of Import Substitution"; Haggard, *Pathways from the Periphery*.
15. Cárdenas, *La industrialización mexicana*; Kaufman, "How Societies Change."
16. Bulmer-Thomas, *Economic History of Latin America*, 263–64.
17. Thorp, "Reappraisal," 186–88; Villarreal, *Industrialización, deuda y desequilibrio externo*.
18. FitzGerald, "Restructuring through the Depression"; Palma, "Export-Led to an Import-Substituting Economy."
19. Similarly, see Silva, "Import-Substitution Model."

ways in which its experience diverged from the ECLA model.[20] But also distinguishing ISI in Mexico were its revolutionary origins, which made Mexico's politicians, technocrats, and industrialists ambivalent about accepting any rigid foreign economic models. Instead, they drew from a range of economic ideas derived from both international schools of thought and Mexico's domestic experience. This intellectual heterodoxy is especially significant since the division between economic liberals and protectionists in Latin America has often been overdrawn, even more so after the mid-twentieth-century triumph of protectionism there. Economic historians, such as John Coatsworth and Jeffrey Williamson, Graciela Márquez Colín, Aurora Gómez Galvarriato, and Edward Beatty, have already shown that the Great Depression was less a turning point in the shift from nineteenth-century orthodox liberalism to twentieth-century structuralism in Mexico than a conjunctural factor that advanced existing protectionist trends. Among other things, they have pointed out that state intervention and tariffs were an entrenched part of purportedly liberal economic policy in the late nineteenth century, even as exports boomed and even if the primary goal often was pursuit of revenue rather than protection of domestic industry.[21] Since that time, even Mexico's most ardent, pro-trade economic liberals had displayed a pragmatic appreciation of tariffs, at the very least for their own industries. Similarly, after the Revolution, neither those who supported state economic intervention nor their liberal rivals viewed the economy in strictly laissez-faire or statist terms. For example, in order to address the mounting trade imbalance and stem the loss of reserves after World War II, self-styled liberals gave nominal support to temporary, limited tariffs, despite their aversion to state economic intervention. In this light, liberalism, rationalization, and protectionism reflected people's visions of modern political and social relations more often than they determined economic policy. As argued by Robert Heilbroner and William Milberg, "'powerful' economic theory is always erected on powerful sociopolitical visions; and that theory retains its power over our intellects only as long as its underlying visions continue to mobilize our moral sympathies."[22]

---

20. FitzGerald, "Restructuring through the Depression." Stephen H. Haber argued that Mexico's ISI was "peculiar" because of its low worker productivity, small market, and high-cost capital goods. Haber, *Industry and Underdevelopment*.

21. Coatsworth and Williamson, "Always Protectionist?"; Beatty, *Institutions and Investment*; Gómez Galvarriato, "Impact of Revolution"; Márquez Colín, "Political Economy."

22. Heilbroner and Milberg, *Crisis of Vision*, 47.

In Mexico, the complexities of reconstructing state and society after the Revolution critically influenced the competing visions for industrialism. The 1920s witnessed extremes of postrevolutionary regional radicalism and initial efforts by the state to rein it in through agrarian reforms and anticlericalism. But it was also a period of rapid urbanization and industrialization. Some scholars depicted this take-off in Gerschenkronian terms. They argued that Mexico's weak national bourgeoisie, unable or unwilling to pursue industrial opportunities, fostered the emergence of a strong developmental state that stepped in to pursue capitalist growth.[23] But along with variants of the revolutionary family thesis, this overstates the coherence, intent, and autonomy of the state in the 1920s and 1930s. Instead, as the authority of rural hacendados gave way to the crosscutting political and monetary ambitions of Mexico's disparate postrevolutionary leaders, social and political conflicts attained a new level of influence over industrial policy and industry-state relations. Some of these conflicts arose within the state itself. For example, a new breed of technocrats brought strong developmental currents to the heart of the 1920s state, and they challenged the rent seeking and radicalism of revolutionary victors. These technocrats also confronted Porfirian merchant-financiers who tried to reassert their historic monopoly over banking and finance by limiting state economic intervention. Some of these technocrats were inspired by positivism and stirred by Catholic teachings, in particular in their support for liberal trade policies and paternalist labor relations. Yet they distinguished themselves from their *científico* forebearers by promoting an activist, autonomous state capable of directing economic development toward both growth and collective welfare. Also bringing a fresh voice into debates over policy and production was the multitude of new industrialists, who emerged in the 1920s amid the loosening of prerevolutionary constraints on land, labor, and capital. Perhaps even more significant was the new political influence of labor unions, some backed by populist leaders seeking a mass base, which helped to destabilize politics and production in key industrial cities.

In this kaleidoscopic era of reconstruction, producers from the industrially vital cities of Guadalajara, Mexico City, Monterrey, and Puebla drew from a cauldron of regional political and class relationships to confront the expansion of postrevolutionary state authority. Of particular concern was the political and economic fallout of growing state intervention in the economy, especially after the consolidating successes of *cardenismo* in the late

---

23. Bennett and Sharpe, "State as Banker."

1930s. Regional elites adapted to these new forms of national political authority and state intervention, and they often collaborated with governors now imposed by the ruling party. Yet, they also drew on regionally rooted interests and alliances to press governors to protect regional political authority, local industry, and their control over labor-employer relations. In the process, they exploited, altered, or contested the national industrial and labor policies that constituted statist industrialization.[24]

The Monterrey Group, in the northern border state of Nuevo León, presented one of the most coherent responses to the postrevolutionary expansion of state authority over regional politics and industry. As one of Mexico's most powerful and autonomous business groups, many of its members shared good relations with ruling-party insiders. From the late 1920s through the 1930s, they nevertheless censured state economic intervention, especially regulations and trade controls, which they felt were an assault on private property rights and were undermining the region's large-scale production linked to foreign markets. They also assailed new corporatist labor politics for weakening the historical cross-class alliances around company paternalism that they argued were responsible for the region's social peace. The postwar economic crisis and consolidation of the ruling party's authority by the late 1940s led them to soften their antagonism to state economic intervention, if only to accommodate what was seen as the inevitable, yet temporary, turn to trade controls. They also redefined traditional company paternalism in terms more consistent with the growing emphasis on modern industrial relations. But even with this détente with the national authorities, they continued to resist formal incorporation into the ruling party. They instead challenged the central government by promoting an identity founded on the region's rugged frontier individualism that they interpreted as the root of its remarkable industrial modernization. In doing so, they cast regionalism as an alternative nationalist project that epitomized Mexico's modern industrial future. Akin to Adrian Lyttelton's portrayal of nineteenth-century Milan, the Monterrey Group created a durable image of the city of Monterrey as the "'moral capital'" and nationalist vanguard of not just Nuevo León but the entire country, in opposition to what it argued were the revolutionary excesses of ruling-party-directed statist development concentrated in Mexico City.[25]

---

24. Similarly, in early nineteenth-century Italy, peripheral regions showed a powerful capacity to accept, modify, or reject the initiatives of the center, incorporating them into local politics and practices on their own terms. Broers, "Myth and Reality."

25. Lyttelton, "Shifting Identities," 48.

In contrast, the highly protected and well-organized cotton-textile industrialists in Puebla produced largely for national markets, and they thus saw the expansion of trade controls and tariffs in less threatening terms. Far more noxious, in their estimation, was the state-backed unions' control of local labor regimes. Paradoxically, the high levels of union privilege within the textile industry in Puebla had been a direct outgrowth not just of revolutionary mobilization but also of prior efforts to help the antiquated industry survive. In the late 1920s, textile industrialists had entered into an unofficial pact with the state that guaranteed protection in return for their acceptance of the collective contracts that the ruling party sought as a means to ensure labor peace and industry competitiveness.[26] As part of this accommodation, the state also slowed the importation of modern machinery, which Pueblan industrialists feared would speed the creation of modern factories far more efficient than Puebla's generally older plants. However, as the industry slid into decline after World War II, Pueblan industrialists switched strategies and began to promote investment in new machinery as a means to force the renegotiation of collective union contracts. They argued that it would enable them to become more competitive, though it would also let them undermine union privilege and reassert authority over their workforce. By pressing for new technology in the late 1940s, they exhibited a keen understanding of the significance of modern industrial capitalism for the state's and the ruling party's power, and potentially for their own survival. However, the Alemán administration largely resisted these pressures and continued to back corporatist labor arrangements while favoring more modern textile sectors. In this manner, it made certain that Puebla's textile industrialists would remain politically marginalized and economically excluded.

Finally, in the third regional case, Guadalajara in the state of Jalisco, the conflicts over state economic intervention centered on the perceived threats of central authority to local political and productive relations. Many large-scale, conservative industrialists in that city predictably resented state intrusion into labor-employer relations, preferring the region's historic, Catholic-inspired class cooperation, which they felt ensured labor peace. But given the complexities of forging class alliances in a region with a heterogeneous industrial base, many of Jalisco's small- and medium-sized producers of consumer goods, by contrast, welcomed the state's influence over labor

---

26. Gómez Galvarriato, "Impact of Revolution," 592–98; Gómez Galvarriato, "Measuring the Impact," 309–10.

as a means to manage labor-employer relations, end class warfare, and control wages. On the other hand, they protested the centralization of authority over industry organizations and biased federal tax-exemption legislation. The producers in Guadalajara contended that each of these was a threat to the regional production and markets that underpinned strong cross-class collaboration built upon a shared faith in a small-scale, varied, and distinctly Jaliscan industry. Ultimately, in some senses, Guadalajaran industrialists entered into the archetypal Mexican pact with the ruling party, wherein regional elites ceded on some issues, including labor relations, while preserving their local authority over others, such as industrialist political representation.

Recovering Regional Industry

During the late nineteenth century, capitalist modernization and political centralization significantly diminished regional political power in Mexico.[27] The acceleration of state consolidation and industrial centralization after the Revolution, coupled with a commitment to social justice through agrarian and labor reforms, further undercut regional industrialists' authority. In this context, the intensification of statist industrialism reignited historic antagonisms between the national state and industrial and political leaders in Guadalajara, Mexico City, Monterrey, and Puebla concerning regional political authority and who would hold power over labor-employer relations. In turn, the contours of their competing projects for industrialism, forged as they were from the regional alliances and class relations that formed Mexico's disparate industrial paths, critically influenced the character of Mexico's midcentury development.

Much like prior historians of nineteenth-century Europe, many early postrevolutionary scholars were unconcerned with the region as a site of study. Most instead celebrated the centralizing triumphs of the postrevolutionary state and the birth of the modern nation-state out of the ashes of the Revolution.[28] For some, given the political chaos that plagued many other

---

27. Claudio Lomnitz-Adler argues that regional power centers have been subjugated to central authority since the colonial era. After Independence, sovereignty continued to reside at the "pinnacle," though political groups struggled against the country's "dismemberment" due to political violence. Managing the power of regional centers and the centralization of authority was an uneven and fractious process. Lomnitz-Adler, *Exits from the Labyrinth*, 286–90.

28. On this trend in the historiography of Europe, see Applegate, "Europe of Regions," 1159–60.

Latin American countries by the 1960s, the PRI's stable endurance seemed to confirm interpretations of the authentically national and revolutionary origins of Mexico's modern state. However, others saw the state's role in midcentury development, and the social inequality and authoritarian politics that accompanied it, in darker hues, similar to the analysis of scholars working on Brazil and Argentina. Shifting their focus to the shortcomings of statist development in Latin America, these scholars turned their attention to assigning blame for the region's problems. Some placed it on the predations of a powerful state that had inflicted forced development while ignoring popular demands.[29] Others located it in the developmental state's reversals and distortions.[30] In the case of Mexico, scholars underscored the exceptionality of Mexico's largely nonmilitarist path to authoritarianism, and the PRI's ability to balance corporatism and exclusion in managing its relationship with popular groups.[31] Marxists, of both the structural and instrumental variety, also weighed in on the nature of midcentury state authority in Mexico. They maintained that the Revolution had created a national bourgeoisie that pursued capitalist expansion and autonomy from foreign capital by colluding with or controlling the state.[32]

By the 1980s, however, historians began to reconsider the emphasis on the monolithic nature of the midcentury Mexican state. Alan Knight contended that the Mexican state prior to 1940 was "weaker, often much weaker than [statolaters] suppose; after 1940 it was much less autonomous."[33] Knight drew from a spate of revisionist regional studies in the 1970s and 1980s that dislodged key postulates of modernization and Marxist theory that had effaced the role of regions in modern nation-state formation. These studies disrupted official and scholarly renderings of the nationalist and revolutionary origins of the ruling party while reflecting on the PRI's bankrupt methods for achieving social peace, political stability, and

29. Leff, *Economic Policy-Making*; Wirth, *Politics of Brazilian Development*; Hansen, *Politics of Mexican Development*; Glade, "Revolution and Economic Development"; Glade, "Party-Led Development."

30. Evans, *Dependent Development*; Haber, *Industry and Underdevelopment*; Waisman, *Reversal of Development*; Kirsch, *Industrial Development*.

31. For a classic study of Mexico as an inclusive authoritarian regime, see Purcell, *Mexican Profit-Sharing Decision*. See also her study of clientelism and corporatism in Mexico, Purcell, "Mexico: Clientelism, Corporatism, and Political Stability." For more about how mobilization strategies modified state incorporation to create a model of radical populism, see Berins Collier and Collier, *Shaping the Political Arena*. On the links between authoritarianism and rapid economic growth and social change, see O'Donnell, *Bureaucratic Authoritarianism*.

32. Leal, *Del estado liberal al estado interventor*; Hamilton, *Limits of State Autonomy*.

33. Knight, "Mexican Revolution," 12.

capitalist modernization.[34] Knight acclaimed their regional insights, but he urged historians to use them to revisit the postrevolutionary state. His appeal anticipated a flood of works that drew on cultural studies to rehabilitate the popular and participatory nature of the Revolution and to recover the centrifugal tendencies that contributed to the fitful process of state formation in the 1920s and 1930s.[35] Ultimately, however, these works stressed how the agrarian and reformist accomplishments of state-building, especially cardenismo, represented dominant political and economic interests by 1940. These accomplishments, in turn, helped to restrain political and social radicalisms while overcoming regional obstacles to state consolidation.

The malleability of statist industrialism as a political project, however, stands as a testament to the complexity of state-building into the 1940s and beyond. For example, the emphasis on 1940 as a major point of reversal for the Revolution has meant that scholars have tended to overlook the historical continuities in the process of state formation after 1940. Most notable was the ruling party's ambition to create a stable political system that could survive enduring social and political opposition. Moreover, although the ruling party incarnated the interests of the dominant class in important ways by the 1940s, industrialists were neither necessarily contributory nor collusive in the construction of a centralized state.[36] Therefore, this book seeks to "decenter" state power by capturing the varied responses of regional industrialists to shifts in state policy and authority. In doing so, statist industrialism appears as a nationalist project that often accommodated, or at least tolerated, the eclectic strains of regional industrialist resistance to the state's consolidating and centralizing pull.[37]

Decentering state authority has implications for understanding industrialization as well. Systematic studies of the politics of Mexican industry are now decades old, and they tend to emphasize consensus about statist development that arose between a national bourgeoisie and a Leviathan state.[38] Much as statolaters (Knight's term) had underscored the ruling party's success in using state power to expand its authority, these scholars had often been enamored of the growth that accompanied midcentury stability, the

34. Carr, "Recent Regional Studies," 7–10.
35. Most notably, see Joseph and Nugent, *Everyday Forms of State Formation*.
36. One study complicating understandings of industrialist pressure on the ruling party is Schneider, *Business Politics and the State*.
37. Rubin, *Decentering the Regime*, 13–14. Similarly, Adrian Lyttelton argues that Italy's diverse regional identities and political relations critically shaped the different ways that regions interacted with the state. Lyttelton, "Shifting Identities," 33–52.
38. Brandenburg, *Making of Modern Mexico*; Mosk, *Industrial Revolution in Mexico*; Vernon, *Dilemma of Mexico's Development*.

so-called stabilizing growth. They therefore were equally sanguine about the ruling party's use of state capacities to nationalize industrial development. Modernization theorists and structuralists from ECLA, too, were enthusiastic about the state's potential to help Mexico overcome backwardness and achieve industrial development, despite admonitions from political economists, such as Albert Hirschman, to be chary of the rigidity of staged development.[39]

But Mexico's regions fared almost as poorly in interpretations of midcentury industrialization as they had in early examinations of the state. By the late 1970s, many scholars became disenchanted with the teleologies of modernization and Marxist theories that emphasized state centralization and capitalist development, as well as with the limits of ECLA's structuralist *desarrollismo* (developmentalism). This disenchantment had already prompted *dependentistas* (dependency theorists) to adapt world systems theory to processes within nation-states to try to understand the evolution of internal dependency and inequality.[40] Some, such as André Gunder Frank, maintained that urban cores created underdeveloped hinterlands by extracting resources and wealth in order to fuel capitalist modernization. Others arguing from within the ECLA school, including Fernando Henrique Cardoso and Enzo Faletto, looked to weak domestic class arrangements to locate the causes of internal underdevelopment and dependency.[41] But although each was correct to highlight that the hinterlands were neither premodern nor precapitalist, they remained content with interpretations of regions wasting away at the expense of the presumably more national core. Regions were products of development in urban areas, and regionality was almost solely passive or reactive.[42]

Although dependency theorists homogenized the national industrial experience, regional studies have tended to ignore industry altogether. Even works from the field of new economic history have only just begun to

---

39. For an appraisal of Hirschman's contributions to the field, see Gootenberg, "*Hijos* of Dr. Gerschenkron?" 59–61.

40. Harding, "Maoism: An Alternative to Dependency Theory?" 62. In Mexico, the theory of internal colonialism echoed loudly in the works of two of its most influential *dependentistas*, Pablo González Casanova and Rodolfo Stavenhagen. See González Casanova, *Sociología de la explotación*, and Stavenhagen, *Las clases sociales*. The use of the core-periphery model to discuss internal development became popular in studies of Tokugawa Japan and imperial China as well. See Wigen, "Culture, Power, and Place," 1185.

41. For an examination of the various schools evolving out of dependency theory, see Chilcote, "Dependency"; Gootenberg, "*Hijos* of Dr. Gerschenkron?" 67.

42. Applegate, "Europe of Regions," 1167.

move beyond a national state focus.⁴³ Among these is the work on crony capitalism by Stephen H. Haber, Noel Maurer, and Armando Razo. Primarily concentrated on the national state, they find that weak state institutions and an absence of limited government in the 1920s induced postrevolutionary political leaders to encourage investment by providing special guarantees and protection to a small group of economic elites. In contrast to the clientelist crony capitalism of the Porfiriato (1876–1911), arrangements in the 1920s were largely institutional and for the first time incorporated labor. Yet they still blurred the boundaries between government and private interests to become the cornerstone of state formation and industrial capitalism.⁴⁴

But other factors at the national level also intervened to significantly influence the state's pursuit of economic growth. Among these were embryonic developmentalist currents within the government in the 1920s. Engineers, economists, and lawyers attained a new status in the postrevolutionary governments and promoted the potential role of the state in spurring economic growth *and* development. By the 1940s, these professionals coalesced into a group of technocrats concentrated in the Office of Industrial Research (Oficina de Investigaciones Industriales, OII) at the Banco de México. By then, their ideas had evolved to include a broader analysis of the ways in which an activist state could function as a substitute factor of production (to put it in Gerschenkronian terms). This, they argued, could enable Mexico to catch up to more developed countries, much in the same way that access to coal or new technologies had earlier allowed many European countries to achieve a marked leap in industrial development.⁴⁵ Technocrats were concerned about the political excesses that had characterized previous state interventions, however, arguing that this had hindered Mexico's long-term development. They therefore promoted economic planning as a means to curb the influence of politics in economic policy making. But the postrevolutionary state never came close to creating an agency that approximated the role of the MITI in coordinating industrial trade and policy in Japan or the role of the Commissariat Général du Plan in leading France's post–World War II indicative planning.⁴⁶ As suggested by Haber,

---

43. For a critique of the problems associated with the new economic history, such as its insistence on the singular value of scientific methodologies over other forms of historical interpretation and the difficulties in the collection of quantitative data in Mexico, see Knight, "Export-Led Growth," appendix, 137–41.

44. Haber, Maurer, and Razo, "Sustaining Economic Performance," 35; Haber, Razo, and Maurer, *Politics of Property Rights*.

45. Gerschenkron, *Economic Backwardness*.

46. Johnson, *MITI*; Kuisel, *Capitalism and the State*; Lynch, "Resolving the Paradox."

Maurer, and Razo, even as many Mexican bureaucrats lauded the virtues of economic planning, they often privileged their ties to economic elites over building a bureaucracy capable of defining, coordinating, or implementing planned development. Their reasons for not pursuing effective large-scale planning were numerous and conflicting. Some might cite a lack of will or vision, whereas others could point to a conviction among some officials that the politicians, themselves, could best guide long-term development. Moreover, the state faced serious limits on its authority over the private sector, which circumscribed its ability to incite or compel compliance with planning.[47] Dependency also played a role, as U.S. influence over the use of loans and aid and the rapid influx of direct foreign investment after the war reduced the state's options for intervening in the economy.

Nevertheless, strong rationalist impulses that emphasized planning and limited political intervention endured, especially among technocrats and some bureaucrats in the OII, Nacional Financiera, S.A. (NAFINSA), and the Secretariat of the Treasury and Public Credit (Secretaría de Hacienda y Crédito Público, SHCP). Their interest in planning stemmed from the Revolution, which had fostered élan about the potential of the state to lead the economy toward long-term development and improved living standards. But this interest was also a product of a particular historic moment, in which planning symbolized the aspirations to wealth, sovereignty, and international influence for officials in both developing countries and those that were recovering in the aftermath of two World Wars. Therefore, the pressure for planning ultimately shaped the evolution of statist industrialization in Mexico, in part because of technocrats' use of economic planning tools, such as tax breaks, subsidies, trade controls, federal financing, planning committees, and resource studies.[48] Furthermore, in 1958, the state finally created its first centralized system of planning to coordinate and direct the efforts of disparate state agencies. To the likely dismay of technocrats, however, it was headed by a bureaucratic ministry, the Secretariat of the Presidency (Secretaría de la Presidencia), directly tied to Mexico's president.[49]

Moreover, the state's pursuit of economic growth was also affected by the variety of arrangements among labor, industrialists, and the state at the regional level. These drew on local alliances and class relations to secure

---

47. Similarly, see Chibber, *Locked in Place*; Evans, *Embedded Autonomy*; Granovetter, "Economic Action and Social Structure."

48. As Kathryn Sikkink contends, ideas that are embedded in state institutions become critical in driving the adoption of new economic projects. Sikkink, *Ideas and Institutions*, 2. See also Goldstein, *Ideas, Interests*.

49. Pichardo Pagaza, *10 años de planificación*, 19–23.

regionally distinct growth and political loyalties. Indeed, if anything characterizes postrevolutionary industrial development, it is the heterogeneity of industrial experiences, as well as the *lack* of political connections for the majority of new entrepreneurs. Scholars of Mexico are hardly unique in their late appreciation of the heterogeneity of regional industrial experiences. For example, until recently, scholars of German industrialization were even more wedded to unitary views of industry, perhaps because of the exceptional influence of the grand theory of Gerschenkron and Schumpeter there. Yet, as Gary Herrigel argues for the German case, regions were the bedrock of the country's "diverse systems of industrial development."[50] In Mexico, too, the vitality of its industrial development and politics rests in its multitude of regional class and productive relations.

In the early 1980s, Nora Hamilton framed her now classic study of the Mexican state in Marxist terms about the autonomy of the state vis-à-vis capital.[51] *Made in Mexico,* in contrast, draws on fresh insights offered by the cultural turn in the study of class relations within the context of changing political preoccupations associated with late twentieth-century neoliberal developments. In doing so, it reexamines the challenges to state intervention made by segments of the capitalist class. In this new light, industrialist reactions appear as an effort to curb the limits placed on their regional political and productive authority by an increasingly, albeit imperfectly, centralizing state.[52] To be sure, the midcentury Mexican state retained its role in reconciling class interests in order to pursue industrial capitalism. However, its efforts were shaped not only by dependent development and radical revolutionary ambitions, such as working-class mobilization, but also by regional resilience generated by shifting local alliances of industrialists, labor, and politicians.

Region, Nation, and Statist Industrialism

President Alemán recast mexicanidad to blend its promise of social justice and economic independence with the PRI's project for statist industrialism.

---

50. Herrigel, *Industrial Constructions,* 1–2, 19–22. Quote is from Applegate, "Europe of Regions," 1169–70. Similarly, Pat Hudson argues for analyzing the "different path[s] or pattern[s] of development" that national-level studies of industry in England have obscured. This is important for understanding both industrial diversity and the role of regional development paths in constituting the national aggregate. Hudson, "Regional Perspective," in Hudson, *Regions and Industries,* 9–10.

51. Hamilton, *Limits of State Autonomy.*

52. Thanks to Sinclair Thomson for this observation.

In the face of persisting labor unrest and industrialist ambivalence, he was seeking to use the broad appeal of revolutionary nationalism to build support for ruling-party power. President Alemán's message of mexicanidad drew on modernist assumptions about progressive development. His political project was to advance Mexico's evolution into a modern nation-state and shed its allegedly backward and provincial past. This project insinuated that lingering regionalism, whether as passive or active resistance to modernization, undermined integrative development.[53] Yet Prasenjit Duara has argued that nationalism is "a phenomenon that registers difference even as it claims a unitary and unifying identity . . . [and] is rarely the nationalism of *the nation,* but rather marks the site where different representations of the nation contest and negotiate with each other."[54] In Mexico, these "different representations of the nation" were manifest in the rival visions for political authority and modern social relations underlying the competing projects for industrialism. These projects, in turn, emerged out of Mexico's longer legacy of regionalism.

The standard Marxist view emphasizes that amid the rise of industrial capitalism, producers shed regional allegiances in favor of joining in national class-based alliances in collaboration with strong, centralized states to promote modernizing growth. Eric Van Young astutely adapted this to the Mexican case, stating that "much of the energy in Mexican history . . . has manifestly revolved around changing the country from a strong regional and weak class structure, to a weak regional and strong class structure: this is certainly at least one aspect of what 'modernization' has meant."[55] But although class conflict has been a hallmark of the modern industrial age, it did not necessarily destroy regional affiliations and consciousness.[56] Rather, during the 1930s and 1940s, industrialists in Guadalajara, Monterrey, and Puebla sometimes deliberately eschewed ties to industrialists in other regions, choosing instead to reinforce regional cross-class and political relations. In part, this was an attempt to mitigate the impact of the centralizing effects of industrial capitalism and political concentration on regional political power. However, although interregional class-based alliances helped to

53. Drake, "Mexican Regionalism Revisited."
54. Duara, *Rescuing History,* 4–8.
55. Van Young, "Introduction," 4, 15–16.
56. John Langton argues that pre-industrial regional differences, and people's consciousness of them, intensified during early industrialization in England, though in the end, national economic integration destroyed regionalism. Langton, "Industrial Revolution." For an exegesis on the evolution of historical approaches to the relationship of regions and nation in the United States, see Ayers and Onuf, "Introduction."

reinforce centralized political authority, state power also was predicated on differences and conflicts among elites, whose interests were rooted in Mexico's culturally and materially distinct regions. Indeed, the ways in which the state accommodated and managed these differences among elites, as well as the diverse, often fluid "affinities and rivalries" that resulted from them, also were critical in the consolidation of state authority.[57]

Mexico's industrial regions comprised unique productive and political relations, which surely shaped the ways in which industrialists understood regionalism. Some scholars have already examined the formation of Mexico's industrial regions through the lens of the geopolitical economy of urban industry. They focus on the ways in which the "process of production, distribution, and consumption of goods has a *spatial dimension* [italics in original] that constitutes the nexus between mode of production and the process of urbanization."[58] This book similarly emphasizes the different political and productive relations that defined Mexico's industrial regions. Yet it goes on to explore the ways in which industrialists constructed affinities from these local political and productive relations as a means to navigate postrevolutionary state formation and industrialization. This sense of affinity was significant in Mexico, where many industrialists in the early twentieth century were recent migrants, whether to a city, a region, or the country. Some, most notably the Barcelonnette network, drew from their common ancestry, region of origin, or ethnicity to forge social and political relations critical for business success. Others, including immigrants from Europe and the Middle East, formed social clubs based on their region of origin. Finally, the family enterprise became a prominent feature of commercial and industrial development, though, as David Walker shows, family alone could not substitute for advantageous social and political connections in securing business success.[59] At the same time, the manifold class, ethnic, and geographic origins of Mexico's industrialists militated against broader professional and personal fraternization. Therefore, regional relations of production, and the meanings attached to them, were central in forging alliances that enabled industrialists to advance their regional interests and economies. These "network[s] of trust" were especially important in Mexico, because they helped

---

57. Gramsci, *Selections from the Prison Notebooks*, 92–100. Similarly, Tulio Halperín-Donghi analyzes the role of the relationship between provincial power holders and central authority, and the blurred boundaries between public and private during the years of political turmoil and institutional breakdown surrounding Independence in Argentina. Halperín-Donghi, *Politics, Economics, and Society*, especially 383–91, quote from 388.

58. Garza Villarreal, *El proceso de industrialización*, 27; Bassols Batalla, *México*.

59. Walker, *Kinship, Business, and Politics*. See also Adler Lomnitz and Pérez-Lizaur, *Mexican Elite Family*.

to substitute for a state that struggled to enforce laws and regulations that could protect investors.[60]

For example, when industrialists and politicians in Guadalajara resurrected notions of the *patria chica* as a rallying cry to defend regional industry in the 1930s, they referenced a faith, held even among large industrialists, in the small-scale and distinctly Jaliscan forms of local industry producing largely for regional markets. A closer inspection of class relations in Jalisco reveals an elite divided by the array of industry types, sizes, labor forces, and markets that characterized the region's diverse industry. Yet this sense of unity based on affirmations of a transcendent regional identity empowered regional industrialists to contest aspects of state consolidation and industrial centralization perceived as affecting local power and production. The embrace of patria chica, in this sense, was neither premodern nor reactive but rather a means for industrialists to negotiate growing state authority.

Nevertheless, government officials did not view all assertions of regionalism as problematic, and at times, they even fostered them. For example, regionalism could help to mitigate local radicalisms and manage conflict among the growing urban classes. This proved important in the decades immediately after the Revolution, when a relatively weak state had only a limited capacity to control the range of challenges coming from, among others, *agraristas,* labor leaders, Catholics, Communists, caudillos, and a host of pretenders to political power. Historians of Italy, with its long and contentious history of regional autonomy movements, have pioneered the study of the discrete roles of regions and states during periods of rapid industrial growth and late nation-state formation.[61] They have found that although countering certain expressions of regionalism, states often concurrently allowed other manifestations that may have something to offer the state or when the costs of overcoming them—for example, when the use of force sacrificed political legitimacy—were too high.[62] Similarly, Mexico's mid-twentieth-century nationalist industrialism neither displaced nor superseded regional identities and interests, and regional industrial paths often thrived amid its expansion. Moreover, competing regional projects for industrialism fulfilled a variety of concurrent and even, at first glance,

---

60. Gómez Galvarriato, "Networks and Entrepreneurship," 476–77.

61. Sidney Tarrow disputed the conclusions of both dependency theory and conservative diffusionist models by demonstrating the ways in which regions, through the development of marginal political power, can moderate the influence of the market in modern states. In the end, however, he reinforced the notion that peripheries have interests distinct from and antagonistic to the center. Tarrow, *Between Center and Periphery.*

62. C. Levy, *Italian Regionalism.*

conflicting roles vis-à-vis nationalist industrialism, often defying it, sometimes substituting for it, and at times functioning as vehicles for it.[63] For example, even as regional industrialists in Guadalajara promoted their identities and interests in ways that countered statist industrialism, they reacted in predictable and nationalist ways to U.S. threats to Mexican industry.

Industrialists were not always confronting the state when they defined regionally oriented industrial projects. They also drew on these projects to avail themselves of protectionist policies while limiting the central government's incursions into regional authority and their own power over labor-employer relations. In the process, statist industrialism evolved as a flexible, nationalist political project. This project, in turn, enhanced both state and ruling-party authority with its capacity to appropriate, tolerate, or marginalize alternative regional industrial paths and the rival visions of political rule and modern social relations attached to them.

Structure of the Book

This book explores conflicts among industrialists, labor, and the state over statist industrialism, and it looks at the roots of these conflicts in the genealogy of regionalism in Mexico. Four of the chapters are a kind of case study of regional politics and industry. These chapters are interspersed with others that trace the national context. Although the book emphasizes the political and social processes underlying the uneven evolution and varied chronologies of statist industrialism across Mexico from the 1920s to the early 1950s, each chapter also foregrounds themes relevant to a cross-section of regional and national contexts.

Chapter 1 explores the politics of economic policy and planning during the tumultuous 1920s. In that decade, technocrats worked to expand state authority over economic policy and stave off Porfirian merchant-financiers seeking to reclaim their past preeminence. The creation of a central bank promised to improve the autonomy of the federal government vis-à-vis domestic and foreign bankers. Yet this did not translate into substantial changes in state authority, as President Plutarco Elías Calles (1924–28) struggled to use tariff policy and planning agencies as a means to incorporate a wider swath of industrialists. Rather, many business elites took advantage of the political chaos, economic tumult, and social unrest of the 1920s to press

---

63. Similarly, see Schoppa, "Province and Nation," 674.

their own visions for national reconstruction and development. As a result, industrial policy languished as a vehicle to achieve political consolidation or even substantial economic transformation.

Chapter 2 traces the labyrinthine path to what became an archetypal, accommodationist pact between the ruling party and Guadalajara's industrialists in the 1930s and 1940s. Elites in Jalisco contested state consolidation with assertions of identity derived from the region's small-scale industry and local class relations. At the same time, government efforts to expand and centralize state authority through federal labor legislation, tax-exemption legislation, and laws regulating industrialist organizing did not always generate uniform opposition in the region. Ultimately, local political leaders mediated tensions between regional industrialists and the state by balancing their commitment to regional industrial growth with their party loyalty. As a result, statist industrialism accommodated identities and practices particular to the Guadalajaran industrial region, expanding the base of federal authority.

Chapter 3 analyzes rival visions of state and society embedded in competing projects for industrialism among groups close to the ruling party in the early 1940s. Although the OII at the Banco de México proposed economic planning as a means to circumscribe the role of politics in economic decision making, CANACINTRA promoted the expansion of state economic intervention led by industrialists themselves. Both OII technocrats and CANACINTRA industrialists drew from an array of international intellectual traditions, yet they conceived of economic policy through the lens of Mexico's postrevolutionary social and political challenges. Consequently, the chapter points to the heterodox ideological and historical foundations of midcentury economic policy.

Chapter 4 examines how the ruling party and textile industrialists in Puebla steered a course between exclusion and accommodation in negotiating the role of these producers in statist industrialism. Thematically, the chapter takes up the state's intrusion into labor-employer relations, and industrialist efforts to import new machinery as a means to regain power over local labor regimes. The Alemán administration largely refused to grant import permits for Puebla's traditional textile industrialists. Instead, it used industrial policy to undermine traditional forms of industrialist authority in order to reinforce corporatist labor relations and state-labor alliances, which were central to the power of both the state and the ruling party.

Chapter 5 considers the political and social conflicts that defined a pivotal moment in the expansion of statist industrialization: the 1947 decision by the Alemán administration to adopt trade controls. The chapter treats Mexico City as an industrial region whose project for protected urban manufacturing was ascendant amid postrevolutionary social dislocation, the economic fallout of the Great Depression and World War II, the nascent Cold War, and ruling-party efforts to achieve labor peace and political stability. In the face of U.S. pressure on Mexico to commit to free trade, a debate erupted between protectionists and their more liberal opponents over the nationalist merits of their distinct industrial projects. As some scholars have argued, the outcomes of this conflict, including the formation of a nationalist alliance of the ruling party with labor and industrialists in Mexico City, contributed to the PRI's authority over the state. The chapter adds to the literature by considering the contested origins of this arrangement, its success in redefining revolutionary nationalism to include class collaboration and cooperation with the state, and the enduring opposition to the expansion of state authority at the perceived expense of the rights of private enterprise.

Chapter 6 examines conflicts between the well-known Monterrey Group and the ruling party that persisted through the mid-twentieth century over economic regulation and state intervention in labor relations. Despite the turn to protected industrialization, economic liberalism remained a prominent force in midcentury politics and development, even as the Monterrey Group itself softened its opposition to protection. After the 1947 implementation of trade controls, the Monterrey Group also redefined company paternalism in terms consistent with the growing emphasis on modern industrial relations. In doing so, Monterrey was assimilated into the Mexican nation as an alternative center of power, whose elites prided themselves on being ideologically conservative and economically autonomous, as well as being opposed to the purported statist excesses of the ruling party.

1

THE POLITICS OF STATE ECONOMIC INTERVENTION FROM THE REVOLUTION TO THE GREAT DEPRESSION

With the full force of economic depression bearing down on Mexico by 1931, officials implored producers to do their part to salvage the Mexican economy and ensure national welfare. They even imagined a manifesto targeting the business community: "When managers realize that it is necessary to employ virility, courage, energy, and intelligence to lead their businesses, then we will save our national industry."[1] These were to be a new generation of revolutionary businessmen—brave, virile, energetic, smart—whose superior aptitudes and masculine attributes privileged their role in national reconstruction. This rhetoric recalled the competences conferred on Porfirian elites by positivists in the late nineteenth century, who saw it as their right to lead the nation to Progress. However, in its 1930s guise, this right had been supplanted by a responsibility of industry and commerce to fulfill the revolutionary goals of economic development and national welfare.

After the Revolution, the growing weight of collective welfare and the incorporation of labor and agrarian groups into national politics reverberated in debates between business and the state over the latter's intervention in the economy. Among those who challenged the rise of mass politics were Porfirian-era merchant-financiers, who correctly perceived the threat it presented to their historic influence over economic and fiscal policy. In some ways, these merchant-financiers were successful in recapturing their prerevolutionary status and wealth in the 1920s. As scholars have shown, in

---

1. "Como deben proceder los hombres de negocios ante la crisis," *Boletín Semanal*, no. 103, SICT, Dirección de Publicaciones y Propaganda, July 27, 1931, Fondo Dependencia Federal (DF)/Serie Secretaría de Industria, Comercio, y Trabajo (SSICT)/Archivo General del Estado de Nuevo León (AGENL), c. 5.

this period, the state, often more preoccupied with political than economic concerns, looked on as a sort of "neo-Porfirian" crony capitalism reestablished itself.[2] An alliance of the revolutionary victors with the surviving Porfirian business aristocracy dominated this new revolutionary capitalism. Seeking to consolidate their hold over the state—including by pacifying parvenu revolutionary generals with financial incentives—Presidents Álvaro Obregón (1920–24) and Plutarco Elías Calles supported these arrangements with tariffs, subsidies, and other guarantees.[3] According to some scholars, the creation of the National Revolutionary Party (Partido Nacional Revolucionario, PNR) in 1929 secured these arrangements by enabling Calles and his backers to funnel favors to party loyalists, laying the foundations for a one-party state dominated by rent-seeking party insiders.[4]

This version of business-state relations attributes a remarkable amount of political coherence, authority, and intent to the clique from Sonora who controlled the state. But, as other scholars have amply demonstrated, the 1920s state faced pressures as diverse as the revolutionary factions themselves, including from agraristas, labor leaders, regional caudillos, the United States, foreign companies, the Church, and a range of political aspirants. Moreover, this version of business-state relations portrays industrialization in relatively narrow, homogeneous, and politically pacific ways.[5] Yet, in reality, Mexico's national bourgeoisie in the 1920s was "a strangely schizoid class" divided by disparate sectoral, political, ideological, and religious interests.[6] The shift from traditional export-oriented production to more dynamic forms of commercial agriculture and industry in the 1920s fed this heterogeneity. Along with commercial agriculture and mining, manufacturing was buoyant through much of the decade, with manufacturing production growing by 71 percent between 1921 and 1927.[7] A disproportionate share of that growth was due to a small cohort of large-scale industrialists. In 1930, although industries whose production value exceeded Mex$100,000

---

2. Knight, "Political Economy," 300.
3. Haber, Maurer, and Razo, "Sustaining Economic Performance," 35; Haber, Razo, and Maurer, *Politics of Property Rights*.
4. Examples include Cockcroft, *Mexico's Hope*, 111–14; J. Meyer, *Estado y sociedad con Calles*, 283–90; Brandenburg, *Making of Modern Mexico*; Hansen, *Politics of Mexican Development*, 158–62, 165–71.
5. Similarly, Thomas Passananti argues that the concept of crony capitalism fails to capture the complexity of early Porfirian economic policy making. Passananti, "'Nada de Papeluchos!'"
6. Knight, "Political Economy," 299.
7. The percentage of growth refers to the volume of manufacturing production. Cárdenas, "Process of Accelerated Industrialization," 178–82; Haber, *Industry and Underdevelopment*, 150–56; FitzGerald, "Restructuring through the Depression," 214–17; Zebadúa, *Banqueros y revolucionarios*, 335; Bortz, *Revolution Within the Revolution*, 34.

per year were only 2.5 percent of the total number of industrial establishments, they employed close to 50 percent of the national industrial workforce and produced 65 percent of the national production value.[8] Nevertheless, small- and medium-sized industries also emerged during the 1920s to take advantage of deeper markets, new sources of investment, better transportation and electric power, and a growing urban labor force. They epitomized the spirit of reconstruction that inspired new and varied forms of entrepreneurial activity, and they contributed to the complexity of business-state relations during the 1920s and 1930s.[9]

The efforts of the *callista* state to manage these diverse industrialists centered on the expansion of state intervention in the economy, in part through the creation of multiple economic planning decrees and agencies. In pursuing this, President Calles drew on a burgeoning technocratic class that carried strong developmentalist currents to the heart of the postrevolutionary state. The most prominent were heirs of the Porfirian era's developmentalist liberals. Yet, inspired by a revolutionary commitment to social justice, they had supported revolutionists like Francisco Madero and Venustiano Carranza because of their disillusion with the authoritarian and exclusionary excesses of the científicos.[10] Therefore, they advocated for the construction of a strong activist state guided not by politics but rather by scientific and technical considerations that could channel economic development toward both growth and collective welfare.

Ultimately, economic policy in the 1920s and 1930s reflected the inchoate nature of the Sonoran group's vision of economic development. It also was influenced by domestic social and political challenges, disputes with the United States over oil and loans, and pressures from dissatisfied foreign and domestic bankers, all of which militated against effective policy making. When the callista state finally turned its attention more concertedly toward industrial promotion, planning, and protection, its goals often centered not on developing the foundations for long-term economic development but on advancing technocratic visions of political legitimacy and state power. By attempting to incorporate industrialists into an array of industrial policy-making and planning commissions, callistas sought to extend their hold over the state while undermining what they argued were the remnants of Porfirian political excess. In this, economic planning commissions in the 1920s and early 1930s became surrogates for industrialist political inclusion at a

---

8. L. Meyer, *El conflicto social,* 81–82.
9. Knight, *Mexican Revolution,* 2:524–26.
10. Knight, "El liberalismo mexicano," 82–86.

moment of limited political representation. These commissions manifested the aspirations of politicians and technocrats to tackle the seemingly endemic challenges of economic dependence and widespread poverty, but they largely functioned as a means for ruling-party leaders to consolidate their corporatist authority.

The Technical Foundations of the Postrevolutionary State, 1920–25

When President Obregón assumed the presidency in 1920, building state power and establishing social peace were principal concerns. Therefore, in many ways, the key markings of Porfirian political economy initially remained in place, including cronyism, the dominion of foreign capital, and the state's conservative fiscal and monetary policies. Citing these continuities and the similarities in the industrial experiences of Mexico, Brazil, and Argentina in the 1920s and 1930s, some scholars saw little of note in terms of the impact of the Revolution on capitalism's advance, except perhaps on its timing and vigor.[11] Nevertheless, the Revolution would leave a real imprint on the evolution of capitalist development, including in the emergence of an energetic labor movement and in the focus on the Revolution's redistributive promise. The revolutionary victors also sought to expand the state's fiscal autonomy vis-à-vis the Porfirian merchant-financiers and foreign lenders who had dominated fiscal policy making in the decades before the Revolution. To accomplish this, Presidents Obregón and Calles called on the support of the last of a generation of nineteenth-century positivists who had joined in the Revolution in part due to their desire to fulfill the goals of scientific politics. Labeled by Alan Knight as neo-científicos, these revolutionary technocrats sought to establish the foundations for a technical state able to guide economic growth toward development and revolutionary collective welfare, free from politics, cupidity, and clientelism.[12] Yet, while posited as apolitical, this technical vision of the state was in truth a form of politics that served to deepen the hold of the Sonoran leaders over the government. It gained legitimacy by drawing on the appeal of scientific and technical forms of knowledge, as well as from the belief that Porfirian científicos and their allies in the financial world had betrayed the developmental goals of scientific politics.[13]

11. For example, see Topik, "La Revolución."
12. Knight, *Mexican Revolution*, 2:525.
13. Similarly, see Weinstein, "Discourse of Technical Competence."

During the Porfiriato, bankers had a monopoly of financial knowledge, capital, and connections to foreign lenders. They secured this privileged position within a highly concentrated system of clientelism, perquisites, and state protection. Though twenty-four private banks had the right to issue paper currency during the Porfiriato, the Banco Nacional de México stood at the apex of the banking system, largely because it was the sole liaison between the Porfirian government and foreign lenders.[14] So commanding was the influence of bankers over fiscal and monetary policy that Stephen H. Haber contends that "financiers *were* the state" during the Porfiriato.[15] Bankers survived the Revolution, though by 1920 they were virtually bankrupt and largely discredited owing to their collaboration with the governments of Porfirio Díaz and Victoriano Huerta (1913–14).[16] Despite this, they remained a powerful business group, and they quickly sought to reestablish their preeminence after Obregón took office.

However, the bankers did not anticipate the growing authority in the postrevolutionary governments of a new breed of technocrat, who admired the economic growth of the Porfiriato but who was inspired by the ideals of the Revolution. Typifying them was Alberto J. Pani, secretary of the Treasury and Public Credit from 1923 to 1927. Pani was part of a generation of late Porfirian intellectuals who readily supported the revolutionary governments of Madero (1911–13) and Carranza (1917–20).[17] Like most in his cohort, he had faith in the order and progress of positivism, and he held classically liberal views in fiscal and monetary matters. Yet, also like many Porfirian *científicos*, he tempered his liberalism with a belief in the power of an activist, centralized state, guided by a technocratic, scientifically oriented elite, could lead the nation toward progress.[18]

Pani's disaffection with the authoritarian excesses and rent seeking by Porfirian elites in alliance with foreign interests shaped his path to the group of revolutionary intellectuals who joined the *carrancistas*. His beliefs therefore stemmed from the scientific politics that he saw as having been betrayed by these elites, as well as from revolutionary calls for social justice and economic independence. In some senses, he sought to consummate what the early exponents of scientific politics dating back to Justo Sierra in the late

---

14. Maurer, *Power and the Money*; C. W. Anderson, "Bankers as Revolutionaries," 116; Haber, Razo, and Maurer, *Politics of Property Rights*, 44.
15. Haber, *Industry and Underdevelopment*, 69.
16. Shelton, "Banking System," 131.
17. C. W. Anderson, "Bankers as Revolutionaries," 114–15.
18. Córdova, *La ideología de la Revolución*, 21; Knight, "El liberalismo mexicano," 85–86.

1870s had failed to accomplish: the creation of a strong, centralized executive guided by scientific and technical considerations and attentive to the material and spiritual improvement of the human condition.[19] Therefore, though Pani and others of the revolutionary right did not see social justice in terms of equality, they nevertheless valued revolutionary social principles.[20] Pani's calls for reform stemmed from the lessons of Revolution itself and, in particular, from the belief that the failure of the Díaz regime to deal adequately with social problems was a central cause of the Revolution. Although he admired the economic progress of the Porfirian era, he also characterized it as a period of "material, transitory, and regressive peace" obtained through bloody repression and the unfettered concentration of wealth.[21] He added that capitalist industrial development inevitably unleashed class conflict and that long-term growth depended on reining in the excesses of this conflict and establishing political stability and social peace. Yet, Pani had little confidence that employers would actually pursue this without being compelled to do so by the state.[22] He therefore favored a version of paternalism wherein the state, rather than free individuals, would be responsible for mediating class conflict and ensuring worker welfare. In doing so, he framed state intervention within Catholic tenets emphasizing class conciliation and social hierarchy. Though Pani's vision was largely conservative and hierarchical, he saw the state as the best means to create the conditions for the advance of both capitalist development *and* collective welfare.[23]

Others on the revolutionary right echoed Pani's sentiments, including those who claimed little exposure to positivism as part of their educational pedigree, such as lawyer and economist Manuel Gómez Morin.[24] Although he was one of the humanistically oriented *Siete Sabios* of the generation of 1915, Gómez Morin distinguished himself with his expertise in fiscal and monetary matters. By the early 1920s, he encountered one of his first moments of disillusionment with the Revolution, when his negotiations with the United States over loan repayments and oil fell apart as a result of politics and chicanery by both U.S. and Mexican bankers and officials. In the wake

19. Silva Herzog, *Nueve estudios mexicanos*, 244–45; Knight, *Mexican Revolution*, 2:525.
20. Silva Herzog, *El pensamiento económico*, 506–7.
21. Pani, *Apuntes autobiográficos*, 1:76.
22. Haynes, "Orden y Progreso," 260–61, 269; Rovzar, "Alberto J. Pani," 219–20.
23. Haynes, "Orden y Progreso," 265, 275. On the developmental proclivities of Pani, see Knight, *U.S.-Mexican Relations*, 56. On nineteenth-century scientific politics, see Hale, *Transformation of Liberalism*.
24. On the early years of Gómez Morin, see Recio, "El abogado y la empresa," chapter 3.

of this experience, he advocated the businesslike organization of the federal government as a way for the state to take up the task of pursuing capitalist opportunities in areas where the private sector had traditionally lagged, including in mining, forestry, and industrial credit.[25]

The group of technocrats that emerged in the 1920s was diverse, and it included intellectuals born not of Porfirian progress but rather of revolutionary promise. Many of them, including Daniel Cosío Villegas and Gonzalo Robles, did not reach the height of their influence until the 1930s and 1940s. But they began their public lives as engineers, researchers, and lower-level officials for the Sonoran-led governments, and they helped to constitute the intellectually heterodox, technocratic wing of the revolutionary family in the 1920s. Though divided over the meanings and practices of social justice and economic nationalism, among other things, these intellectuals from across the political spectrum were united by their common belief in the power of an activist state guided by technical and scientific knowledge—rather than politics, class warfare, and corruption—that would bring about social transformation and long-term capitalist growth.

This technocratic vision of state-guided economic development was a powerful countercurrent to the Porfirian bankers, who sought to use their expertise in the financial sector and ties to foreign lenders to reestablish their influence over fiscal and monetary policy. Pani believed that a central bank had the potential to curb their influence, since it would provide the state with fiscal autonomy from private interests and with a mechanism for more centralized economic policy making.[26] Pani's predecessor as head of the SHCP, Adolfo de la Huerta (1920–23), had tried to secure international credit to finance a central bank, but he had been rebuffed, ostensibly due to ongoing loan and oil disputes with the United States. According to Pani, however, de la Huerta's alliance with the head of the Banco Nacional de México, Agustín Legorreta, in support of reasserting the private sector's control over central banking had also undermined state efforts to extend its authority over fiscal affairs. Pani cited the 1922 De la Huerta–Lamont Treaty with the United States as evidence of de la Huerta's ineffectiveness, since it set up unrealistic debt repayment conditions, with no proviso for future loans from foreign banks. With few other options and possibly deceived by de la Huerta as to the treaty's limitations, President Obregón reluctantly

---

25. J. Meyer, "Revolution and Reconstruction," 218–19; Krauze, *Caudillos culturales*, 47–48, 115–18, 137–40.

26. Haynes, "*Orden y Progreso*," 266–67.

ratified it. He hoped that it would prompt the U.S. government to grant him diplomatic recognition, something that failed to occur.[27]

Adherence to the schedule of debt repayments laid out in the treaty was short-lived. In 1923, de la Huerta rebelled after discovering that Obregón's choice for Mexico's next president was Calles rather than de la Huerta himself. Under pressure to find international backing and financing to put down the revolt, Obregón more aggressively sought a compromise with the United States, and he authorized a quick resolution to the oil crisis. The August 1923 Bucareli Accords included significant concessions to foreign-owned oil companies, most notably the pledge that article 27 of the 1917 Constitution governing subsoil rights would not be applied retroactively. With U.S. recognition, and the financing that soon followed, President Obregón was able to quash de la Huerta and his rebel backers.

The 1923 revolt highlighted the political and economic constraints facing the postrevolutionary state, and it became a turning point in ending the stalemate between the Obregón administration and the financial sector. Though most elites did not actively participate in the rebellion, many in the banking and business community had supported de la Huerta. In response, and at the urging of Pani, President Obregón proposed the 1924 First National Banking Convention (Primera Convención Nacional Bancaria) as a platform to open up a dialogue between bankers and his government. The arrangement that resulted granted the financiers a privileged position in shaping banking and finance laws and policies. It also protected monopolistic aspects of the banking sector by creating high barriers to the formation of new banks. In return, bankers began to cooperate more fully with the president, including being minority investors when a central bank was created a year later.[28]

Although welcoming the détente with both the bankers and the United States, Pani remained convinced that the state's most pressing issue was fiscal autonomy from domestic and foreign lenders.[29] However, the Obregón government was still financially strapped owing to the costs of the rebellion and the strains of postrevolutionary recovery. By 1924, President Obregón once again suspended debt repayments, while the international lending community remained reluctant to grant loans to Mexico. This was particularly true of funds to establish a central bank, since some U.S. financiers

---

27. Kane, "Bankers and Diplomats"; Oñate, "La batalla," 657–59; Collado Herrera, *Empresarios y políticos*, 57, 73, 84, 111–12.

28. Haber, Maurer, and Razo, "Sustaining Economic Performance," 50–53; Collado Herrera, *Empresarios y políticos*, 99–103.

29. Pani, *La política hacendaria y la Revolución*, 75–83.

suggested that a central bank was unnecessary in a country of Mexico's stature. Some domestic bankers, including Agustín Legorreta, added that if a central bank were created, it should not be under state control.[30] Consequently, to generate revenue to start the bank, Pani imposed an income tax and austerity measures on the federal government. He stated that the income tax took aim specifically at regressive aspects of previous taxes, which he argued historically had favored a small cohort of elites to the detriment of the majority.[31] The tax provoked the ire of the business community. Bankers predictably opposed it because of Pani's intention to use the revenue to expand the state's fiscal authority.[32] Merchants and some industrialists railed against excessive taxation, and they expressed skepticism about the state's motives and ability to administer taxes. Their biggest objection may simply have been that the income tax was a blatant assertion of the power of the federal government over both business and regions. Not only was the tax enacted by emergency decree, but it was also a direct tax imposed by the federal government, even though direct taxation historically had been the exclusive domain of regional governments. Some industrialists added that the tax was unconstitutional, anti-economic, and even communistic for its assault on individualism.[33]

Despite this broad opposition, revenue from the income tax, as well as from the diversion of oil and railroad taxes that according to the 1922 De la Huerta–Lamont Treaty were supposed to be used to service the foreign debt, allowed the Calles administration to establish the Banco de México in 1925.[34] Though it remained relatively weak in its early years, the bank helped to stabilize public financing, augmented the state's regulation of the banking sector, and offered the federal government limited autonomy from private lenders.[35] Moreover, it enabled the state to enhance its tutelary role in stimulating the private sector to invest in industry or other productive fields, something the Calles administration also pursued through investment

---

30. Oñate, "La batalla," 634, 655.
31. Alberto J. Pani to gobernador, Nuevo León, July 22, 1925, Fondo Correspondencia Ministerios Federales (MF)/Serie Correspondencia Ministerio de Hacienda (MH)/AGENL, c. 38; Pani, *Apuntes autobiográficos*, 1:323–26, 333; Pani, *Apuntes autobiográficos*, 2:16–22. See also Córdova, *La ideología de la Revolución*, 351–57; Collado Herrera, *Empresarios y políticos*, 166–71, 191–97.
32. Haynes, "*Orden y Progreso*," 268.
33. Aboites Aguilar, *Excepciones y privilegios*, 133–43; Cárdenas, *La hacienda pública*, 80–81; Collado Herrera, *Empresarios y políticos*, 57, 73, 111–12, 162–71, 185–89, 198. Merchants, especially from Monterrey and Puebla, pressed for the total repeal of the income tax into at least the 1950s. Urquidi, "El impuesto sobre la renta," 424.
34. Oñate, "La batalla," 663.
35. Buchenau, *Plutarco Elías Calles*, 119–21.

in and regulation of transportation and public utilities.³⁶ Predictably, technocrats enthusiastically welcomed the creation of the Banco de México. Pani argued that it symbolized the fulfillment of the Revolution by laying the foundation for the economic independence of Mexico based on technical competence and domestic financing. He was joined by Gómez Morin, whom Pani had invited to spearhead the writing of the new central banking legislation. Gómez Morin, who served as the first chairman of the board of the Banco de México, averred that it represented the destruction of "earlier excesses" and would "make the existence of [financial] institutions like that which have always operated here impossible; pawnshops disguised as banks, unable to give sound service to those who deserve it and plagued by favoritism and other forms of corruption."³⁷

According to Gómez Morin, "technocrat" was an increasingly popular term in the 1920s, signifying skill, knowledge, and control in setting and achieving realistic goals.³⁸ As he and other intellectuals and officials envisioned it, technocrats would assist an interventionist state in pursuing industrial development without succumbing to the passions and corruption that had marked the Porfirian era. Claiming that Mexico needed more technocrats, one official at the Department of Labor (Departamento del Trabajo) asserted, "Our century is the century of efficiency, the century of specialists, of technocrats, not that of masters and lords who . . . try to survive, despite the times in which they live, by clinging to their traditions and customs."³⁹ Gómez Morin's élan soon faded, however. Already by the late 1920s, the Banco de México had become a lender to several revolutionary insiders, including Aarón Sáenz; Presidents Obregón and Calles; Luis N. Morones, who was the head of the Regional Confederation of Mexican Workers (Confederación Regional Obrera Mexicana, CROM) and, from 1924 through 1928, served as the top official of the Secretariat of Industry, Commerce, and Labor (Secretaría de Industria, Comercio, y Trabajo, SICT); and even Pani himself.⁴⁰ Gómez Morin, discouraged with the cronyism and corrupt lending practices that had taken over the Banco de México, resigned from his position as head of the bank in 1928. Although the fiscal

---

36. This contrasted with the Porfirian state, which had developed infrastructure by granting monopoly rights to private companies, many of them foreign. C. W. Anderson, "Bankers as Revolutionaries," 118–19.
37. Manuel Gómez Morin to Valentín R. Garfias, September 25, 1925, Archivo Manuel Gómez Morin (AMGM), v. 232, exp. 742.
38. Krauze, *La reconstrucción económica*, 13.
39. Jefe, Departamento del Trabajo, SICT, report, August 15, 1923, DT/AGN, c. 680, exp. 15.
40. Cavazos Lerma, "Cincuenta años de política monetaria," 67; Zebadúa, *Banqueros y revolucionarios*, 256–58; Buchenau, *Plutarco Elías Calles*, 93; Rodríguez Garza, "Cambio institucional," 30.

base of the state remained fragile and subject to clientelism and political interference, Gómez Morin had nevertheless been right to emphasize the significance of technocrats to postrevolutionary governments. To be sure, the compromise with Porfirian merchant-financiers conceded significant privileges to the banking sector based in part on political considerations. And the postrevolutionary state never became the domain of technocrats instead of politicians, as Pani had urged. However, technocrats helped to overcome the oligarchic tendencies and factionalism of Porfirian rule and to expand the capacity of the revolutionary victors to build a broader base of political support by institutionalizing their relations with emerging groups, including industry and labor.

The Politics of Protectionism, 1917–34

In 1916, to address problems with scarcities, Venustiano Carranza lowered tariffs on a range of primary materials, textiles, and foodstuffs. Though this was part of his effort to secure social peace as the violence of the Revolution waned, it drew sharp opposition from industrialists, especially from Mexico's influential textile companies. This friction over tariff modifications foreshadowed the outcome of President Carranza's attempts to strengthen his relationship with industrialists at the First National Congress of Industrialists (Primer Congreso Nacional de Industriales) in late 1917. Sensing the cloud of muted antagonism that hung over the event, Pani, secretary of Industry, Commerce, and Labor in 1917 and 1918, opened the event by emphasizing that its purpose was to build ties between government and industry. Despite his calls for cooperation, however, the oil, mining, and textile industrialists who dominated the congress responded by condemning articles 27 and 123 of the 1917 Constitution, arguing they constituted an illegitimate statist assault on individual rights over property and labor. When Pani rebuked them for improperly trying to induce federal legislators to modify the Constitution, their attacks on articles 27 and 123 intensified. In the end, the only tangible result of the congress was an agreement to form the Confederation of Industrial Chambers (Confederación de Cámaras Industriales, CONCAMIN).[41]

41. Haber, Razo, and Maurer, *Politics of Property Rights*, 44–47. See also Haber, Maurer, and Razo, "Sustaining Economic Performance," 25–46; Córdova, *La ideología de la Revolución*, 365–67; Shafer, *Mexican Business Organizations*, 16, 25–41, 147–48, 240 n. 68; Ramírez Rancaño, "El Primer Congreso de Industriales," 84, 94–95, 105–8; Puga, "La Confederación de Cámaras Industriales," 106–8, 123–24; Alcazar, *Las agrupaciones patronales,* 33–34; Juárez González, "Una década en la organización," 258.

The hostilities that erupted at the congress reproduced industrialists' fears that constitutional changes would facilitate the expansion of state economic intervention. These worries resounded through debates over protectionist policies in the 1920s and 1930s. Tariffs themselves were not at issue. Even Mexico's most ardent supporters of economic liberalism, including the Monterrey Group, had long had a pragmatic appreciation of the role that limited tariffs could play in advancing industrialization, even as they advocated for stronger trade links with foreign markets.[42] Therefore, disagreements over protectionism frequently were less about specific policy than about the political and social aspirations of industrialists amid the reconstruction of the state and society in the 1920s. As part of his effort to manage his relationship with Mexico's industrialists, President Calles created tariff commissions in the late 1920s. Although these commissions outwardly demonstrated the state's commitment to industrial development, they also served as a proxy for the incorporation of the private sector at a time of limited political representation. Yet, President Calles also underscored that their members were to employ a technocratic emphasis on the science, study, and analysis of Mexican industry. Therefore, these commissions functioned to incorporate industrialists politically while restraining their ability to influence the state.

Most industrialists suffered production and sales setbacks during the armed phase of the Revolution due to transportation problems, endemic violence, social upheaval, and predation by different revolutionary factions. Yet, in part, the economic impact of the Revolution was mitigated by World War I, because it led to continued, and even higher, demand for some Mexican goods, including agricultural exports. It also inflated the prices paid for Mexican minerals and thereby offset the temporary decline in the volume of mineral exports.[43] By the late 1910s and early 1920s, most industries recovered production and sales, many still with the same owners. Like bankers, these industrialists sought to reestablish protection and the crony arrangements that had ensured profits during the late Porfirian period.[44] In some ways, they succeeded. Tariffs and tax breaks remained in place, many secured loans, and in some sectors, the government tolerated monopolistic practices. Consequently, companies with Porfirian origins continued to dominate many industrial sectors in the 1920s, including cement, textiles,

---

42. Beatty, *Institutions and Investment*, chapter 3.
43. Kuntz Ficker, "Export Boom"; Coatsworth, "United States and Democracy," 145.
44. Womack, "Mexican Economy." See also Reynolds, *Mexican Economy,* 28–29; Haber, *Industry and Underdevelopment,* 5, 44, 67–69, 124–39.

steel, beer, dynamite, soap, paper, glass, and cigarettes. Joining them was a wave of foreign subsidiaries, such as Ford Motor Company, Bayer, DuPont, and Palmolive, and new entrepreneurs, including William Jenkins, Carlos Trouyet, and Raúl Bailleres.[45]

The response of Mexico's large-scale industrialists to the efforts of the Obregón and Calles administrations to intervene in the development of industry varied. The industrialists and merchants of the socially conservative, economically autonomous Monterrey Group expressed disquiet about state economic intervention, and in particular about its impact on their rights over labor and their access to U.S. markets and supplies. Arguing from a classic liberal position, they contended that protectionism inhibited capitalist industrial development by eliminating the free and fair competition of individuals and abrogating the rights of private property. They added that protectionism allowed for inefficient production, which contributed to higher prices and lower-quality goods that could not compete with foreign manufactures. Monterrey's businesspeople concluded that tariffs and other protectionist policies consequently were prejudicial because they placed the well-being of a few producers ahead of consumers and workers, a sentiment that President Calles later echoed. To an extent, Pani and others in the Obregón administration backed them. Pani, for example, condemned protectionism for unjustly favoring some industrialists over others and thereby slowing market-oriented progress. Officials in the Department of Labor criticized protection that helped industries that could neither compete with foreign manufacturers nor pay a fair wage.[46] Yet, akin to many nineteenth-century liberals, Pani also maintained that there were exceptions, specifically for some infant industries, as well as for new industries that had come into existence with tariffs and needed time to adapt to international trade conditions.[47] Similarly, and despite their ideological position, the businessmen of the Monterrey Group also accepted the need for limited tariffs, at the very least for their own industries, and they regularly requested them from both the state and federal governments. They bolstered these requests with attestations about their contributions, as captains of industry, to the collective welfare. For example, when the cement producers in Monterrey requested more protection, they emphasized that their industry provided jobs for a

45. Haber, *Industry and Underdevelopment*, 6–7, 26, 124, 141–43, 151–52.
46. Jefe, Departamento del Trabajo, SICT, report, August 15, 1923, DT/AGN, c. 680, exp. 15.
47. Pani, *Apuntes autobiográficos*, 2:22–24; Cámara Nacional de Comercio, Industria, y Minería del Estado de Nuevo León to Secretario de Industria, Comercio y Trabajo Aarón Sáenz, November 8, 1930, Fondo Industria y Comercio (IC)/AGENL, c. 4; Córdova, *La ideología de la Revolución*, 319.

large number of workers.[48] In the end, their professed belief in economic liberalism was often more about contesting the growing power of the state and the threat that it posed to the rights of individuals than it was about policy itself.

By contrast, textile industrialists, who historically had enjoyed tariff protection for their products, assailed what they alleged was the market-oriented, export focus of the Sonoran-dominated governments and their merchant backers. As early as 1916, textile industrialists had confronted the Carranza government over tariff reductions, condemning his administration's commitment to laissez-faire principles.[49] They also criticized President Obregón for what they claimed was his emphasis on free trade and apathy toward national industry. During the final months of 1922, Puebla's textile industrialists complained vigorously to both the state and federal governments about the crisis in their industry. They attributed it to a number of factors, including problems with cotton supplies; the inundation of U.S. contraband across the northern border; high energy costs; and worker theft, absence, and opposition to management.[50] In 1923 under heavy pressure from textile owners, and coincidentally facing fiscal crisis, President Obregón raised tariff rates and compelled domestic cotton growers to supply the textile industry before exporting any surplus. But the impact of these measures was negligible. Between 1920 and 1924, imported cloth as a percentage of total national consumption of cloth actually rose from 16.16 percent to 22.42 percent.[51]

For an array of reasons, labor groups also often supported protectionist policies.[52] Some were readily apparent, such as when workers in the textile and sugar industries backed employers' bids for tariffs in return for salary guarantees.[53] Other workers did so out of a sense that unfair competition caused by an influx of U.S. textiles was undermining their industry, especially because owners exploited the crisis by cutting wages, shortening hours, and closing factories. But labor leaders soon reached the limits of

48. Cementos Portland Monterrey, S.A. and Cementos Hidalgo, S.A. to Secretario de Industria, Comercio, y Trabajo Manuel Puig Casauranc, September 19, 1928, IC/AGENL, c. 3.
49. Puga, "La Confederación de Cámaras Industriales," 108–9; Gómez Galvarriato, "Impact of Revolution," 604, 608.
50. Centro Industrial Mexicano to gobernador, Puebla, memorandum, October 22, 1922, and "Memorandum sobre la crisis actual del trabajo," Centro Industrial Mexicano, November 9, 1922, both in DT/AGN, c. 488, exp. 9.
51. SEN, Departamento de Estudios Económicos, *La industria textil en México*, 151–52.
52. "Notas sobre las actividades del estado en materia de fomento industrial," 1939, Fondo Gonzalo Robles (GR)/AGN, c. 84, exp. 5.
53. Haber, Razo, and Maurer, *Politics of Property Rights*, 154.

their ability to pressure the Obregón administration to intervene. For example, in 1921, union leaders wrote to President Obregón to complain that U.S. competition was causing a deterioration of labor-employer relations. While advocating for more protection, they also maintained that the state needed to enact federal enabling legislation for article 123 of the 1917 Constitution. In an unusual and perhaps foolhardy coda to their letter, they stated that if the government did not step in to help the industry's impoverished workers, they could not be responsible for the worker unrest that might ensue. In a stinging rebuke, President Obregón's representative stated that Mexico's lower salaries meant that owners should have no difficulty competing with U.S. manufacturers and that no further protection was needed. He added that the president would not be swayed by threats, and should the workers choose unrest, they would regret their decision.[54]

Workers also backed some industrial policy simply because it explicitly promoted the creation of jobs. For example, a 1926 tax-exemption decree specified that to qualify, 80 percent of an established company's workforce must be Mexican workers (for new companies, the figure was 50 percent). By creating more jobs in the formal sector, protected industrial growth would likely expand the power base of organized labor as well as benefit unions politically. The payoff for politicians was also potentially high. For example, when the government conferred a package of tariffs on the cotton textile industry in the late 1920s, it did so contingent on employers' acceptance of a collective contract that protected jobs and enforced higher salaries. Not only did this garner broad support from textile unions and assurances of social peace; it also helped the antiquated, albeit economically crucial, industry survive despite its bloated workforce.[55]

In the early 1920s, industrialists struggled for political influence as the Obregón administration focused on developing mining, oil, and agriculture. Once accords with the United States allowed the oil and loan issues to be temporarily deferred in the mid-1920s, however, President Calles turned his attention to Mexico's rapidly developing industrial sector. His goal was not just to satisfy Mexico's large-scale, established industrialists. He and his immediate successors, and perhaps to a lesser extent President Obregón, had also sought to foster small industry and build an enduring base of support

---

54. Federación Obrera de Hilados y Tejidos del Distrito Federal to Obregón, April 4, 1921, and August 28, 1921, and Palacio Nacional to Juan J. Durán, secretario general, Confederación Obrera de Hilados y Tejidos, et al., September 3, 1921, all in Fondo Álvaro Obregón-Plutarco Elías Calles (OC)/AGN, 407-H-2.

55. SEN, Departamento de Estudios Económicos, *La industria textil en México*, 73–104; Gómez Galvarriato, "Impact of Revolution," 154–57, 171, 602–16.

among Mexico's burgeoning and increasingly diverse small- and medium-scale industrialists.[56] Thus, President Calles's 1926 federal tax-exemption legislation specifically targeted small-scale producers. Before the 1920s, Mexico had already experimented with various iterations of federal tax-exemption legislation. The most prominent was the 1893 New Industries (Industrias Nuevas) decree, which granted tax exemptions to new industries with a minimum capital investment of Mex$250,000 (reduced to Mex$100,000 in 1898, or about US$50,000 at that time).[57] By comparison, the 1926 law offered three-year exemptions only to companies capitalized with less than Mex$5,000. President Calles supported this lower limit by citing the obstacles to the launch of small industry in Mexico, especially the lack of credit. However, few companies applied for the exemption, even after the state slightly loosened the restriction on capitalization in 1932.[58] The significance of the law therefore had less to do with industrial promotion than with the ambition of President Calles to harness the political potential of the owners of the legion of small- and medium-sized industrial companies emerging in the 1920s.

Under President Calles and his successors, tariffs became one of the most active and interventionist arenas of industrial policy. The political facets of protectionism are evident in the shifts that occurred in tariff policy from the late nineteenth to the early twentieth century. Some scholars have argued that the primary factor shaping tariff rates in Mexico from the nineteenth century through much of the 1930s was the state's need for revenue.[59] For the nineteenth century, when import and export taxes constituted more than 50 percent of federal revenue and governments often adjusted rates to raise revenue in response to economic crises, this assertion has merit.[60] Revenue remained a primary motive during the Revolution as well. For example, in 1916, when Carranza lowered tariffs on a range of primary materials, textiles, and foodstuffs, he concurrently raised them on some other consumer items and intermediate goods in order to generate revenue, even though inflation erased any protectionist gains.[61]

56. SICT, *Memoria de los trabajos*, 14–20, 147; A. Vázquez del Mercado, subsecretario, SICT, Departamento de Fomento Industrial y Comercial, March 1923, DT/AGN, c. 680, exp. 12; "Plan financiero que se propone desarrollar el Sr. Ing. Pascual Ortiz Rubio para el arreglo definitivo de las diversas deudas con banqueros o ciudadanos americanos y para el resurgimiento económico de México," 1930, Fondo Pascual Ortiz Rubio (POR)/AGN, 1931, 68/7110.
57. Beatty, *Institutions and Investment*, 152.
58. Cordero H., *Concentración industrial*, 10; King, *Mexico: Industrialization and Trade*, 99; Mosk, *Industrial Revolution in Mexico*, 63.
59. For example, see Story, *Industry*, 33; Mosk, *Industrial Revolution in Mexico*, 68–69.
60. Márquez Colín, "Political Economy," 2, 202–4.
61. Márquez Colín, "Protección y Cambio Institucional," 381–83; Gómez Galvarriato, "Impact of Revolution," 609.

Recently, though, scholars have shown that the desire for revenue in the nineteenth century did not occur to the exclusion of developmental considerations. By the late Porfirian period, a cascading tariff structure that placed higher tariffs on manufactured goods than on inputs and machinery for most industries underpinned an incipient form of import substitution that sheltered domestic manufacturers from foreign competition.[62] Even Daniel Cosío Villegas, who in the early 1930s condemned the ignorance that had shaped tariff policy since independence, noted that tariffs had always served a dual purpose of generating revenue and developing industry.[63] But the balance between the goals of revenue and industrial development was not stable across the nineteenth and early twentieth centuries. As shown by Graciela Márquez Colín, the shifting political weight of protectionists and free traders during the Porfiriato had a significant effect on tariff rates, with each of the three factors concurrently reflected to some degree in tariff policy at all times. The balance shifted decisively away from revenue after the Revolution, however. Between 1918 and 1930, import tariffs as a percentage of federal income dropped below 30 percent, whereas between 1900 and 1910, they still represented 45 percent. This occurred even as average tariff rates recovered during the 1920s, reaching late Porfirian levels again by 1930.[64] In their place, the state tried to impose more reliable forms of internal taxes, such as the 1925 income tax, which aimed in part to make state revenue impermeable to the vagaries of import and export taxes. Thus, President Pascual Ortiz Rubio (1930–32) could confidently state that his administration had designed the 1930 general tariff revision, which was the first substantial overhaul of tariff policy since the Porfiriato, not to earn revenue but rather to develop industry.[65]

As tariffs became more weakly moored to revenue, issues surrounding postrevolutionary reconstruction and development surged to the fore of tariff debates. Though the economy had rebounded by the mid-1920s, it was a recovery clouded by agrarian reform demands, *cristero* violence, and labor radicalism, all of which conspired with the early onset of the Great Depression in Mexico to make investors cautious. Moreover, resentment about the influence of U.S. investors in Mexico predated the Revolution,

---

62. Beatty, *Institutions and Investment*, 63–65, 74.
63. Cosío Villegas, *La cuestión arancelaria*, 20–21, 33–34. See also Salvucci, Salvucci, and Cohen, "Politics of Protection."
64. Esquivel and Márquez Colín, "Some Economic Effects," 337.
65. Márquez Colín, "Political Economy," 2, 8–9, 15–73, 202–4; Márquez Colín, "Protección y cambio institucional," 385–89, 394.

but by the 1920s, it was intensifying over Mexico's complicated and dependent relationship with the United States, as evidenced in loan disputes and Mexico's pronounced nationalist sentiment regarding oil. Presidents Obregón and Calles both supported the goal, as stated by Manuel Gómez Morín, of turning foreign capital into "'the servant rather than a master of the Mexican economy.'"[66] Yet, characteristic of the national bourgeoisie in the 1920s, neither president saw the need to limit foreign investment or sever economic ties with the United States. Rather, their nationalist sensibilities remained ardently capitalist, shaped by both their appreciation of the model of U.S. development and their recognition of the importance of U.S. investment to economic recovery and state-building. Therefore, though oil policy would turn much more radical in the 1930s, Obregón and Calles both continued in the 1920s to promote outward-oriented growth that focused on the revival of foreign-owned oil companies and renewed access to foreign loans. Additionally, President Calles courted foreign direct investment using tax and other incentives.[67]

In this context, economic nationalism connoted the ambition to establish a balanced trade relationship with the United States by reducing Mexico's dependence on manufactured imports and primary material exports.[68] President Calles therefore targeted economic policy to diversify domestic industry and agriculture. For example, the 1926 federal tax-exemption legislation made exemptions available solely to companies that were nationally owned and that favored the use of domestic raw materials.[69] But efforts at diversification did little to fundamentally alter Mexico's trade relationship with the United States, as evidenced when the Great Depression hit with full force in 1929. In the three following years, as trade with the United States fell off, the volume of exports dropped a stunning 37 percent and a "demand shock" led to an 18 percent decline in the GDP.[70] It is no coincidence, then, that as part of an economic stimulus package designed to respond to the crisis, the 1930 Tariff Code revised rates in a way that explicitly aimed to lessen dependence by increasing the protection of Mexican industry and diversifying its industrial base. The code raised tariff rates and expanded the number and variety of goods covered to 2,771 categories. Clothing and textiles received the highest levels of protection, followed by agricultural

66. J. Meyer, "Revolution and Reconstruction," 218–19.
67. Buchenau, *Plutarco Elías Calles*, 121–22; Knight, "Political Economy," 299.
68. Córdova, *La Revolución en crisis*, 55–56; Collado Herrera, *Empresarios y políticos*, 213–14.
69. Cordero H., *Concentración industrial*, 10; King, *Mexico: Industrialization and Trade*, 99; Mosk, *Industrial Revolution in Mexico*, 63.
70. Cárdenas, "Process of Accelerated Industrialization," 178–79.

products and foodstuffs, which at that time were among the largest contributors to the national economy. Also included were steel and iron products, alcoholic beverages, cotton, some oils and chemicals, motion pictures, paper, and a variety of other manufactures, raw materials, and equipment.[71]

The impact of the 1930 Tariff Code on economic recovery and dependence remains under debate. Even with broader coverage and higher rates of protection, E. V. K. FitzGerald maintains that the revisions contributed more to the federal budget and the balance of payments than to fostering industry.[72] Enrique Cárdenas adds that by the early 1930s, a drop in imports and a monetary contraction led to higher demand for domestically produced goods. This set off a series of monetary and fiscal policies that, rather than tariffs, were responsible for accelerating import-substituting industrialization.[73] Consequently, although the average tariff rate appears protectionist at first glance, its overall effect on industry remains ambiguous. Indeed, tariff modifications enacted on some intermediate inputs, such as chemicals, had the corollary of hurting manufacturing sectors that relied on those goods. Ultimately, the cascading tariff structure that had protected final manufactured goods since the Porfiriato remained intact but with great variation across different industries.[74]

However, the function of tariffs transcended their impact on economic recovery. As their importance to federal revenue diminished, they became more subject to the politics of postrevolutionary reconstruction, and, in particular, to the Sonoran leaders' efforts to manage their relationship with industrialists. The Carranza administration took an initial step when it formed a tariff commission in 1919 with industrialist, merchant, and labor representation. But the tariff commission accomplished little under President Obregón, confining itself to vague recommendations.[75] With its sights set on oil and foreign loans, the Obregón administration developed no substantive institutional means to compose tariff policy or integrate industrialists into policy making. Not coincidentally, in 1920, 1921, and 1922, effective tariff rates on imports were among the lowest in Mexico's history.[76] Moreover, during those years, CONCAMIN railed against the SHCP for failing

---

71. Cosío Villegas, *La cuestión arancelaria*, 18–19, 43; Kate and Wallace, *Protection and Economic Development*, 21–22; Mosk, *Industrial Revolution in Mexico*, 68.
72. FitzGerald, "Restructuring through the Depression," 223–24.
73. Cárdenas, "Great Depression," 201–8; Cárdenas, "Process of Accelerated Industrialization," 178–82; Haber, *Industry and Underdevelopment*, 150–56; Zebadúa, *Banqueros y revolucionarios*, 335.
74. Márquez Colín, "Protección y cambio institucional," 388; Haber, Razo, and Maurer, *Politics of Property Rights*, 152–53.
75. Collado Herrera, *Empresarios y políticos*, 219–23.
76. Cosío Villegas, *La cuestión arancelaria*, 60–61.

to provide it with representation on tariff commissions. It even requested the creation of a permanent tariff commission that would include industry representation and would consult with the government's technocrats. CONCAMIN pessimistically concluded, however, that the president would never recognize its members' expertise on tariff issues.[77]

In part to alleviate the dissension that had arisen between President Obregón and disgruntled industrialists, President Calles refocused his administration's efforts on helping industry and on developing opportunities for the private sector to participate on official commissions. In 1925, Pani formalized the tariff commission originally established in 1919, stating that part of his intent was to give a fuller voice to private-sector interests in advising on tariff rates. The new tariff commission included five government representatives, one representative from the Confederation of National Chambers of Commerce (Confederación de Cámaras Nacionales de Comercio, CONCANACO), and one nonvoting representative from CONCAMIN. In 1927, Calles modified the commission to include three more government representatives, as well as one representative each from the agrarian and labor sectors. As part of its responsibilities, the restructured commission was to assimilate scientific and technical considerations into tariff decisions through the analysis of industry and resources. Its primary task was to recommend revisions of the current tariff law, in effect since 1891, in order to normalize tariffs and taxes on trade.[78] In cooperation with other agencies, such as the SICT, the commission dispatched teams of delegates to conduct technical studies of those companies seeking, or already enjoying, tariff protection, including in the steel, cement, textile, beer, glass, chemical, soap, and paper industries. With the information culled from these studies, the commission generated reports that analyzed the production process, from the acquisition of primary materials through distribution and marketing. From 1925 to 1927, the SICT delegates conducted 4,478 factory visits to more than two hundred types of factories.[79]

Pani supported the restructuring of the commission because he believed that the technical analysis of industry and resources would limit the influence of politics over tariff policy and ultimately advance the interests of free trade. During the early and late Porfirian periods, when tariff policy was

77. Annual reports for 1920–21, 1921–22, and 1923, in CONCAMIN, *La Confederación de Cámaras Industriales*, vol. 1.
78. Márquez Colín, "Protección y cambio institucional," 384–85, 394–95; annual reports for 1924–25, 1926–27, and 1927–28, in CONCAMIN, *La Confederación de Cámaras Industriales*, vol. 1.
79. Comisión de Aranceles, Secretaría de Hacienda y Crédito Público (SHCP), memorandum, March 2, 1928, MF/MH/AGENL, c. 38; SICT, *La industria, el comercio y el trabajo*, 118, 133–41.

more important than rates of exchange and price trends in determining effective rates of protection, a variety of people close to the Díaz administration had informally shaped policy, including industrialists, politicians, foreign diplomats, and customs officials.[80] But despite Pani's efforts to formalize the commission and prevent the reassertion of similar influence peddling, limited state resources and weak institutional controls allowed clientelism and politics to reinsert themselves in the tariff-setting process. This was exacerbated because the executive could change tariff rates without congressional approval.[81] Thus, CONCAMIN regularly pressed various state agencies to modify tariffs in order to help its members.[82] And cement manufacturers from Monterrey lobbied multiple government officials and agencies, urging them to pressure the executive to better protect their industry. They began with the tariff commission, requesting both higher tariffs and the termination of an exemption that allowed foreign companies to sell cement to border cities. This exemption had originally been enacted to supply urban beautification projects along the border, though foreign cement soon spread into the rest of Mexico due to lower production costs abroad and high rail transport costs in Mexico that made it cheaper to ship cement to Yucatán from Europe than to bring it from Monterrey. Producers in that city also took their case to the SICT and Nuevo León governor José Benítez (1928), asking them to intervene on their behalf. Governor Benítez subsequently contacted no fewer than three government secretariats to request a cancellation of the exemption for foreign producers, pointing out that an advantage of enhancing domestic production was the possibility of paving Mexico's roadways. In March 1929, after years of pleas, Monterrey's producers finally succeeded in having the exemption cancelled.[83]

In his well-known history of tariff policy published in the early 1930s, Daniel Cosío Villegas contended that this pressure from industrialists and merchants had deformed tariff policy in the 1920s into an instrument of elite interests. Rather than leading to free trade, as had been Pani's original hope when he formalized the tariff commission, the private sector's advisory role in setting tariff rates led to steady tariff increases during the late 1920s.[84]

80. Márquez Colín, "Political Economy," 204; Márquez Colín, "Protección y cambio institucional," 381; Beatty, *Institutions and Investment*, chapter 3.
81. Esquivel and Márquez Colín, "Some Economic Effects," 336–37.
82. Numerous annual reports for the 1920s, in CONCAMIN, *La Confederación de Cámaras Industriales*, vol. 1.
83. Cementos Portland Monterrey, S.A., Cementos Hidalgo, S.A., SICT, SHCP, Secretaría de Comunicaciones y Obras Públicas, and Gobernador José Benítez, correspondence, September 19, 1928–March 8, 1929, IC/AGENL, c. 3.
84. Cosío Villegas, *La cuestión arancelaria*, 97–101; Márquez Colín, "Daniel Cosío Villegas," 888.

Businesspeople from Monterrey agreed, arguing that the commission had not applied the proper technical criteria when assigning tariffs, had responded too rapidly to transitory incidents, and had succumbed to the personal interests and ideological convictions of a select few connected to the executive, to the detriment of economic stability, investor confidence, and national interest.[85]

The politics of industrial protectionism in the 1920s and early 1930s revealed the complexities of postrevolutionary state-building and economic reconstruction. In the arena of economic policy, technocrats claimed a special place, asserting that scientific analysis and technical knowledge, as the basis for industrial policy, would encourage the rise of industries able to compete freely in international markets. Advocates of free trade, especially from Monterrey, backed them, even as their pragmatic and opportunistic support of tariffs betrayed their liberal demands. When President Calles formalized the tariff commission in 1925, however, his intention had not been to encourage free trade. He instead sought to appeal to industrialists by giving priority to industry and providing a means for private-sector representation in policy making at a time when formal political inclusion did not exist.

Regionalism and Economic Planning, 1925–34

In 1928, President Calles demonstrated his confidence in technocrats when he declared that economic policy based on calculations, statistics, and experience would be the basis for future development.[86] With the early effects of the Great Depression hitting Mexico by 1926, President Calles most likely was seeking to generate faith in the state's ability to lessen the impact.[87] He and his successors attempted to employ technocratic means to

---

85. Cámara Nacional de Comercio, Industria, y Minería del Estado de Nuevo León to Secretario de Industria, Comercio, y Trabajo Aarón Sáenz, November 8, 1930; Cámara Nacional de Comercio, Industria, y Minería del Estado de Nuevo León to Secretario de Hacienda y Crédito Público, November 25, 1930; Cámara Nacional del Comercio, Industria, y Minería del Estado de Nuevo León to Cámara Nacional de Comercio, December 17, 1930, all in IC/AGENL, c. 4; editorial, *Excélsior*, December 16, 1930.

86. Secretaría de Programación y Presupuesto, *Los primeros intentos de planeación*, 19.

87. Enrique Cárdenas finds that various depressive forces were already affecting the Mexican economy by 1925. Cárdenas, *La industrialización mexicana*, 32. Stephen H. Haber adds that a general economic contraction due to falling demand and declining output and investment began in 1926, with GDP dropping 5.9 percent in 1927 alone and 30.9 percent overall between 1926 and 1932. Haber, *Industry and Underdevelopment*, 150–56.

manage the economy with a spate of planning commissions and decrees. These commissions were to coordinate the various factors of production and allocate resources to maximize growth and distribution, including by collecting information about industry, mining, and agriculture from across Mexico. But the regional focus of many of these studies and commissions indicates that federal intervention also sought to integrate regional producers and consumers into a national project for economic development as a means to undermine state-level challenges to callista authority. This motivation was especially decisive after the formation of the PNR in 1929, when it became evident how some populist regional governments remained out of step with the conservative callista currents that dominated the new ruling party. Indeed, even though the PNR had a strong regionalist structure made up of a loose confederation of state and national parties, its operation was authoritarian and strived to contain regional and factional rivalries.[88] Many industrialists welcomed its efforts to suppress regional radicalism and the populist governors who supported it. Yet, they nevertheless expressed concern about the intrusion of the federal government into regional forms of authority and were alarmed by what they saw as the efforts of the state to use these planning commissions and decrees to subvert the right of private enterprise to determine local production. In this climate, an array of business elites and regional politicians responded with opposition or noncompliance to the planning endeavors of President Calles and his immediate successors.

Though President Calles referenced the technocratic appeal of planning and efficiency, the administrations of the 1920s and 1930s struggled to move planning beyond the political, partly because President Obregón and especially President Calles used these planning commissions explicitly to incorporate industrialists, labor, and other groups into the policy-making process. Most planning agencies included not just technocrats but also representatives of industrialists, merchants, campesinos, consumers, cultural groups, and the working class. This provided the state with a means to manage these diverse interests, but it also invited conflicts over various groups' competing demands into the core of economic decision making. One classic example was the abortive National Economic Council (Consejo Nacional Económico), which formed in 1928. Designed to be an independent consultant to the government, its mission was to foster collaboration between the public and private sectors for economic development. Its representatives came from government ministries; the business, educational, scientific, and cultural communities; consumer groups;

---

88. Middlebrook, *Paradox of Revolution*, 26; Hamilton, *Limits of State Autonomy*, 76–77.

campesinos; and the working class. In laying out the mission of the council, President Calles made clear that the information and insights it generated would be the foundation of his new economic plan.[89] However, the business community balked at taking part. Reflecting the president's belief that these commissions should contribute to the consolidation of the state, his administration in response condemned the business community, not for impeding economic development, but for missing a prime opportunity to exercise influence in the Calles government.[90]

Economic planning commissions and decrees often explicitly focused on Mexico's diverse regions and on overcoming regional political and productive arrangements that were seen as undermining national economic development.[91] Pani, in particular, perceived an active state as important to reining in regional radicalism. Like other developmentalist liberals, he saw local and regional governments as especially susceptible to the pull of political passions.[92] As evidence, he and other technocrats pointed to the multitude of distinct, arbitrary, and vague state-level protectionist laws, fiscal legislation, and planning ventures, which they argued lacked technical criteria. For example, between 1926 and 1930, ten states enacted protectionist legislation for industry. By 1933, that number had grown to nineteen. The laws protected an array of activities important on a regional level, some of which were only tangentially industrial, such as mining, transportation, electric energy, agriculture, forestry, tourism, construction, urban development, and even health and cultural services.[93] In light of this diversity at the regional level, national legislation could have only a weak impact on promoting industrial development.

The statist zeal to coordinate regional variations of industrial development became especially prominent in the early 1930s, as the state pursued economic recovery. Among those most committed to the idea of creating a more planned economy was Primo Villa Michel, from 1932 to 1934 the head of the Secretariat of the National Economy (the Secretaría de la Economía Nacional [SEN] succeeded the SICT in 1932). He captured planning's dual mission when he told state governors that if they wanted Mexico

89. Secretaría de Programación y Presupuesto, *Los primeros intentos de planeación,* 19.
90. SICT to gobernador, Nuevo León, July 6, 1927, DF/SSICT/AGENL, c. 2.
91. Similarly, Mark Wasserman shows how some Porfirian elites allied with new elites in regional settings in order to challenge the efforts of the nascent national ruling party to consolidate its authority in the late 1920s and early 1930s. Wasserman, *Persistent Oligarchs.*
92. Haynes, *"Orden y Progreso,"* 265; Knight, "El liberalismo mexicano," 61.
93. Banco de México, "Análisis de las leyes de protección y fomento industrial," 1946, GR/AGN, c. 77 bis (2), exp. 3, pp. 4–13.

to distinguish itself from other colonial countries while helping their regional economies, they needed to submit to a national economic plan. According to Villa Michel, it would aim to stabilize financing and avoid market disruptions by determining industry locations and organizing the distribution of supplies and loans. Many lauded the nationalist intent of this effort. Yet, Villa Michel met mostly opposition when he suggested that the states begin asking new industries to register with the federal government and provide information about their location, capitalization, machinery, primary materials, projected production, number of workers, and the owner's nationality. Though he averred that the information was solely for planning purposes, doubts about the federal government's fiscal, regulatory, and political intentions fostered skepticism.[94]

The nature of economic planning during the late 1920s and early 1930s highlights the crosscutting institutional, political, and cultural forces shaping the consolidation of state authority after the Revolution. Most obvious was the limited or conflicting institutional and financial support provided by the state to launch its various planning decrees and commissions. Quite simply, the state usually failed to provide resources and clear guidelines when it issued planning decrees or pledged to constitute planning commissions, despite the intentions of some federal bureaucrats to establish the legal foundations to regulate planning. As part of this, some agencies, such as the SEN, pursued planning despite lacking sufficient authority, knowledge, or resources to actually do so. Most planning decrees and commissions were poorly designed or never got off the ground because of the strains that the Great Depression placed on federal resources, the vagaries of political turmoil and administrative turnover, or apathy among federal and regional authorities. This included not just the National Economic Council but also the 1930 National Law on General Planning (Ley Sobre Planeación General de la República) and the 1933 National Council of the Economy (Consejo Nacional de Economía), among others.[95]

Other factors also conspired against economic planning, not the least of which was suspicion among industrialists and other business elites about the state's motives. Many argued that the expansion of state monitoring and economic planning would come at the expense of the private sector's rights

---

94. Primo Villa Michel to Gobernador Francisco A. Cárdenas, February 6, 1933, Serie Documentos Fuera de Sección, SEN, AGENL, c. 1; SEN to Gobernador Sebastián Allende, February 6, 1933, Archivo Histórico del Estado de Jalisco (AHJ), Ramo Fomento, F-9–933, 10, 727; "Impulsa el estado el funcionamiento de nuestras fuentes productoras," *El Universal*, August 10, 1934; "Notas sobre las actividades del estado en materia de fomento industrial," 1939, GR/AGN, c. 84, exp. 5.

95. L. Meyer, *El conflicto social*, 94–95; Solís, *Planes de desarrollo*.

and autonomy. In Jalisco, for instance, alcohol producers argued that a proposed national planning agency would not take into account regional variations in the industry and would weaken industrialist authority over local production.⁹⁶ The long-standing belief that the state collected data about businesses generally in order to regulate them and increase taxes fed their distrust. For example, when merchants criticized Pani's income tax proposal, they protested that it would expand state oversight of their businesses, especially through financial audits.⁹⁷ Similarly, in 1929, the Federal District's chamber of industry accused the SICT of sending inspectors into factories on the pretext of examining weights and measures when the real purpose was to find an excuse to extort the factory owners. Behind these accusations was some industrialists' resistance to conversion to a national system of weights and measures, even though that system had been obligatory for nearly a quarter of a century.⁹⁸ In recognition of this historic distrust of state motives and in anticipation of future census taking, in 1929, President Emilio Portes Gil (1928–30) decreed that data collected by census takers be used solely for statistical purposes. At the same time, he urged industrialists to fulfill their responsibility to the collective by cooperating with the data collectors. He concurrently imposed a fine for those who failed to do so. Nonetheless, when the federal government tried to obtain data from regional industrialists in 1930, it still faced suspicions. Many industrialists balked at supplying the information, even though budget shortfalls had meant that the federal government requested it by correspondence rather than by sending data collectors. Only after the government sent multiple assurances of confidentiality was it able to obtain some information.⁹⁹

But noncompliance with federal planning agencies and regulations should not be read solely as opposition to the expansion of federal authority over regional production. At times, it simply represented apathy on the part of industrialists, a lack of local resources, or the distinct ways in which the federal and regional governments conceived of production and politics. An example was the failed 1930 National Law on General Planning. In 1985, then Secretary of Programming and Budget (Secretario de Programación y

---

96. Unión Alcoholera de Occidente, S.A. to Gobernador Allende, July 25, 1933, AHJ, Ramo Fomento, F-9–933, 10, 726; "Que la Unión Alcoholera de Occidente, S.A. somete a la ilustrada consideración del Sr. General de División Don Plutarco Elías Calles de quien se pide su valiosa intervención," memorandum, July 25, 1933, AHJ, Ramo Fomento, F-9–933, 10, 726.

97. Collado Herrera, *Empresarios y políticos*, 198.

98. *Boletín Semanal*, no. 69, SICT, Dirección de Publicaciones y Propaganda, September 30, 1930, DF/SSICT/AGENL, c. 3.

99. Departamento de la Estadística Nacional and industrialists, correspondence, April 1, 1930, AHJ, Ramo Estadística, Sección de Industria y Comercio, ES-9–930, 5201.

Presupuesto) Carlos Salinas de Gortari described that law as Mexico's "first formal effort at planning."[100] Technocrats had designed it to carry out an inventory of natural resources and coordinate economic activities across Mexico.[101] During the Porfiriato, elites had already completed some studies of natural resources, especially in mining and agriculture, and they had intended but failed to survey forest resources.[102] Their efforts did little to coordinate development activities during those years. When the state returned to this effort with the 1930 law, it considered the country in broadly topographical terms. However, in doing so, its plans cut across political boundaries in a way that paid little attention to the political and social facets of regional development. Consequently, it received negligible support from state governments. More effective were regionally based undertakings to direct local production, such as the Pro-Economy Committee of Western Mexico (Comité Pro-Economía del Occidente de la República). Formed by local business leaders with state and municipal backing, it gained some popular support because its mission originated in an understanding of local needs and included the goal of improving regional conditions by promoting industry that used local primary materials and supplied regional markets.[103]

Some noncompliance with national efforts also stemmed from antagonism between the federal and state-level governments over the constitutional boundaries of their authority. States' rights over taxation and fiscal expenditures were often at the center of these conflicts, reflecting and reinforcing what many local and national politicians saw as "'fiscal anarchy'" in the decades after the Revolution.[104] In one protracted case, a dispute erupted over the failure of the state government of Nuevo León to subsidize the state's Regional Consulting Board for Commerce and Industry (Junta Regional Consultiva del Comercio y de la Industria). The federal-level central consulting board accused callista governor Jerónimo Siller (1925–27) of evading his moral and material obligation to form the regional board. Governor Siller responded that he did not have the authority to approve the expense, citing provisions in the state constitution that mandated legislative approval for all expenditures. He emphasized that the federal government lacked jurisdiction to decide how state and local governments should allocate their budgets, adding that federal mandates should be supported by

---

100. Secretaría de Programación y Presupuesto, *Los primeros intentos de planeación*, 12.
101. Ceceña Cervantes, *La planificación económica*, 57.
102. Boyer, *Vanishing Woods*, chapter 1; Tenorio-Trillo, *Mexico at the World's Fairs*, chapter 8.
103. Comité Pro-Economía del Occidente to Presidente Municipal de Guadalajara Luis Alvarez del Castillo, January 18, 1939, MGSGG, File I-1-00-4.
104. Díaz-Cayeros, *Federalism, Fiscal Authority, and Centralization*, 47.

federal funding. Ultimately, under pressure from federal agencies and local business leaders, Siller relented and sought legislative approval, but not before he reiterated that the federal request for funds was unconstitutional and that his actions did not set precedent whereby state budgets would fund federal initiatives.[105] In this case, Governor Siller likely did not want to comply with this federal mandate for political reasons related to its centralizing implications rather than out of opposition to planning itself.[106]

The state was largely frustrated in its attempts to broaden its reach through the creation of planning agencies and decrees in the 1920s and 1930s. In 1935, the Secretariat of the Interior (Secretaría de Gobernación) was still pressing regional governments to cooperate in forming local economic councils and to assist in synchronizing state and federal planning.[107] Throughout the 1930s, economic crises, conflicts over state authority, industrialist reticence, administrative fragmentation, and regional noncompliance would inhibit the effectiveness of federal planning commissions and decrees in achieving political centralization or economic growth.

Conclusion

By 1933, officials in the SEN had concluded that allowing private enterprise to take part in economic planning had fostered disorder and inefficiency.[108] And indeed, in the 1920s, cronyism, along with vague laws, a weak central bank, poor institutional backing for planning decrees and commissions, and fiscal privation had circumscribed the state's interventionist capacities and the ability of technocrats to direct economic growth. Nevertheless, industrial policy and economic planning commissions served as arenas of negotiation through which Mexico's diverse and competing industrial and political interests attempted to influence the postrevolutionary state. The biggest

---

105. Gobernador de Nuevo León, Junta Central Consultiva del Comercio y de la Industria, Junta Regional Consultiva del Comercio y de la Industria, SICT, and Secretaría de Gobernación, correspondence, April 2, 1927–June 22, 1929, DF/SSICT/AGENL, c. 2.

106. Just a couple of years earlier, Pani had urged the federal and state governments to subject themselves to technical oversight in order to coordinate their competing tax laws and turn them into a coherent national fiscal regime that demarcated the fiscal jurisdictions of federal and state governments. Alberto J. Pani to gobernador, Nuevo León, July 22, 1925, MF/MH/AGENL, c. 38.

107. SEN, Gobernador de Jalisco, and Secretaría de Gobernación, correspondence, April 5, 1935, AHJ, Ramo Gobernación, G-1–935, 16.

108. Primo Villa Michel to Gobernador Francisco A. Cárdenas, February 6, 1933, Serie Documentos Fuera de Sección, SEN, AGENL, c. 1; SEN to Gobernador Allende, February 6, 1933, AHJ, Ramo Fomento, F-9–933, 10, 727; "Impulsa el estado el funcionamiento de nuestras fuentes productoras," *El Universal*, August 10, 1934.

challenge for some established businesspeople was the way in which the Sonoran-led federal governments attempted to gain legitimacy by drawing on a vision of technocratic governance that purportedly was apolitical, yet which promoted the corporatist aims of the Obregón and, especially, the Calles administrations. Economic planning commissions and industrial policy, even if largely unrealized, represented the intention of the callista state to intervene in economic affairs while undermining legacies of Porfirian rule rooted in alleged rights derived from the power and legitimacy of property holding. In this light, industrial politics and economic planning commissions were not mere tools of elite rent seeking. Rather they were, among other things, a surrogate for political representation and a reflection of emerging postrevolutionary developmentalist currents, both of which contributed to the corporatist intentions of the callista state.

Another challenge for economic planning and policy during the 1920s and early 1930s were the diverse labor, industrial, and political arrangements that constituted the multitude of regional industrial experiences across Mexico. In fact, when the SEN lamented the country's economic disorder in 1933, it specifically cited regional industrial dispersion as an impediment to national planning. Consequently, throughout the 1930s, the state continued its struggle to manage regional opposition to and noncompliance with economic planning commissions and industrial policy. Along the way, industrial policy and economic planning became expressions of ruling-party efforts to centralize and consolidate its authority by associating regionalism with Mexico's politically divided and socially chaotic past.

2

"JALISCO, OPEN YOUR ARMS TO INDUSTRY"
Industrialism and Regional Authority in Guadalajara in the 1930s and 1940s

In the mid-1930s, citing article 33 of the 1917 Constitution, President Lázaro Cárdenas (1934–40) tried to expel from Mexico foreign-born entrepreneur Enrique Anisz, a successful Jaliscan alcohol merchant, on the grounds that he engaged in activities destructive to the nation.[1] When Anisz soon after learned of President Cárdenas's failed efforts to buy land from a Texas businessman on which to develop the Hidroeléctrica de Chapala, the merchant saw an opportunity. He offered to broker the land deal and leave the alcohol trade if he could remain in Mexico. President Cárdenas and his secretary of the Treasury and Public Credit, Eduardo Suárez (1935–46), were wary, but Anisz's success in negotiating the deal soon impressed them. Suárez subsequently urged Anisz to apply his business acumen to a more constructive venture, suggesting that he complete a feasibility study on rayon production. In his report, Anisz concluded that Mexico lacked only financing and technical assistance to launch the industry. Suárez put him in contact with the Banco Nacional de México and NAFINSA, which provided start-up loans, and with the Celanese Corporation of America, which agreed to be a partner in setting up a plant.[2] Established in Ocotlán, Jalisco, Celanese Mexicana quickly grew into one of Mexico's premier chemical companies.

The formation of Celanese epitomized the dense network of business, financial, political, personal, and technical relationships behind many of Mexico's large companies in the postrevolutionary years. But although revealing much about business growth and political authority, the story of

---

1. Article 33 of the Mexican Constitution grants the Federal Executive the competence to expel any foreigner without legal justification.
2. Suárez, *Comentarios y recuerdos*, 126–30.

companies like Celanese tells us less about the industrial experiences of most Mexicans at that time. In Jalisco, small- and medium-sized factories and workshops, employing most of the region's industrial workers and supplying local and regional markets, were far more common than large-scale firms.

Some scholars justifiably contend that the varied and dispersed nature of Jalisco's industry militated against the formation of a regional bourgeoisie with coherent class interests and an express political project.[3] Indeed, a close inspection of class relations in Jalisco reveals an elite that was internally differentiated by an array of industry types, sizes, labor forces, and markets. Yet the prevalence of small- and medium-sized factories manufacturing a wide selection of consumer goods for local markets fostered a sense of a transcendent regional identity that empowered regional industrialists to contest aspects of state consolidation and industrial centralization perceived as affecting local power and production. In many ways, this sense of a unique regional industrial culture substituted for the class-based or political alliances that were dominant in other regions. Moreover, it critically shaped the way in which Jaliscan industrialists balanced their accommodation of central authority with their defense of local forms of control.

In the 1930s and 1940s, the federal government enacted legislation on labor, business chambers, and tax exemptions. Each bespoke the federal government's intention to manage regional radicalism and political ambivalence while encouraging regional adherence to national industrial priorities. The state's intervention in labor-employer relations provoked especially fervid dissonance among Jalisco's industrialists. Traditional industrialists, in particular, objected that state regulation of labor relations was an unjustified and unnecessary assault on the rights of individuals in a region where Catholic-inspired, cross-class fraternity—with its origins in Catholic social action and emphasis on mutual responsibility and respect between owners and workers—historically had ensured social peace. By contrast, other industrialists perceived advantages in using state capacities to manage labor-employer relations. The state, they believed, was capable of reining in labor radicals who, sometimes backed by sympathetic regional governments, had exacerbated Depression-era production problems. These industrialists supported corporatist labor arrangements as a way to temper the radicalism, which they saw as even more threatening to regional political and productive relations than a consolidating state. Despite these different responses to labor

---

3. Arias, "El proceso de industrialización," 106.

legislation, Jalisco's industrialists united against state efforts to regulate industrialist organizing and force compliance with national industrial priorities. From the late 1930s through the 1940s, they joined together to oppose aspects of the new legislation and to defend regionally oriented production and their authority over it.

In this contentious climate, the ability of Jalisco's governors to balance their loyalty to the ruling party with their defense of regional industry was critical in restraining potential antagonisms between the federal government and Jaliscan industrialists. The alliances between these governors and local industrialists undoubtedly contributed to the centralization of ruling-party authority, in part because by the 1930s the alliances empowered regional leaders to check remaining labor radicalism and Catholic conservatism that had survived the 1920s. Yet these alliances also sustained distinctly regional forms of industrialist authority and affinities rooted in alternative industrial paths and interests. They therefore required the ruling party to build a supple political machine that could accommodate regional variations of political and class relations. Porous industrial legislation and its flexible enforcement facilitated accommodation by providing a bounded means for regional industrialists to influence policy and the institutionalization of state-industry relations. Consequently, by the late 1940s, enduring regional allegiances and local industrialist authority were in some senses incorporated into the ruling party. The hesitant accommodation on which this was predicated in turn contributed to the centralization of the party's authority through much of the mid-twentieth century.

Radicalism and Regional Authority in the 1920s and 1930s

As the violence of the Revolution waned, many of Jalisco's large-scale merchant-industrialists looked to reassert their regional political and economic dominance. They quickly discovered, however, that the Porfirian state's indifference to labor-employer relations was now a relic of Mexico's discredited positivist past. In its place was a more interventionist regional government intent on mobilizing radical labor groups in order to expand its populist legitimacy and thereby counter the political aspirations of conservatives, Catholics, and callistas. Many large-scale industrialists predictably opposed the expansion of both federal and local state authority over labor and the rights of private enterprise. Instead, they touted cross-class collaboration, informed by Catholic social action but forged by the experiences of

Jalisco's provincially loyal workers and employers. They argued that this labor regime had historically obviated the need for government labor protection in the region. But as the number of Jalisco's small- and medium-sized companies grew in the 1920s and 1930s, and as the callista state eventually ousted the region's populist governors, an increasing number of industrialists backed federal mediation of labor-employer relations. Importantly, this support did not necessarily signify collaboration with the callista strains that now dominated the national ruling party. Rather, it reflected an adaptation of regional power and production to nascent corporatist labor relations.

By 1800, a large regional market and supply area had grown up around Guadalajara, as an offshoot of its role as a colonial commercial and administrative center. At that time, a local oligarchy united by strong commercial, social, credit, familial, and political ties dominated the region.[4] Although the upheaval of independence eroded their dominion, even more threatening was the arrival between the 1830s and the 1850s of immigrant merchants from England, Germany, France, and South America.[5] Led by French arriving from the Barcelonnette region, these immigrants built on existing artisan and textile manufacturing to set up large-scale clothing stores and warehouses, including the influential department store Fábricas de Francia. By the 1870s, they had become a local gentry of merchant-industrialists embedded in Guadalajara's society and economy. The Porfirian peace only contributed to their wealth and power, since it allowed them to branch out into new areas of production, such as hides, soaps, hardware, shoes, beer, and paper, and to extend the distribution chains that linked producers and consumers from across the region.[6] The industrial growth that ensued included not just large-scale ventures, such as the textile manufacturers Compañía Industrial de Guadalajara and Compañía Industrial Manufacturera, but also a rash of small- and medium-sized businesses. By 1902, Jalisco had 825 industrial establishments, slightly more than 13 percent of the total nationwide, which provided close to 5 percent of the total value of national industrial production.[7]

Most large-scale businesses in Jalisco survived the Revolution. Yet while production quickly rebounded, for a number of reasons, the dominance

4. Van Young, *Hacienda and Market*; Miller, "Social Dislocation and Bourgeois Production," 26–36; Lindley, *Haciendas and Economic Development*, chapter 4.

5. Heath, "British Merchant Houses," 261–67.

6. Alba Vega and Kruijt, *Los empresarios y la industria*, 125–26; Olveda, "Banca y banqueros," 293; Olveda, *Guadalajara*, 150–64; Lindley, *Haciendas and Economic Development*, 21–22.

7. Aldana Rendón, "El derrumbe del Porfiriato," 61–62.

that Porfirian-era merchant-industrialists had over local politics and production did not. Some businesses passed on to heirs, whereas others were sold after the Revolution. Some scholars cite Cárdenas-era agrarian reforms as the cause of the loss of authority of the region's nineteenth-century business groups, especially in the heavily agricultural region in southern Jalisco.[8] But even before the cardenista reforms, dislocations caused by revolutionary social change and political conflict, as well as by the onset of the Depression, had already undermined their authority. The rapid growth of industry from the 1920s to the 1940s further undercut the authority of the formerly powerful merchant-industrialists by generating shifts in patterns of ownership and class relations.

Industry surged in Jalisco in the 1920s, and the state listed 4,200 industrial establishments in the 1930 national census; food manufacturing generated close to 42 percent of the value of Jalisco's production at that time, with textiles a distant second at about 19 percent.[9] An expanding urban labor force and stronger urban and rural markets fed this growth. Both were the result of a massive rural-to-urban migration driven by agrarian reform and cristero violence. During the 1920s, Guadalajara's population grew by 25 percent while the rest of Jalisco grew by just 2.5 percent.[10] As migrants poured into Guadalajara, they brought with them capital, labor, skills, and a knowledge of regional markets. In addition to increasing consumer demand, they helped to feed the city's industrial expansion.[11] In 1903, Guadalajara was home to just 10 percent of Jalisco's industries, an indication of the rural, subsistence-oriented character of regional production at the end of the Porfirian period.[12] However, across Mexico, the 1920s and 1930s generally witnessed the concentration of industrial production in urban centers. In Jalisco, for example, of the 143 registered establishments that made up the state's prominent shoe manufacturing industry in 1935, 139 were in Guadalajara.[13] The investment brought by a new wave of French, German, and

8. For example, see G. de la Peña, "Populism, Regional Power, and Political Mediation," 191; Alba Vega and Kruijt, "La burguesía industrial," 298; Alba Vega and Kruijt, "Urban Hacendados," 178.

9. López Malo, *Ensayo sobre localización*, 87 n. 1; Aldana Rendón, *Desarrollo económico de Jalisco*, 231–32.

10. Alba Vega and Kruijt, *Los empresarios y la industria*, 53–54.

11. Arias, "La industria en perspectiva," 85–90; Arias, "El proceso de industrialización," 77, 82–86, 94–96; Alba Vega, "Las regiones industriales," 115; Alba Vega and Kruijt, *Los empresarios y la industria*, 57, 243–44; Arias, "Presentación," 13–14; Alba Vega and Kruijt, "La burguesía industrial," 305.

12. Aldana Rendón, *Desarrollo económico de Jalisco*, 179.

13. Arias, "Talleres, comerciantes e industriales," 223.

Spanish immigrants—and in the 1930s and 1940s, increasingly Lebanese and Jewish immigrants—fed this urban industrialization.

Most new industries that emerged in the 1920s and 1930s were quite small, such as corn and wheat mills or small-scale shoe manufacturers that replaced artisanal production. In 1930, Jalisco's 4,200 industrial concerns constituted about 8.6 percent of the national total, though they contributed just 3.7 percent of the value of national production. By comparison, Mexico City, with 3,476 factories, had 7.1 percent of the total of industries nationwide, but they produced 27.3 percent of total national production. Nuevo León, also notable for its larger industries, had just 1,201 industries listed in the 1930 census, or about 2.5 percent of the national total, but they generated 7.6 percent of the total value nationwide. Moreover, although factories in Mexico City averaged 14.7 workers (*obreros*) each and those in Nuevo León averaged about 11.5 workers, Jalisco's factories averaged just 4.1. Even Puebla's factories, which were notable for their relatively small size compared to mills in other regions, averaged almost six workers each.[14] The growth in the number of small industries producing for regional markets nevertheless helped to cement Guadalajara's status as an industrial center. Moreover, Jalisco's unique industrial demographics meant that capital, markets, and labor responded largely to the imperatives of small-scale, rather than large-scale, production. By the 1930s and 1940s, though, some of these small-scale entrepreneurs had managed to become large-scale industrialists, and by the mid-twentieth century, they constituted a new generation of regional industrial elites, including the Aranguren, Martínez Güitrón, López Chávez, Gutiérrez Nieto, Garciarce, and Urrea families.[15]

Nevertheless, postrevolutionary industrial relations in Guadalajara became comparatively diffuse and diverse, with no single industrial leader or

---

14. SEN, Dirección General de Estadística, *Primer censo industrial de 1930*, vol. 1, *Resumenes generales*. The figures for workers do not include professional workers but do include women and children. Use of statistics from the 1930 industrial census is problematic since it aimed to include only those establishments whose production was valued at Mex$500 or higher. Yet, the SEN found that of the 48,850 establishments from which it gathered information, about 21,032 had annual production valued at less than Mex$500. Statistics for 1935 and 1940 are even more problematic, as the threshold for inclusion grew to a minimum production value of Mex$10,000. Therefore, while the 1930 census reported 48,850 manufacturing industries, the 1935 and 1940 censuses had just 7,035 and 12,861, respectively. Thus, in 1935, the number of factories in Guadalajara appears to drop to 558, and the number in Nuevo León declines to 254. Clearly, evaluating change in manufacturing industries across that time span or the characteristics of small industry is problematic. The 1935 census even opens with a warning about the provisional nature of the data, given that the set of data is incomplete and it needs further clarification. Thus, census data should be used with great caution. SEN, Dirección General de Estadística, *Segundo censo industrial 1935* (1937).

15. Alba Vega and Kruijt, "La burguesía industrial," 313–15, 323; Alba Vega and Kruijt, *Los empresarios y la industria*, 126–27, 152–93.

business group dominating the region. This distinguished Guadalajara from both Monterrey, where a clique of established owners of large businesses controlled politics and industry, and Puebla, whose industrialists were well organized due to the weight of the textile sector there. In Guadalajara, by contrast, ownership and production patterns engendered a political and ideological project founded on a faith in Jalisco's varied, small-scale, regionally oriented production. The tendency toward the production of traditional consumer goods for local consumption reinforced the class dimension of this project. Mexico City and Monterrey, to the contrary, had significant large-scale industry that included not only nondurable consumer goods but also capital goods, intermediate goods, and consumer durables produced for local, national, and international markets. Regional solidarity in Guadalajara hence stemmed in part from perceptions of both class difference and economic competition with entrepreneurs in other regions. A sense among some businesspeople in Jalisco that federal legislation frequently subjected them to unfair competition from industrialists in other regions enhanced this solidarity. For example, they persistently defied efforts to establish a national minimum wage from the 1910s to the 1930s, arguing that it would be prejudicial because of the lower costs of living and higher production costs in Jalisco than in other industrial cities, such as Monterrey and Mexico City.[16]

The relatively small size and diversity of Jalisco's industries contributed to the splintering of its organized labor force and complicated the corporatist endeavors of callistas in the state. In the early 1920s, revolutionary victors in Jalisco seized on the mobilizations of some local labor groups to fashion a particularly radical and deep-seated populism. This mirrored arrangements in other states, where populist governors allied with radical regional labor organizations in order to build independent political bases.[17] Typified by the political career of Jalisco's Governor José Guadalupe Zuno Hernández (1923–26), these politicians forged populist coalitions with agraristas, workers, teachers, professionals, and women's groups to underpin their tenuous and often combative ascents to office.[18] Zuno, for example, helped to create the Communist-dominated Confederation of Libertarian Workers Groups of Jalisco (Confederación de Agrupaciones Obreras Libertarias de Jalisco,

---

16. "Memorandum que sobre las condiciones especiales de la industria azucarera en los estados de Michoacán, Colima, Jalisco, y Nayarit presentan ante el C. Presidente de la República, General Lázaro Cárdenas, los productores de la Región Centro-Occidente del país," February 1, 1935, AHJ, Ramo Fomento, F-9-933, 10, 748; Keremitsis, "La doble jornada de la mujer," 121.

17. Ruiz, *Labor and the Ambivalent Revolutionaries*, 79–80, 95–100.

18. Gruening, *Mexico and Its Heritage*, 440–44.

CAOLJ), with which he formed an alliance. He did so in part to defend his government's autonomy from the intrusions of both the CROM and the Catholic Church.[19] In the process, he aggravated the CAOLJ's conflicts with its conservative, Catholic, and *cromista* labor counterparts.

Though now weakened, many of Jalisco's traditional industrialists condemned the state government's sanction of radical union authority as an assault on owners' rights over their factories and workers.[20] They framed their opposition within the tenets of positivist individualism and Catholic class fraternity, which together, they argued, obviated the need for state intervention in labor-employer relations. They added that the historic cooperation between the region's employers and their individual workers had its origins in the regionally oriented nature of Jaliscan production, and this cooperation was nurtured by a shared heritage, culture, and religion.[21] Therefore, when Governor Zuno interposed the state as the mediator between employers and labor and passed state labor laws that protected workers and union authority, he was threatening the legal, cultural, and intellectual foundations of the region's paternalistic labor relations.[22] Many unions were less enthusiastic about the benefits of employer paternalism however. Now empowered by revolutionary rhetoric and protected by state-level labor laws, unions became increasingly audacious in demanding that economic reconstruction guarantee workers' rights. Therefore, in the 1920s, employers found themselves operating with significant constraints on their political influence and property rights.[23]

Amid a callista purge of radical and independent regional governments, Governor Zuno chose to resign from office in 1926. He made the move ostensibly to preserve state autonomy and engineer the election of an *anticallista* state government from behind the scenes.[24] Consequently, even with his resignation, industrialists found little to celebrate. Indeed, ex-union activist Governor Margarito Ramírez (1927–29) continued to encourage radical labor unions as a means to further curtail the influence of the CROM. He thus backed the transformation of the CAOLJ into a broader Communist-dominated coalition, the Labor Confederation of Jalisco (Confederación Obrera de Jalisco, COJ), which aggregated almost all unions in the state against the CROM. Ongoing labor strife and the outbreak of the

19. Fernández Aceves, "José Guadalupe Zuno Hernández," 98–99.
20. Romero, "El movimiento obrero en Jalisco," 19–20; Tamayo, "Movimiento obrero y lucha sindical," 137–38, 141–45.
21. Alba Vega and Kruijt, "La burguesía industrial," 323.
22. Durand, "Siglo y medio en el camino," 174–76.
23. For example, see Hamilton, *Limits of State Autonomy*, 68, 102, 107–8.
24. Fernández Aceves, "José Guadalupe Zuno Hernández," 101–2.

Cristero War in 1926 continued to destabilize regional politics and production.[25]

The volatility of national labor politics and the impact of the Great Depression fed labor unrest in the region. Even at the peak of the CROM's national power from 1924 to 1928, it struggled with internal dissent and worked to undermine competing labor groups, such as those organized by Communists, anarchists, radicals in the General Confederation of Workers (Confederación General de Trabajadores, CGT), Catholic workers, and employers themselves, with the last two often closely tied.[26] Moreover, agrarian reform, enduring revolutionary and religious violence, and political upheaval, combined with the Great Depression's negative effect on living standards and formal employment opportunities, fostered insecurity among Mexico's workers during the late 1920s and early 1930s.[27] The impact of the Depression on overall employment is difficult to estimate. However, in the cotton textile industry, which at that time was Mexico's largest manufacturing industry, employment declined by 24 percent between 1926 and 1932. The return of more than three hundred thousand Mexican workers expelled from the United States, in that country's attempt to address its own troubles with excess labor, aggravated the employment problem.[28]

Mexico's increasingly mobile and often-underemployed population fed callistas' unease about labor radicalism and its impact on state consolidation and economic recovery. This only grew after Luis Morones and the CROM fell out of national political favor in the wake of president-elect Obregón's assassination in 1928. As the CROM splintered and the central government lost its primary means to control labor, radical unions surged. This included the anarcho-syndicalist CGT, although by then it was less radical than it had been in its early days, and in just a few years, it would break apart. Populist governors who had survived the callista purges continued to back some of these unions.[29] When General José Gonzalo Escobar revolted in March

25. Though many traditional businesspeople shared the conservative vision of social relations promoted by the region's Catholics, they decried the cristeros' radical fervor and shunned its mass base. González Navarro, *Masones y cristeros*, 54–55; Bailey, *Viva Cristo Rey!* 79–85; J. Meyer, *Cristero Rebellion*, chapter 3; Gabayet, "La industria textil," 69; Tuck, *Holy War in Los Altos*, 14–23.

26. J. Meyer, "Revolution and Reconstruction," 228–32; Tamayo, "La aurora roja," 71.

27. Unemployment statistics for the 1930s are problematic for many reasons, including a lack of data, poor estimates, and the vagaries of defining "unemployed" in a population that has large sectors working in both the informal and agricultural sectors. I thank Jeffrey Bortz for clarifying some of these limitations.

28. Haber, *Industry and Underdevelopment*, 152–54.

29. J. Meyer, "Revolution and Reconstruction," 228–32; Hart, *Anarchism*, 175–77. For a discussion of the currents of radicalism and mass politics at the regional level in the 1920s and their relationship to political shifts at the national level, see Benjamin, "Laboratories of the New State, 1920–1929."

1929, with significant support from labor groups, it confirmed Calles's fears about the impact of an independent labor movement on political stability and social peace.[30] In Jalisco, by contrast, callistas largely had already succeeded in suppressing both labor radicals and political Catholics by 1929. They did so through a mix of political manipulation and violent repression that forced Governor Ramírez from office and the COJ underground.

The codification of article 123 of the 1917 Constitution at the national level in 1931 revealed Jaliscan industrialists' profound differences in attitudes toward postrevolutionary shifts in local labor politics. When federal labor law began to look like it would become a reality in the late 1920s, the most vocal opposition had come from industrialists from Monterrey. In 1929, they had formed the Mexican Employers Association (Confederación Patronal de la República Mexicana, COPARMEX) explicitly to pressure for the protection of the interests of employers in federal labor legislation. Some large-scale industrialists in Jalisco had sympathized with their counterparts in Monterrey. In 1930, a group that included textile industrialists Carlos and Manuel Dávalos; Carlos Medina, who held interests in hide tanning; and food industry owners Antonio and Trinidad Martínez Rivas had joined to form a COPARMEX regional affiliate (Centro Empresarial de Jalisco). Some of these industrialists therefore protested the 1931 Federal Labor Law simply because they opposed any legislation that aided unionization drives and workers' rights. As when they earlier had challenged Governor Zuno's efforts to expand the state government's role in labor-employer relations, they characterized the 1931 Federal Labor Law as an unjustified and unnecessary intrusion of the federal government into local labor affairs. However, they now framed their opposition within a regionalist perspective that censured that law's centralizing tendencies and the ruling party's bid to consolidate callista authority over Jalisco. They added that it was a shortsighted attempt to achieve social peace by asserting the rights of the collective at the expense of individuals.[31] Nevertheless, Jaliscan businesspeople refrained from joining the Monterrey Group in outright opposition to the Federal Labor Law. Possibly outweighing their resistance to federally protected labor rights were concerns about ceding their autonomy to the powerful entrepreneurs in Nuevo León.[32]

30. Middlebrook, *Paradox of Revolution*, 77–83.
31. For an elaboration of the federal government's justification for intervening to defend workers, see "Doctrina social en que se basa el proyecto de Ley Federal del Trabajo," *Boletín Semanal*, no. 93, SICT, Dirección de Publicaciones y Propaganda, May 18, 1931, DF/SSICT/AGENL, c. 5.
32. Luis G. Sada to Enrique Sada Muguerza, July 21, 1930, AMGM, v. 442, exp. 1443; Camp, *Entrepreneurs and Politics*, 163; González González and Alba Vega, *Cúpulas empresariales*, 11; Alba Vega and Kruijt, *Los empresarios y la industria*, 205; Alba Vega and Kruijt, "La burguesía industrial," 323.

Yet, other industrialists in Jalisco saw potential in the 1931 Federal Labor Law, which superseded the roughly ninety state-level labor laws and decrees enacted across Mexico between 1918 and 1928.[33] Since at least March 1925, when ninety representatives of various industries from across Mexico had come together in the Second National Congress of Industrialists (Segundo Congreso Nacional de Industriales), some industrialists began to point to the advantages of national-level labor legislation. Many argued that it was preferable to the variety of state-level laws that they saw as protecting abusive unions to the detriment of owners, workers, and production itself.[34] They believed the 1931 Federal Labor Law had the potential to curb the arbitrary and often political interpretations of state-level labor laws, would allow owners to reassert authority over production and workers, and could weaken alliances between regional labor and political leaders. Federal authorities' involvement in local labor relations would facilitate the imposition of regimes at the state level backed by the ruling party, but some businesspeople considered this less of a threat to their regional authority and class relations than were the radical local unions and the populist regional governors who backed them.[35]

Among those who saw the benefits of federal labor legislation were the owners of small-scale or family-run workshops. Like the owners of large-scale industries, the owners of these smaller firms often fostered paternalistic labor relations and many touted class fraternity. Yet, unlike their wealthy counterparts, most had few protections from profiteering merchants, corrupt union bosses, labor factionalism, or politically motivated local leaders.[36] For some small-scale employers, class fraternity may merely have been a way to exert their prerogative amid the unstable power dynamics within small factories. For others, it was more likely a reflection of their sharing class origins and similar living conditions with their workers. Though the close setting of workshop production undoubtedly added to the potential for abuses of paternal authority, class fraternity was an affirmation of a shared commitment among these employers and their workers to a workplace on which both relied for their survival.[37] Amid the economic and political tumult of the early 1930s, many of these employers and workers did not see

33. Middlebrook, *Paradox of Revolution*, 48–49.
34. CONCAMIN, Ponencia de la Sección Textil sobre la Capacidad y Responsabilidad de las Asociaciones Profesionales Obreras, March 5, 1925, DT/AGN, c. 856, exp. 2; Juárez González, "Una década en la organización," 263–65.
35. Haber, Razo, and Maurer, *Politics of Property Rights*, 146–47.
36. Arias, "Presentación," 13–14; Arias, "La industria en perspectiva," 94–96; Gómez, "Una burguesía en ciernes," 35–36.
37. Arias, "La industria en perspectiva," 98–99; Lailson, "De mercaderes a industriales," 191–218.

state intervention as a threat to class fraternity but rather as a means to sustain it. For example, both workers and employers often willingly came together in the Central Board of Conciliation and Arbitration (Junta Central de Conciliación y Arbitraje, JCCA) to negotiate resolutions to production problems in embattled factories in a way that would ensure the long-term survival of the workplace. Many of the resolutions involved the temporary suspension of collective contracts as well as layoffs that provided partial salaries to affected workers.[38]

When tensions did erupt, both employers and workers turned to the JCCA for mediation. Efforts by employers to subvert collective contracts were a key worker grievance. But many workers at small factories and laboring under individual, often verbal, contracts also appealed to the JCCA over issues like pay irregularities, lack of vacation time, and firing disputes. Although many employers evaded the call to meet with the JCCA, others used the JCCA and the 1931 Federal Labor Law to assert their rights. Indeed, the JCCA was important to owners of smaller factories, many of whom saw the state as a potential ally in managing their workers.[39] For example, in June 1936, one faction of an ironworkers union declared a strike in workshops owned by José G. Ramírez, accusing him of not responding to its demands. Ramírez, who allegedly was colluding with a second faction of workers that had sent him a letter advising him of the looming problems with the first faction, disputed the legality of the strike before the JCCA. Citing paperwork proving the legality of the second faction, the JCCA ultimately sided with Ramírez, and it ordered the workers back to work under threat of losing their jobs.[40] Employers and their allied unions won their cases so often that workers regularly, and with some justification, complained of JCCA bias toward employers. Moreover, under the leadership of COJ labor leader and callista Heliodoro Hernández Loza, the

---

38. For example, see JCCA agreement between the Sindicato de Trabajadores en la Industria del Calzado y Similares and Porfirio Francisco Fuentes, 1947, AHJ, Ramo Secretaría General de Gobierno, Gobernador Silvano Barba González, Legajo 1, exp. 73, 1940; José María Sánchez to JCCA, May 10, 1937, AHJ, Ramo Trabajo, Sección 2, Conciliación y Arbitraje, T-2-937, T-19 bis D3, 7700.

39. For example, see Atanasio Díaz (owner, Fábrica de Calzado El León) to JCCA, March 23, 1936, AHJ, Ramo Trabajo, T-3-936, 7917; Heladio Navarro to JCCA, June 5, 1936, AHJ, Ramo Trabajo, T-3-936, 7906; Sindicato de Trabajadores en la Industria del Cartón y Similares and JCCA, correspondence, October 1936–February 1937, AHJ, Ramo Trabajo, T-3-936, 7911; Pedro Cuellar to JCCA, February 9, 1937, AHJ, Ramo Trabajo, T-3-936, 7911; José Díaz de Sandi to JCCA, December 17, 1936, AHJ, Ramo Trabajo, T-2-936, c. T-19 bis B1, 7578.

40. Ignacio Hernández et al. of the Unión de Trabajadores del Hierro, Victor R. Corona et al. of the Unión de Trabajadores del Hierro, JCCA, and José G. Ramírez, correspondence, June 10–19, 1936, AHJ, Ramo Trabajo, T-3-936, 7906.

JCCA often defended the power of callista unions to the detriment of workers' rights, especially those in unions soon to affiliate with the CTM.[41]

Even more than the resolution of individual disputes in favor of employers, the election of callista governor Sebastián Allende (1932–35) moderated industrialist opposition to the centralizing tendencies of the 1931 Federal Labor Law. Winning them over was Governor Allende's commitment to defending regional political and industrial relations, even when they conflicted with national goals. Although his defense of regional politics and industry to some extent grew out of the institutional weakness of the federal government in the 1930s, it nevertheless brought social peace and political stability to the region. With the ascent of Governor Allende, the business community enjoyed a return to regional political influence, in particular through the institutionalization of moderate political and social groups in the state. Governor Allende also promoted industry through the development of infrastructure, financial assistance, protectionist legislation, and even the occasional use of political influence to intercede on behalf of aggrieved industrialists.[42] Although many industrialists remained chary of the impact of *callismo* on regional authority and their rights as employers, they supported the demobilizing aspects of labor co-optation and repression under Governor Allende, as well as the highly controlled unionism of Hernández Loza and the now more moderate COJ.[43]

Significantly, though he favored large industry, Governor Allende understood the importance of small-scale production in the state. Most notably, he recognized its role in bringing together Jalisco's varied and dispersed producers and consumers after the Revolution, when political instability, industrial modernization, and migration from both rural areas and abroad were rending apart traditional political and social ties.[44] For example, he

41. Frente Único de Trabajadores to Gobernador Everardo Topete, July 29, 1935, AHJ, Ramo Trabajo, T-1–935, c. T-9 bis A, 6767; Unión Sindical de Obreros y Empleados, Fábrica de Calzado Cometa, Secretario General de Gobierno, and JCCA, correspondence, August 15–September 4, 1935, AHJ, Ramo Trabajo, T-1–935, c. T-9 bis A, 6664; Cámara Nacional del Trabajo de la República Mexicana to JCCA, August 26, 1935, AHJ, Ramo Trabajo, Secc. 1, T-1–935, c. T-9 bis A, 6679; Federación de Trabajadores de Jalisco to Gobernador Topete, January 7, 1938, AHJ, Ramo Trabajo, T-1–938, c. T-9 bis B, 6931; Fernández Aceves, "En-gendering *Caciquismo*," 216.

42. Cámara Nacional de Comercio, Industria, y Minería de Guadalajara to gobernador, March 22, 1933, AHJ, Ramo Fomento, F-9–933, 10, 729; Tamayo, "La Confederación Obrera de Jalisco," 29–32, 36–37, 49–50; Tamayo, "Movimiento obrero y lucha sindical," 137–38, 146–49; Romero, "El movimiento obrero en Jalisco," 37–38; Gómez Fregoso, "Los orígenes del sindicato de panaderos," 164.

43. Tamayo, "Los obreros," 79–82; Romero, *El Partido Nacional Revolucionario en Jalisco*, 54–56, 75; Arias, "Talleres, comerciantes e industriales," 242–43; Arias, "La industria en perspectiva," 97–98.

44. Gómez López, "Los empresarios y el estado," 66–67; Arias, "La industria en perspectiva," 91; Arias, "Talleres, comerciantes e industriales," 242.

announced plans to dedicate two pavilions at the state museum in Jalisco to a permanent exhibit honoring small industry. By so doing, he appealed not only to popular perceptions about the region's small-scale, locally oriented production but also to affinities emerging from the purported common political, ethnic, religious, historical, and class heritage of Jalisco's industrialists. In the early 1930s, pride in local productive autonomy was especially important to industrialists trying to recover from the Depression. Not only did the region's business community organize the country's first business fair outside of Mexico City to advertise local industry and agriculture,[45] but it also lauded the "virtues and advantages" of local products and justified pressures to buy local goods with moralistic intonations about regionalism. *La Verdad* even ran two regular columns titled "Regionalist Campaign" and "Patria chica," with articles that concluded, "Protect regional industries and do Pro-Patria work!"[46] Although this propaganda referenced a faith among even large-scale industrialists in the small industries producing largely for regional markets, it concurrently projected the notion that a defense of regional industry was essential to national recovery and independence. In this climate, callista penetration of the state depended in part on the ability of Governor Allende to protect regional industry and the authority of regional industrialists in matters of local production, even if at the expense of political centralization.

This collaborative interlude ended, however, as cardenistas extended their authority over Jalisco in the late 1930s. In fact, the political survival of Governor Everardo Topete (1935–39), who originally had risen to power with callista backing, rested largely on his subsequent cooperation with cardenista mass organizations.[47] This included the CTM-allied Federation of Jaliscan Workers (Federación de Trabajadores de Jalisco), which formed in 1936 to supplant the corrupt, internally divided, and weakened COJ as the most powerful union organization in the state. Reinvigorated by state support for labor, union membership and labor mobilizations surged in the late 1930s.[48] Along with cardenista efforts to secularize and socialize education,

---

45. Manuel Dávalos and Ignacio Padilla to Gobernador Sebastián Allende, December 30, 1933, AHJ, Ramo Fomento, Sección 7, Exposiciones, F-7-933, 9548; Gómez López, "Los empresarios y el estado," 67.

46. Gómez López, "Los empresarios y el estado," 65–66.

47. Alan Knight mentions these "'girasoles,'" or "sunflowers," whose allegiances followed the brightest light across Mexico's "political sky" in the 1930s in a "tactical" effort to survive national ruling-party shifts. Knight, "Cardenismo," 104–5.

48. Romero, *El Partido Nacional Revolucionario en Jalisco*, 79.

this state-sponsored labor activism piqued many employers. Many resurrected arguments about the statist assault on their individual rights.[49] Some even accused labor arbitration boards of being agents of labor interests and reestablished employers' unions to try to undercut state-backed organizations.[50] Others, however, responded in a more measured way and continued to support the state as a mediator in labor-employer relations. They often felt that the state was still the best check on labor militancy, even as they condemned perceived cardenista bias toward workers. Therefore, though many employers now conceded that the state would, and even should, be a permanent fixture in labor-employer relations, cardenista labor politics rekindled widespread industrialist opposition to the ruling party. This resistance critically shaped the ruling party's subsequent bids to incorporate industrialists.

Defending Regional Representation

In 1941, the federal government passed the Law on Chambers of Commerce and Industry (Ley de las Cámaras de Comercio y de las de Industria, hereafter the 1941 chambers law). Jalisco's industrialists immediately perceived this law to be the state's attempt to break down regionally rooted alliances and overcome enduring regional political authority. The most contentious parts of the law were its stipulations that all chambers for national industry be located in Mexico City and incorporated into the state as public institutions. Not only did this undermine the rights of private enterprise to organize independently, but it also provided Mexico City industrialists with privileged political access and enhanced their ability to promote forms of industry ascendant in the capital. In response, Jalisco's industrialists availed themselves of a provision in the law that allowed them to organize regional industrial chambers if at least twenty-five producers from the same industrial sector requested it. In this case, the small size and diversity of Jalisco's companies enabled industrialists to retain discrete representation in the face of

---

49. Gómez López, "Los empresarios y el estado," 64–66.
50. For example, see letters dealing with the sugar industry, October 1936, AHJ, Ramo Gobernación, G-14-936, no exp. So many employers had established employers' unions that in 1938, the ruling party urged governors to intervene to cancel the unions. Comité Central Ejecutivo, PRM, to Gobernador Topete, AHJ, Ramo Trabajo, T-1-938, c. T-9 bis B, 6928.

the expansion of state power. In the process, they subverted the law's original intent and critically influenced the institutionalization of state-industry relations.

The 1888 formation of the Jalisco Chamber of Commerce (Cámara de Comercio de Jalisco) launched business organizing in Jalisco.[51] Though the chamber regularly lobbied the state on behalf of business, only with the 1908 Law on Chambers of Commerce (Ley de Cámaras de Comercio) did the state formalize its relationship with the business community. Even then, however, business chambers remained private, voluntary organizations and continued to unite industrialists and merchants in a single association. When merchants and industrialists were split into separate chambers at the national level in 1917 and 1918, their joint representation at the regional level survived.[52] Subsequently, the National Chamber of Commerce, Industry, and Mining of Jalisco (Cámara Nacional de Comercio, Industria, y Minería de Jalisco) became the primary representative of all business interests in the state, and it served as the key conduit for business-state contact through the mid-1930s. Alongside it were business organizations with no legal charter, including Jalisco's regional affiliate of COPARMEX, the National Union of Industry and Commerce of Guadalajara (Unión Nacional de Industria y Comercio de Guadalajara), and clubs that connected businesspeople along social, ethnic, and cultural lines, such as the Círculo Francés, Círculo Español, and Círculo Libanés (French, Spanish, and Lebanese Circles, respectively). Moreover, groups like the Western Sugar Producers Union (Unión de Azucareros de Occidente) and the Chamber of Mezcal Producers of Jalisco (Cámara de Mezcaleros de Jalisco) represented sector-specific interests.[53] By the 1930s, then, businesspeople in Jalisco were well organized in myriad groups that represented them at the national, regional, and local levels in both broad and specific ways.

In the early 1930s, the callista state initiated the centralization of organizing in some industrial sectors, rankling a handful of business owners. However, the passage of the 1936 Law on Chambers of Commerce and Industry (Ley de Cámaras de Comercio e Industria, hereafter the 1936 chambers law) elicited more general reprobation from the business community, both because it was a more comprehensive attempt to exert state regulation of

---

51. Aldana Rendón, "El derrumbe del Porfiriato," 65–66.

52. Ramírez Rancaño, "El Primer Congreso de Industriales," 83–122; Alba Vega and Kruijt, Los empresarios y la industria, 202–3; Juárez González, "Una década en la organización," 256–57, 260–65; Story, Industry, 82.

53. Círculo Libanés Mexicano de Guadalajara to Presidente Municipal de Guadalajara, March 24, 1943, MGSGG, I-1-09-36; Gómez López, "Los empresarios y el estado," 62–63, 67–68.

business representation and by reason of its explicitly political aims. The 1936 chambers law joined industrialists and commercial interests into a single national organization, the Confederation of National Chambers of Commerce and Industry (Confederación de Cámaras Nacionales de Comercio y de Industria, CONCANACOMIN), which was to serve as the representative for all businesses. Legally defined as having a public character, its membership and internal organization were determined by law.[54] Though some scholars have maintained that this was to be the employers' counterpart to the CTM, the organization had no formal ties to the ruling party.[55] Rather, through the changes implemented with this law, the state sought to draw entrepreneurs closer and to establish a foundation for business-state collaboration. Accordingly, some chambers gained political leverage with regard to legislation and policy.[56]

The semi-official status of business chambers set off a wave of resistance to state intervention in the private sphere and over the rights of individuals to free association. Most vexing was the requirement that all businesses capitalized at more than Mex$500 join a chamber.[57] This was an important change from the 1908 law, which had protected the voluntary nature of business organizations and claimed to respect the rights of private enterprise. Some businesspeople were so incensed with the 1936 chambers law that they agitated for the creation of more extra-official organizations. For example, Pueblan textile industrialist Jesús Rivero Quijano stated that the 1936 chambers law had "denaturalized" business chambers since it enabled the state to circumscribe the range of issues that members could discuss. He urged businesspeople to instead join autonomous organizations, such as the Association of Industrial and Commercial Businesses (Asociación de Empresas Industriales y Comerciales), of which he was then president, to defend the business sector from the corporatist assault of the state.[58]

The modification of the 1936 chambers law ultimately was not spurred by business hostility, but rather by the rise to dominance of conservative commercial interests within CONCANACOMIN. Soon after the passage of the 1936 law, the Cárdenas administration realized that the political clout of these conservative merchants gave them considerable influence over the economy as well as autonomy from the state. Therefore, when ruling-party

54. Brandenburg, *Making of Modern Mexico*, 88–89; Padgett, *Mexican Political System*, 129.
55. Centro de Información y Estudios Nacionales, *La Cámara Nacional*, 1–2.
56. Presidente Municipal de Guadalajara and Cámara Nacional de Comercio e Industria de Guadalajara, December 15, 1938, and January 3, 1939, MGSGG, I-4-30-2.
57. Juárez González, "Una década en la organización," 274.
58. Jesús Rivero Quijano to Manuel Gómez Morin, July 21, 1937, AMGM, v. 276, exp. 944.

leaders incorporated labor, peasant, and middle-class groups into the newly formed Party of the Mexican Revolution (Partido de la Revolución Mexicana, PRM), which they created out of the reorganization of the PNR in 1938, they tested the idea of bringing in business chambers as well. But opposition from the business community, as well as popular perceptions that President Cárdenas was abandoning his mass base, soon led the party to drop the idea. One faction of industrialists even responded to the ruling party's populist turn under President Cárdenas by calling for its dissolution, arguing that it was both a "'threat to democracy'" and a "'cyst of the Revolution.'"[59] Quite simply, as the ruling party sought to rebuild itself along more corporatist and populist lines, the incorporation of the ambivalent and often conservative business community presented too many obstacles.[60]

The reality of this threat to ruling-party consolidation became manifest during the 1940 presidential elections, when opposition candidate Juan Andreu Almazán garnered broad backing from labor, the middle class, and business groups. In the months before the election, many businesspeople supported the conservative National Action Party (Partido Acción Nacional, PAN). The PAN had been co-founded in September 1939 by Manuel Gómez Morin and Efraín González Luna, the latter of whom served as legal advisor to some of Guadalajara's wealthiest industrialists. Its Catholic, pro-business platform and support for political decentralization was a rejection of the ruling party's anticlerical, interventionist, and centralizing character in the 1930s. Though Gómez Morin had a secular vision of politics, his disillusion with official corruption and cronyism in the 1920s led him to view Catholicism as the only means to restrain the abuses and disruptions attending economic modernization and political consolidation. Though the PAN did not officially endorse Almazán, he did receive the party's support.[61] But this conservative patronage probably had less to do with his political platform, which differed little from that of ruling-party candidate Manuel Ávila Camacho, than with his offering a moderate alternative to the ruling party.[62] And ultimately, many business owners in Jalisco and elsewhere abandoned Almazán amid concerns about his mass following and

---

59. Garrido, *El partido de la revolución institucionalizada*, 242.

60. "Observaciones que la Confederación de Cámaras Nacionales de Comercio e Industria, somete a la consideración del C. Presidente de la República, del H. Congreso de la Unión y del C. Secretario de la Economía Nacional, acerca del proyecto de Ley de Cámaras de Comercio y de las de Industria," February 7, 1941, Fondo Manuel Ávila Camacho (MAC)/AGN, 545.2/7, leg. 1 al 5.

61. Gómez Morin, *La nación y el régimen*; interview with Manuel Gómez Morin, in Wilkie and Monzón de Wilkie, *México visto en el siglo XX*, 176–80; Loaeza, *El Partido Acción Nacional*, 116–22, 168–74.

62. González, *Los días del presidente Cárdenas*, 259.

because of the ruling party's pro-business overtures in the run-up to the election.[63] Yet, despite this hemorrhage of support, electoral estimates indicate that Almazán probably took Guadalajara as well as Mexico City and Monterrey.[64] Therefore, even though Ávila Camacho won the fraudulent election, the voters showed the PRM that its authority was fragile and its relations with some of Mexico's fastest growing groups, including the working class, the middle class, and business interests, were tenuous.[65] This realization was especially significant in Guadalajara, a city undergoing a rapid expansion of its working and middle classes and still carrying the fresh scars of the government's anticlerical crackdowns and agrarian upheaval.

In the aftermath of the election, ruling-party leaders revived their efforts to build a more cooperative relationship with the business community in order to undercut conservative challenges to their control of the state. The 1941 chambers law sought to do this by dividing commercial and industrial interests into separate chambers defined as public, autonomous institutions overseen by the SEN. The response of the conservative commercial interests who dominated CONCANACOMIN was swift. As Congress was debating the law, CONCANACOMIN president Leopoldo Palazuelos railed against the government's failure to consult the private sector when designing the law. He singled out head of the SEN Francisco Javier Gaxiola Jr. (1940–44) and accused him of purposefully withholding the legislation from the private sector in order to block its input. Palazuelos then appealed directly to Congress and to President Ávila Camacho to urge legislators to take private sector opinion into account, but he was largely ignored.[66] Similarly, when CONCAMIN tried for two months to arrange a meeting with President Ávila Camacho to discuss the legislation, he rebuffed the organization.[67] From February to May 1941, hundreds of telegrams protesting the 1941 law from chambers of commerce and industry from all over Mexico reached President Ávila Camacho. Most portrayed the law as an attack on the rights of the private sector and a thinly veiled attempt by the PRM to

---

63. Puga, "Las elecciones de 1940," 281–82; Hamilton, *Limits of State Autonomy*, 261–69; Contreras, *México 1940*, 137, 154–57, 167–68; Camp, *Entrepreneurs and Politics*, 212; Sherman, *Mexican Right*, 117–31; Cockcroft, *Mexico's Hope*, 134–35. González González and Alba Vega state that Jaliscan entrepreneurs have generally refused to join opposition parties. González González and Alba Vega, *Cúpulas empresariales*, 11–12.

64. Davis, "Uncommon Democracy in Mexico," 177.

65. Contreras, *México 1940*, 154–56.

66. Leopoldo Palazuelos to Javier Gaxiola, telegram, February 1, 1941, and Palazuelos to Cámara de Diputados al Congreso de la Unión and Ávila Camacho, telegrams, February 3, 1941, all reprinted in *Carta Semanal* 5, no. 205 (February 8, 1941).

67. CONCAMIN to Ávila Camacho, telegram, February 28, 1941, MAC/AGN, exp. 111/1790.

bolster its power by making the business community more dependent on the state. CONCANACOMIN argued that defining business chambers as "autonomous" public institutions was absurd because they would be accountable to the SEN. It added that its members would be transformed into "simple bureaucratic dependencies" whose primary purpose would be to collect taxes, while their leaders essentially would be public functionaries, representing state rather than private sector interests.[68] Also at issue was the desire of both merchants and the Ávila Camacho administration to co-opt the political potential of industrialists, whom each viewed as "still in diapers."[69] Therefore, commercial interests objected to the division of merchants and industrialists into separate chambers, seeing that industrialist autonomy would diminish the political weight of business chambers and establish more direct ties between industrialists and the state.

Unlike merchants, industrialists were split in their response to the 1941 chambers law. Leaders of CONCANACOMIN stated that 3,243 industrialists complained about the legislation.[70] They added that industrialists were satisfied with CONCANACOMIN due to genuine unity within the organization and its ability to settle differences internally.[71] Yet, some industrialists felt CONCANACOMIN underrepresented them. They had even formed their own group within the organization after it failed to defend them against cardenista labor radicalism.[72] Therefore, although concerned about the statist implications of the 1941 chambers law, most industrialists supported the partition of merchants and industrialists into distinct chambers. The 1941 chambers law offered them the possibility of more effective and discrete representation after years of political marginalization, even if it facilitated co-optation by the state.[73]

Yet, the law's mandate that industrial chambers be headquartered in Mexico City and have national jurisdiction checked regional industrialists' enthusiasm. They feared that Mexico City industrialists would have privileged political access, to the detriment of regional industrialists. However, the 1941 chambers law did not result from collusion between industrialists

68. CONCANACOMIN, telegram, February 4, 1941, and CONCANACOMIN to Ávila Camacho, 1941, both in MAC/AGN, exp. 545.2/7, leg. 1 al 5; CONCANACOMIN, telegram, February 7, 1941, MAC/AGN, exp. 545.2/7.
69. L. Medina, *Del cardenismo al avilacamachismo*, 294.
70. *Carta Semanal* 5, no. 219 (May 17, 1941), 8. Though the origins of this figure are unknown, evidence indicates that an array of industrialists lodged complaints. See MAC/AGN, exp. 545.2/7.
71. *Carta Semanal* 5, no. 207 (February 15, 1941), 8.
72. Martínez Nava, *Conflicto estado empresarios*, 105–9.
73. Juárez González, "Una década en la organización" 263–65; Shafer, *Mexican Business Organizations*, 30, 34; Story, "Industrial Elites in Mexico," 364.

in the capital and the ruling party. Rather, the law represented the desire of a faction of PRM leaders to harness the political energy of the burgeoning industrial sector, particularly those industrialists operating in Mexico City. When the state went on to create CANACINTRA in December 1941, it did precisely that. CANACINTRA was to serve as a single national chamber joining all manufacturing industries from across Mexico, but its location in Mexico City allowed the industrialists in the capital to dominate it.

Outside of Mexico City, however, many remained convinced that the law represented an effort by Mexico City industrialists to assert their dominance over national industry. CONCANACOMIN seized on these concerns to urge the government to reconsider the law's national impact: "The centralizing tendency of specialized chambers is not compatible with the enormous plurality of interests that exist in the vast national territory."[74] Confirming this, many of the regional chambers that objected to the law were quite small in size, and they represented business interests in places as geographically distant as Chiapas and Chihuahua. Some argued, as in the case of the business chamber in León, Guanajuato, that the law was being forced through the legislature by a small group of Mexico City business owners intent on usurping control of national industrialist representation.[75] Others, notably the Pátzcuaro, Michoacán, chamber, alleged that the law was an attack on regional industrialists and in the "bastard interest" of businesspeople in the capital.[76] These chambers emphasized that the legislation would be most damaging to smaller industrialists located in provincial settings who, they argued, relied on regional business organizations for representation. CANACINTRA was especially targeted, since it grouped a wide array of manufacturing industries into a single national organization headquartered in the capital. CONCANACOMIN deemed it absurd to presume that shoe manufacturers from León or Monterrey would have anything in common with ice or soap producers from Yucatán.[77] Moreover, the creation of CANACINTRA exacerbated fears that the central government was

74. CONCANACOMIN to Ávila Camacho, December 3, 1941, MAC/AGN, exp. 545.2/7, leg. 6 al 9; "Nuevas observaciones al proyecto de Ley de Cámaras de Comercio y de las de Industria, en lo que respecta a la agrupación de esos 2 ramos en cámaras diferentes," CONCANACOMIN, February 14, 1941, MAC/AGN, 545.2/7 leg. 1 al 5.
75. Cámara Nacional de Comercio e Industria de León, Guanajuato, telegram, February 28, 1941, MAC/AGN, exp. 545.2/7.
76. Cámara Nacional de Comercio e Industria de Pátzcuaro, telegram, March 3, 1941, MAC/AGN, exp. 545.2/7.
77. CONCANACOMIN to Ávila Camacho, December 3, 1941, MAC/AGN, 545.2/7 leg. 6 al 9.

seeking to regulate regional industry by providing privileged access to industrialists who advocated broader state economic intervention and who had overt sympathies for the PRM. These two tendencies excluded industrialists from areas with a long history of autonomous regional organizing, such as Guadalajara and Monterrey.[78] Consequently, when CANACINTRA tried to establish delegations in Jalisco and Nuevo León in the mid-1940s, some regional industrialists tried to block that.[79]

The 1941 chambers law formed part of a long struggle by the state to break down regional political and class alliances viewed as threatening to its consolidation. In response, many small- and medium-sized industries in Jalisco took advantage of a provision in the law that allowed them to form a regional chamber if a minimum of twenty-five businesses from the same industrial sector requested it and if the SEN approved. The law therefore provided for distinct representation for some regional industrialists within the institutional confines of the state, though this also allowed for tighter regulation in areas where concentrations of industry justified closer monitoring. Since 1941, the SEN has authorized sixteen regional industrial chambers in Jalisco, including chambers dedicated to industries that manufacture corn; shoes; foodstuffs; tequila; textiles; hides; jewelry and silver; clothing; wood; graphic arts products; and oils, fats, and their derivatives.[80] In this case, the proliferation and diversity of small- and medium-sized companies, as well as the lack of a controlling business leadership in the region, actually benefited regional industrialists by providing them with the sheer numbers and autonomy needed to contest the centralization of representation in Mexico City.[81] The SEN nevertheless continued to exercise authority over the chambers when, for example, it compelled Guadalajara industrialists to consider provincial producers when naming chambers and in assigning membership quotas.[82]

The formation of these regional chambers diluted the law's original intent and influenced the institutionalization of state-industry relations. The law had the potential to undermine regional alliances, some of which had

78. CONCANACOMIN to Ávila Camacho, March 8, 1941, MAC/AGN, 545.2/7, leg. 1-5; Shadlen, *Democratization Without Representation*, 40. CANACINTRA has jurisdiction throughout Mexico except in regions where regional manufacturing chambers later formed, such as Jalisco and Nuevo León. Alcazar, *Las agrupaciones patronales*, 26.

79. Lavín, *Actividades durante el año de 1945*, 25.

80. Alba Vega and Kruijt, "La burguesía industrial," 320; Alba Vega and Kruijt, *Los empresarios y la industria*, 311-12.

81. González González and Alba Vega, *Cúpulas empresariales*, 28.

82. SEN, Mexico City to Ricardo Aguilar and Indalecio Núñez, Guadalajara, January 10, 1944, Cámara Regional de la Industria de Transformación del Estado de Jalisco (CRIT-J).

supported conservative opposition to the ruling party in the 1940 election. Resistance to the law and the pressure for industry-specific regional chambers therefore demonstrated the persistent ambivalence of Jalisco's industrialists to state consolidation, and their aspiration to defend their distinct, regionally grounded interests and authority. Jalisco's industrialists were not unique in pressing for regionally based representation. For example, textile industrialists in Puebla and Tlaxcala fervently defended their right to have a regional chamber to represent the textile industry, despite pressures from the federal government to join the national textile chamber. In Puebla and Tlaxcala, the overwhelming dominance of textiles and the long history of strong, politically active regional industrial chambers made national organizations unattractive. By contrast, Monterrey's industrialists were concentrated in a single regional chamber that represented a variety of companies, indicating the political autonomy of a narrow and powerful group of allied northern businesspeople. Therefore, despite federal efforts to institutionalize and centralize the representation of industrialist interests through the creation of public chambers located in Mexico City, industrialist representation in the end continued to reflect the varied forms of industry and local class relations across Mexico.

The Social and Political Geographies of Protectionism

Almost concurrent with the passage of the 1941 chambers law, the federal government promulgated the Law on Manufacturing Industries (Ley de Industrias de Transformación, hereafter the 1941 federal exemption law). Passed on April 21 of that year, it provided tax exemptions to national industries. As we have seen in chapter 1, this was not the first postrevolutionary tax-exemption law for industry. Unlike its predecessors, however, the 1941 law included in its scope not just new industries but also "necessary" industries, as defined by the agencies involved in granting the exemptions. Officials intended these exemptions to stimulate production in order to lower prices and meet consumer demand while fulfilling the goal of achieving independent, coordinated, sustainable industrial growth. Yet vague language, poor planning, and ineffectual institutional mechanisms for its enforcement complicated the execution of the 1941 federal exemption law. Therefore, despite its framers' intentions to use the law to coordinate growth by promoting the production of a narrow range of goods directly tied to consumer demand, the challenges of postrevolutionary state-building and economic nationalism during World War II soon grew to play a prominent role in determining which producers would receive exemptions. Renowned Banco de México economist Víctor Urquidi was so troubled at this distortion of industrial policy that he dubbed the process of granting tax exemptions a sort of "Roulette Law" ("Ley de la Ruleta"), because the federal and state governments haphazardly doled out exemptions to encourage the manufacture of an array of random and inconsequential items.[83] Further inhibiting the effectiveness of the 1941 federal exemption law were the disparate state laws promoting industry. State officials generally had not designed these laws to counter federal legislation, but they nevertheless advanced regionalist visions of industrialization at odds with national priorities. In turn, they defended local forms of production in the face of the consolidating tendencies of the federal law, and they asserted the authority of state-level politicians and industrialists over regional industrial paths.

The 1941 law granted five-year exemptions from income taxes, excess-profits taxes, import taxes, and commercial-earnings taxes to any "new and necessary" industry producing finished and semifinished articles to satisfy consumer demand, excluding mining, metallurgy, and oil companies. It also allowed exemptions for imports of machinery and certain primary materials not available domestically. However, the definition of "new and necessary" was vague, and the Industrial Affairs Office (Dirección General de Industrias) issued application guidelines that emphasized that the SEN, at its own discretion, would deem companies "new and necessary." As with other legislation whose "interpretation [could] only be validated at the center," the law had the potential to contribute to the centralization of state authority, in this case, over industrial development.[84] However, the guidelines also asked applicants to indicate the advantages to Mexico of establishing their proposed industry.[85] Whether due to a lack of knowledge about national industry or ambiguity among technocrats and officials about developmental priorities, the government in effect was open to suggestions about what

83. Urquidi, "Espejismos económicos actuales," 26. See also Bravo Jiménez, *Planeación industrial en México*, 26–27.
84. Purcell and Purcell, "Mexican Business and Public Policy," 206.
85. These guidelines were located in multiple files in the DGI/AGN. Once the DGI recommended a company for an exemption, the SHCP then either granted the exemption or provided evidence for its rejection. Among the hundreds of cases from the 1940s reviewed for this book, no evidence indicated that the SHCP participated in the collection of information, review of applications, and initial decision making. The SHCP's role was limited to offering fiscal analyses, granting final approval to petitions already accepted by the Dirección General de Industrias, and fining companies that exceeded the approved import limits. See also Mosk, *Industrial Revolution in Mexico*, 64.

industries were necessary to satisfy unmet demand. It thereby created a legislative and discursive space for industrialists to pressure to have their production declared "new and necessary" based on conditions often unrelated to consumption. Consequently, vague wording, a fragmentary understanding of national industry, and jurisdictional overlaps among agencies involved in the process of writing and administering the 1941 federal exemption law diluted its effectiveness as a tool for industrial planning.

Further conspiring against the clear identification of consumer demand were concerns about wartime scarcities provoked by inflation, the interruption of normal trade relations, and U.S. manipulation of Mexican production to meet the war effort. As the various agencies involved in the administration of the law, including the SEN, the SHCP, industrial chambers, and the Banco de México, debated how to allocate resources and production, scarcity itself—rather than a clear understanding of popular consumer demands—became a primary determinant in defining unmet need.[86] Wartime industrial growth fed this confusion about the identification of unmet need, as shortages of producer goods, such as corrugated iron, iron and steel for tools, calcium carbide, and rawhide, induced technocrats and officials to broaden the definition of "new and necessary" even further.[87]

Some industrialists hewed closely to the original intent of the law when appealing for exemptions. They argued that projected production would meet domestic demand and mitigate problems with scarcity, inflation, or insufficient primary materials.[88] More commonly, however, industrialists

---

86. "Decretos que establecen el control sobre la venta, producción o distribución de diversos artículos" and "Decretos que establecen restricciones a la exportación de diversos artículos," MAC/AGN, exp. 545.22/160–1–33; SHCP, memorandum, September 23, 1942, MAC/AGN, exp. 545.22/160.

87. SEN, Oficina de Barómetros Económicos, *El desarrollo de la economía*, 49–53; Agencia General del SEN in Pachuca, Hidalgo, report, October, 21, 1939, DGI/AGN, v. 133, exp. 31/332.2 (03)/1; Primera Convención para el Estudio de Problemas Económicos de México, *Escasez y carestía*, 19–23; Secretaría Particular del Presidente Ávila Camacho, "Organismos de emergencia en la administración económica," October 19, 1943, MAC/AGN, exp. 545.22/160–1–33, pp. 26–27; Torres, *México en la segunda guerra mundial*, 289–91.

88. Celanese Mexicana, S.A., correspondence, March 12, 1942, and March 18, 1946, DGI/AGN, v. 126, 391/332.0/-47-A; Celanese Mexicana, S.A., SHCP, and Enrique Anisz, general director of Fomento Industrial y Mercantil, S.A., correspondence and application, July 15, 1941, DGI/AGN, v. 126, exp. 31/332.0/29; Productora de Artisela, S.A., application, June 10, 1941, DGI/AGN, v. 126, exp. 31/332.0/29; Carburo, S.A., March 27, 1942, GR/AGN, c. 74, exp. 11; La Perfeccionada, S.A. and SEN, Dirección General de Industria y Comercio, correspondence, December 16, 1944–April 30, 1945, DGI/AGN, v. 134, exp. 31/332.3/-3; Industria Nuevo León, S. de R.L. and SEN, correspondence, April 3–16, 1943, DGI/AGN, v. 25, 24/300 (03)/-1-10, letra I.

capitalized on the mutable and expanding concepts of necessary consumption during the war to introduce a range of political and ideological pressures into the application process. For example, nationalist reactions against U.S. control of Mexican production, including limits placed by the United States on machinery, primary material, and equipment exports, played a prominent role in shaping the evolution of tax exemptions. Industrialists and labor leaders from across Mexico blamed U.S. export restrictions for scarcities and high prices and condemned U.S. policies as a threat to fledgling industries. They even accused the United States of using wartime trade quotas to curb the development of certain industries in order to facilitate U.S. reentry into Mexican markets after the war and to ensure the long-term supply of Mexican primary materials for U.S. producers.[89]

Accordingly, applications for tax exemptions often became nationalistic statements that linked unmet demand to U.S. bids to influence Mexican production. Some simply touted their company's use of domestic primary materials or how their manufactures would soon displace imported goods.[90] Others addressed Mexican dependency more explicitly. For example, Productos Químicos de San Cristóbal, a producer of potassium chloride, won tax exemptions partly because it offered to "create a truly national industry within the territory" for a product that was unavailable because of wartime trade limits. The Banco de México backed the application, adding that domestic potassium chloride production would liberate Mexico from the high prices and supply problems that resulted from dependency on imports.[91] In another application, the head of Ancona-Ederer, Hernando Ancona, requested a tax exemption for the manufacture of fishing nets and thread to sew shoes. With U.S. production focused on netting for camouflage and large artillery covers, Ancona proposed to initiate production to assist Mexico's fishing industry. He supported his application by arguing that a U.S. fishing trust was trying to prevent Mexican fishermen from acquiring the rights and machinery necessary to develop the netting industry as a way to reserve the Mexican market for U.S. manufacturers after the war. Thus, the development of the industry, Ancona argued, was critical for defending

---

89. Ávila Camacho, Antonio Ruiz Galindo, F. Javier Gaxiola Jr., and Francisco Castillo Najera (Mexican Ambassador to the United States), correspondence, June 26, 1941, to October 28, 1942, MAC/AGN, exp. 564.2/27; tripartite commission of the Secretaría del Trabajo y Previsión Social (STPS), report, November 12, 1941, MAC/AGN, exp. 523/30; "Repercusiones de la guerra en la situación de los trabajadores," 1941, MAC/AGN, exp. 523/30.

90. Mauricio Roger Salle to Secretario de la Economía Nacional, Dirección General de Industria y Comercio, October 23, 1944, DGI/AGN, v. 130, exp. 31/332.1/-26.

91. Fermín Espinosa Aguilar, Oficina de Investigaciones Económicas (OIE), Banco de México to Jefe, OIE, Banco de México, report, July 26, 1941, GR/AGN, c. 73, exp. 6.

Mexico from foreign dependence and intervention. He concluded, "The power to determine the movement and capacity of [the fishing] industry should not be left to the arbitration of foreign nations."[92]

The instability of wartime production and its impact on the labor force meant that concerns about labor peace also influenced applications. During the war, labor organizations deluged President Ávila Camacho with complaints about problems in their industries, including deteriorating wages and work conditions. Many suggested that a further erosion of workers' rights would affect law and order, social peace, and even the legitimacy of the PRM as a party of the masses. In response, in November 1941, the Secretariat of Labor and Social Welfare (Secretaría del Trabajo y Previsión Social, STPS) initiated a campaign to endorse industries that would preserve jobs and maintain good work conditions. It predicted that if industry conditions continued to worsen "not only the economic, but also the social problem [would] become awful, since . . . the salaries of hundreds of thousands of workers" would be affected.[93] The SEN's Industrial Affairs Office and the SHCP thereafter requested that all applicants for tax exemptions include the projected number of workers. In addition, the agencies brought in the STPS to verify that applicants had honored all labor laws and codes. Subsequent applications invoked the Ávila Camacho administration's emphasis on labor peace.[94] Most applicants referred to their company's large workforce or their payment of a family wage.[95] For example, Enrique Anisz argued that Celanese should receive exemptions in order to prevent numerous factory closings, which he pointed out would lead to layoffs.[96] Another rayon producer urged the government to more closely regulate the establishment of new factories, asserting that excessive competition would lead to reduced wages.[97]

---

92. Ancona-Ederer, S.A., SHCP, and SEN, correspondence, September 1945–August 1946, DGI/AGN, v. 123, exp. 31/331.0/-16.

93. Tripartite commission of the STPS, report, November 12, 1941, and "Repercusiones de la guerra en la situación de los trabajadores," 1941, both in MAC/AGN, exp. 523/30.

94. For example, see La Perfeccionada, S.A. to SEN, Dirección General de Industria y Comercio, December 16, 1944, and April 30, 1945, DGI/AGN, v. 134, exp. 31/332.3/-3; Agencia General del SEN, Pachuca, Hidalgo, report, October 21, 1939, DGI/AGN, v. 133, exp. 31/332.2 (03)/1.

95. Ancona-Ederer, S.A., SHCP, and SEN, correspondence, September 1945–August 1946, DGI/AGN, v. 123, exp. 31/331.0/-16; El Bordador, S. de R.L., correspondence, September 1944–June 1945, DGI/AGN, v. 130, exp. 31/332.1/-26; Super-Malla, S.A. to Secretario de la Economía Nacional, Departamento de Industrias, Sección de Control Industrial, May 24, 1939, DGI/AGN, v. 136, exp. 31/332.3/46, leg. 1.

96. Celanese Mexicana, S.A. and SEN, correspondence, March 12, 1942, DGI/AGN, v. 126, 391/332.0/-47-A.

97. Giovanni Naselli, representative of Productora de Artisela, S.A. to SEN, September 22, 1943, DGI/AGN, v. 126, exp. 31/332.0/29.

The 1941 federal exemption law also aimed to encourage regional commitment to national development priorities. The goal of the law's creators was not explicitly to erode the authority of regional industrialists and politicians over local production. But they did seek to counteract the negative impact of the diverse state protectionist laws on national development. Despite their intentions, the 1941 federal exemption law and federal initiatives to shape state-level protectionist legislation to complement national laws generated opposition from regional industrialists who sought to defend regional production and their authority over it. In responding to federal pressure, regional political leaders had to balance their allegiance to the federal government with their loyalty to the local business community. Although these leaders stated that they did not seek to contest national development priorities, they often implemented state-level exemption legislation that ignored or contradicted federal legislation. Consequently, regional legislation often thwarted federal efforts to standardize protectionist policies and extend national authority over the economy.

Since at least the late nineteenth century, national policy makers had struggled to deal with the problem of standardizing federal legislation so that it took regional differences into account.[98] But even into the 1920s and 1930s, federal agencies simply pressed regional governments to pursue industrial development, often in vague, conflicting, or redundant ways. For example, in 1934, the SEN urged state governments to create protectionist legislation, even though nineteen states already had laws in place. A year later, the same secretariat directed states to enact trade measures to protect goods made with domestic primary materials that satisfied domestic demand. But just as the SEN was pressing states to enact legislation, technocrats at the Banco de México began to be concerned about the potential economic problems that could result from broad and uncoordinated protectionist policies. In 1935, they initiated a study of state-level protectionist laws with the goal of creating a national law that would supersede the diverse state laws, legislate a uniform national standard for granting exemptions, and produce a template on which all states could base their own legislation.[99] This study became the backbone of the federal exemption law passed in April 1941.

The 1941 law bore little resemblance to most regional legislation, however. On June 30, 1941, cardenista governor Silvano Barba González (1939–

---

98. Márquez Colín, "Political Economy," 44–45.
99. Banco de México, "Análisis de las leyes de protección y fomento industrial," 1946, GR/AGN, c. 77 bis (2), exp. 3, pp. 5, 62.

43) pushed through Jalisco's Law on Industrial Promotion (Ley de Fomento Industrial, hereafter Jalisco's 1941 exemption law), a law that diverged greatly from the federal one. In 1910, 1928, and 1932, the state had also passed legislation to promote industry. The 1910 law was largely a dead letter, however, falling victim to the vagaries of revolutionary violence, postrevolutionary populism, and fiscal constraints. In 1928, former provisional governor Barba González (1926–27) and Governor Ramírez observed the negative impact of industrial stasis on Jalisco's treasury, and a new tax-exemption law was enacted. Decree No. 3564 recognized "the public utility of establishing new industries in the State and promoting those already in existence."[100] Like Jalisco's 1941 exemption law, the 1928 decree demonstrated little inclination on the part of the Jaliscan government to mimic national policies. As we saw in chapter 1, the 1926 federal exemption law was relatively narrow, and it granted three-year tax exemptions to small industries that employed a high percentage of Mexican workers and relied on domestic primary materials. The 1928 Jaliscan law, in contrast, granted new and established industries exemptions that ran from two to fifteen years and from 25 percent to 90 percent of taxes. Only alcoholic beverage manufacturers were excluded. Yet, as occurred with the 1926 federal variant, few companies applied, due partly to the impact of the Great Depression, regional political conflicts, poor harvests, and the Cristero War.[101]

When Governor Allende passed the 1932 Industry Protection Law (Ley de Protección a la Industria), tax exemptions finally became crucial to industrial policy in Jalisco. The 1932 law, among other things, offered significant tax reductions for new industries and steep discounts on electricity rates.[102] It also promoted industries vital specifically to the local economy and to links between regional producers and consumers. It granted exemptions to industries that proposed to produce goods not manufactured in the state or which were produced in insufficient quantity to meet local demand. It also provided exemptions for companies that sought to boost efficiency in ways that would improve quality or lower prices and to intrastate transport or communications companies that developed links between communities in the region. Finally, it provided exemptions for existing companies that invested in machinery or improved worker hygiene, comfort, and security.[103]

100. Arias, *Fuentes para el estudio*, 15–17.
101. Ibid., 18.
102. Gómez López, "Los empresarios y el estado," 67.
103. Ley de Protección a la Industria, AHJ, Ramo Fomento, F-10-932, 11, 237.

In contrast to the tepid response to the 1928 Jaliscan law, the 1932 law was enthusiastically received. Between 1932 and 1940, the state government approved fifty-two requests from companies throughout Mexico trying to expand production into Jalisco, even though most exemptions went to companies already active in the state. Although data about the recipients are incomplete, large firms, including those in Jalisco's textile and food sectors, were among the recipients, but small-scale producers were the majority. Companies receiving exemptions ranged from the small soap factory of Enrique García Sherman, which had a stated capital of Mex$500, to Nestlé's plant in Ocotlán, capitalized at Mex$1,250,000. Of the forty-four factories for which data are available, just five were capitalized above Mex$50,000, while twenty-two were valued at Mex$10,000 or less.[104] Recipients included sixteen food producers, ten chemical companies, and six textile manufacturers, most of whom (thirty-six of fifty-two requests) expressed their intent to set up business in the state capital, Guadalajara, and to produce for local and regional consumption. The law was so successful that in 1935, Governor Topete doubled the length of the exemptions granted to six years.[105]

According to Patricia Arias, Governor Barba González revised Jalisco's tax-exemption law in 1941 in response to earlier pressure from his political collaborator, President Cárdenas, to encourage industries needed for the war effort.[106] But though loyalty was a prerequisite to gubernatorial survival by the late 1930s, Governor Barba González's success also depended on his ability to defend the companies and political authority of regional industrialists, even when it occasionally meant challenging the federal government's bids to shape national industrial development.[107] In this light, the timing of Jalisco's 1941 exemption law was suspicious, coming as it did fewer than three months after the promulgation of the federal exemption law. At the time, Governor Barba González tried to pass off the revision as a consequence of legislative bungling. He argued that a 1940 decree annulling all previous fiscal legislation had been applied incorrectly to the 1932 tax exemption law, forcing him to enact new legislation in order to reestablish industrial exemptions. But Jalisco's 1941 exemption law adhered less faithfully to the federal exemption law than had the 1932 legislation. Moreover, the governor stated that the law aimed explicitly to aid industry that took advantage of Jalisco's natural resources and contributed to the region's development, and he made little mention

---

104. Derived from data in Arias, *Fuentes para el estudio,* table 1, 64–69.
105. Arias, "La industria en perspectiva," 91–93; Arias, *Fuentes para el estudio,* 21.
106. Arias, "La industria en perspectiva," 105.
107. On the loyalty of governors, see Brandenburg, *Making of Modern Mexico,* 150–52.

of wartime demands.[108] And while the 1941 federal exemption law sought to tightly delimit the range and length of exemptions while contributing to national production and consumption goals, Jalisco's 1941 law expanded the list of industries targeted for protection, and it included local industries that only promised to supply regional markets. Jalisco's 1941 exemption law was a twenty-year project to promote new industries and those that would produce goods or services to satisfy demand currently unmet by regional companies. It also benefited industries that introduced more efficient or modern production methods, lowered production costs by at least 25 percent, or improved work conditions.[109] With this broad and vague list, Governor Barba González aimed to improve the local economy on all fronts by encouraging an array of both new and well-capitalized established industries.[110] He was so convinced of the importance of this legislation to the development of regional industry that it became a centerpiece of his propaganda to attract foreign investors, as demonstrated by a 1941 pamphlet titled "Jalisco, Open Your Arms to Industry."[111]

In the end, Jalisco's 1941 exemption law often benefited existing industries in areas of production already predominant in Jalisco, including oils, soaps, food products, chemicals, and clothing, although exemptions for established companies were lower than those for new ventures.[112] Depending on the size of the company and novelty of the product, exemptions lasted up to twenty years and from 100 percent of taxes. The largest industries received the most generous exemptions, with a 100 percent exemption from taxes for fifteen years for companies capitalized at between Mex$200,000 and Mex$1,000,000. For those whose capitalization was more than Mex$1,000,000, the exemption was for twenty years. For smaller companies, the exemptions were still significant, though they decreased incrementally over the course of the concession.[113] From 1942 to 1945, the state

108. Acta de la Sesión celebrada por la H. XXXV Legislatura del Estado, Jalisco, June 17, 1941, in Libro 185, Actas, H. Congreso del Estado, January 20–December 31, 1941, Biblioteca del Congreso Valentín Gómez Farías (VGF).
109. Decreto No. 4757, Ley de Fomento Industrial, *Periódico Oficial, El Estado de Jalisco*, July 3, 1941.
110. Barba González, *Informe*, 115–16; Gobernador Silvano Barba González, report, February 1, 1942, AHJ, Ramo Gobernación, G-1-942; Gobernador Silvano Barba González, report, February 1, 1943, AHJ, Ramo Gobernación, G-1-943.
111. Secretaría de Gobierno, "Jalisco, abre los brazos a la industria" (Guadalajara, August 1941), AHJ, Biblioteca, F338.1 Jal.; Arias, "La industria en perspectiva," 106.
112. Arias, "La industria en perspectiva," 106–7.
113. Decreto No. 4757, Ley de Fomento Industrial, *Periódico Oficial, El Estado de Jalisco*, July 3, 1941.

government granted 118 tax exemptions for an assortment of new and existing industrial products and services. Five other exemptions went to companies that had taken mortgages to develop their physical plant, including some of Jalisco's most prominent companies, such as Aceites, Grasas y Derivados, Nacional Textil Manufacturera, and Fomento Industrial y Mercantil.[114] Recipients ranged from a few companies with just Mex$1,000 up to the Compañía Industrial de Atenquique, which was capitalized at Mex$6,000,000.[115]

Because of the variety of companies that received state-level exemptions across Mexico, technocrats concluded that the 1941 federal exemption law had failed to induce states to enact uniform protectionist legislation geared to advance national industrial objectives. Rather, many states continued to pass broad tax-exemption legislation during the 1940s with no sense of the dangers of building an economy under haphazard protection. By 1945, twenty-eight states and the Federal District had legislation in place to stimulate industry. As with the federal exemption law, most state laws provided no clear definition of "new and necessary" or left its definition to the discretion of the state executive. "New and necessary" hence incorporated many activities that had little to do with the novelty or necessity of a proposed industry and which reflected regional as opposed to national criteria. Moreover, the exemptions extended not just to manufacturing industries but also to agriculture, ranching, mining, construction and urbanization, communications, transportation, commerce, tourism, forestry, credit institutions, service industries, and cultural projects, such as movie theaters. For example, in Hidalgo, the law favored companies that offered housing to poorer workers, sought to improve distribution, participated in extractive or agricultural activities, or provided transport to previously underserviced communities. In Chihuahua and Morelos, exemption laws targeted companies that proposed to build medical or cultural centers. In Veracruz, the state offered exemptions to companies that provided housing in areas with tenant problems.[116] Finally, Jalisco's 1941 exemption law aided in the construction of a hospital and the creation of a messenger service.

More than ten years after they had commissioned their 1935 study of regional laws, Banco de México technocrats were still pressing state governments to promote and protect industries in accordance with national goals,

---

114. "Empresas con franquicias fiscales concedidas," AHJ, Ramo Fomento, F-1-942-955, 7591. Patricia Arias's data also indicate that 118 exemptions were granted between 1942 and 1945. Arias, *Fuentes para el estudio*, table 2, 70–83.

115. "Empresas a las que se le concedieron extenciones [sic] fiscales," AHJ, Ramo Fomento, F-1-942-957, 7590.

116. Banco de México, "Análisis de las leyes de protección y fomento industrial," 1946, GR/AGN, c. 77 bis (2), exp. 3, pp. 60–61, 135–36, 109–10.

even as these officials failed to elaborate on those goals.[117] Almost twenty years later, a study co-authored by Mexican economists with ties to the Banco de México concluded that state tax-exemption laws still focused almost exclusively on regional issues "as if each state were its own country." They consequently undermined national development by discouraging interregional competition, limiting the scale of production, and supporting industries in regions where access to labor, supplies, and markets was not optimal.[118]

The 1941 federal exemption law ultimately encouraged the centralization and consolidation of national industry, though not because state-level laws imitated it. Rather, industries that qualified as "new and necessary" and received federal exemptions were disproportionately companies and types of production concentrated in Mexico City. Of the 938 federal exemptions granted between 1941 and 1946, more than one-half were for products manufactured in companies located in Mexico City.[119] The emerging metal and chemical industries, both of which were particularly prominent in the capital, together received about 50 percent of the exemptions granted.[120] Other industries to receive exemptions included historically strong sectors such as food processing, textiles, steel, soaps, glass, paper, construction materials, and cement, as well as relatively new areas of production, such as medical equipment and electronics.

Additionally, between 1941 and 1946, only about twenty federal exemptions, 2 percent of the total, went to Jaliscan companies.[121] Of these, many went to large companies, especially those targeted by the Ávila Camacho and Alemán administrations as "basic and necessary" and already enjoying extensive political and financial subsidies. This included Celanese Mexicana, which received exemptions from a variety of taxes for at least seven different products between 1942 and 1957.[122] Along with the Compañía Industrial de Atenquique, a paper and cellulose producer located in the municipality

---

117. Banco de México, "Análisis de las leyes de protección y fomento industrial," 1946, GR/AGN, c. 77 bis (2), exp. 3, pp. 16, 25, 30, 40–41, 60–62, 75–78, 98–99, 108, 126–41.

118. Romero Kolbeck and Urquidi, *La exención fiscal*, 19–20.

119. Data compiled from Banco de México, Departamento de Investigaciones Industriales, *Directorio de empresas industriales*. Without comprehensive data on applications, it is unknown if a proportional percentage of applications came from companies in Mexico City.

120. NAFINSA, *La política industrial*, 261.

121. Data compiled from Banco de México, Departamento de Investigaciones Industriales, *Directorio de empresas industriales*. The inexactitude in the Jalisco figures is due to a small number of companies whose location was unknown. In 1945, Jalisco had 6.3 percent of the nation's manufacturing establishments, producing 2.8 percent of the value of national production. López Malo, *Ensayo sobre localización*, 92–99.

122. Banco de México, Departamento de Investigaciones Industriales, *Directorio de empresas industriales*.

of Tuxpan in the south of Jalisco, Celanese was also among the top six recipients of federal aid to industries during the Ávila Camacho administration, mostly through NAFINSA.[123]

Not surprisingly, some owners of Jalisco's small- and medium-sized industries objected to federal protectionist policy, which they argued disproportionately benefited industry in Mexico City. They pointed to the federal government's partiality toward modern industries at the expense of the nondurable consumer goods industries that dominated in Jalisco. For example, in 1946, the Western Regional Chamber of Oils, Soaps, Fats, and Similar Products (Cámara Regional de la Industria de Aceites, Jabones, Grasas, y Similares de Occidente) accused the federal government of not protecting Jalisco's vital oil and soap industry in the same way that it protected industries that dominated in other regions.[124] The chamber requested new price controls and trade limits, and it pressed the federal government to develop a plan to save the industry.[125]

In the end, the 1941 federal exemption law failed to bring about regional commitment to national industrial goals, and not just because it favored industrial concentration and centralization in Mexico City. In truth, its impact on development was relatively minor. Some scholars have even argued that tax exemptions did more to increase profits than to encourage industry. They have noted that other factors, such as market size and labor organizations, have a more decisive impact on industrial development.[126] Moreover, during the 1940s, piecemeal national planning and vague wording in the 1941 federal exemption law let the challenges of postrevolutionary state-building and economic nationalism play a prominent role in the law's execution. In this climate, federal tax-exemption legislation did not become a template for regional laws. Rather, state-level laws continued to reflect local social and political priorities, including the promotion of production closely tied to regional markets in places like Jalisco. By passing their legislation, regional leaders were not necessarily defying the state and its right to intervene in the economy, though that may have been a factor at times. Rather, they were defending local forms of production in the face of the consolidating tendencies of federal laws, and asserting the right of state-level politicians and industrialists to determine regional industrial paths.

123. Cue Cánovas, "Economía de emergencia," 309; Gabayet Ortega, "Diferenciación social," 240–42.
124. Arias, *Fuentes para el estudio*, 26–27.
125. Cámara Regional de la Industria de Aceites, Jabones, Grasas, y Similares de Occidente to SEN, June 24, 1947, AMGM, v. 302, exp. 1050.
126. Romero Kolbeck and Urquidi, *La exención fiscal*, 20, 69.

An Archetypal Pact: Regional Industry and Ruling-Party Authority in the 1940s

Struggles over tax exemptions and industrialist representation reflected the complex, often ambivalent relationship between Jaliscan industrialists and the ruling party in the decades after the Revolution. As demonstrated by the governorships of Allende and Topete in the 1930s, Jalisco's governors became critical mediators balancing ruling-party loyalties with local commitments. Their success depended in great measure on their alliances with regional business leaders and the ability to embody regionalist perceptions and practices grounded in shared interests and economies. By the 1940s, the growth of Guadalajara increased their ability to traverse these two often-conflicting worlds. It did so by allowing industrialists to deepen and expand regional production and markets, as well as their regional political roles. As a result, the emergence of Guadalajara as a regional metropolis enabled industrialists to sustain local allegiances founded on a belief in their common economic, class, political, and religious interests, even as industrial growth, migration, and political centralization brought great social and economic change to the region and transformed the meanings and functions of these alliances.

Even more than the dislocations caused by the Revolution and the Depression, World War II threatened to alter the nature of locally oriented production in Jalisco. Because of the limited availability of foreign goods, some producers moved into national and international markets during the war. This included producers of goods such as textiles, tequila, and even soaps, whose manufacturers produced the glycerin needed for explosives.[127] Foreign demand for Mexican goods grew, accounting for almost 79 percent of total manufacturing growth in Mexico during the war. This counters common claims that the import-substituting effects of World War II were the primary stimulus to manufacturing growth in the early 1940s.[128]

Despite the influence of the war in drawing producers into new markets, however, much industry in Jalisco remained focused on producing nondurable consumer goods for regional markets. Indeed, the diverse and dispersed nature of the regional market continued to play a defining role in

---

127. Arias, "El proceso de industrialización," 88–89. Purportedly, much of the tequila exported to international markets during the war, including to troops, was bottled under questionable conditions, was of poor quality, and even had bits of glass or garbage in it. Muriá, *Breve historia de Jalisco* (1988), 549.

128. Cárdenas, "Process of Accelerated Industrialization," 184–85.

the survival of local industry, since it provided a consumer base even for traditional manufacturers.[129] To be sure, by the 1940s, Jalisco had also witnessed the emergence of a new wave of large-scale industry in the region, especially in agro-industry and exemplified by the formation of Nestlé, the Cremería La Danesa, and the paper-manufacturing complex at Atenquique.[130] But the majority of businesses in Jalisco were unregistered, small-scale, and home-based workshops concentrated in areas such as knitwear, shoes, and leather tanning.[131] Even among registered industries, Jalisco's companies were smaller than those in Mexico City and Monterrey. For example, in 1950, Jalisco had 525 machine shops averaging just 3.47 workers each. Comparatively, the average shop nationwide had 6.67 workers. Jalisco's 525 machine shops employed 1,822 workers. By comparison, Nuevo León had only 337 establishments, but they employed 5,287 workers.[132] More broadly, in 1950, Jalisco had 5.5 percent of the country's industrial establishments, employing just 4.4 percent of the workers and producing only 3.9 percent of the total national production value. By comparison, Mexico City had 21.8 percent of the nation's industries with 30.3 percent of its workers generating 28.6 percent of Mexico's production value.[133]

Jalisco's small- and medium-sized industries depended on local political leaders to protect their regional markets and opportunities. In the 1940s, the ability of Jalisco's governors to meet both the demands of local industry and their obligations to the ruling party that put them in office depended in part on the rapid expansion of Guadalajara. Spurred by agrarian reform, the lingering effects of cristero violence, industrial development, improved roads, and educational and cultural opportunities, the percentage of Jaliscans living in urban areas grew from 41 percent to 48 percent between 1940 and 1950. Guadalajara alone absorbed 44 percent of the state's growth in that decade, as the city's population surged from roughly 235,000 to 380,000 residents.[134] While Jalisco's population grew by slightly more than 23 percent between 1940 and 1950, the population of Guadalajara grew by more

129. Arias, "La industria en perspectiva," 103–7.
130. Alba Vega and Kruijt, "La burguesía industrial," 299.
131. Manuel Bravo Jiménez to Daniel Cosío Villegas, report, June 2, 1943, GR/AGN, c. 84, exp. 1.
132. I. Medina, "Un dinamismo frustrado," 253–55.
133. López Malo, *Ensayo sobre localización*, 92–99.
134. Alba Vega, "Las regiones industriales," 115; Alba Vega and Kruijt, *Los empresarios y la industria*, 57, 243–44. Even though growth rates were more rapid during the 1950s, the decade of the 1940s saw a departure from 1930s urbanization rates. Estimates of population growth in Guadalajara vary, although only slightly. Patricia Arias claims that the population surged from 244,406 to

than 60 percent, resulting in more than one-fifth of Jaliscans living in the capital by 1950.¹³⁵

Governors Marcelino García Barragán (1943–47) and Jesús González Gallo (1947–53) were both acutely aware that their political survival lay in part in stimulating the expansion of urban industry geared toward local producers and markets.¹³⁶ Each therefore focused on managing Guadalajara's rapid growth. Governor González Gallo in particular expanded housing, roadways, electricity, and other public services. As part of this support for regional industry and urban development, generating secure, long-term regional sources of investment was paramount. Often a result of state-business collaboration, nine regional banks were created between 1930 and 1945, including the Banco Industrial de Jalisco.¹³⁷ Both governors also acclaimed their use of regional tax-exemption legislation to promote new and necessary industries, especially in Guadalajara. Given that between 1948 and 1952, 80 percent of tax-exemption requests came from companies located in the state's capital, the emphasis on Guadalajara is understandable.¹³⁸

Governors García Barragán and González Gallo ultimately took divergent political paths, largely due to their management of regional labor radicalism. In the 1940s and beyond, some employers in Jalisco continued to endorse Catholic social action and its emphasis on class cooperation as a means to achieve social peace and economic prosperity.¹³⁹ The acceptance by many industrialists of state intervention in labor-employer relations increasingly marginalized this conservative opposition, especially after the election of the more moderate President Ávila Camacho. Some employers

---

403,982 inhabitants between 1940 and 1950. Arias, "La industria en perspectiva," 105. John Walton states that Guadalajara grew from 229,234 residents in 1940 to 377,016 in 1950. Walton, *Elites and Economic Development*, 38.

135. Walton, *Elites and Economic Development*, 38.
136. Arias, *Fuentes para el estudio*, 26.
137. Banco Capitalizador de Guadalajara, documents, April 12, 1940, and January 7, 1941, AMGM, v. 352, exp. 1222; Alba Vega and Kruijt, "La burguesía industrial," 323–24; Alba Vega and Kruijt, *Los empresarios y la industria*, 217–18; González González and Alba Vega, *Cúpulas empresariales*, 27.
138. Statistics on the number of state-level tax exemptions granted vary and data are incomplete. Governor García Barragán claims to have granted exemptions to 148 companies, whereas Governor González Gallo probably granted 82 exemptions between 1948 and 1952. Because only 205 requests for exemptions were submitted between 1941 and 1950, Governor García Barragán's number seems inflated. Also, the location of a number of companies is not provided, so it is impossible to fix a more exact percentage of Guadalajaran companies seeking tax exemptions. See Arias, *Fuentes para el estudio*.
139. Herrera Rossi, "Defensa de la pequeña industria," 17–21; Alba Vega and Kruijt, *Los empresarios y la industria*, 189–90.

were so confident in the state's ability to control labor that they even requested that unions organize their factories.[140] State management of labor-employer relations was put to the test during World War II, however, as Jalisco experienced a wave of union organizing, protests, and strikes. Rather than quelling the unrest, Governor García Barragán purportedly fostered it by endorsing a dissident faction of workers amid labor strife that rent the CTM-backed Federation of Jaliscan Workers. With these accusations, Governor García Barragán suffered a serious blow to his revolutionary credentials, to his relationship with regional industrialists, and to his ties to the PRM.[141] When he subsequently defied the ruling-party presidential selection process by backing the region's military commander, General Miguel Henríquez Guzmán, for president of Mexico, Governor García Barragán fell out of favor. Removed from office just eleven days shy of the end of his term amid a disagreement with Congress over the term length of the governorship, Governor García Barragán left in political disgrace.[142]

Governor González Gallo, by contrast, became an archetypal ruling-party politician and governor, as shown by his agility in balancing the often-competing claims of regional industrialists and the federal government. Even though Governor González Gallo had lived in Mexico City since the late 1930s, his ties to Jalisco were impeccable. He had been born and educated in Jalisco, and he had married a woman from one of the state's most prominent families. He had also been a federal senator, president of the PNR in Jalisco in the early 1930s, head of the Comité Pro Ávila Camacho in Guadalajara in 1939, and private secretary to President Ávila Camacho. Moreover, Governor González Gallo had strong ties with the local labor movement, since he had worked with Heliodoro Hernández Loza in 1932 to create the workers' section of the PNR.[143] Finally, he was a close friend of President Ávila Camacho's wife, Soledad Orozco. As a ruling-party insider, he never placed his loyalty to the party in doubt, yet he managed the demands of local industrialists through personal contacts and a willingness to defend regional interests, even when they countered those of the ruling party.

The relationship of regional industrialists with the ruling party therefore was founded less on popular support than on a faith in local politicians.

140. Arias, "El proceso de industrialización," 90.
141. Fernández Aceves, "En-gendering *Caciquismo*," 216–17; Tamayo, "Movimiento obrero y lucha sindical," 152–53; Muriá, *Breve historia de Jalisco* (1988), 539–40.
142. Muriá, *Breve historia de Jalisco* (1988), 541–42; Camp, *Mexican Political Biographies*, 260–61, 303–4. For more on *henriquismo* in the 1940s and 1950s, including Henríquez Guzmán's relationship with Governor García Barragán, see Servín, *Ruptura y oposición*.
143. Fernández Aceves, "En-gendering *Caciquismo*," 216; Tamayo, "Los obreros," 89–93.

Some of this faith was borne of the fact that both politicians and labor leaders increasingly became investors in local industry by the 1940s, just as industrialists were gaining new opportunities to move into regional politics. For example, mixed public-private initiatives to foster industrial and urban development, such as the Commission for Industrial Promotion (Comisión de Fomento Industrial) and the Guadalajara Council on Municipal Collaboration (Consejo de Colaboración Municipal de Guadalajara), became more common in the 1940s. Moreover, Governor González Gallo endeavored to include the private sector in public decisions, especially those affecting industrial growth and city planning. Beginning with his administration, the position of vice president of the municipality of Guadalajara was reserved for a local representative from the private sector. After 1959, only local merchants or industrialists occupied the position, transforming it into a key channel of communication between the public and private sectors in Guadalajara.[144]

The accommodation between the ruling party and Jalisco's industrialists rested not just on the regional adaptation of national authority but also on the evolution of the national ruling party into an organization of technocrats and politicians. They signaled the ruling party's move toward moderation when they reorganized the PRM into the PRI in 1946. Throughout the 1940s, these technocrats and politicians would focus their efforts on harnessing the political energies of Mexico's growing urban middle classes, professionals, and businesspeople. They acknowledged the importance of Guadalajara in accomplishing that when, in 1943, they selected the city as the site for the founding meeting of the National Confederation of Popular Organizations (Confederación Nacional de Organizaciones Populares), which was to become the popular arm of the ruling party. The confederation grouped an array of middle-class and professional interests, and it attracted Guadalajara's business community because the organization pledged to defend private property, foster small industries and landholdings, and combat fanaticism. The ruling party's appeal to small business owners and professionals in the region also grew after the 1940 election, when the PAN failed to design a platform for industrial development. After 1949, that party increasingly retreated into issues related to religious doctrine, although it retained a significant following in Jalisco and the region supplied a number of PAN candidates for public office.[145]

144. Velasco, "La vicepresidencia municipal de Guadalajara," 37–38; Alba Vega and Kruijt, *Los empresarios y la industria*, 204, 227–28.
145. Davis, *Discipline and Development*, 309–10; Loaeza, *El Partido Acción Nacional*, 192–95, 201.

Governor González Gallo represented the shift away from cardenista radicalism and toward political moderation and middle-class incorporation within the ruling party. However, in this region of complex religious and political loyalties, he maintained personal ties to some of Guadalajara's most conservative and Catholic forces, which was another indicator of the flexibility of ruling-party authority at the regional level. His prior years of study for the priesthood at a Catholic seminary facilitated this. For example, even as Efraín González Luna ran as the PAN candidate for president in 1952, Governor González Gallo remained close friends with him, a friendship that dated back to their participation in the Mexican Association of Catholic Youth in Guadalajara many years earlier.[146]

But the path to the political incorporation of Guadalajara's industrialists was not smooth, and in 1954, Guadalajara's regional chamber representing the shoe industry highlighted the reasons for the enduring ambivalence of industrialists toward state centralization. Complaining of the excessive individualism of large producers and statist attacks on the rights of private enterprise, the chamber suggested that morally responsible, balanced development should entail the promotion of small-scale and artisanal producers.[147] This assertion points to the obstacles faced by the ruling party as it sought to extend authority over Mexico's diverse regional industrialists after the Revolution. In Jalisco, it faced industrialists who both welcomed the opportunity to use the state's corporatist capacities to manage labor radicalism and decried what they saw as excessive state intervention in the rights of private enterprise. In some senses, the party used regionalism in Jalisco to manage fluid political and class arrangements, though this demanded that it become a supple political machine. This included at times allowing regional industrialists to adapt or appropriate state capacities for regionalist ends, as demonstrated by regional responses to federal chambers and tax-exemption laws. Even though legislation ostensibly aimed to curb regional authority, it often was spongy and accommodated, or at least tolerated, regional challenges to its centralizing and consolidating objectives. The relationship between the state and regional elites in Jalisco therefore reinforced forms of regionalism rooted in local class relations and affinities. Technocrats both celebrated and were troubled by regionally oriented development. They saw the potential advantages of decentralized growth, but

---

146. González González and Alba Vega, *Cúpulas empresariales*, 10, 55; Camp, *Mexican Political Biographies*, 304.
147. Herrera Rossi, "Defensa de la pequeña industria," 5–15.

they concurrently criticized its impact on efforts to research, develop, and implement national economic planning. These concerns shaped debates about statist industrialism in the early 1940s and spurred new ones about the impact on state authority of defining nationalist development in either regionalist or centralizing terms.

3

THE PASSION AND RATIONALIZATION OF MEXICAN INDUSTRIALISM
Rival Visions of State and Society in the Early 1940s

In September 1941, discontented workers from Materiales de Guerra, a government arms and munitions manufacturer, marched to President Ávila Camacho's residence to petition for higher salaries and to lodge complaints against the company manager. With the women in front carrying flowers for the president's wife, about two thousand workers, union members, and supporters made their way on foot from the factory to Los Pinos, the presidential mansion. Waiting at the presidential gates was a military battalion. Versions vary as to how the skirmish began, but by the end, between seven and thirty-three workers had been killed and fifteen to sixty injured. In response, railroad, mining, petroleum, telephone, and transport workers organized a demonstration in front of the National Palace, while labor leaders Vicente Lombardo Toledano and Fidel Velázquez scrambled to assuage the workers' anger in order to preserve wartime national unity.[1] Nevertheless, national protests continued, underscoring one of the most active periods of labor mobilization in Mexican history.

The surge in labor mobilizations in the early 1940s resulted mostly from wartime scarcities and deteriorating real wages. Yet widespread poverty and the daily flood of migrants arriving in Mexico City transformed these protests from narrow demands for workers' rights into a critique of the state's efforts at political incorporation, agrarian redistribution, and labor reform in the 1930s. In this climate, industrialism increasingly appeared as a solution to perceived problems with postrevolutionary reconstruction.

1. Campa, *Mi testimonio*, 169–70; Bernal Tavares, *Vicente Lombardo Toledano y Miguel Alemán*, 115; Niblo, *Mexico in the 1940s*, 106–8.

During the 1940s, bureaucrats, politicians, and the business community held differing views of the proper role of the state in economic development, just as had been the case in the 1920s. Technocrats in the Banco de México's Office of Industrial Research (Oficina de Investigaciones Industriales, OII) heavily favored economic planning, but they also had reservations about the state's ability to pursue it without succumbing to the self-interested machinations of politicians. Many of these technocrats, including Daniel Cosío Villegas and Gonzalo Robles, had moved through the bureaucratic ranks in the 1920s and 1930s, and they had seen bureaucrats' well-intentioned introduction of planning into policy making fall victim to economic crises, political intrigue, and the uncoordinated development projects of multiple state agencies. They therefore sought to supersede the heirs of the positivists, who had dominated policy making in the 1920s, by emphasizing rationalization as the means to counter politics and cronyism in economic planning. Their self-anointed mission was to define an economic plan that could coordinate industrial activities and rationalize the state's role in the economy while promoting regionally balanced industrial development with a focus on basic industry. By the late 1940s, the Alemán administration recognized this mission and even at times encouraged it.[2] Moreover, along with the Ávila Camacho administration, it often remarked on the potential benefits of planning as it extended state regulation over the economy. However, to the disappointment of Robles and others, the state under Alemán never authorized the creation of a single planning agency empowered to coordinate national industrial development.

In contrast to the technocrats in the OII, the leaders of CANACINTRA pressured the state to intervene aggressively in the economy. In their view, Mexico's burgeoning group of urban-based manufacturers of consumer goods should determine state intervention, not the bureaucratic and technocratic elite. Untroubled by the potential perils of unequal development, they urged the state to promote the concentration of industry in a few key urban settings.

Both the OII and CANACINTRA sought to incorporate Mexico's growing urban working class into their industrial projects in a way that could generate national wealth, improve standards of living, and bring social peace. With this in mind, technocrats at the OII proposed to transform workers into modern, capitalist producers by reshaping labor-employer relations according to an objective economic plan that alluded to social justice

---

2. Secretaría de Programación y Presupuesto, *La programación de la inversión pública*.

but obscured the perpetuation of traditional forms of social control. CANACINTRA, by contrast, focused on building a domestic market for Mexican manufactures based on worker commitment to consumption and production. It proposed to foster this commitment by co-opting labor into an urban-industrial alliance led by the ruling party and founded on hierarchical political relations and patronage masked by assertions of equality. This alliance, in turn, would guarantee a place for industrialists in future economic decision making.

The OII and CANACINTRA were only two among many groups trying to shape the future of industrialism in Mexico. However, their distinct visions for the state's role in industrial development were emblematic of rifts among groups close to the state, and their debate echoed arguments taking place in other Latin American industrializing nations in the 1940s and 1950s. Neither CANACINTRA nor the OII fit neatly into the national populist or developmentalist camps. Like national populists and developmentalists in other countries, both advocated protection for industry, though to different extents, and both were concerned about the export-oriented focus of liberalism. CANACINTRA was more in tune with national populism, with its entrenched anti-export and anti-foreign-capital bias and focus on domestic consumption and markets, all of which led it to favor small- and medium-sized industry. By contrast, the OII reflected developmentalist ideas that advocated limited state involvement and the use of foreign capital and technology to foster basic industries that later could move competitively into export markets. For developmentalists and the OII, "not all forms of industrialization were equal or contributed equally to development." Thus, development efforts should first focus on basic industry and infrastructure that would serve as the foundation for more integrated, dynamic industrial growth.[3]

These distinctions are significant given that many scholars of mid-twentieth-century Mexico have identified a relatively stark ideological fault line between economic liberals and those advocating state economic intervention, which led to an assumption that a consensus existed within the state on protected growth by the 1940s. Yet, the national state was hardly a monolith by the 1940s, similar to the situation during the 1920s and 1930s, when regional political currents often ran counter to national ruling-party trends. Indeed, strong reformist strains, some of which were holdovers from

---

3. On the distinction between national populism and developmentalism, see Sikkink, *Ideas and Institutions*, 29–33.

the Cárdenas period, continued to play a prominent role in shaping policy. Moreover, economists, engineers, politicians, and businesspeople commonly took a heterodox approach to economic policy, rarely viewing it in strictly liberal or statist terms. Rather, they drew from Marxist, Keynesian, and neoclassical schools while addressing economic policy through the lens of Mexico's unique postrevolutionary social and political challenges. Consequently, while most believed that industrialism could fulfill the revolutionary guarantee of social justice, establish social peace and political stability, and build a disciplined and productive workforce, they nevertheless presented a remarkable array of visions for state and society in defining an industrial project to accomplish these goals.

The Origins of the OII and CANACINTRA

Both the OII and CANACINTRA were established during President Ávila Camacho's first year in office. The OII emerged from the desire to meet the technical demands of the new state through professionalizing the management of economic development. In contrast, the origins of CANACINTRA were explicitly political and lay in state efforts to ally with urban manufacturers in order to undermine regional industrialist opposition and quell wartime labor unrest. The distinct origins and divergent missions of the two organizations demonstrate dissonance about the state's role in economic development in the early 1940s.

The predecessor of the OII was the Office of Economic Research (Departamento [or Oficina] de Investigaciones Económicas, OIE). Created in 1932 to study banking and monetary matters, the OIE had only about twelve employees throughout the 1930s. With the emergence of the professional fields in Mexico, especially economics, the OIE thrived despite its small size.[4] In 1929, a politically diverse group of public officials and intellectuals who were committed "to building national state institutions in the service of economic development" had come together to design and implement an economics curriculum in the Law School at the National Autonomous University of Mexico (Universidad Nacional Autónoma de México, UNAM).[5] The group included a number of people who would be prominent in industrial research, banking, and finance in the 1940s, including

---

4. Cleaves, *Professions and the State*, 2–7.
5. Quote from Babb, *Managing Mexico*, 29; Camp, "National School of Economics and Public Life in Mexico," 138.

Narciso Bassols, Eduardo Villaseñor, Jesús Silva Herzog, Manuel Gómez Morin, and Daniel Cosío Villegas. The curriculum they designed was so successful that by 1935, economics had grown into a stand-alone program, the National Economics School (Escuela Nacional de Economía). The school's graduates, actively recruited by the state, soon filled government agencies, including the SHCP, the Secretariat of Agriculture (Secretaría de Agricultura), the SEN, and, of course, the Banco de México. For example, at the urging of Cosío Villegas and others, President Portes Gil established a list of mid-level public administrative positions that could be filled only by people with a university degree in economics.[6] Out of the work of these intellectuals and officials, Mexico became a leader in economic research in Latin America in the 1930s. In 1934, Cosío Villegas and Villaseñor initiated publication of *El trimestre económico* and founded the Fondo de Cultura Económica, which quickly took their places among Latin America's most esteemed economics journals and publishing houses, respectively. By the early 1940s, other economics journals appeared in Mexico as well, and economics became a prominent field at the newly founded El Colegio de México, where many Banco de México employees taught.[7]

When the OII spun off from the OIE in 1941, it comprised a small coterie of administrators, economists, and engineers committed to regionally balanced industrial, mining, and agricultural growth. Its initial mandate was to address concerns among bankers about their lack of preparedness when faced with decisions about long-term credit for industrial projects. Consequently, in its early years, it focused on the production and diffusion of technical knowledge about industry. It performed copious studies of basic industry and natural resources, surveyed development projects taking place in other state agencies, established a scholarship program that sent Mexicans abroad to study in technical fields, and assisted in the formation of technical institutions. The OII subsequently became an influential advisor to the SEN, the SHCP, NAFINSA, and other government agencies and banks, especially over issues such as credit, machinery, and production and distribution controls.[8]

In contrast to the professional and technical origins of the OII, the beginnings of CANACINTRA were largely political. As we have seen in the

6. Rodríguez Garza, "Cambio institucional," 189–211, 240; Babb, *Managing Mexico*, 23.
7. Love, "Institutional Foundations," 146–47.
8. The OII's focus on research reflects that economic planning is perceived, in part, to be a response to the imperfections of the market that occur due to inadequate economic information. On the SEN's ideas about industrial growth, see "Una patriótica excitativa para la industrialización de la República Mexicana," *El Universal*, June 11, 1938.

previous chapter, the 1940 presidential elections proved that extensive opposition to the ruling party still existed among industrialists. Though the official tally stated that opposition candidate Juan Andreu Almazán had received only 15,101 votes across Mexico, most agreed that he had actually won in Mexico's three most industrially vital cities: Guadalajara, Mexico City, and Monterrey. Many of his supporters came from the working class and popular sectors, which included professionals and owners of small- and middle-sized businesses.[9] The PRM thus realized the limits of its legitimacy in the seat of national politics and among the city's most rapidly growing and economically important groups.

In the aftermath of the rigged, violent election, the ruling party sought an alliance with industrialists in the capital to foster stronger relations with its burgeoning urban manufacturing sector and to assimilate it into the state's industrial project. In this light, CANACINTRA was an outgrowth of the transformation of Mexico City into an industrial metropolis in the decades after the Revolution and of the ruling party's recognition that it needed to manage this transformation.[10] The industrial impulse provided by World War II complicated the organization's mission. During the war, Mexico became a key supplier of war materials for the United States, while it also moved into Central and South American markets abandoned by Japan, Europe, and the United States. Domestic scarcities and rationing also stimulated industry and lessened worries about quality and prices. As a result, from 1940 to 1950, the number of industrial establishments in Mexico City exploded from 4,920 to 12,704. During that same decade, the percentage of establishments located in Mexico City grew from just 8.7 percent of the national total to approximately 20 percent, though notably, their contribution to the total national value of production dropped between 1945 and 1950, from 32.3 percent to a still significant 28.6 percent.[11]

CANACINTRA provided an efficient means to manage forces associated with this rapid urban expansion and to undercut opposition from some regional industrialists. Its mandate to act as a "mixed-activity industrial chamber for firms of all sizes," and the legal requirement that all companies of a certain size join an industrial chamber, meant that the organization

9. Contreras, *México 1940*, 143; Davis, *Urban Leviathan*, 97–99.
10. Scholars who emphasize cooperation between CANACINTRA and the ruling party and the origins of their relationship in the conditions in Mexico City include Davis, *Urban Leviathan*; Shadlen, *Democratization Without Representation*; Mosk, *Industrial Revolution in Mexico*; Lütke-Entrup, "Business, Labour, and the State."
11. Garza Villarreal, *El proceso de industrialización*, 143; López Malo, *Ensayo sobre localización*, 98–99.

grew swiftly. From its formation with ninety-three members in 1941, CANACINTRA expanded to 6,700 members by 1945 and to 8,970 by 1950. In 1945, 4,585 of its members were located in Mexico City.[12] With this growth, it morphed into a representative of small industry, especially those businesses located in Mexico City. The reasons for this are numerous, but perhaps most simply, small industry dominated CANACINTRA because their numbers in Mexico City had grown most quickly during the 1930s and 1940s, especially in textile production.[13] Moreover, although it represented all national manufacturers, CANACINTRA was located in the capital, thereby enhancing the dominance of the city's manufacturers. Finally, as we have seen in the previous chapter, many regional industrialists took advantage of a loophole in the 1941 chambers law to create their own regionally based chambers. This offered them autonomy from CANACINTRA, but it had the corollary of concentrating the chamber's authority in the hands of its industrialist members in Mexico City.

As Kenneth Shadlen has noted, "material and organizational weakness" led CANACINTRA to forfeit its political autonomy and ally with the state. However, its members received significant benefits in return, not the least of which was "regularized access to state officials and policy-making forums" for small manufacturers.[14] Furthermore, throughout the 1940s, tax exemptions favored the manufacturing and service industries located in Mexico City that dominated CANACINTRA's membership. Between 1941 and 1946, on average 60 percent of all tax exemptions for new and necessary industries went to companies based in Mexico City (the highest point was 78 percent in 1942; the lowest, 47 percent in 1945).[15]

The formation of CANACINTRA also addressed the problem of labor unrest, since it became a key player in the urban-industrial alliance between industrialists, workers, and the ruling party. Political solutions for labor unrest were not new. In 1938, President Cárdenas had designated the CTM as the official labor representative in the newly reconstituted ruling party. Although offering workers official recognition and representation, this corporatist shift had concurrently facilitated the control of the working class, including by enhancing the authority of labor leaders over their members. But by the early 1940s, the empowerment of these labor leaders translated

12. Shadlen, *Democratization Without Representation*, 37–38; Lavín, *Actividades durante el año de 1945*, 24–25; Centro de Información y Estudios Nacionales, *La Cámara Nacional*.
13. Haber, *Industry and Underdevelopment*, 185–87.
14. Shadlen, *Democratization Without Representation*, 32.
15. Statistics calculated based on information from Banco de México, *Directorio de empresas industriales*.

into a serious threat to the ruling party, and the PRM became concerned about its ability to control the direction of union management. In response, the party took advantage of rivalries among union leaders in order to undermine their authority over labor. It concurrently reached out to other, more conservative national labor federations.[16]

Diminishing the power of the central labor authority encouraged local and statewide union bosses to pursue work actions independent of the approval of national labor federations. And amid the economic difficulties brought on by World War II, they did precisely that. Between 1940 and 1945, mobilizations rocked major industries, including the petroleum, textile, mining, film, tramway, and railroad industries. For example, in December 1943, more than 50,000 textile workers from approximately 250 factories struck in the wake of a breakdown in negotiations over wage increases.[17] More common than strikes in major industries were small, isolated ones taking place all over Mexico. In 1944, conservative estimates that only take into account official strikes had labor unrest peaking at 887 strikes comprising 165,744 strikers. This was more active than any single year during the tumultuous Cárdenas presidency. By 1945, official strikes began to taper off, but workers still took part in 220 strikes in that year.[18]

As with political incorporation, economic solutions to labor unrest also had only limited success in demobilizing labor, due largely to wartime conditions. Strikes during World War II most often were in response to spiraling prices, declining real wages, interunion rivalries, and shortages. For example, in Mexico City, the annual increase in the cost of living for workers was close to 18 percent during World War II; during 1943 and 1944, it spiked to between 27 percent and 30 percent.[19] Even basic foods like corn were scarce.[20] The state tried to stem the decrease in real wages with price, supply, and trade controls. It also introduced Social Security to Mexico City in 1943.[21] The government had minimal success in improving standards of living, however. Restrictions on Mexico imposed by U.S.-Mexican trade

16. Carr, *Marxism and Communism*, 115–16, 130.
17. "Mexican Textile Workers Strike for Living Level of Wages," *Mexican Labor News*, December 22, 1943.
18. Wilkie, *Mexican Revolution*, 184.
19. Middlebrook, *Paradox of Revolution*, 113–14, 214–15; Bortz and Aguila, "Earning a Living," 122–29. For worker complaints about rising prices and the impact on labor-employer relations, see "Economic Crisis Menaces Mexican Working Class," *Mexican Labor News*, February 16, 1943; "Mexican Textile Workers Strike for Living Level of Wages," *Mexican Labor News*, December 22, 1943; "Los trabajadores de Puebla contra la carestía de los artículos de subsistencia," *Germinal*, May 23, 1942.
20. Suárez, *Comentarios y recuerdos*, 253.
21. Roxborough, "Mexico," 195–97.

treaties constrained President Ávila Camacho's ability to slow the rise in prices. In addition, distribution controls were often ineffective, since some distributors failed to comply with presidential directives regarding transport and supply. For example, despite a 1941 order, Mexico's national railroad refused to grant priority to shipping basic goods, as defined by the Nacional Distribuidora y Reguladora, the government-run distribution and regulatory company. Moreover, administrative inefficiency, economic instability, and hoarding and speculation by politicians and businesspeople seeking to profit from wartime shortages fueled the black market and subverted wartime price and distribution controls.[22] In one sensational case, while he was head of the SEN, Francisco Javier Gaxiola allegedly participated in schemes to manipulate rayon, grain, corn, and meat prices, as well as to speculate in leather prices.[23] Even repression could not stem the tide of labor unrest. Emergency wartime and antifascist legislation that circumscribed the right to strike and individual political rights and that criminalized social dissolution did little to slow labor's momentum.

World War II provided a propitious climate to forge a new political solution to the labor problem, one that departed greatly from cardenista tactics that had incorporated and empowered union leaders. Specifically, in 1942, President Ávila Camacho proposed National Unity (Unidad Nacional), a pact among labor, business, and the state wherein each consented to honor wartime production goals and maintain wartime peace. Diane Davis asserts that National Unity "restructur[ed] . . . the relationship between capital, labor, and the state in order to promote more rapid industrial development, economic growth, employment, and wage prosperity."[24] Under National Unity, labor unions pledged to diminish interunion conflict and end work actions. In a show of further compliance, many unions, including the CTM, the CROM, and the CGT, also signed the Labor Unity Pact (Pacto de Unidad Obrera) and formed the National Labor Council (Consejo Nacional Obrero), wherein they pledged to cooperate toward these objectives. Industrialists, for their part, agreed to protect standards of living, while the government gave its assurances that it would respect the gains made by labor in the 1930s.[25]

22. Eduardo Villaseñor, address to the Eleventh Convention of the Asociación de Banqueros de México (ABM), Guadalajara, Jalisco, April 20, 1945, GR/AGN, c. 20, exp. 8; Primera Convención para el Estudio de Problemas Económicos de México, *Escasez y carestía*, 24–43.

23. Niblo, *Mexico in the 1940s*, 124–31.

24. Davis, *Urban Leviathan*, 110.

25. Niblo, *Mexico in the 1940s*, 121.

In the end, the success of the National Unity pact in achieving labor peace was uneven, since the labor council predicated its support on an extensive list of demands. It also complained of unwillingness on the part of the business community to sacrifice to meet the war effort.[26] Yet, by forging a nationalist political alliance that revolved around wartime production demands, President Ávila Camacho created a powerful tool for the ruling party to manage popular and industrialist dissension. In doing so, he gained CANACINTRA as an ally in the PRM's political consolidation.

Rationalizing the Masses: Poverty and the Reconsideration of Agrarianism

According to Gonzalo Robles, head of the OII in its early days, "To plan is to realize the most important work of the economy: that of rationalizing activities that man develops to satisfy his needs. Without rationalization—which is nothing more than, in short, an economic plan—the economy will be converted into an anarchic and heartless struggle in which some privileged people will prosper, while the vast majority of citizens will succumb or vegetate."[27] Albert Hirschman captured the spirit of Robles and other OII technocrats when he stated that the faith of Latin Americans in rationalization and economic planning was a "concrete expression of the universal aspiration toward better living standards."[28] Yet, the technocrats never specified who, exactly, was to benefit from improved living standards or what "better living standards" even entailed. Reflecting on the ambiguity and potential hollowness of attestations about the public good, Gunnar Myrdal proclaimed, "One might also say that the ultimate aim of all policy is the public weal."[29] Yet, with an eye toward achieving industrial growth and development, OII technocrats had serious reasons for concern about the well-being of the Mexican population. Most significant, in their view, was the failure of agrarian reform to transform the Mexican people into modern citizens and producers.

---

26. Middlebrook, *Paradox of Revolution*, 111–12; Consejo Nacional Obrero, memorandum, June 30, 1942, MAC/AGN, exp. 437.3/165; Consejo Nacional Obrero to Secretario del Trajabo y Previsión Social, June 18, 1942, MAC/AGN, exp. 437.3/165.
27. Robles, "Los pueblos atrasados," 61. For more on the thought of Gonzalo Robles, see Bravo Jiménez, "Con Gonzalo Robles."
28. Hirschman, "Economic Policy in Underdeveloped Countries," 362–70.
29. Myrdal, *Political Element*, xv–xvi. See also Schumpeter, "Communist Manifesto in Sociology," 208–9.

At the onset of the Revolution, hacendados still dominated Mexico's political landscape and presided over rural social relations. By the 1930s, however, they had been supplanted by a group of progressive entrepreneurs intent on fostering capitalist agricultural and industrial production through mass political incorporation and land reform. Their task was made more challenging by agrarian unrest, as well as by popular political mobilization through peasant leagues, labor unions, and multiple political parties, all of which contributed to the instability of postrevolutionary politics. Once in office, however, President Cárdenas brought formal political power to previously disenfranchised rural groups by uniting campesinos in the National Campesino Confederation (Confederación Nacional Campesina), which became the agrarian wing of the ruling party. This mass rural integration gave the state the political weight to pacify remaining rural unrest and suppress conservative opposition during the late 1930s, including remaining hacendado recalcitrance. Moreover, the PNR's mobilization of agraristas was critical in the denouement of callismo in 1935.[30]

Alongside political incorporation, President Cárdenas pursued land redistribution as a means to achieve rural economic and social transformation. By the time he left office, 41.5 percent of Mexico's agriculturally active population had received some form of a land grant. He alone was responsible for more than one-half of those grants. While in office, he distributed close to eighteen million hectares of land to more than eight-hundred thousand campesinos.[31] As agrarian reform tore apart the fabric of traditional rural social relations and upset the political and economic dominance of hacendados, rural social hierarchies eroded further.[32] In turn, campesinos regained some of the authority that they had lost with the land seizures of the late nineteenth century.[33]

Elevating the cultural, hygienic, and moral condition of the Mexican masses by means of social reform and socialist education was also at the heart of the cardenista project. In the 1930s, agraristas and socialist teachers went to the countryside with an almost evangelical zeal, seeking to root out "backwardness" and the host of characteristics and behaviors ascribed to it, including laziness, alcoholism, illness, fanaticism, and political apathy.[34] Armed with a social science ethic, these reformers targeted Mexico's clergy

30. Knight, "Rise and Fall of Cardenismo," 255–56.
31. Wilkie, *Mexican Revolution,* 189–94.
32. Tobler, "Peasants," 517–18.
33. For a classic study of postrevolutionary agrarianism, see Simpson, *Ejido.*
34. Knight, "Popular Culture," 404–5.

as charismatic atavists opposing rational professionals who could aid in enhancing the well-being of Mexico's masses.[35] Although they carried the same faith in science that inspired late nineteenth-century positivists, their projects for secularization, literacy, and even racial advancement now carried the weight of cardenista authority, including the promise of social justice.[36] And as the turn-of-the-century allure of biological determinism gave way to environmental explanations for racial degeneracy, reformers were able to claim even more authority to challenge what they saw as the conservative and Catholic bases of rural inequality and poverty.

Increased access to land, education, and political power did not translate into a sudden decrease in rural poverty, however. The first *Plan sexenal*, published by the PNR in 1934, tied land reform to more equitable wealth distribution in rural areas.[37] Yet, from 1900 to 1950, the number of lower-class Mexicans, defined by income, only dropped from 91 percent to 84 percent of the overall population.[38] The reasons for this enduring poverty are abundant, but clearly, land reform alone failed to bring about a widespread redistribution of wealth, at least over the short term. Some scholars have argued that land redistribution did not produce the anticipated results in part because it was not given time to mature.[39] Moreover, by the time land redistribution hit its stride in 1936–37, poverty as an impetus for land reform had become secondary to the goal of transforming communal *ejido* production into the engine of commercial agriculture.[40] Agricultural production, however, remained disappointing during much of the Cárdenas period, with 1940 production levels mirroring those of the mid- to late 1920s.[41] Contributing to this stagnation were insufficient ejidal credit and irrigation, as well as land grants too small to support Mexico's burgeoning rural population.[42]

In addition to the material constraints of land redistribution, agraristas and socialist educators encountered other difficulties in their attempts to craft modern citizens and producers in the countryside, including popular

35. For more on Max Weber's ideas about religious rationalization, see Ritzer, "Professionalization, Bureaucratization, and Rationalization"; Kalberg, "Max Weber's Types of Rationality," 1146, 1152–55.
36. For the influence of science on politics in the late nineteenth century, see Hale, *Transformation of Liberalism*.
37. PNR, *Plan sexenal*, 23, 26–27.
38. NAFINSA, *50 años de Revolución*, 153–54.
39. Larroa Torres, "Cárdenas y la doble vía," 295.
40. Tobler, "Peasants," 514.
41. NAFINSA, *50 años de Revolución*, 52.
42. De Oliveira, *Migración y absorción de mano de obra*, 5, 9.

recalcitrance to state-sponsored reforms.[43] Despite their efforts to achieve the cultural and moral redemption of the masses, they found that indigenous resistance or apathy to the cardenista project often ran high.[44] Perhaps most troubling, they discovered that popular groups were persistently, and perhaps even rationally, committed to the Catholic Church.[45]

Consequently, by the late 1930s, many discerned a failure among agraristas, socialist teachers, and other reformers to deliver the "backward" masses from poverty and the clutches of fanaticism. These included OII technocrats, many of whom were struggling to understand why the cardenista project, in particular land redistribution, had not succeeded in bringing about a widespread change in rural economic and social conditions. Rather than blaming agrarian reform itself, however, they criticized its execution. Some cited problems with production that resulted from the failure to plan land reform, including poor irrigation, low-quality land, and lack of agricultural inputs. They attributed this lack of planning to the fact that the fervor of postrevolutionary agrarian demands had taken the country by surprise. Gonzalo Robles noted that there had been little rumination about whether it was prudent or even possible to have private property and ejidos coexisting in the countryside. He added that the private sector had access to land, labor, and investment capital, but *ejidatarios* had only land and their own labor. The speed and poor planning of land redistribution had left ejidatarios without seeds, work animals, tools, and even food to keep them alive until the first harvest. Robles suggested that the mistake had been in not transferring entire haciendas to campesinos and not providing sufficient credit to jumpstart production.[46]

Even if there had been time to plan agrarian reform, according to Robles, political factors, such as poorly conceived agrarian reform legislation, would have created other obstacles. Most damning was Robles's contention that agrarian reform had been perverted by the political and economic ambitions of revolutionary leaders, who had abused their power to gain possession of

---

43. See Knight, "Revolutionary Project."

44. Two conceptually distinct works detailing the popular reaction to cardenista attempts to remake the Mexican nation are Vaughan, *Cultural Politics in Revolution*; Becker, *Setting the Virgin on Fire*. For an overview of the postrevolutionary education project as a tool for social engineering, and the indigenous impact on it, see Lewis, "Nation."

45. Jean Meyer suggests that historians reveal a sort of analytical parochialism when they condemn campesino support for the Catholic Church and claim that it demonstrates a lack of class consciousness or is a type of simplemindedness or irrationality. J. Meyer, "Idea of Mexico," 288.

46. Becerra, "Recordando a Robles," 272–73; Robles, "Los pueblos atrasados," 32–33.

lands with superior access to water in the 1920s and 1930s.[47] In some instances, Robles also claimed that the clergy had influenced campesinos to refuse land grants in an attempt to challenge agraristas and the authority of the ruling party at the local level.[48] Others at the OII viewed the problems with agrarian reform in more somber terms. Emilio Alanis Patiño argued that poverty had resulted from past mistakes, including land misuse, natural disasters, and huge tracts of land left "at rest." He quantified the resulting lost opportunities and interpreted them through the lenses of *"Pérdidas"* (Waste) and *"Miseria"* (Poverty).[49]

The OII employees' reconsideration of agrarianism was striking since many had originally trained in agricultural studies, including Gonzalo Robles and Daniel Cosío Villegas. The latter headed the Department of Economic Studies in the early 1940s and had to approve OII initiatives. Others included Robles's assistant, Manuel Bravo Jiménez, who had begun his career as a rural schoolteacher.[50] During the late 1910s and 1920s, these professionals had spent considerable time consulting for various administrations on land redistribution and the transition from hacienda to ejido production. Their focus after the late 1930s on industrial development is, therefore, all the more notable because it resulted from a personal reassessment of the role of agrarianism in Mexico's future. In an increasingly urban and industrial society, agrarian reform necessarily could have only a limited capacity to engender widespread wealth redistribution and cultural transformation. During the 1930s, industry became the leading dynamic economic sector in Mexico. Between 1932 and 1940, industry was responsible for 38 percent of GDP growth, even though it accounted for only on average 17 percent of the GDP.[51] Though the import-substituting effects of the Great Depression fostered a growth in consumption of domestically produced goods, it took the deepening of markets due to agrarian reform, education, urbanization, and labor reform in the 1930s for industry to expand rapidly.[52] The political and intellectual climate of the late 1930s consolidated this transition. For example, the slowing of reforms by President Cárdenas and the conservative

47. Gonzalo Robles, "Ideario sobre industrialización y política industrial," c. 1959, GR/AGN, c. 77 bis (3), exp. 3.
48. Becerra, "Recordando a Robles," 273.
49. Emilio Alanis Patiño, "Planeación nacional," 1944, GR/AGN, c. 46, exp. 53.
50. Víctor Urquidi, pers. comm., August 27, 1998.
51. Cárdenas, "Great Depression," 204; Haber, *Industry and Underdevelopment,* 171; Cárdenas, *La industrialización mexicana,* 194–97.
52. Knight, "Export-Led Growth," 136.

turn within the ruling party by 1940 ensured that forces attuned to industrialization would supersede agraristas in determining national development priorities. An international community that encouraged industrialization in Mexico and a growing social science literature emphasizing the links between comparative advantage and persistent dependency corroborated the need for Mexico to industrialize. As an elegy to past agrarian practices, CONCANACOMIN concluded that Mexico's ejidatarios were social parasites, while traditional hacendados, as a class, "had passed into history."[53]

Despite urbanization and the growth of industry, the challenges of social reform remained the same.[54] Lured by the new promise of factory jobs and fleeing rural violence and the dislocations associated with the transition from hacienda to ejidal production, campesinos flooded into urban areas in the 1930s and 1940s. Between 1940 and 1950 alone, the population of the metropolitan area of Mexico City surged from 1,757,530 to 3,050,442.[55] In that same decade, the number of industrial workers grew from 89,358 to 156,697.[56] The boom of migrants in the 1930s and 1940s radically altered the capital's urban landscape. Wealthy Mexicans abandoned their luxurious downtown mansions in an exodus to outlying areas, and these buildings were often converted into tenements (*vecindades*) that at times held up to one thousand people; their run-down condition only worsened with the imposition of rent controls in 1942.[57] Moreover, factory jobs could not keep pace with the growing urban population, and many soon found themselves working in the rapidly expanding informal sector. These migrants strained public services, consumer and basic-goods supplies, and employment opportunities in the growing city.[58] Though almost 60 percent of Mexicans

53. CONCANACOMIN, "Estudio sobre las causas del alza de los precios," October 1937, AMGM, v. 42, exp. 1439.
54. Knight, "Popular Culture," 395–402, 440–44.
55. Pick and Butler, *Mexico Megacity*, 54. Different sources cite different figures for the same year, but the population grew from roughly 1.6 million inhabitants in 1940 to 3.1 million inhabitants in 1950. Muñoz, de Oliveira, and Stern, *Mexico City*, 16, 18, 38; de Oliveira, *Migración y absorción de mano de obra*, 10.
56. Garza Villarreal, *El proceso de industrialización*, 142.
57. Cornelius, *Politics and the Migrant Poor*, 27; Ward, *Mexico City*, 37; Eckstein, *Poverty of Revolution*, 45.
58. The themes of industrialization, migration, construction, and poverty have received extensive attention by scholars of mid-twentieth-century Mexico City, who use the Federal District as an example of urban overpopulation and the perils of unimpeded, unregulated growth. A few examples include Cornelius, *Politics and the Migrant Poor*; Kandell, *La Capital*; Kemper, *Migration and Adaptation*; Ward, *Mexico City*. In contrast, Gustavo Garza Villarreal argues that Mexico City also made possible the efficient reproduction of a modern workforce and the concentration of technological innovation, entrepreneurial spirit, finance, and bourgeois and governmental power. Garza Villarreal, *El proceso de industrialización*, 27; Garza Villarreal, "Desarrollo económico," 159–60.

were still laboring in agriculture, fishing, hunting, and forestry by 1950, many politicians and intellectuals were disturbed by what they saw as the degeneracy associated with this burgeoning urban blight.[59] In a sense, urban poverty, especially in Mexico City, became a testament to the political, cultural, and material limits of agrarianism, socialist education, and anticlericalism. It confirmed the need to approach social reform using new avenues that reached the rapidly urbanizing population.

For OII technocrats, industrial rationalization promised to carve this new path to social change. It could not only achieve economic growth and improve standards of living but also engender the wholesale social and cultural transformation of the masses. However, economic policy did not always imply the protection of workers as much as it did the reinforcement of elite paternalism that ignored rural concerns amid efforts to create a modern industrial labor force. For example, in debates over the benefits of agricultural versus industrial labor, one OIE report posited industrial labor as a positive substitute for lower-paying agricultural work. The report argued that even though campesinos resented industries that paid higher wages and drew from the rural labor pool, eventually they would appreciate the benefits of higher-paid factory labor and leave behind agricultural work.[60] This sentiment reverberated within the OII, as when Robles stated, "An economic plan . . . must project itself into the distant future and think in *higher levels of culture*" (italics in original). By reining in the clientelist passions of politicians and the arbitrary authority of the clergy, rationalization could free development to elevate the material and cultural condition of the disinherited masses.[61] In turn, OII technocrats insinuated that economic planning and the pursuit of scientific knowledge could bring about the secularization, social reform, and material progress essential to a modern, productive citizenry. As Manuel Bravo Jiménez concluded, scientific observation was the best "offensive and defensive weapon to improve the material and cultural living conditions of the Mexican people."[62]

In the end, agrarian reform laid the bases for the rapid capitalist expansion that would occur in the 1950s, by making society more fluid, by freeing capital for investment in industry, and by transforming rural Mexicans into

59. Comisión de Planeación Industrial de la CANACINTRA, *Proceso ocupacional*, 219.
60. OIE, Banco de México, report, July 26, 1941, GR/AGN, c. 73, exp. 6.
61. Robles, "Los pueblos atrasados," 61–62, 79; Gonzalo Robles, "Ideario sobre industrialización y política industrial," c. 1959, GR/AGN, c. 77 bis (3), exp. 3.
62. Manuel Bravo Jiménez, "Planeación económica: Urgencia de su aplicación en México y reseña de una visita a Instituto de Planeación en Holanda, Francia, e Inglaterra," 1951, GR/AGN, c. 43, exp. 12.

market-oriented producers.⁶³ Technocrats at the OII recognized agrarian reform's importance in this regard, and they argued throughout the 1940s and 1950s that agricultural, mining, and industrial production were interrelated in terms of markets and resources.⁶⁴ They concluded that the concerted development of all three was the optimal way to accomplish the task of raising wages in both urban and rural areas amid the transition from a predominantly agricultural economy to one that was largely industrial.⁶⁵ In turn, OII technocrats assumed that the accompanying capitalist transformation would ultimately accomplish the material and cultural advances that the revolutionary state had failed to achieve. However, for them, the factory, rather than the school, would be the "crucible of nationalism, moralization, and development."⁶⁶

Rival Visions of Politics: Passion Versus Rationalization

CANACINTRA and the OII agreed that the solutions to widespread poverty and economic dependence lay in industrialization. They also agreed that the state had a potentially important role to play in its development. They differed, however, over defining exactly what the state's role in the economy should be. While OII technocrats promoted industrial rationalization to supersede the role of politics in state economic intervention, CANACINTRA advanced political prescriptions determined largely by industrialists themselves.

The vogue of rationalization in early to mid-twentieth-century Latin America revealed a desire among professionals to use the legitimacy of scientific forms of knowledge to advance their developmental and reform projects. Although having universal origins in the human condition, as Max Weber argued, rationalization varied widely across and within geohistorical contexts. At the same time, while he rejected the idea that rationality was a "unilinear evolutionary process," Weber nevertheless maintained that a relatively new type of rationality had emerged consonant with the industrial age. It was distinguished by its focus on the "economic, legal, and scientific spheres, and the bureaucratic form of domination." Its allure rested in its

---

63. Knight, "Mexican Revolution," 25–27.

64. Víctor Urquidi, "Mexican Industry, a Descriptive Survey—Its Recent Evolution," January 1943, GR/AGN, c. 23, exp. 17 and c. 22, exp. 5, pp. 1–2.

65. Robles, "Los pueblos atrasados," 36, 59; Gonzalo Robles, "Ideario sobre industrialización y política industrial," c. 1959, GR/AGN, c. 77 bis (3), exp. 3.

66. Knight, "Revolutionary Project," 230–31, 242.

subjugation of self-interested action to the rationality implied by rules, laws, and regulations.[67]

Historians of Latin America most often associate industrial rationalization with U.S.-born scientific management, a correlation justified by the array of experiments with Taylorism in factories throughout the Americas.[68] However, OII technocrats were part of an intellectual generation that, although it emerged during World War I, came of age during the postwar "rationalization era," when economists and industrialists increasingly focused on devising far-reaching plans for national industrial growth. Though neither rationalization nor American-style efficiency were clearly defined concepts, OII technocrats took inspiration from German ideas about industrial rationalization. In Germany, these ideals literally referred to the rationing of production amid conditions of high inflation and excess capacity right after World War I.[69] At that time, Germans attempted to control output to correspond with market demand while reducing the costs of production. During the 1920s, industrial rationalization shifted and expanded to imply the "national control and regulation of whole industries," aimed at achieving efficiency (in production; distribution; and the use of resources, including labor, primary materials, technology, and capital), lowering costs, and increasing productivity.[70] Despite disagreement among Germans about the definition of industrial rationalization, including arguments by some that company profits were the best indicator of rationalization and criticism by others that rationalization was an age-old concept new in name only, economists across the globe seized on it.[71]

When the OII formed in 1941, technocrats agreed on little in terms of a specific plan for industrial development. Their thinking had advanced beyond the nineteenth-century concept of *fomento,* or general economic promotion imbued with a vague faith in modernization and progress. But, as Banco de México economist Víctor Urquidi stated, "development" had yet to even enter the OII lexicon in the early 1940s.[72] Therefore, rationalization

67. Kalberg, "Max Weber's Types of Rationality," 1146, 1150–51, 1158.
68. Examples include Winn, *Weavers of Revolution*; Farnsworth-Alvear, *Dulcinea in the Factory*.
69. Mary Nolan demonstrates that Germans themselves drew on American efficiency, and particularly Fordism, in their efforts to rationalize industrialization. Nolan, *Visions of Modernity,* quote from 165.
70. Meakin, *New Industrial Revolution,* 7–9, 16–18, 21. See also Brady, *Rationalization Movement,* xii.
71. Meakin, *New Industrial Revolution,* introduction; Brady, "Meaning of Rationalization," 529, 539–40.
72. Urquidi, *Otro siglo perdido,* 91.

emerged to symbolize technocrats' aspiration to achieve independent, sustainable economic development free from clientelism and political motives. They turned to rationalization in part because of their frustration at the continuing failure of the state to coordinate economic planning throughout the 1930s. Even the PNR's *Plan sexenal* included only a vague listing of what the Cárdenas government intended to accomplish.[73] The PRM's more elaborate *Segundo plan sexenal, 1941–1946* (1939) also fell short of being a coherent, comprehensive economic plan. World War II compounded technocrats' frustrations, as they watched the government create no fewer than ten agencies and commissions between 1941 and 1943 to monitor and administer the wartime economy. These included distribution companies, economic planning commissions, and trade and production-control offices.[74] In response, Urquidi condemned what he saw as the plague of economic, administrative, and planning organisms that were undermining the implementation of a comprehensive plan for economic development.[75]

Urquidi was not alone in his criticism of the state. Both conservatives and leftists spoke out to challenge uncoordinated state economic intervention. For COPARMEX, the Mexican employers association, perhaps the most troubling aspect of wartime intervention was the absence of industrialist representation on economic planning commissions. Indeed, during the war, the Ávila Camacho administration revamped the National Council of the Economy, reducing the representatives from 107 to 20 and giving government ministries a much more prominent role. In protest, COPARMEX declared that these changes would extend the "tendency of the State to direct the economy . . . with the aim that the State . . . and the workers will be those most directly acting in it."[76] When the council was replaced by the Federal Economic Planning Commission (Comisión Federal de Planificación Económica) in 1942, further shrinkage resulted in a seven-member body with representatives from six government ministries and the head of the government of the Federal District, although a Coordinator of Production was added later. There were also representatives for workers,

73. Víctor Urquidi, pers. comm., September 4, 1998. See also Guillén, *Planificación económica*, 57–59; Ceceña Cervantes, *La planificación económica*, 61–70.
74. Secretaría Particular del Presidente, "Organismos de emergencia en la administración económica," October 19, 1943, MAC/AGN, exp. 545.22/160–1–33; Azpeitia Gómez, *Compañía Exportadora*, 33–41.
75. Urquidi, "Espejismos económicos actuales," 27.
76. COPARMEX, *Boletín Confidencial*, no. 13 (August 30, 1941), AMGM, v. 442, exp. 1442.

campesinos, and employers, but they were all nonvoting members.[77] Some labor leaders also renounced the clientelism and political motives that pervaded state economic intervention. For instance, Vicente Lombardo Toledano founded the short-lived Mexican Economic Planning Association (Asociación Mexicana de Planificación Económica) in 1941, consisting of bankers, scholars, technocrats, and labor leaders, including Robles and Cosío Villegas. He created it to forge an international capital-labor alliance that could devise an economic plan suitable for the entire continent "without the intervention of governments."[78]

Assessing the European context, Robert A. Brady aptly characterized the "'rationalization era'" as being remarkable for its rationality, egalitarianism, secularism, and "naïve" optimism.[79] And indeed, amid this rapid and uncoordinated expansion of the state in the economy, the promises of industrial rationalization produced an almost pious commitment among OII technocrats to modernize Mexico through apolitical decision making and economic planning. Gonzalo Robles embodied this commitment. In 1935, he had been forced to resign from his position as general director of the Banco de México for refusing to fulfill President Cárdenas's request for more government credit, which he believed would lower reserves to a point that threatened the peso. As a result, when he was invited to join the OII in 1941, he declined to join as a salaried official, claiming that politics would potentially jeopardize his intellectual freedom. He agreed to join only as a consultant.[80]

When Robles characterized rationalization as "nothing more than, in short, an economic plan" (however much Weber might have objected!), he was echoing sentiments already expressed by others in Europe and the United States caught up in its promise.[81] But rationalization was more of a credo than any sort of prescriptive economic agenda. Therefore, though models of state planning, such as indicative planning and command economies, are useful referents, in practice, economic planning was as diverse as the countries that took it up in the early to mid-twentieth century. For

77. SEN, *Planificación Económica*, no. 1 (March 6, 1943); SEN, "Los organismos de coordinación económica en México," *Planificación Económica*, no. 18 (August 14, 1944).
78. Vicente Lombardo Toledano to invited members of the association, GR/AGN, c. 44, exp. 29.
79. Brady, "Meaning of Rationalization," 539–40.
80. Becerra, "Recordando a Robles," 272–73, 282–84; Víctor Urquidi, pers. comm., August 27, 1998.
81. Robles, "Los pueblos atrasados," 61. Similarly, see Brady, *Rationalization Movement*, viii.

example, in Germany in the 1920s, rationalization was promoted by a well-organized private sector that created a central rationalization bureau (the Reichskuratorium für Wirtschaftlichkeit) that focused on improving productivity and technical efficiency within corporations and across industries.[82] By contrast, in Mexico, rationalization was mainly the province of technocrats and some bureaucrats, and it did not become prominent until the 1940s. Even then, it focused more on efficiency across industrial sectors than within factories.

By the 1940s, political stability and economic growth coupled with the inspiration drawn from the international intellectual community put OII technocrats on new footing to tackle the problem of planning. As mentioned, when the OII first initiated operations, it focused on the production and diffusion of technical knowledge about industry, including through extensive studies about industry and natural resources. It also sent Mexicans abroad to study technical fields and helped to form technical institutions that studied industrial and technological processes. In perhaps its first broad initiative, in 1944, the Banco de México took the lead in the creation of the Federal Commission for Industrial Promotion (Comisión Federal de Fomento Industrial) to replace the Federal Economic Planning Commission. The commission's task was to promote new industries and plan industrial development. However, it soon became obsolete amid the rapid industrial growth and expansion of state planning agencies during the war.[83] To offset the uncoordinated growth of state agencies and economic intervention, OII technocrats pressed for a "standardization of methods and procedures," which could "set Mexican industrialization on the right economic path and prevent it from falling [victim to] politics and personal favoritism."[84] For OII technocrats, planning and rationalization became antidotes to disorganized and ill-conceived state intervention in the economy.

OII technocrats sought to limit the damaging influence of politics and clientelism in economic policy making by defining a limited, rational role for the state. A key facet of this, according to OII technocrats, included coordination across government agencies and with private-sector groups

---

82. Only after its formation did the bureau begin to seek public funding. Shearer, "Reichskuratorium für Wirtschaftlichkeit," 569–602. See also Maier, "Between Taylorism and Technocracy," 45–46, 54–59.

83. Pichardo Pagaza, *10 años de planificación*, 16–17; Ceceña Cervantes, *La planificación económica*, 59–61, 77–79; Bravo Jiménez, *Planeación industrial en México*, 20–21. On the war as an impetus to studying industrialization, see Quintana, "Problemas fundamentales"; Gonzalo Robles, "Ideario sobre industrialización y política industrial," c. 1959, GR/AGN, c. 77 bis (3), exp. 3.

84. R.F. Castelán, of R.F. Castelán e Hijos, "El plan de investigación industrial necesario para México en la época actual," September 24, 1945, GR/AGN, c. 77 bis (2), exp. 3.

involved in planning.⁸⁵ This could be accomplished with the formation of a single planning and coordinating institution "removed from political hazards wherein select, capable people would dedicate themselves to pondering issues and preparing short- and long-range programs, with a high sense of responsibility and patriotism. Tying the function and execution of those plans to an efficient and incorruptible administration would be one of the most important successes of each government."⁸⁶ Ultimately, technocrats believed that a technically advanced state could play an honest and efficient, albeit circumscribed, role in economic modernization.

Conservatives, drawing on critiques common in many areas of the world at that time, condemned the OII planning proposals as a Soviet-inspired effort to facilitate communism's infiltration of Mexico.⁸⁷ These critics were not completely wrongheaded in their accusations, although they mistook ideological inspiration for political dogma. In Mexico in the 1930s, Marxism was the only broadly available economic theory that critiqued "the defects of free-market capitalism."⁸⁸ OII technocrats recognized their debts to Marx and admired aspects of Soviet-style planning. But by the 1940s, the economic theories of scholars like John Maynard Keynes and even the more conservative Joseph Schumpeter also shaped the thinking of OII technocrats. The writings of Keynes, Schumpeter, Colin Clark, and others were not widely available in translation at that time in Mexico, but many Banco de México employees, including Cosío Villegas, Robles, Urquidi, and Eduardo Villaseñor (general director of the Banco de México, 1940–46) had studied abroad and regularly attended international conferences. Moreover, though ECLA was still a few years away, Raúl Prebisch visited Mexico in 1944 and delivered lectures at both the Banco de México and El Colegio de México. He came to Mexico once again, in 1946, to attend a meeting of central bankers from across the Americas.⁸⁹ Therefore, OII technocrats were influenced by an intellectually eclectic group of international economists who were especially attentive to the social and political context surrounding the rise of capitalism. Confirming this, Víctor Urquidi stated that although many in Mexico's government focused on narrowly conceived projects,

---

85. For example, see Mario J. Ordaz, "La Oficina de Investigaciones Industriales como centro coordinador en la industrialización del país?" December 26, 1944, GR/AGN, c. 23, exp. 14; "Reglamento interior del Departamento de Estudios Económicos de la Economía Nacional," September 1, 1938, GR/AGN, c. 44, exp. 25. Ordaz argued that the OII should become Mexico's central industrial planning agency.

86. Robles, "Los pueblos atrasados," 63–64.

87. Lorwin, "Some Political Aspects," 723.

88. Babb, *Managing Mexico*, 57–58.

89. Love, "Rise and Fall of Structuralism," 161.

such as roads and irrigation, there was a group of OII employees who thought in broad terms and met regularly to discuss the ideas of economists such as Clark and Schumpeter.[90]

With regard to the role of the state in the economy, Keynes stood out among OII technocrats who disagreed with classical assertions that government intervention in production and distribution inevitably slowed capitalist development. Keynes appeared in translation in Mexico in 1934 with an article in *El trimestre económico*. By 1943, the journal had published two other articles by Keynes, as well as four more about his theories.[91] His seminal *The General Theory of Employment, Interest, and Money* was released in translation in 1942.[92] OII technocrats appreciated Keynes's idea that capitalist economies could benefit from government management that allowed for "a measure of state intervention but preserved the capitalist organization of production." They especially valued his contention that limited state intervention could be a "middle way . . . between the complete socialization of the means of production and the excesses of unbridled capitalism" and could protect the collective well-being of the nation. Critical to the state's success in this regard, according to Keynes, was the creation of a technocratic elite, who could pursue state economic intervention guided by scientific principles. In reconciling state economic intervention and rationalization, Keynes proffered a solution to the excesses of both laissez-faire growth and statist economic management.[93]

Keynes's ideas were not seen as prescriptive by OII technocrats, however. In particular, they were attentive to the fact that the ideas of Keynes and other intellectuals of the developed world overlooked important global differences, especially in relation to dependence. For example, OII employee Emilio Alanis Patiño agreed that the state should play a role in the economy. However, he argued from a position of rights, stating that developing countries had a right to use the state to accomplish the goal of catching up to developed countries, since so far, private enterprise had failed in that regard.[94] He and others emphasized that Mexico was entitled to use the state to compensate for past errors, missed opportunities, and its disadvantage in comparison to more developed countries. Anticipating Gerschenkron's later musings about "substitutes" and the potential role of the state

90. Víctor Urquidi, pers. comm., September 4, 1998.
91. Love, "Rise and Fall of Structuralism," 161.
92. Babb, *Managing Mexico*, 57–59.
93. Quotes from Hall, "Conclusion," 366; Topik, "Karl Polanyi," 93. For Schumpeter's position, see Smithies, "Schumpeter and Keynes."
94. Emilio Alanis Patiño, "Planeación nacional," 1944, GR/AGN, c. 46, exp. 53.

in late-comer development, the state itself could become a resource in production.[95] It could offset a lack of resources in other realms, especially in areas where the private sector was unwilling or unable to take the lead, such as those industries with prohibitive start-up costs or whose product served the national interest. Thus, OII technocrat Manuel Bravo Jiménez argued that "one of the most salient characteristics of the industrial process in economically backward countries consists of government intervention in order to fill the lacuna created by a lack of resources."[96] Ultimately, OII technocrats concluded that the state's legislative power and its capacity for oversight could ensure that any adopted economic plan would be just and fair for all Mexicans.[97]

By subjecting the economy to laws and regulations derived from an economic plan and enforced by the state, industrial rationalization was a powerful assault on the rights of private enterprise. CANACINTRA agreed with the OII about the need for economic planning, but it argued for a much more prominent role for entrepreneurs. It stated that businesspeople were especially prepared to take part in planning because they were driven by the objective criterion of profits and they performed the nationally important task of wealth production. It added that state intervention was only legitimate if it was in accordance with industrialists' requests, especially if those requests were made through industrial chambers.[98]

However, through the mid-1940s, CANACINTRA displayed a curious ambivalence about the role of both business and the state in economic planning. CANACINTRA president José R. Colín (1946) asserted that due to their selfish interests, private enterprise usually was inept at economic policy making. This seemed to support state economic intervention, as he pointed to laissez-faire growth as the reason for the creation of huge industries that were operating independent of the collective national interest. In contemplating the state as an economic administrator, however, Colín was equally elusive. He argued that the state was "indispensable and necessary for all activities of coordination and direction," yet he added that it was the most damaging economic administrator, due to corruption and bureaucratic inefficiency.[99] Along with OII technocrats, CANACINTRA also censured politicians who used their power to reap great profits and then reinvested them

---

95. Gerschenkron, *Economic Backwardness*.
96. Bravo Jiménez, *Planeación industrial en México*, 10, 14.
97. Robles, "Los pueblos atrasados," 64.
98. CANACINTRA, *Conclusiones sobre los puntos*, 3–5, 19–20.
99. Colín, *Requisitos fundamentales*, 39–40, 46–47.

in their political futures rather than in the economy.[100] Consequently, Colín proposed the formation of a national commission to coordinate industrial planning, led by an industrialist or technocrat rather than a government functionary, in order to guarantee that it would be autonomous and operate honorably, efficiently, and with minimal bureaucracy. He added that if a politician were to lead it, it would invariably succumb to careerist motives rather than the dictates of the collective good. However, predicting liberal opposition, Colín mused that if a businessperson led it, it would "create a feeling of discord and [would] bother a sector of industrialists, who in company with almost all merchants have fought against State intervention in all economic spheres."[101]

By 1947, CANACINTRA abandoned its ambivalence about state economic intervention, as will be seen in chapter 5. However, it is worth noting here that this shift most likely occurred in response to postwar changes, including its closer ties to the ruling party, the U.S. reluctance to support Mexican industry, the conservative turn under President Alemán, and economic concerns related to balance-of-payment problems and plunging monetary reserves. All of this contributed to a sense of national urgency about industrial development, and perhaps even to the perception that only the state had the power to intervene against foreign economic aggression. In that year, CANACINTRA argued that there should be a National Industrial Planning Commission (Comisión Nacional de Planeación Industrial) that would include government, banking, labor, agrarian, and private sector representatives but which would operate solely at the discretion of the president.[102] Even with the shift in position, however, CANACINTRA did not advocate unharnessed state economic intervention. It maintained that the state should limit itself to targeted price and distribution controls; the stimulation and protection of industrial investment; and specific tariffs, subsidies, tax breaks, or other types of protection when requested by industrialists. CANACINTRA even listed the industries that should receive protection.[103] Like the OII and conservative critics of state economic intervention, the organization emphasized that the state should protect and promote industry, but it should never compete with it. It instead should restrict its ownership

---

100. Lavín, "La industria química nacional," 97.
101. Colín, *Requisitos fundamentales*, 43–46.
102. CANACINTRA, "Conclusiones generales del Primer Congreso Nacional de la Industria de Transformación," April 29, 1947, MAV/AGN, 433/99, 1–2.
103. Colín, *Requisitos fundamentales*, 10–11.

and involvement to cases when private enterprise could not take the lead.[104] In this light, the midcentury alliance that emerged between the state and CANACINTRA in defense of statist industrialization appears both contingent and fluid.

Despite its pretensions to being apolitical, rationalization was a form of politics that used the power of science and objectivity in order to rein in the ruling-party politicians who controlled the state. As with espousals of scientific rationality in other realms, such as medicine, demography, and military planning, industrial rationalization asserted a scientific-based authority that excluded all other forms of rationality, including ethical and value-oriented forms.[105] But OII technocrats did not turn to rationalization in order to channel the state's power toward the fulfillment of their own goals for economic modernization to the exclusion of all others. Rather, especially in their early days, OII technocrats were, to paraphrase Robert Brady, naively optimistic about industrial rationalization and its power to oblige the state to fulfill the revolutionary promises of social justice and improved standards of living.[106] Moreover, in the early to mid-1940s, OII technocrats were hardly alone in their efforts to influence the state's role in economic development. CANACINTRA leaders also had designs for the state, though their goal was to secure a role for industrialists in economic decision making in order to secure their future political authority.

Rival Visions of Wealth: Labor

The OII and CANACINTRA both took prominent positions with regard to labor in the 1940s. Each contended that their desire was to improve workers' standards of living while meeting the demands of industrial modernization. Their discussions often centered on the issue of wealth, especially how to optimize labor's contribution to the creation of national wealth. The OII advocated maximizing wealth through increased production. Its technocrats proposed to transform workers into modern, capitalist producers by rationalizing the worker as a factor of production. In doing

---

104. CANACINTRA, "Conclusiones generales del Primer Congreso Nacional de la Industria de Transformación," April 29, 1947, MAV/AGN, 433/99, 1–2; "El Lic. Gómez Morin habla de la intervención estatal," *Excélsior*, February 15, 1945.

105. For a description of Weber's typology of rationality, see Kalberg, "Max Weber's Types of Rationality," 1173–75.

106. Brady, "Meaning of Rationalization," 539–40.

so, they recommended reshaping labor-employer relations according to an objective economic plan that alluded to social justice but obscured the perpetuation of inequality. In contrast, CANACINTRA emphasized that the consumption of domestically produced goods, and therefore workers' buying power, was the driving force behind the creation of national wealth. Yet, the chamber also revealed that despite its assertions of equality and commitment to an alliance with labor, its members continued to believe that any improvement in workers' buying power should result from owner patronage rather than from a legal obligation compelling them to pay a higher wage.

Examining the OII and CANACINTRA proposals regarding labor and the creation of national wealth reveals the boundaries of foreign intellectual penetration in the mid-twentieth century. Although engaged with the ideas of foreign scholars, economists, engineers, industrialists, and others put forth proposals that often reflected an intellectual agnosticism born of Mexico's unique postrevolutionary realities. For example, the arguments of CANACINTRA about labor closely reflected Keynesian ideas, especially pertaining to the links between higher consumption, employment, and the creation of national income, but neither it nor the OII sought prescriptive solutions to the labor issue. CANACINTRA leaders, in particular, displayed deep-seated biases against the working class, and their solutions to the "worker problem" often drew from late nineteenth-century positivism and Social Darwinism. OII technocrats, for their part, took inspiration from Keynes as well, yet questioned the efficacy of activist economic policies designed to stimulate demand in times of high unemployment, such as through public works projects.

CANACINTRA leaders were deeply concerned about the impact of production cuts and lost wages on consumption during World War II. José Domingo Lavín, predecessor of Colín as president of CANACINTRA, ascribed great power to workers as consumers. He argued that they could drive the creation of a strong domestic market, which in turn would generate national wealth and enhance standards of living.[107] To stimulate consumption, the leaders of CANACINTRA at times advocated higher wages and benefits. For example, they backed proposals to extend Social Security benefits to the parents of workers, to grant time to working mothers to nurse their babies, and to initiate the construction of more hospitals and clinics by Mexico's Social Security agency.[108] To reflect a new era of modern

---

107. Lavín, *Plan inmediato*, 4; CANACINTRA, *Conclusiones sobre los puntos*, 4–5, 7–8.
108. CANACINTRA, "Conclusiones generales del Primer Congreso Nacional de la Industria de Transformación," April 29, 1947, MAV/AGN, 433/99, 24–33.

labor relations, Lavín even suggested that Mexicans banish the use of terms like "patrón" and "worker" in favor of "employer" and "employee."[109]

More commonly, however, CANACINTRA leaders alleged that the working class itself was the key obstacle to industrial growth and higher consumption.[110] Specifically, they argued that with their demands, laborers discouraged individual initiative and raised costs. Colín recognized that some employers hurt the working class through corruption, bribery, and selfishness.[111] In general, however, he and Lavín held conservative notions about the innovative investor or entrepreneur hindered by a self-interested working class.[112] Colín and Lavín stated that all Mexicans should understand that the collective national good superseded their particular interests. They concluded that national welfare could be secured only by enabling industrialists to "pursue their wealth-creating activities."[113]

Backing these arguments was a surfeit of conservative, paternalistic ideas about the proper roles of workers and employers. Tellingly, though CANACINTRA leaders conceded that workers needed steady salaries to become modern consumers and publicly supported demands for wage increases, Lavín also maintained that higher wages only produced vice.[114] With this, he revealed a host of ethnic and cultural biases about Mexico's "backward" masses that CANACINTRA used to denounce labor. For example, Lavín decried the excessive number of days of rest and the reduction in the legal workday in Mexico City to 7.5 hours. He and Colín further contended that by failing to take the economy into account when making demands, union leaders contributed to rising costs of living and poor worker morale and efficiency. Colín even denounced union leaders as dishonest traitors to their class who amassed great fortunes through blackmail and bribery. Colín had some paternalist concern about the working class, and he cited the high unemployment rate as the cause of crime and prostitution. However, he ultimately blamed the labor movement for high unemployment, since it had failed to "work intelligently" to create new jobs.[115]

With these accusations, Colín and Lavín implied that workers were too irresponsible to participate in a modernizing industrial project without the

109. Lavín, "Relaciones obrero-patronales," 28–29.
110. Niblo, *War, Diplomacy, and Development*, 196–98.
111. Colín, *Requisitos fundamentales*, 14, 16–20; Lavín, "La industria química nacional," 97–98.
112. For more on conservative ideas about the critical role of the entrepreneur in capitalist growth, see Dahms, "From Creative Action to the Social Rationalization of the Economy," 3–5.
113. CANACINTRA, *Conclusiones sobre los puntos*, 4–5, 7–8; Lavín, "La industria química nacional," 97–98, 104–5; Colín, *Requisitos fundamentales*, 5, 12.
114. CANACINTRA, *Conclusiones sobre los puntos*, 4–5, 7–8.
115. Colín, *Requisitos fundamentales*, 14, 16–20; Lavín, "La industria química nacional," 97–98.

guidance of employers. It therefore fell to employers to educate workers about their responsibilities to the production process while ensuring their welfare.[116] Rhetorically, CANACINTRA leaders supported social reform and income redistribution in order to jump-start consumption. In practice, however, they were much more conservative and regarded reform and redistribution as eventual outcomes of increased national wealth by means of industrialist innovation, increased profits, and higher productivity.[117]

Like Colín and Lavín, OII technocrats were troubled that labor unrest and strikes impeded production. Echoing earlier technocrats, such as Pani in the 1920s, they viewed collective welfare and social peace as prerequisites to long-term capitalist economic growth, though they were much more explicit in trying to outline prescriptions to rectify social injustice. Importantly, they recognized poor income distribution as a factor in worker unrest. Moreover, Gonzalo Robles expressed appreciation for activist policies aimed at immediately improving the impoverished masses' levels of consumption. Yet, he added that government efforts to redress distribution inequities and improve mass consumption inevitably had an inflationary effect, which in turn only aggravated poverty.[118]

Although rejecting activist economic policies that promoted rapid income redistribution, OII technocrats considered fair salaries and improved purchasing power as necessary to increase consumption and production and ensure labor peace. Yet, they argued that the egotism, paternalism, and partisan politics of both industrialists and labor leaders continued to depress workers' wages.[119] For OII technocrats, labor peace and higher wages could be accomplished only by respecting the role of both employers and workers within a rational plan for economic development. For example, Alanis Patiño posited humans as a factor of production, whose function needed to be rationalized alongside other factors of production like primary materials. As he underscored the misuse of natural resources, he pondered the economic costs of Mexico's high mortality. In a slightly morbid tone he professed, "The loss of human life is in the millions of pesos, if judged by the money invested in raising and educating or in the value of the lost work of individuals who have died prematurely."[120]

116. Lavín, *Plan inmediato*, 4; Colín, *Requisitos fundamentales*, 15–16.
117. This was a prominent position at the time. See Schumpeter, *Theory of Economic Development*.
118. Robles, "Los pueblos atrasados," 43.
119. Robles, "Obstáculos a la industrialización."
120. Emilio Alanis Patiño, "Planeación nacional," 1944, GR/AGN, c. 46, exp. 53.

OII technocrats advanced classical tenets that advocated the moderation of social reform and the delay of redistributive policies in order to foster the growth of production. They recognized that their proposals would require sacrifices by the masses, but the technocrats argued that this was only for the short term and necessary to guarantee a safe investment climate for entrepreneurs. Eduardo Villaseñor even hinted at abandoning social reform altogether, noting that leaders of the Russian Revolution had renounced social reform in order to focus on production in the face of widespread starvation.[121] More commonly, OII technocrats believed that increased production would generate the national income needed to improve standards of living and, eventually, to implement the redistributive policies promised by the Revolution.

In a 1943 conference, Gonzalo Robles explained two distinct attitudes toward labor in Mexico. The first viewed the worker as a living factor of production. Machines, technology, and instruments were simply auxiliary features. The net income of production should be paid to workers as remuneration, not only because it was just but also because it would facilitate the expansion of consumption and consequently production. The second envisioned labor as a commodity subject to the laws of supply and demand. Workers should be paid the minimum permitted by the labor market. This would maximize profits for individual companies and allow for more exports, both of which were fundamental to a strong national economy and would therefore improve living standards.[122] The ideas of neither the OII nor CANACINTRA neatly conformed to these definitions, even as they drew from both. This demonstrates the eclecticism of technocratic and industrial attitudes toward labor during the 1940s. Even more, despite their stances, the OII never dedicated much energy to the labor question, while CANACINTRA ultimately settled on political solutions. Consequently, the voice of labor and the redistribution of wealth remained subordinate to the midcentury push for economic growth.

Rival Visions of Mexico's Industrial Geography: Region Versus Center

One of the core differences between the rival industrial projects of the OII and CANACINTRA was their distinct approaches to the concept of

---

121. Eduardo Villaseñor, address to the Eleventh Convention of the ABM, Guadalajara, Jalisco, April 20, 1945, GR/AGN, c. 20, exp. 8.
122. Robles, "Obstáculos a la industrialización," 40–45.

wealth. Since OII technocrats argued that the creation of wealth occurred at the moment of production, they championed basic industry and its large-scale transformation of primary materials. CANACINTRA's leaders, to the contrary, promoted the manufacture of consumer articles, especially nondurables, such as food and drink, textiles, shoes, and chemicals. They contended that this would foster the rapid circulation of goods and consequently the creation of wealth.[123] As Lavín stated, "All goods that satisfy needs and are rapidly consumed have the economic advantage of promoting more frequent domestic circulation, thereby sustaining productive activity, which means an improvement in standards of living for the masses."[124]

Distinctions about national wealth had significance in light of geographical disparities in Mexico in the 1940s. Partly due to concerns about the exacerbation of regionally based inequalities, OII technocrats supported the regionally balanced development of industry, agriculture, and mining for both export and domestic consumption. Carlos Novoa, general director of the Banco de México from 1946 to 1952, affirmed that the rational expansion of domestic consumption and production could only occur with the integrated, decentralized development of all regions of Mexico.[125] These proposals for industrial decentralization appealed to many ruling-party insiders. For instance, Secretary of the Treasury and Public Credit Eduardo Suárez embraced the balanced growth of agricultural and industrial production, which he argued would foster basic industry, regional autonomy, and industrial decentralization.[126] Gustavo Serrano, head of the SEN from 1944 to 1946, claimed that regional industrialization was more rational than centralized industry because producers would be closer to primary resources and population and infrastructure pressures would be better distributed. He added that industrial decentralization would increase the buying power of the masses, improve standards of living, and expand the domestic market.[127] And Antonio Ruiz Galindo, the head of the Secretariat of the Economy (Secretaría de Economía, successor to the SEN beginning in 1946) from 1946 through 1948, lamented that Mexico City had been transformed into

123. CANACINTRA, *Conclusiones sobre los puntos*; Colín, "Requisitos fundamentales"; Lavín, "La industria química nacional," 81–105.
124. Lavín, *Plan inmediato*, 5.
125. Carlos Novoa, "Planeación económica de México," GR/AGN, folletería, c. 20, folleto 1132.
126. Eduardo Suárez to Ávila Camacho, memorandum, May 26, 1943, MAC/AGN, exp. 550/44-2.
127. Serrano, *Centralización o descentralización*.

a "huge head" sustained by a "weak skeleton," consisting of the rest of Mexico. He concluded that the Alemán administration needed to pursue industrial decentralization in order to achieve equity among the provinces and limit the disorder, inefficiency, corruption, and immorality that had accompanied massive industrial buildup in Mexico City.[128] His observations reflected tensions within the Alemán administration between those who sought to slow the excesses of urban growth and those who continued to amass political and economic power in the capital.

CANACINTRA countered the OII by promoting urban-based consumer manufacturing. It even suggested that government policy should force industrial concentration in Monterrey, Guadalajara, and Mexico City.[129] For CANACINTRA, agricultural regions would provide the raw materials to factories in a few key cities, thereby transforming agricultural production into an appendage of a regionally concentrated consumer-manufacturing sector.[130] By emphasizing rural development designed to feed urban-industrial concentration, CANACINTRA promoted a form of national economic growth that would ultimately exacerbate internal dependency and regionally differentiated, unequal development.[131]

For Mexico's technocrats, including Jewish Hungarian-born immigrant and UNAM economist László Radványi, an economic plan for regionally balanced development would optimize the use of Mexico's primary resources, not just in basic industry but also in the manufacturing, mining, and agricultural sectors.[132] Therefore, OII technocrats focused on generating technical and economic data by inventorying Mexico's natural resources, since they believed data and knowledge were the foundations of rational

128. "Descentralización industrial y libre competencia," *El Nacional*, June 26, 1947. See also Secretaría de Economía, "El esfuerzo económico de México," December 8, 1947, MAV/AGN, exp. 523/1; Secretaría de Economía, Dirección General de Estudios Económicos, *Industrialización y planeación regional de México*.
129. CANACINTRA, *Conclusiones sobre los puntos*, 27–28.
130. Ibid., 24; Colín, *Requisitos fundamentales*, 5–6.
131. Later dependentistas, adapting world systems theory to the national context, condemned this as internal colonialism and argued that it resulted from global dependency. Sternberg, "Dependency, Imperialism," 79, 82.
132. Radványi, "Planeación del desarrollo económico," 135; László Radványi, "Posibilidades y tareas de la planificación de ramas industriales," mid-1940s, GR/AGN, c. 85, exp. 19, p. 5; anonymous, "La obra inmediata por realizar," early 1940s, GR/AGN, c. 47, exp. 67. Radványi, a Communist, had been a member of the Budapest Sunday Circle (led by Georg Lukács and including Karl Mannheim and Karl Polanyi, among other bourgeois intellectuals). He was also the husband of the well-known communist poet and novelist Anna Seghers. After he was briefly interned in Europe, he and Seghers, along with their two children, fled to Mexico in 1941, where he stayed until 1952. Moreno and Sánchez-Castro, "Lost Decade," 3–8.

resource usage.[133] CANACINTRA industrialists, in contrast, shunned calls for rationalization. Instead, they argued that industrialists were the most appropriate arbiters for determining resource usage. José R. Colín even asserted that industrial chambers should be responsible for determining what constituted a basic primary material. Moreover, Colín averred that primary materials should be sold to national manufacturers without limits and at "Mexican" (that is, lower) prices. Along with Lavín, he insisted that the export of primary materials should occur only after the needs of Mexican industry had been met.[134]

These conflicts about the availability and rationing of Mexico's natural resources briefly revived the hoary debate about Mexico's purported natural riches. Porfirian elites had already dispelled the notion, disseminated in the late colonial period by Alexander von Humboldt, that Mexico was a wealthy nation due to its resources. Instead, they "emphasized the realm of production, particularly the central roles of capital, technology, and labor in generating wealth."[135] By February 1940, however, Daniel Cosío Villegas was disturbed enough by lingering perceptions of Mexico's fantastical wealth that he publicly condemned Mexicans and foreigners who highlighted national riches, arguing that they did so at the expense of efforts to expose the grinding poverty, inequality, and underdevelopment that continued to plague the country.[136] Cosío Villegas celebrated the possibilities of development through industrial production just as had the Porfirian positivists. He was wary of their exuberance, however, and believed that Mexico's limited natural resources would remain a permanent impediment to industrialization that no amount of human intervention could master.[137]

Planning in Practice

Technocrats embarked on a project that included the wide-scale inventory of Mexico's natural resources, as well as industrial research, assessments of

133. Bravo Jiménez, *Planeación industrial en México*, 14, 70; Robles, "Los pueblos atrasados," 31–32.
134. "Un plan inmediato para la industrialización nacional," *Novedades*, July 6, 1945; Colín, *Requisitos fundamentales*, 9–10.
135. Weiner, *Race, Nation, and Market*, 53–54. For a more developed discussion of Humboldt's vision and the científico challenge, see Weiner, "El declive económico"; Salmerón Sanginés, "El mito de la riqueza."
136. Cosío Villegas, "La riqueza legendaria de México."
137. Weiner, "Economic Thought and Culture."

regional industrial possibilities, the education of technicians, and the publication of studies detailing industrial and technological expertise.[138] The scope of their efforts demanded the coordination of an array of individuals and organizations involved in economic development in Mexico. In its early days, the OII showed interest in using the data collected during the war by the U.S. Foreign Economic Administration. Part of the U.S. Metals and Minerals Procurement program, it had completed an extensive study of natural resources that might contribute to the war effort, including metals, minerals, lumber, fiber, fats and oils, drugs, and agricultural products.[139] In addition, at the suggestion of Manuel Bravo Jiménez, Gonzalo Robles hired two Spanish engineers, Luis Torón and Adrián Esteve, to conduct a national exploration of resources needed for the steel industry, especially coal and iron reserves. The OII soon expanded its program by hiring young geological engineers, many of whom it sent to the United States to do postgraduate work. Others completed a range of industrial and primary resource investigations. Furthermore, the Banco de México contracted at least three foreign consulting groups, including Higgins Industries, Inc., the Armour Research Foundation, and Ford, Bacon & Davis, to complete industrial, transportation, and natural resource studies and to make recommendations about industrialization.[140] The OII also placed a priority on advancing technical education within Mexico, and it played a prominent role in the creation of the Mexican Institute for Technological Research (Instituto Mexicano de Investigaciones Tecnológicas) and in the development of domestic laboratories for industrial research. Importantly, the OII argued that the institute should remain outside of government control, because it feared that bureaucratization and political abuse would undermine it. However, it lauded other government efforts to set up laboratories, such as the Secretariat of the Economy's Standards Laboratory (Laboratorio de Normas).[141]

At the heart of its efforts, the OII worked to coordinate industrial planning and standardize the procedures that various agencies used to promote and protect industry. In its first fifteen years of existence, it was responsible for writing, editing, and soliciting hundreds of industrial and natural resource studies. It focused on basic industries, such as iron and coal, as well

138. Rodríguez Garza, "Cambio institucional," 71; Mario J. Ordaz, "La Oficina de Investigaciones como centro coordinador en la industrialización del país?" December 26, 1944, GR/AGN, c. 23, exp. 14; Hernández Delgado, "El pensamiento pragmático," 230.
139. William G. Kane to Banco de México, memorandum, June 12, 1945, GR/AGN, c. 20, exp. 2.
140. For example, see Higgins Industries, Inc., *Estudio sobre México*.
141. "Proposición para la creación de un Instituto Mexicano de Investigaciones Tecnológicas," 1947, GR/AGN, c. 48, exp. 4.

as on agriculture and fishing. But it also branched out into the fields of transportation, mining, canning, refrigeration, and electric energy, as well as into industries like cement, ceramics, sugar, chemicals, plastics, textiles, and foodstuffs.[142] Additionally, it expanded its advisory role to the ruling party. It also established links with other government entities and private institutions involved in economic planning, such as, among others, the Secretariats of Agriculture, Communications and Public Works, Hydraulic Resources, Economy, and Treasury and Public Credit; NAFINSA; the Banco Nacional de Comercio Exterior; the Banco Nacional de Crédito Ejidal; the Instituto Geológico; the Comisión de Fomento Minero; Henequeneros de Yucatán; and the Unión de Productores de Azúcar. Its primary goal in building these ties was to facilitate cooperation and coordination among the multiple agencies involved in planning.[143] Furthermore, by 1949, the OII officially began to collaborate with the SHCP and the Secretariat of the Economy to help in decisions about tax-exemption applications. In the next year, it conducted factory visits to 209 of the 610 factories enjoying federal exemptions. It concluded that 14.8 percent had committed violations that contravened the conditions of their exemption.[144] Finally, by the late 1940s, the OII was even working with CANACINTRA, which had become involved in economic planning by forming its own industrial planning commission.

In the early 1950s, technocrats at the Banco de México considered the OII, along with CANACINTRA, the Secretariat of the Economy, and NAFINSA, to be the four organizations capable of studying and planning long-range industrial development.[145] To the dismay of OII technocrats and even some members of CANACINTRA, however, industrial planning continued to run into obstacles throughout much of the 1950s, whether due to the constraints of dependence on foreign investment, a lack of resources, or official apathy.[146] Even worse, when the state finally did create its first centralized planning system in 1958 to coordinate and direct the

142. Bravo Jiménez, *Planeación industrial en México*, 52. For a list of these studies, see Bullejos, *Índice bibliográfico de obras*.
143. Manuel Bravo Jiménez, draft for discussion of the General Policy of the Industrial Research Office, Banco de México, April 16, 1949, GR/AGN, c. 23, exp. 16.
144. Bravo Jiménez, *Planeación industrial en México*, 55–58; Banco de México, "Informes elaborados por la sección de industrias nuevas," May 31, 1950, GR/AGN, c. 23, exp. 12; Manuel Bravo Jiménez, "Sección de vigilancia de exenciones," June 1, 1950, GR/AGN, c. 23, exp. 12; "Bases para la calificación de industrias nuevas o necesarias," late 1940s/early 1950s, GR/AGN, c. 85, exp. 18; report on tax exemptions, early 1950s, GR/AGN, c. 25, exp. 2.
145. "El desarrollo industrial en México," February 29, 1952, GR/AGN, c. 77 bis (3), exp. 3.
146. Bravo Jiménez, *Planeación industrial en México*, 21–23; Ceceña Cervantes, *La planificación económica*, 82–92.

efforts of disparate state agencies, it was led by a bureaucratic ministry, the Secretariat of the Presidency, which answered directly to the president.[147]

A Rational Plan for Realistic Development

By the late 1940s, OII technocrats pressed for economic planning as they argued that "spontaneous industrialization" was a luxury that Mexico, as a backward country, could no longer afford.[148] Yet Gonzalo Robles recognized that structural impediments to economic planning existed in Mexico and many Latin American countries, including weak legislative authority, the poor organization of the private banking sector, the absence of national development banks, fiscal disarray, institutional fragmentation, and liberal opposition to state economic intervention.[149] He contended that if haphazard state intervention continued, it would further dilute the efficacy of attempts at economic rationalization.[150] In 1945, CANACINTRA leader José Domingo Lavín similarly concluded, "The state dictates contradictory measures when on the one hand, it helps private enterprise with appropriate legislation, and on the other, it dismisses it with conflicting legislation. In this terrain, it is necessary to define a policy and follow it, since what is not possible is the coexistence of policies that cancel each other out."[151]

Regardless of their convictions, the realities of the wartime and postwar economies stymied the OII's proposals for the planned development of basic industries. Despite the diversity of industrial growth during World War II, the textile industry remained fundamental to the national economy during the mid-1940s. With the threat of diminished postwar foreign exchange earnings, and U.S. reluctance to provide loans or to export machinery and goods needed to industrialize, the OII and the ruling party redefined plans for industrial modernization to incorporate traditional industries. As a result, alongside basic industry, the rationalization of textile manufacturing became one focus of the OII. In effect, *rational* industrialization sought the growth

147. Pichardo Pagaza, *10 años de planificación*, 19–23, 40. In 1962, the government supplanted the Secretariat of the Presidency with the more wide-reaching and centralized Comisión Intersecretarial para la Formulación de Planes Nacionales de Desarrollo. It brought together representatives from the Secretariat of the Presidency and the SHCP to formulate short- and long-range plans for economic and social development, although in practice, it achieved little.
148. Quintana, "Problemas fundamentales," 21–23.
149. Robles, "Los pueblos atrasados," 50–55.
150. Hernández Delgado, "El pensamiento pragmático," 231–32.
151. Lavín, "La industria química nacional," 100.

of basic industries. *Realistic* industrialization demanded the maintenance of industries vital to national earnings, including textiles.

Mexico's political climate in the 1940s also tempered OII plans for industrial rationalization. During the war, the Ávila Camacho administration justified its indifference toward industrial rationalization by stating that wartime economic imperatives precluded long-term planning.[152] Although President Ávila Camacho was accurate that the wartime economy hindered planning, federal officials were also reluctant to be constrained by OII proposals or, even more threatening, a broad-based economic plan. Moreover, while the heterodox approach to economic policy by economists, engineers, politicians, and businesspeople allowed for a vibrant intellectual life in Mexico, some, such as Communist László Radványi, argued that the lack of a "comprehensive theory and methodology of national economic planning" militated against "systematic planning work." Radványi added that so long as the spirit of free enterprise reigned in Mexico and Latin America, governments would refuse to force the private sector to comply with planning initiatives, and planning would inevitably fall short of its goals.[153] Ultimately, in the 1940s, the ruling party focused not on economic planning but on engineering a state-led alliance with CANACINTRA and urban labor that could demobilize workers while undermining recalcitrant industrialists. To accomplish this while defending Mexican industry in the face of a postwar economic downturn, the state rapidly expanded its program of tariffs and trade controls in 1947. These protectionist policies promoted the production of consumer goods, but this shift concurrently expanded state authority and the power of politicians to influence economic policy.

---

152. Cue Cánovas, "Economía de emergencia," 306–7.
153. László Radványi, "A Brief Memorandum Concerning the Possibilities and Tasks of Industrial Planning in Mexico," March 7, 1949, GR/AGN, c. 77 bis (3), exp. 3; Radványi, "Planeación del desarrollo económico," 132–33.

4

SOWING EXCLUSION

Machinery, Labor, and Industrialist Authority in Puebla in the 1940s

According to lawyer and textile-industry investor Francisco Doria Paz, on the night of July 23, 1943, labor leader Luis Morones called him over to his table at a restaurant in Puebla where both happened to be dining. As Doria Paz later recounted the story to the Association of Textile Entrepreneurs of Puebla and Tlaxcala (Asociación de Empresarios Textiles de Puebla y Tlaxcala, AETPT), Morones proposed a toast to celebrate the recent, albeit fleeting, settlement of an extended labor dispute at the Fábrica La Trinidad. Doria Paz did not explain how things heated up, but soon, Morones and his friends, likely emboldened by drink, began hitting the lawyer over the head with their bottles. The next day, an irate Doria Paz wanted to protest directly to President Ávila Camacho, but his fellow AETPT members urged restraint.[1]

Doria Paz had a long and turbulent history with labor. In his earlier days, he had been part of a group of business leaders in Monterrey who had supported the PNR's ouster of the CROM from the revolutionary family. That coupled with his antilabor stance in some high-profile labor conflicts in Puebla led both the CTM and the CROM to assail him for dealing unfairly with unions.[2] Morones, for his part, was one of the most corrupt and violent labor leaders in Mexico. His memories of the late 1920s assault on the CROM by business and political leaders, as well as the CROM's later conflicts with Doria Paz and other industrialists in Puebla, probably were fresh in his mind that evening as he spoke with the lawyer. Regardless

---

1. Junta de la Directiva, AETPT, meeting minutes, July 24, 1943, and August 3, 1943, CITPT, F-VI/LAJD-3.
2. "La Bonetera Avant y las cc. separadas," *Acción*, June 28, 1941; "Doria Paz, enemigo de la CROM," *Germinal*, February 21, 1942; Saragoza, *Monterrey Elite*, 163.

of his motives, this incident reflects a monumental shift away from the prerevolutionary era, when labor had little or no legal recourse when subjected to managerial whims. By the 1940s, the historic dependence of textile workers on employers had been supplanted by a state-labor alliance that expanded union and state authority within factories and communities at the expense of paternal forms of managerial autonomy. Industrialists' loss of local authority was made more bitter by the state's growing focus on large-scale production using modern technology. This occurred to the detriment of the traditional, small-scale textile manufacturing that predominated in Puebla. Furthermore, Puebla's textile industrialists had good relations with the regional political leaders who constituted the *avilacamachista cacicazgo*. According to Wil Pansters, this was a sort of "collective *caciquismo*" that, rather than being forged around a single individual, was made up of a group of allied individuals, who built "a stable system of loyalties and patronage" that dominated regional authority, beginning with the governorship of Maximino Ávila Camacho (1937–41) and lasting until the 1960s. In contrast to earlier periods, however, Alan Knight argues that these modern caciques now were "usually members and servants" of the ruling party and its electoral machine. This provided them with access to the substantial patronage that the ruling party commanded during the mid-twentieth century, but their ability to mediate the intervention of the state at the regional and local levels was now more circumscribed.[3] This, in turn, weakened the role of regional alliances in guaranteeing the interests of Puebla's industrialists.

Amid Puebla's postwar economic crisis, textile industrialists' concerns about their political and economic marginalization transformed into resentment against the new populist forms of state power and nationalist development that were displacing traditional labor regimes. The postwar crisis also provided the justification to invest in new machinery after decades of technological stagnation. The allure of modern machinery lay not just in its potential to raise the industry's status within the national project for statist industrialism. State-of-the-art machinery would also allow employers to undercut the collective contracts that had protected the labor force and allowed for union control over the production process since the 1920s. In this context, the Alemán administration's almost total refusal to grant import permits for machinery to traditional textile industrialists demonstrates how protected industrialism enabled the state to challenge the authority of regional industrialists. By rejecting the modernization of traditional sectors of

---

3. Knight, "*Caciquismo* in Twentieth-Century Mexico," 30, 45; Pansters, "Building a *Cacicazgo*," 302.

one of Mexico's most important industries, the government substantively disempowered a technologically backward, highly protected, and historically autonomous group of regional industrialists who were recalcitrant to emerging corporatist populism.

The Erosion of Industrialist Autonomy in the 1920s

Esteban de Antuñano founded Puebla's first mechanized textile factory in 1835, and ever since, cotton textiles played a steadily expanding role in the state and national economies of the nineteenth century. Accompanying the industry's rise to prominence was the emergence of a small, but politically and socially cohesive, group of textile industrialists who exercised significant autonomy over local labor relations. However, in the 1920s, labor legislation and collective contracts broadened the power of both unions and the state in labor-employer relations and created the legal foundations for the transformation of these local labor regimes. Puebla's textile industrialists fiercely opposed these changes, which soon threatened to erase labor's postrevolutionary gains. Consequently, the federal government conceded to an array of tariffs, tax breaks, and supply guarantees for the industry. This ensured its survival over the short run, but ultimately fostered the political and economic conditions for enduring stagnation.

Though it started out with great promise, Mexico's mechanized textile industry faltered under the Liberal and Conservative governments of the mid-nineteenth century. Most supported the industry with tariffs, tax exemptions, loans, and cotton subsidies, but all too often, they designed these policies to generate revenue for federal coffers rather than to foster long-term industrial development.[4] Porfirian political stability and economic progress soon created a more propitious climate for industry, however, allowing the textile sector to enter a period of sustained expansion in the late nineteenth century. Nevertheless, from the outset, Puebla's textile industry was distinct from that of other regions. It had more mills, but they tended to be smaller and grow more slowly. Indeed, despite Puebla being home to one of Mexico's largest mills, Metepec, the size of the state's factories grew more slowly than the national average during the Porfiriato. Between 1878 and 1912, the average increase in spindles per mill across the

---

4. Thomson, "Protectionism and Industrialization," 136; Potash, *Mexican Government and Industrial Development*.

nation was 116 percent. Yet, in Puebla, it was just 68 percent. The difference is even more pronounced when Metepec is excluded from Puebla's figures: the growth of spindles per mill drops to just 20 percent. Specifically, in 1878, the average mill in Mexico had 2,918 spindles, while Puebla's mills averaged 3,294. By 1912, the national average had grown to 6,299 spindles per mill. In Puebla, it had grown to just 5,527 per mill (and only 3,954 if we exclude Metepec). Although the cotton textile industry overall was larger in Puebla, it was less concentrated than in other regions.[5] By 1921, Puebla's textile industry had the highest fixed investment in the country, with its fifty-six mills worth Mex$25,890,824. Veracruz was in a distant second place, at Mex$18,850,847, but it had only eleven mills.[6]

During the Porfiriato, a small group of textile industrialists emerged in Puebla who, along with their heirs, would dominate the industry into the mid-twentieth century. Many of them came from Spain or were of Spanish descent. Not only did they own many of the large- and medium-sized factories in the region, but they also invested heavily in banking, haciendas, and other commercial ventures. By the early 1900s, these industrialists had fashioned a coherent and closed interest group based on their common heritage and close personal relationships cemented by patronage. They were members of a number of business organizations, including Puebla's first textile-industry association, the Mexican Industrial Center (Centro Industrial Mexicano, CIM), as well as the Puebla Chamber of Commerce (Cámara de Comercio de Puebla), the Spanish Chamber of Commerce of Puebla (Cámara Española de Comercio de Puebla), the Chamber of Owners (Cámara de Propietarios), and the Agricultural Chamber of Puebla (Cámara Agrícola de Puebla). Consequently, the apparent array of political pressure groups in the state in reality expressed only a limited range of opinions held by a narrow segment of its business elite.[7] In the decades after the Revolution, ownership became more diverse, thanks to the arrival of new immigrants, frequently Lebanese. By the 1930s and 1940s, some of these recent arrivals had even moved into the industry's sectoral organizations, such as the AETPT. Yet, most remained outside the CIM and other groups.[8]

5. Between 1878 and 1912, the national aggregate for spindle increase was 155 percent, while in Puebla it was 210 percent (158 percent with Metepec excluded). Gómez Galvarriato, "Impact of Revolution," 80, 82.
6. Bortz, *Revolution Within the Revolution*, 35–36.
7. Gamboa Ojeda, "El mundo empresarial," 504–12; Gamboa Ojeda, *El perfil organizativo*; Gamboa Ojeda, *Los empresarios de ayer*, 121–200.
8. Kenny et al., *Inmigrantes y refugiados españoles en México*; Gamboa Ojeda, "El mundo empresarial," 504–12.

Before the Revolution, Puebla's industrialists enjoyed significant autonomy over local labor relations due to the importance of the industry to the state's economy. The unity forged from the industrialists' organizational, social, and ethnic ties enhanced this autonomy. Because many companies provided worker housing, the industrialists' control over workers extended both inside and outside the factory gates. This helped to secure a stable workforce in part by increasing labor's dependence on employers.[9] Employer control of the workforce went largely unchecked because Mexico had no minimum wage requirements, collective contracts, labor offices, or even limits on shift lengths. By the early 1900s, unions were beginning to make inroads in organizing and lobbying for better pay and work conditions. But many industrialists still felt a proprietary right to run their factories and the lives of their workers.[10]

Puebla's factory owners were so concerned about labor organizing and its threat to their paternalist authority that they formed the CIM in November 1906. It aimed in part to overcome conflicts among employers about unequal pay and work conditions in order to unify them in their struggle with labor. The organization's first task was to codify regulations governing salaries and labor relations. The resulting Internal Work Regulations (Reglamento Interior de Trabajo) included provisions that defined shift lengths and worker responsibilities. But when labor challenged the regulations with a counterproposal, it surprisingly did not tackle work conditions. Instead, the counterproposal weakened or eliminated those provisions that perpetuated employers' paternal influence over workers' lives, including provisions that called for worker indemnities for defective cloth; prohibited guests in worker housing without administrative approval; banned any type of literature, pamphlet, or weapon in the factory; and gave employers the right to expel labor agitators.[11] Employers rejected labor's counterproposal, however, setting off the industry's first general strike on December 4, 1906. By early 1907, it had spread to textile factories throughout much of Puebla and Veracruz, climaxing in the Río Blanco massacre of January 7, 1907.[12]

Strikes and labor radicalism during the Revolution and the 1920s soon enabled textile workers to make significant legal gains, which contributed to the forging of new political pacts and labor regimes that dramatically

9. Gamboa Ojeda, "La trayectoria de una familia," 74.
10. Bortz, "Legal and Contractual Limits," 256–59.
11. Ramírez Rancaño, "Un frente patronal a principios del siglo XX," 1358–59, 1372–74.
12. Gamboa Ojeda, *La urdimbre y la trama*, 219–38; R. Anderson, *Outcasts in Their Own Land*, 137–71; Gutiérrez Álvarez, *Experiencias contrastadas*, chapters 8–9.

altered labor-employer relations in the industry. As early as 1912, textile workers secured the equivalent of an industrywide collective contract that provided for permanent unions and curbed managerial authority within factories.[13] But revolutionary violence complicated labor-owner relations in the region. During the Revolution, workers often found themselves on the side of employers, defending their mills from attacks by various revolutionary factions. From fall 1914 to winter 1915, revolutionary forces attacked and even sometimes burned more than one-half of Puebla's textile mills, including Metepec. In response, employers and labor collaborated to protect their factories while demanding that Constitutionalist forces intervene to ensure security and jobs. At the same time, however, both state and federal officials enacted labor reforms in an effort to gain military backing and personal favor from textile workers, which exacerbated conflicts in the industry.[14]

The inclusion of article 123 in the 1917 Constitution confirmed the gains made by labor during the Revolution. Highly progressive at the time, article 123 set up a tripartite relationship among labor, employers, and the state that stripped industrialists of much of their authority. Though the federal government did not codify article 123 until 1931, Puebla issued a state labor code on November 14, 1921. Among other things, it guaranteed unions and the state a role in the workplace and in settling labor-employer disputes. It also granted unions rights over hiring and firing and the production process.[15] But employers and even some workers soon bristled at the perceived abuse of authority by the newly empowered union leaders. For example, the textile section of CONCAMIN complained of unions that unjustly and even illegally took over direction of production to the almost total exclusion of owners. It added that some unions were using excessive punishment against their own members. Workers similarly protested that while they had recently been able to "break the chains of capitalist slavery" through revolutionary struggle, they now were suffering under a "new oppression" created by union leaders trying to enslave workers for their own political purposes. The textile section of CONCAMIN concluded that employers were the only suitable guardians and disciplinarians of the workforce.[16]

13. Bortz, "Legal and Contractual Limits," 261–73.
14. LaFrance, *Revolution in Mexico's Heartland*, 120–23.
15. Bortz, *Revolution Within the Revolution*, 146–47.
16. CONCAMIN, Ponencia de la Sección Textil sobre la Capacidad y Responsabilidad de las Asociaciones Profesionales Obreras, March 5, 1925, DT/AGN, c. 856, exp. 2. On worker complaints, various unions and peasant leagues to Calles and other government agencies, September 5–24, 1928, DT/AGN, c. 1460, exp. 4–10; Bortz, *Revolution Within the Revolution*, chapter 8.

Many states promulgated labor laws augmenting workers' rights and union authority during the early 1920s, though with substantial variations between them. These variations, along with uneven adherence to the 1912 agreement with workers, soon provoked dissension among textile industrialists. Interregional conflict among them had predated the Revolution. For example, on December 24, 1906, ninety-three of the country's one hundred and fifty textile mill owners had participated in a one-day lockout in solidarity with their Puebla counterparts during the general strike.[17] Despite that, in 1907, Pueblan and Tlaxcalan industrialists refused to join an association representing textile industrialists from across Mexico, the Centro Industrial de México, not to be confused with the Mexican Industrial Center, or CIM, which represented only industrialists from Puebla and some of its immediate environs. Puebla's industrialists justified this by arguing that a bias existed against the type of factories in Puebla—which were smaller and less modern than those elsewhere in the country—which would put them at a disadvantage in voting in the organization.[18] In 1912, tensions came to a head with a clear organizational split in the industry. On one side were textile industrialists in the Puebla- and Tlaxcala-dominated CIM, which tended to represent small- and medium-sized factories. On the other side was the Mexican National Manufacturing Confederation (Confederación Fabril Nacional Mexicana), formed in 1912 by larger, more modern factories like the Compañía Industrial Veracruzana and the Compañía Industrial de Orizaba. The confederation was designed to be an alternative, more aggressive representative of industrialist interests. In its early years, it represented factories in Mexico City, Veracruz, Jalisco, Querétaro, and Guanajuato, but none from Puebla.[19]

Problems with labor and between the two sides resurged in the mid-1920s, especially over regional wage disparities. Therefore, between 1925 and 1927, the industry convened a new round of collective contract negotiations. The primary issue under debate at the Industrial and Labor Convention for the Textile Sector (Convención Industrial y Obrera del Ramo Textil) was the standardization of salaries, though the subtext of the discussions was the expansion of state-backed union power and the intervention of federal authorities in the textile industry.[20] The resulting contract created

17. Ramírez Rancaño, *Burguesía textil*, chapter 1.
18. Gamboa Ojeda, *El perfil organizativo*, 5–9.
19. Ramírez Rancaño, *Burguesía textil*, 62–65.
20. SEN, Departamento de Estudios Económicos, *La industria textil en México*, 40–104; "El fracaso de una industria," *El Universal*, September 16, 1934; "Problemas de la industrial textil," *El Universal*, April 8, 1934.

labor-employer commissions to manage conflict arbitration and a closed shop that gave unions power over hiring and firing. Although employers resisted the loss of authority over their factories and workers, according to Jeffrey Bortz, they often supported the contracts since these promised "peace in factories and low wages."[21]

The wage schedule agreed on in the contract, however, continued to generate problems. At the outset of the negotiations, the owners of large, technologically modern factories in Mexico City, Veracruz, and the Estado de México contended that the lower salaries paid to workers in smaller, less modern factories, like those of Puebla and Tlaxcala, provided them with a form of protection. The larger firms therefore pushed for a national, uniform minimum wage in the industry. However, the less-modern firms, whose owners were a majority at the convention, opposed the proposal. After a rancorous debate, the majority prevailed, and wage inequalities were preserved.[22]

Despite their success in retaining regional wage disparities, by 1927–28, Puebla's industrialists were again protesting the wage schedule in the contract. Part of their resistance can be ascribed to the dire situation for Puebla's textile industry at the onset of the global downturn in textiles in 1926, even though it affected the industry throughout Mexico. More likely, the opposition was due to the stipulation that Puebla's employers pay a greater increase than would the owners of the large, modern factories, where owners already paid wages that exceeded their contractual obligations. To forestall disaster in the industry, as well as a crisis that might lead to the abrogation of the contract, the Department of Labor allowed Puebla's employers to shorten and eliminate shifts for a few months in 1928. Dissatisfied with this temporary solution, the employers responded that conditions in the industry were forcing them to ignore contracts and close factories. The state-labor alliance required that President Portes Gil meet the industrialists with a show of strength, which he did when he ordered employers and labor to honor their contracts. Yet, he concurrently gave employers the right to shorten hours and rid themselves of unnecessary personnel, thereby curbing some of the gains made by labor in the collective contract.

President Portes Gil also provided textile industrialists with a protectionist package that assured their survival, at least temporarily. It included lower taxes and a mandate that compelled cotton growers to supply domestic

---

21. Bortz, "Genesis," 51.

22. Ibid., 49–50, 53–55; M. T. de la Peña, *La industria textil*, 23–24. For an analysis of the evolution of wages in the industry, see Gómez Galvarriato, "Measuring the Impact," 300–302.

textile producers before exporting the fiber, which meant that cotton sold at lower prices.[23] Consequently, by the early 1930s, protection for domestic textiles exceeded the rates of effective protection reached during the Porfiriato, when a cascading tariff structure had fostered a period of sustained growth in the industry.[24] These levels of protection helped to hold imports of cotton textiles to only about 12 percent of total Mexican consumption in terms of value between 1890 and 1930.[25] The Great Depression further depressed cotton textile imports, after which high rates of effective protection held imports to less than 10 percent of total production value in Mexico throughout the 1930s.[26]

Tariff protection enabled Mexican textile manufacturers to dominate the domestic market without having to invest in modern machinery. In return, President Portes Gil and his successors gained the quiescence of traditional textile industrialists. In the years after President Portes Gil made his informal arrangement with textile industrialists, textile machinery imports slumped, frustrating the emergence of new competition in the industry. For example, between 1926 and 1928, the United States and the United Kingdom jointly exported more than one million dollars (in 1929 U.S. dollars) annually in textile machinery to Mexico. By 1932, that had dropped to just US$163,623, with the Great Depression speeding this decline.[27] During the 1930s and 1940s, there was little new investment in machinery in the cotton textile industry. The 1925–27 collective contract further deterred industry modernization, since it fixed wage standards based on piecework and set a maximum number of machines per worker. Any introduction of new machinery or modification of the old machinery would have led to prohibitively high wages and production costs.[28]

One of the enduring results of the collective contract was that it confirmed both the role of state-backed unions in negotiating with employers and the loss of industrialist authority over their factories and workers. The

---

23. SEN, Departamento de Estudios Económicos, *La industria textil en México*, 73–104.

24. Beatty, *Institutions and Investment*, 63–65, 74; Gómez Galvarriato, "Political Economy of Protectionism," 365–67. Gómez Galvarriato adds that by taking factors like transportation costs into account, Mexican textiles produced at large factories, such as the Compañía Industrial Veracruzana, during the Porfiriato may have been competitive without tariffs. Thus, tariffs simply increased profits.

25. Gómez Galvarriato, "Impact of Revolution," 154–57, 171, 602–16.

26. Miguel A. Quintana (STPS) and Fernando Pruneda (SHCP), "Estudio sobre la modernización de la industria nacional textil del algodón para la Comisión Federal de Planificación Económica," April 27, 1943, GR/AGN, c. 76, exp. 9, pp. 49–50; L. Meyer, *El conflicto social*, 78–79.

27. Haber, Maurer, and Razo, "Sustaining Economic Performance," 68–69.

28. Gómez Galvarriato, "Measuring the Impact," 309–10.

promulgation of the 1931 Federal Labor Law, which codified laws protecting union power over hiring and firing, work rules, job assignments, and even factory housing, secured this loss for industrialists. Consequently, though textile industrialists gained protection for their industry as the federal government sought to quell their discontent, it was at great cost to both the long-term competitiveness of the industry and the authority of employers over their factories.

Ambivalent Relations: The Political Limits of the Regional Cacicazgo

Despite the legal and political arrangements underpinning the industry by the late 1920s, economic crisis, political turmoil, and labor factionalism continued to hamper the restoration of social peace in Puebla during the 1930s. The emergence of the conservative avilacamachista cacicazgo in the late 1930s promised to resolve social unrest in the state, as well as affirmed the region's historic alliance of business and political elites. But the limits of modern caciquismo, as well as the reluctance of Puebla's textile industrialists to cede authority to the state and industrialists beyond the region, hindered the ability of owners to exert their influence at the national level. When the post–World War II economic downturn hit the industry, they consequently had few options for addressing the crisis.

During the 1920s, Puebla's textile industry suffered waves of strike activity, especially in Atlixco, the heart of its industry.[29] The reasons for this are numerous and include union factionalism stemming from the CROM's corrupt domination of its labor force, as well as employer efforts to break unions and limit concessions to the industry's workers.[30] Until the late 1920s, Puebla lacked a political leader capable of uniting and restraining the region's diverse social movements. The weakening of the CROM after it lost favor with national leaders in 1928 and the rise of Governor Leonides Andreu Almazán (1929–33) seemed to mark an end to the contentious 1920s. Specifically, Governor Almazán forged an alliance with the predecessor of the Regional Workers and Campesinos Federation (Federación Regional de Obreros y Campesinos of Puebla, FROC), seeking to harness its militancy to his budding populist political machine and to overcome labor unrest in the state.

29. Crider, "Material Struggles."
30. Ruiz, *Labor and the Ambivalent Revolutionaries*, 81–85.

Both the CROM and textile industrialists chafed at this progressive alliance. Consequently, labor conflicts in the textile industry persisted as unions continued to compete to expand their influence over factory and community life and as owners sought to reassert their authority. The conflicts were also driven by the Great Depression's effects on both rural and urban employment and the crackdown by the newly formed national ruling party on unions that refused to align with it. Moreover, state and federal labor legislation allowed only one union to be designated as the official union per each factory shift, enabling two and sometimes three unions to be officially recognized within a single factory, though for different shifts. Consequently, seeking to extend their own authority, union bosses struggled to gain influence over workers (both through elections and force) in order to win official state recognition as a shift's majority union.[31] These turbulent political and economic conditions of the late 1920s and early 1930s fueled interunion rivalries in Puebla, especially because, by the 1930s, it was one of the few remaining CROM redoubts after the organization's expulsion from the revolutionary family.

Seeking a resolution to national labor unrest, President Cárdenas attempted to forge tighter ties with workers by means of social reforms and the institutionalization of state-labor relations. However, the strength of callismo in Puebla complicated the president's project for incorporating workers there into the ruling party. Indeed, violence in the textile industry exploded in the mid-1930s between old-school cromistas, who backed Morones and Calles, and those who supported Morones's former ally, now turned cardenista, Vicente Lombardo Toledano. To handle the task of settling labor conflicts in the region and establishing a stable, cardenista-allied government, the president chose Maximino Ávila Camacho, the conservative brother of the then secretary of National Defense, Manuel Ávila Camacho. The president had known Maximino since at least the early 1920s, when Maximino served as Cárdenas's personal aide. Later, Cárdenas would be impressed by Maximino's military exploits in defense of the Obregón government during the de la Huerta rebellion. In the following decade, Ávila Camacho built a successful military career and ascended to the army's second-highest rank, leaving behind a trail of betrayal, corruption, cruelty, and even murder.[32] By 1935, President Cárdenas appointed him *jefe militar* (military chief) of Puebla, and following fraudulent elections, he became

---

31. On legislation regulating union formation and function, see Zapata, "Afiliación y organización sindical en México"; Franco, "Labor Law and the Labor Movement in Mexico."
32. Henderson and LaFrance, "Maximino Ávila Camacho," 159–60.

state governor in 1937.³³ Counting on military force, the backing of both President Cárdenas and the CROM, and a detente with textile industrialists, Governor Ávila Camacho worked to end political rifts and persistent labor conflicts, if only to consolidate his own regional authority.³⁴ In return for his allegiance to the president and his success in ousting callismo and quieting labor unrest, which facilitated the consolidation of ruling-party authority in Puebla, Governor Ávila Camacho and his cronies—the avilacamachista cacicazgo—were rewarded by the ruling party with virtually unchecked regional power for the next two to three decades.

Textile industrialists had much to celebrate about the rise to power of Governor Ávila Camacho and his successors, not least their antireformism and willingness to use force and even murder to curb labor radicalism. In return, the avilacamachista governments supported the industry, largely because of its continued importance to the state economy. By 1945, textiles provided slightly more than 69 percent of total industrial production in Puebla, with cotton textiles responsible for roughly three-quarters of that amount.³⁵ However, clientelistic networks between Puebla's political leaders and textile industrialists also led the state governments to back the industry. The exchange of favors, including industrialist funding for public works projects, cemented these links.³⁶ For example, in May 1944, Governor Gonzalo Bautista Castillo (1941–45) requested assistance from textile industrialists to pay for the reconstruction of the regional hospital. His motive, he claimed, was to rid the hospital of its asylum character and transform it into a modern, professional institution. Unable to complete the project owing to a budget shortfall, he asked industrialists to pay an extraordinary tax calculated according to each factory's number of looms and spindles. When one industrialist asked to spread the payments out over six months, Governor Bautista responded that the state would give a 15 percent tax break to any industrialist who paid in under two months and charge 15 percent extra to any who took longer. The AETPT voted unanimously in favor of the tax.³⁷ A few years later, at an AETPT meeting in April 1948, members unanimously approved a request by Governor Carlos Betancourt (1945–51) to fund the building of a school as part of the government's school-construction campaign. Though some industrialists complained

33. Enríquez Perea, "Gilberto Bosques," 206–21.
34. Valencia Castrejón, *Poder regional*.
35. Estrada Urroz, "El poder de compra," 355.
36. Pansters, "Building a *Cacicazgo*," 302.
37. Asamblea General, AETPT, meeting minutes, May 19, 1944, CITPT, F-VI/LAAG-3.

about the tax—in part, a ploy to delay having to pay it while the terms were negotiated—the AETPT backed the governor in the dispute and offered to provide the names of those who contributed to the project and the "amount of their cooperation."[38]

Conflicts between regional politicians and textile industrialists were at times more substantial than disagreements over fees and taxes. For example, textile industrialists challenged a 1943 state law that punished anyone guilty of crimes against industry, agriculture, business, or economic stability by claiming that it was unconstitutional and potentially arbitrary.[39] More commonly, industrialist discontent resulted from the strikes and factional violence that remained a mainstay of labor relations in the late 1930s and early 1940s. Although the CROM found succor by allying with Governor Ávila Camacho, the more radical FROC refused to cooperate with him. Initially, it continued to dominate key labor sectors and to use targeted strikes to challenge *avilacamachismo*. This ultimately weakened the FROC, however, since both President Cárdenas and the CTM, with which the FROC was affiliated, declined to support its militancy against the governor. The FROC's exile from ruling-party politics was completed when it refused to back the PRM candidate, Manuel Ávila Camacho, in the 1940 presidential elections. Soon thereafter, the FROC broke from the CTM, and it remained one of the more militant mainstream labor federations in Puebla into the mid-1940s.[40] Even with state repression and the marginalization of labor radicals, however, textile industrialists continued to protest what they maintained was the state's pro-labor partisan intrusion and its ineffective efforts to quell unrest. The AETPT even tried to prevent a 1944 conflict at the Fábrica La Trinidad from becoming widely known, fearing that official intervention would inevitably hurt the owners' cause.[41]

Nevertheless, the backing that textile industrialists provided to the regional government through the 1940s brought them important benefits. In contrast to large-scale industrialists, such as sugar and alcohol magnate William O. Jenkins, who appealed directly to federal contacts for concessions, textile industrialists depended on their privileged access to the governor and

38. Asamblea General, AETPT, meeting minutes, April 28, 1948, and June 8, 1949, CITPT, F-VI/LAAG-3.
39. Junta de la Directiva, AETPT, meeting minutes, April 19, 1943, CITPT, F-VI/LAJD-3.
40. On the intersection of regional and union politics in Puebla, see Pansters, "Paradoxes of Regional Power," 135–40; Valencia Castrejón, *Poder regional*. On the history of labor conflict in Puebla, see Malpica Uribe, "La derrota de la FROC"; Talavera Aldana, "Organizaciones sindicales obreras"; Ventura Rodríguez, "La FROC en Puebla, 1942–1952"; Estrada Urroz, *Del telar*.
41. Asamblea General, AETPT, meeting minutes, May 15, 1944, CITPT, F-VI/LAAG-3.

his willingness to intervene on their behalf with the president. Through the governor, they pressed their interests, including complaints about the rising tax burden.[42] Furthermore, both Governors Bautista and Betancourt occasionally alleviated the economic impact of federal mandates. For example, in 1944, Governor Bautista offered to help the textile industry by forgoing the state's portion of a new federal tax on the industry. He proposed to sacrifice the income, which amounted to 25 percent of the total tax, in favor of leaving current local and regional tax structures in place.[43]

Yet, the benefits that accrued to textile industrialists as a result of these links with the regional government had limits due to what Alan Knight terms the Janus face of institutionalized caciquismo under the ruling party. Regional leaders could soften potential points of conflict between industrialists and the federal government. But as part of the official political structure, they ultimately were bound by the ruling party. Admittedly, this mediatory position was not new, in that caciques almost by definition had historically derived their power by operating as "link-men" between those above and below them.[44] What was new, however, was the shift away from civic society toward the institutions of the state in legitimizing and sustaining *cacical* authority. With caciques beholden to a powerful ruling party and facing an increasingly interventionist state, their ability to represent the interests of their supporters below them was limited, though the sheer nature of caciquismo necessitated that they continue to have some ability to guarantee patronage to their followers. This was perhaps even truer of Maximino Ávila Camacho, whose rise to governor was dependent, possibly more than most, on the favor granted him by President Cárdenas and the ruling party and whose style of rule favored often illegal intervention in local politics over building popular legitimacy.[45]

Puebla's textile industrialists also continued to struggle because of their mercurial relationship with industrialists from other regions, as seen earlier in this chapter in the 1925–27 collective contract negotiations. The industrialists from Puebla had often cooperated with other business organizations,

---

42. Junta de la Directiva, AETPT, meeting minutes, October 13, 1943, and January 19, 1944, CITPT, F-VI/LAJD-3.

43. Junta de la Directiva, AETPT, meeting minutes, January 7, 1944, CITPT, F-VI/LAJD-3.

44. Knight, "*Caciquismo* in Twentieth-Century Mexico," 18; Lomnitz-Adler, *Exits from the Labyrinth,* 297; Pansters, *Politics and Power,* 166; Cornelius, "Contemporary Mexico," 145–48. Paul Friedrich shows that not all cacicazgos in the middle of the twentieth century were equally institutionalized. Some agrarian caciques were not regularly active in the official party structure, though they did draw their legitimacy more from informal ties to ruling-party insiders than from their base, and at times, they would rotate into party politics. See Friedrich, "Legitimacy of a Cacique."

45. Henderson and LaFrance, "Maximino Ávila Camacho," 163–64.

even joining various national ones in their capacities as bankers or landowners. Moreover, some of Puebla's wealthiest textile industrialists entered into business ventures with entrepreneurs from other regions, including Jalisco, Veracruz, Mexico City, and Nuevo León. But when they tried to exert their influence at the national level, they often felt frustrated. For example, one of Puebla's most prominent industrialists, Jesús Rivero Quijano, was a founder of CONCAMIN and had served as its president. Yet, Puebla's industrialists left the organization on at least two occasions, including once in the early postrevolutionary period, when they received no leadership positions in the confederation and, later, when they felt CONCAMIN was not adequately representing their interests.[46] In October 1943, they also informed various government agencies, the National Association of Textile Industry Entrepreneurs, and the national textile chamber that the regional AETPT and the Puebla and Tlaxcala Chamber of the Textile Industry (Cámara de la Industria Textil de Puebla y Tlaxcala) would be handling all future matters pertaining to textile industrialists in Puebla because neither of the national textile organizations represented those interests.[47] Meanwhile, some industrialists and federal officials even considered the mere existence of the regional Puebla and Tlaxcala Chamber of the Textile Industry to be an affront to the national organization and the ruling party. The chamber had formed from the CIM in 1936, immediately following the promulgation of the Law on Chambers of Commerce and Industry, which the Cárdenas administration had implemented in order to organize all private interest groups into professional organizations that were tied to the state and preferably located in Mexico City. The factory owners in Puebla and Tlaxcala founded their chamber months before the creation of the national textile chamber in Mexico City, preempting the government's attempt to control regional industrialists. According to César Franco P., manager of the national textile chamber in the late 1930s, officials in the SEN were angered at what they considered to be a subversion of the spirit of the law, and they attempted to cajole, and later threaten, Puebla's industrialists to disband and join their counterparts in Mexico City in one large chamber.[48] In an affront to President Cárdenas, Puebla's owners refused.

Despite government concessions protecting the industry in the 1930s, Puebla's owners continued to rail against what they argued was bias against

---

46. Gamboa Ojeda, *El perfil organizativo*, 26–29; Aguirre Anaya, *El horizonte tecnológico de México*, 74–76.

47. Junta de la Directiva, AETPT, meeting minutes, October 13, 1943, CITPT, F-VI/LAJD-3; Asamblea General, AETPT, meeting minutes, December 10, 1949, CITPT, F-VI/LAAG-3.

48. César Franco P., Mexico City, pers. comm., May 12, 1998.

them. At times, they even attempted to circumvent laws meant to regulate the industry, even if they did not violate them outright. For example, in 1938, the federal government levied a new tax on the consumption of cotton in order to subsidize embattled cotton producers. Cotton prices had always been a key factor in determining textile-industry profitability. Government regulation of cotton prices and distribution therefore had long served as a means to manage levels of industry protection. At the same time, textile industrialists regularly complained about excessive taxation and expressed suspicion about the fiscal motives of the postrevolutionary state. Citing this, as well as what they asserted was the unconstitutionality of levying a tax on one industry to subsidize another, the industrialists protested the 1938 cotton tax. To assuage them and prove that the taxes would not just end up in federal coffers, Eduardo Suárez, secretary of the Treasury and Public Credit, proposed to deposit the taxes into an account in the Banco de México and give back any unused part in the form of a subsidy. In return, Suárez asked that industrialists refrain from interfering with the sale and pricing of cotton, and that they maintain normal consumption levels.[49] They agreed to the compromise, though it soon became irrelevant. During the war, cotton consumption increased dramatically, and the federal government repealed the tax.[50] The government initially returned a small amount of the tax revenue to the industrialists, but most of it remained out of reach. Finally, in February 1950, AETPT president Rafael Miranda informed the membership that a person, who insisted on remaining anonymous, was willing to recoup the money for an honorarium equivalent to 50 percent of the recovered funds. The members agreed to this.[51] In this case, textile industrialists resorted to clientelism to counter what they viewed to be institutional bias against their industry.

The industrialists felt that a spate of new taxes in the 1940s confirmed their suspicions of bias. For example, in 1943, the government implemented a new tax on cotton textiles produced on automatic machines. With this, the federal government sought to take advantage of the wartime textile-export boom in order to fund public works projects. Industrialists who produced for export predictably opposed the tax. They declared that the need for funds during the wartime emergency should not fall unfairly on their shoulders but rather on the textile industry more generally. To the further

---

49. "Iniciativa de ley que suprime el impuesto sobre el algodón," December 19, 1941, MAV/AGN, exp. 564.1/309.

50. Francisco Doria Paz, memorandum, January 20, 1947, MAV/AGN, exp. 151.3/241.

51. Asamblea General, AETPT, meeting minutes, February 22, 1950, CITPT, F-VI/LAAG-3.

consternation of industrialists, in 1944, the government launched a new tax on cotton consumption, which aimed to create a fund that would allow the government to stabilize erratic cotton prices.[52]

The postrevolutionary institutionalization of political representation and state-labor relations eroded the historic autonomy of Puebla's textile industrialists. Even though they had good relations with regional leaders, the new forms of caciquismo that evolved in the 1930s were often heavily dependent on the ruling-party machine, which limited what regional political leaders could do for the industry. A growing breach between Puebla's textile industrialists and the federal government over the state's role in industrial modernization also hindered any durable accord. In the 1930s, some government technocrats began to argue that textile industrialists held an ingrained bias against statist development. They added that cyclical crises in the industry, including overproduction, resulted partly from industrialist resistance to state regulation of production and consumption. According to these technocrats, postrevolutionary problems reflected "an interesting phenomenon of a lack of doctrinal adaptation [as demonstrated by] the conflict between the anachronistic liberal thesis supported by most [textile] industrialists and the progressive thesis of state interventionism connoted by a collective contract and a federal labor tribunal." Anticipating the clash between industrialists and the government that would come to a head in the late 1940s, one contemptuous economist observed, "The current crisis [of overproduction], like that of 1924 and 1928, . . . is a consequence of the stubbornness or lack of vision of [textile] industrialists and of an absurd rejection of an interventionist government."[53]

Boom and Bust in the 1940s

The economic fate of Mexico's textile industry followed a serpentine path through the 1940s, with the highs that accompanied the wartime boom followed by the lows that resulted from a postwar loss of foreign markets and the return of global competition at home. As the postwar crisis in traditional sectors of the cotton textile industry unfolded, the efforts of Puebla's textile industrialists to promote their interests at the national level foundered. Moreover, in a political climate that favored large-scale basic industries and modern consumer-manufacturing sectors, Puebla's industrialists

---

52. Camiro, "La industria textil," 62–65; Camiro, "Ponencia," 187–94.
53. M. T. de la Peña, *La industria textil,* 6–7, 20.

found that the accommodation that they had forged with the ruling party in the early 1930s appeared increasingly archaic.

During the 1940s, textiles remained one of the largest industries in the country. Nationally, it was second only to foodstuffs in terms of the value of its production, and it was first in the manufacturing sector.[54] The growth of wartime markets was largely responsible for the industry's buoyancy during the first part of the decade. As the U.S., Japanese, French, and British governments channeled textiles toward the war effort, Mexican textile manufactures expanded to replace imports, as well as to penetrate markets in Central and South America abandoned by the United States. Between 1942 and 1945, 15 percent to 20 percent of Mexican cotton-textile production was exported to Central and South America.[55] The volume of Mexico's textile exports grew from Mex$5,771,000 in 1941 to Mex$51,455,000 in 1945 (values at constant 1937 prices).[56] Though cotton textiles experienced among the highest rates of growth, almost all types of textile production increased during the war.[57] However, the textile industry suffered a contraction in the volume of its exports after the war, as the United States and Japan recaptured international markets with high-quality, low-priced cloth. By 1948, the volume of textile exports had dropped to Mex$25,942,000 (values at constant 1937 prices).[58] The textile industry suffered relative stagnation compared to other industries in Mexico as well. According to census statistics, the percentage of textile establishments as a part of the total of national industries declined from 8.2 percent to 6.8 percent between 1945 and 1950, while the number of workers in the industry dropped from about 29 percent to slightly more than 21 percent of total industrial workers in Mexico.[59] Even with a brief reprieve during the Korean War, the relative decline continued into the 1950s. Between 1940 and 1955, the value of textile production as a portion of national manufacturing dropped from approximately 30 percent to about 18.5 percent. In 1955, the construction industry surpassed textiles for the first time.[60] The size of the cotton textile

---

54. Cárdenas, *La hacienda pública,* appendices A.5 and A.6; Arroio, "El proceso de industrialización," 104, 106–8; "La mayor industria en México es la de hilados y tejidos," *Novedades,* January 2, 1946.

55. Gamboa Ojeda, "Los últimos años de predominio," 306.

56. CEPAL, "El desarrollo económico de México," 138.

57. SEN, Oficina de Barómetros Económicos, *El desarrollo de la economía,* 50–51.

58. CEPAL, "El desarrollo económico de México," 138.

59. "Informe sobre la situación actual de las diversas industrias de transformación de México: Política nacional al respecto, problemas más importantes y los medios empleados o que se intenta emplear para resolverlos," 1947, GR/AGN, c. 77, exp. 1; Sr. Garfias to Manuel Gómez Morin, August 1, 1944, AMGM, v. 232, exp. 743; Arroio, "El proceso de industrialización," 104, 106–8.

60. INEGI, *Estadísticas históricas de México,* 2:498.

workforce contracted in absolute terms as well, from 42,026 workers in 1940 to 32,847 in 1957.[61]

Puebla, in particular, was hard-hit by the postwar slump, since textiles were central to the state's economy. In 1937, Puebla had ninety-nine cotton textile factories, which generated approximately 30 percent of the nation's textiles.[62] Puebla's dependence on textiles deepened with the industry's wartime expansion, as the number of cotton textile factories grew to 109.[63] After the war, textiles slipped from providing about 69 percent of Puebla's total industrial production in 1945 to just below 49 percent in 1950, though the Korean War brought a temporary rebound to almost 66 percent in 1955.[64] In that year, Puebla still produced about one-third of the total national production value of cotton textiles, though, as seen, the importance of textiles to the national economy was diminishing by that time.[65] This dominance therefore did little to help the state. From 1945 to 1950, while the national manufacturing industry grew by 14.4 percent, in Puebla it grew by just 1.5 percent. It slowed even further between 1950 and 1955, when it grew by less than 1 percent. Significantly, during these years, the Estado de México, Coahuila, and Jalisco surpassed Puebla in terms of their contributions to national industry.[66]

Industrialists and unions joined to confront the Alemán administration about how it was meeting the industry's postwar problems. They were especially troubled by a crisis of overproduction and sinking prices, as cloth was increasingly being stockpiled in warehouses.[67] They contended that problems with primary materials, high taxes, and rising food prices were undermining production, profitability, and sales.[68] Underconsumption became a core complaint, since most industrialists relied on national or local

---

61. SEN, Dirección General de Estadística, *Compendio estadístico*, 344–45; Barajas Manzano, *Aspectos de la industria*, 26. Because of the war, the size of the workforce had climbed to 55,811 by 1946, but it soon began a precipitous decline.

62. SEN, Dirección General de Estadística, *Segundo censo industrial 1935*, vol. 3, book 1, *Hilados y tejidos de algodón*, 24; Pruneda R., "La industria textil," 68–69; Gamboa Ojeda, "El mundo empresarial," 504–5.

63. Secretaría de Economía, Dirección General de Estadística, *Cuarto censo industrial*, 227.

64. Estrada Urroz, "El poder de compra," 355.

65. López Malo, *Ensayo sobre localización*, 112.

66. Pansters, *Politics and Power*, 89.

67. Antonio Ruiz Galindo to Alemán, memorandum, September 10, 1947, MAV/AGN, exp. 433/133; Gamboa Ojeda, "Los últimos años de predominio," 310.

68. Asociación Nacional de Empresarios de la Industria Textil de la Seda, Artisela, y Derivados to Alemán, telegram, March 9, 1950, MAV/AGN, exp. 111/6327; Consejo Nacional de Empresarios de la Industria Textil, memorandums, September 21, 1949, MAV/AGN, exp. 151.3/241; Consejo Nacional de Empresarios de la Industria Textil to Alemán, telegram, December 30, 1948, MAV/AGN, exp. 545.22/239; Casimiro Jean, presidente de la Cámara Textil de México to Alemán,

markets to sell their goods. These included *manta,* or the plain white cotton cloth used in campesino clothing, and *mezclilla,* the coarse blue cotton cloth that went into workers' overalls and other clothing. Both of these types of cloth were usually manufactured by older, traditional factories, such as those that predominated in Puebla.[69]

The response of the Alemán administration to postwar crisis in the industry was erratic. Policies enacted to assist the industry at times seemed poorly conceived or even contradictory. Textile manufacturers had lauded President Ávila Camacho's administration for holding tariff protection steady in the 1942 Reciprocal Trade Agreement with the United States. And they backed the Alemán government when it arranged with cotton producers to guarantee supplies to the domestic textile industry before exporting any surplus.[70] But protection and financing for much of the industry became increasingly uneven during the late 1940s. For instance, in 1947, the Alemán administration put in place a new tariff schedule to protect national industry. However, its effectiveness was diluted by the 1948–49 peso devaluation, the rapid expansion of trade quotas, and the government's new reliance on an official price list to assess tariffs at a time when prices were increasing.[71] In another example, in an attempt to hold onto export markets and reduce stockpiles, in June 1947, the federal government exempted cotton textiles from some export taxes (specifically, the Tarifa del Impuesto de Exportación). Yet, when some export-oriented industrialists lobbied for additional export quotas and for a lowering of other export taxes, they were largely frustrated.[72] In response to their complaints about the rising tax burden, the federal government stated only that in real terms, total taxes for the industry had not risen during the late 1940s.[73]

---

telegram, December 30, 1948, MAV/AGN, exp. 545.22/239; Asamblea General, AETPT, meeting minutes, December 28, 1948, February 10, 1949, November 7, 1949, December 22, 1949, and February 22, 1950, CITPT, F-VI/LAAG-3; "La industria textil fija su posición actual frente a los problemas nacionales," *Excélsior,* September 26, 1948.

69. Consejo Nacional de Empresarios de la Industria Textil to Alemán, August 20, 1951, MAV/AGN, exp. 511/2675; Unión de Empresarios de la Industria Textil de Lana, memorandum, January 13, 1949, MAV/AGN, exp. 545.22/239.

70. Antonio Ruiz Galindo to Alemán, May 7, 1948, MAV/AGN, exp. 705.2/1; Confederación Nacional de Productores Agrícolas to Alemán, May 8, 1948, MAV/AGN, exp. 705.2/1; AETPT and labor unions to Alemán, May 5, 1948, and May 6, 1948, MAV/AGN, exp. 705.2/1; Asamblea General, AETPT, meeting minutes, April 28, 1948, CITPT, F-VI/LAAG-3.

71. Gómez Galvarriato, "Political Economy of Protectionism," 395.

72. See various textile unions and employers organizations to Alemán, January 1947, MAV/AGN, exp. 564.2/12; Asamblea General, AETPT, meeting minutes, March 17, 1947, CITPT, F-VI/LAAG-3; Antonio Ruiz Galindo to Alemán, September 10, 1947, MAV/AGN, exp. 433/133.

73. Secretario Particular Rogerio de la Selva to Alemán, January 3, 1948, MAV/AGN, exp. 545.22/239.

The Ávila Camacho and Alemán administrations were cognizant of the textile industry's continuing prominence in the national economy. But during the 1940s, politicians and technocrats were intent on industrial modernization, and thus, they focused on developing basic industry and large-scale and modern consumer manufacturing. They favored modern industry in part because the postwar economic and loan situation limited the available resources for capitalizing industrial development, which narrowed their options. However, other factors also intervened that explain their focus on modern industry. Many of their decisions were derived from a desire to protect sources of labor in order to ensure social peace. Moreover, especially under the Alemán administration, the owners of modern and larger factories were better able to leverage their political or personal influence to garner government aid and assistance. In the textile sector, the intersection of these factors meant that the government tended to provide financing and protection to industries that produced artificial fibers, as well as to large-scale producers, especially those that used modern technologies. Celanese Mexicana is a prime example of this, since it was among the top six recipients of federal aid under President Ávila Camacho and regularly received tax exemptions and other protection in the 1940s and 1950s.[74] By contrast, the traditional, small- and medium-sized factories that dominated Puebla's textile industry received little that was new.

Deus ex Machina: The Modernization of Labor-Employer Relations

The subdued response of the Alemán administration to the postwar crisis in traditional sectors of the industry heightened resentments among Puebla's textile industrialists about the loss of authority in their factories and communities. With most political avenues blocked, Puebla's textile industrialists turned to investing in new technology as a means both to force a renegotiation of collective contracts, which would undermine unions and diminish state authority within their factories, and to counter the effects of their economic exclusion. Their goal, therefore, was not just to improve efficiency, as they alleged, but also to weaken the corporatist labor relations that were responsible for undercutting traditional labor regimes in the region.

The cotton textile industry was an older industry equipped with antiquated machinery and plagued by technical and administrative inefficiency.

74. Banco de México, Departamento de Investigaciones Industriales, *Directorio de empresas industriales*; Cue Cánovas, "Economía de emergencia," 309.

By 1942, about three-fourths of the looms used in Mexico had been installed before the Revolution; in 1935, only 1 percent of active looms in the country was automatic.[75] Around that time, in Puebla, approximately 69 percent of the textile carding machines (*cardas*), close to one-half of warping machines (*estiradores*), and about 70 percent of its looms (*telares*) had been manufactured before the Revolution.[76] In fact, the most modern machinery being used in textile factories in Mexico in the 1940s had originally been used in French factories in the 1920s.[77] This is not surprising, considering the global economic downturn in the textile industry that began in the late 1920s, as well as the high protection put in place in the aftermath of the 1925–27 contract negotiations. Factory-visit reports produced by the Banco de México in 1945 supported these data about machinery. They found that even at some of Puebla's most competitive factories, such as El Molino de Enmedio and El Mayorazgo, the machinery dated to the mid-1920s. Even at the renowned Metepec factory, in Atlixco, Puebla, the Banco de México reported that most of the machines were of English origin dating from 1900–1902, which required great care by operators to keep them working. The report concluded that the biggest challenge facing industrialists remained the modernization of machinery, work processes, and factory conditions.[78] Industrialist Aurelio Lobatón added that the repair of machinery with domestically produced, non-original parts during World War II sped its deterioration.[79]

Textile industrialists in Puebla had a sporadic history with investing in factory upgrades, spending instead on luxuries or on investments in land,

---

75. Gamboa Ojeda, "Los últimos años de predominio," 307. A study conducted by NAFINSA concluded that roughly 60 percent of the cotton textile factories that responded to its questionnaire were old factories with machinery that had been in use for more than twenty-five years whereas 14 percent of responding factories were modern or semi-modern. Lacking precise definitions for those terms and information about the origins of the machinery, these statistics can only be rough guides. OII, "Respuestas al 'Cuestionario sobre la industria textil' enviado por la Nacional Financiera," February 27, 1951, GR/AGN, c. 76, exp. 8. A study commissioned by the SHCP added that although there had been investment in machinery between 1935 and 1939, little went for labor-saving equipment because labor unions had pressured against that to protect jobs. Pruneda R., "La industria textil," 75–80.

76. Barajas Manzano, *Aspectos de la industria*, 54, 59, 153, 155, 172. Percentages are not exact since the data include a small amount of machinery whose date of manufacture is unlisted.

77. Gamboa Ojeda, "El mundo empresarial," 505; César Franco P., Mexico City, pers. comm., May 12, 1998.

78. Report of visits by Máximo Ramírez I., Banco de México to Textiles El Molino de Enmedio, Puebla, December 13, 1945, to El Mayorazgo, Puebla, December 14, 1945, and to Textiles Metepec, Atlixco, December 11, 1945, GR/AGN, c. 75, exp. 5. For industrialist Jesús Rivero Quijano's account of the spirit of modernization that drove the desire for new machinery at El Molino de Enmedio in 1927, see Rivero Quijano, *La revolución industrial*, 2:419.

79. Aurelio Lobatón, "Modernización de la industria textil," October 4, 1943, GR/AGN, c. 75, exp. 6.

banking, or real estate.⁸⁰ Many therefore relied on their control of a cheap, dependent labor force, as well as tariffs and supply controls, to ensure profits. OII employee Víctor Urquidi cautioned against overemphasizing the impact of protectionist policies on slowing investment in machinery, however. Many foreign textiles had no equivalent Mexican product, whereas some Mexican textiles at the heart of the industry had no foreign competition. This included manta and mezclilla, the former of which constituted roughly one-third of cotton textile consumption in Mexico through the 1930s. According to Urquidi, the lack of foreign competition for some types of cloth likely played a larger role in deterring investment in machinery, since it minimized the impact of tariffs and helped to guarantee markets.⁸¹ Guaranteed domestic and international markets for Mexican textiles during World War II, regardless of quality or cost, further reduced incentives to invest in new technology or other types of factory modernization. The average annual investment in textile machinery in Mexico between 1939 and 1944 was about Mex$5 million, a period during which total annual output for the industry rose from Mex$258 million to Mex$604 million.⁸²

During the war, a small group of prominent textile industrialists in Puebla and Veracruz was concerned about the industry's backwardness.⁸³ They predicted that demand for their textiles would dry up once the United States and Japan reentered international markets after the war. To preempt a crisis in the industry, they began to press the federal government to facilitate the importation of machinery that they hoped might be available in the United States after the war. They argued that modern machinery would allow them to attain new levels of productivity and efficiency characterized by higher profits, salaries, and quality, as well as lower costs and prices.⁸⁴

Yet, they did this with little recognition of the possible problems and pitfalls associated with importing new machinery. First, the late Porfirian experience of the Compañía Industrial Veracruzana suggests that machinery upgrades did not always lead to increased profits. The cost savings from introducing new machinery for U.S. and British firms were offset in Mexico by cheap labor, rigid wage schedules, high costs for technical support, and

---

80. Gamboa Ojeda, "El mundo empresarial," 505.
81. Víctor Urquidi, "Mexican Industry, a Descriptive Survey—Its Recent Evolution," January 1943, GR/AGN, c. 23 exp. 17 and c. 22, exp. 54, p. 9; Pruneda R., "La industria textil," 10–13.
82. King, *Mexico: Industrialization and Trade*, 23–24.
83. Banco de México interview with Lucien Dubois and Marcelino Sors (Río Blanco, Veracruz) and José Rivero Quijano (Atoyac Textil and Almacenes Textiles, Puebla), February–March 1942, GR/AGN, c. 75, exp. 4.
84. Robredo, "Cuarta ponencia"; Aurelio Lobatón, "Modernización de la industria textil," October 4, 1943, GR/AGN, c. 75, exp. 6.

high transportation costs.⁸⁵ By the 1940s, labor conditions and technical support had changed significantly, but industrialists advocated investing in new machinery without any clear sense of its potential impact on efficiency. Second, there was little indication that the United States would allow machinery exports to Mexico after the war. Industrialists understood that during the early 1940s, machinery was funneled to the war effort, but many were caught by surprise when, amid efforts to recapture postwar markets, the United States resisted shipping machinery abroad in the late 1940s. Third, even as some industrialists argued for new technologies, others contended that a lack of capital impeded their ability to invest in it. Some large-scale industrialists had business connections that let them attract investors, or they had mills that were part of joint-stock companies through which they could raise capital. Many others, however, maintained that they did not have access to the needed funds.⁸⁶ Confirming this, advisors like lawyer Manuel Gómez Morín counseled their business clients that poor factory conditions in the textile industry in the 1940s made investment risky.⁸⁷

The failure of textile industrialists to fully recognize these problems may have been real and a result of having been cosseted by tariffs and political support for so long. But it also may simply have been a political maneuver by industrialists in their negotiations with labor and the state. In either case, discussions over modern machinery revived divisions within the industry between large-scale, modern producers and smaller, more traditional manufacturers. The president of Puebla's AETPT underscored these differences when he noted the especially heavy financial burden that Puebla's producers faced when considering the modernization of their overwhelmingly outdated factories.⁸⁸ Although the owners of larger, more modern factories tended to speak out in support of new machinery, there was a tension among traditional industrialists between their assertions that they lacked the

---

85. Gómez Galvarriato, "Impact of Revolution," 154–57, 171; Gómez Galvarriato, "Political Economy of Protectionism," 390–91.

86. "Es lo que requiere ahora la industria textil de México," *La Opinión*, November 12, 1954. Some businesspeople may have had the capital, but preferred to invest in other ventures while relying on traditional textile business practices that included the use of older machinery, collective contracts, and government protection to keep their factories afloat.

87. Consejo de Administración, Atoyac Textil, S.A. and Manuel Gómez Morín, correspondence, September–October 1944, AMGM, v. 313, exp. 1093 and v. 312, exp. 1089; Sr. Garfias to Manuel Gómez Morín, August 1, 1944, AMGM, v. 232, exp. 743; Héctor Argüero Ramírez (Departamento de Inspección, STPS) to Ávila Camacho, study, August 4, 1944, MAC/AGN, exp. 523/116.

88. "Esta será provocada por el problema de la modernización de la maquinaria," *La Opinión*, March 8, 1947.

capital to modernize and their demands that collective contracts be renegotiated in anticipation of the arrival of new machinery. The most recent round of collective contract negotiations, from 1937 to 1939, had preserved regional wage disparities, much to the frustration of President Cárdenas and the large-scale, modern producers. During the contract discussions, labor leaders had joined with small-scale industrialists to reject automatic looms, in the former's case because they felt it would jeopardize jobs.[89] But Puebla's owners still cited collective contracts and the privileges they conferred on state-backed unions as the cause of crisis and inefficiency in the industry.[90] This was despite the presence of evidence indicating that worker productivity actually improved in the years after the collective contract of 1925–27.[91] Nevertheless, employers insisted that collective contracts and union control of the shop floor were to blame for frequent production interruptions and for the disequilibrium between production and consumption, since contracts limited the ability of employers to respond to changes in industry conditions.[92] Both employers and workers recognized that contracts narrowed their range of options for responding to crises, for example, by making salary adjustments impossible.[93] Employers also contended that collective contracts forced them to employ surplus workers, and protected workers who were uneducated, could not operate machinery, lacked a work ethic, and had a tendency to show up to work drunk or not show up at all on "Saint Monday" due to weekend revelry.[94] Prominent industrialist José Rivero Quijano exaggerated that only eighteen thousand out of the forty thousand workers in the industry were necessary.[95]

In the mid-1940s, the growing interest in machinery modernization as a salvation for the industry gave industrialists new fuel in their struggles to

---

89. Bortz, "Genesis," 62, 67.

90. Pruneda R., "La industria textil," 60–61; M. T. de la Peña, *La industria textil*, 26–27, 36. Protection for small-scale producers remained in place until 1951, after which it underwent only slight changes until 1972. Gómez Galvarriato, "Impact of Revolution," 625; Gómez Galvarriato, "Political Economy of Protectionism," 402.

91. SEN, Departamento de Estudios Económicos, *La industria textil en México*, 138–39, 268–69.

92. Reports of visits by Máximo Ramírez I., Banco de México, to Textiles El Volcán and Textiles El León, December 1945, GR/AGN, c. 75, exp. 5.

93. "La industria textil en peligro de paralizarse," *La Prensa*, August 20, 1940; "Las pláticas en el problema de las fábricas de hilados," *El Nacional*, August 20, 1940; Consejo Nacional de Empresarios de la Industria Textil to Alemán, August 20, 1951, MAV/AGN, exp. 511/2675.

94. Reports of visits by the Banco de México to Textil Algodón La Unión, S.A., to Textil Algodón El Rosario, to Textiles de Lana, and to Hilados y Tejidos de Lana Manchester, S. de R.L., all in Puebla, February 1945, GR/AGN, c. 76, exp. 13; reports of visits to Textiles El León and to Textiles El Volcán in Atlixco, December 1945, and to Fábrica de Tejidos de Artisela San Pablo in Tlaxcala, February 1946, GR/AGN, c. 75, exp. 5. See also Robredo, "Cuarta ponencia."

95. Banco de México interview with José Rivero Quijano, March 5, 1942, GR/AGN, c. 75, exp. 4.

renegotiate contracts, since the current collective contracts would have made it prohibitively expensive.[96] Collective contracts mandated pay scales based on piecework for skilled labor. This meant that if workers operated more machines or produced more during their shifts, their salaries could grow to unsustainable levels.[97] Therefore, as the postwar crisis unfolded, employers demanded a renegotiation of collective contracts, which would allow them to install new machinery while holding salaries steady and dismissing a portion of their workers. They used this as an opportunity, as well, to argue that any contract revision should enable employers to move workers between jobs at the management's discretion rather than at the union's.[98] ECLA supported the employers, as did the Armour Research Foundation, which the Banco de México had hired to do an industry study. The foundation concluded that collective contracts would force employers to carry anywhere from 20 percent to 50 percent excess labor were modern machinery to be introduced. It also blamed powerful labor organizations for the industry's inefficiency, stating, "Fearing that new automatic equipment would displace men, [unions] have resisted the installation of modern machinery . . . fiercely."[99] Indeed, when some factory owners, including of the Compañía Industrial Veracruzana and Compañía Atoyac Textil in Puebla, had tried to introduce automatic machinery in the early 1920s, the CROM had turned to violence, intimidation, and even murder to prevent it.[100]

Union opposition to industry modernization remained strong during the mid-1940s. Labor leaders almost universally argued against employers' proposals for industry modernization, instead giving precedence to the protection of worker authority and jobs.[101] Unions therefore fought the renegotiation of wage rates in collective contracts that were necessary to

96. Banco de México interviews with Lucien Dubois, Marcelino Sors, and José Rivero Quijano, February–March 1942, GR/AGN, c. 75, exp. 4.
97. Aurelio Lobatón, "Modernización de la industria textil," October 4, 1943, GR/AGN, c. 75, exp. 6; Camiro, "La industria textil," 67–68; M. T. de la Peña, *La industria textil*, 37–38.
98. "Resoluciones y acuerdos," in *Memoria de la Primera Convención*.
99. Godwin, Nelson, and Villaseñor, *Technological Audit*, 79. See also CEPAL, "El desarrollo económico de México," 167–71.
100. Gómez Galvarriato, "Political Economy of Protectionism," 389–90.
101. CTM to Alemán, May 25, 1949, MAV/AGN, exp. 111/4010; Héctor Argüero Ramírez (Departamento de Inspección, STPS) to Ávila Camacho, study, August 4, 1944, MAC/AGN, exp. 523/116; "Problemas de la industria textil," *Germinal*, July 24, 1943; Fidel Velázquez, Blas Chumacero, and Sindicato de Trabajadores de la Industria Textil y Similares de la República Mexicana to Ávila Camacho, November 30, 1944, MAC/AGN, exp. 523/116; report of visit by Máximo Ramírez I., Banco de México, to Textiles Metepec, December 11, 1945, GR/AGN, c. 75, exp. 5; "Sobrevendrá un desastre en la industria textil," *Novedades*, November 29, 1943; "Temen que desplace la nueva maquinaria a numerosos obreros," *El Nacional*, December 13, 1944; Camiro, "La industria textil," 68–69.

make investment in new machinery economically feasible. The workforce had already been put on the defensive during World War II due to declining real wages, production halts, and scarcities, all of which fostered deep resentments and fears of layoffs. In conjunction with a loss of markets, postwar scarcities of primary materials and electric energy exacerbated worker insecurity. Inflationary pressures caused in part by a mounting trade deficit and the 1948–49 peso devaluation compounded anxieties by imperiling already declining living standards. This was especially significant in the cotton textile industry, where real wages dropped faster than the overall average for manufacturing between 1940 and 1950.[102] Factory paralyzations and pressure for machinery imports after World War II only worsened workers' perceptions that their jobs were threatened. In 1946, *El Sol de Puebla* estimated that the labor force had decreased by approximately 50 percent since the end of the war. Census sources indicated that the decline was much smaller, with the textile workforce dropping from 21,357 laborers in 1945 to 20,857 in 1950.[103] Though the census statistics are certainly more accurate, the public perception that extensive shutdowns and layoffs loomed was more important in shaping labor politics, including the position of union leaders regarding new machinery.[104] A typical reaction came from workers at the textile factory La Luz, who asked their union to pressure the government to act to avoid a postwar unemployment disaster for textile workers.[105] Others were more proactive, as in the case of one youth from Atlixco, Puebla. Fearing unemployment, he wrote to the Secretariat of the Economy to request information about commercial activities he could pursue, stating that he and his friends realized that they no longer could count on one day getting a textile job, as so many had in the past.[106] Perhaps inadvertently, employers supported labor's contention that investment in new machinery would lead to unemployment when, in 1947, they argued that workers displaced by new machinery could be compensated by Social Security.[107]

102. Estrada Urroz, "El poder de compra," 353–57; Barajas Manzano, *Aspectos de la industria*, 31.
103. Estrada Urroz, *Del telar*, 24–25.
104. CTM to Alemán, May 25, 1949, MAV/AGN, exp. 111/4010.
105. "Sobrevendrá un desastre en la industria textil," *Novedades*, November 29, 1943. See also "El maquinismo en la Fábrica de Xaltepec provoca un problema," *La Opinión*, May 22, 1949; "Consejo Nacional de Textiles," *La Opinión*, July 2, 1950.
106. Guadalupe Mino to Departamento de Industria y Comercio en General, SEN, June 30, 1947, DGI/AGN, v. 26, exp. 24/300 (03)/-1–15, letra M.
107. Comisión Mixta Especial de Modernización de la Industria Textil del Algodón y sus Mixturas to STPS, letter and report, August 15, 1947, Instituto de Investigaciones Dr. José María Luis Mora (IM).

Beyond the protection of workers' jobs, labor leaders also deployed technical arguments to question employers' motives for seeking modern machinery. According to CTM leaders Fidel Velázquez and Blas Chumacero, labor's opposition to a revision of the collective contract was not based on a desire to earn excessively high salaries or protect union authority. Rather, workers were in opposition because employers had proposed a salary revision without even understanding the nature of the machinery they sought to import or its potential impact on the production process, productivity, and salaries. Velázquez and Chumacero added that employers were seeking salary adjustments based on the most modern machinery in use in highly industrialized countries, but their only knowledge about it came from sales catalogues. They concluded that industrialists' motives for seeking wage revisions therefore were suspect.[108]

By the end of the war, some labor unions did begin to tentatively support the idea of industry modernization, and they joined with employers to study the issue.[109] The first step was the formation of a joint labor-employer commission, the Special Joint Commission on the Modernization of the Cotton and Cotton Blends Textile Industry (Comisión Mixta Especial de Modernización de la Industria Textil del Algodón y sus Mixturas). The joint commission visited textile factories in the United States to study industry modernization. On their return, however, workers and employers failed to arrive at any joint recommendations. They even disagreed about whether they had a right to make recommendations, with employers supporting the idea and labor opposing it.[110] During that same period, they joined in the Arbitration Commission (Comisión Arbitral), formed in 1946 at the Joint Review Convention for the Cotton Textile Industry (Convención Mixta Revisora de la Industria Textil del Algodón). The goal of the commission was to negotiate a mutually acceptable salary revision that might make machinery modernization viable.[111] Instead of resolution, however, a four-year conflict ensued, during which each side insisted that the other was sabotaging the commission. Labor accused industrialists of exaggerating crises in

108. Fidel Velázquez, Blas Chumacero, and Sindicato de Trabajadores de la Industria Textil y Similares de la República Mexicana to Ávila Camacho, November 30, 1944, MAC/AGN, 523/116.

109. "Acuerdo de las partes para lograr modernizar la industria textil," *El Nacional,* November 16, 1949.

110. Comisión Mixta Especial de Modernización de la Industria Textil del Algodón y sus Mixturas to STPS, August 15, 1947, IM; "Salió de México la Comisión Obrera de la Industria Textil," *Germinal,* September 21, 1946; "Dictamen que formula la Comisión Técnica Textil Mexicana," 32–34.

111. Asamblea General, AETPT, meeting minutes, November 3, 1948, CITPT, F-VI/LAAG-3.

the industry in order to gain salary reductions and impose productivity goals that exceeded even those in more highly industrialized countries. In response, a group of industrialists accused the STPS of intervening to encourage workers to avoid the commission, though other industrialists recognized that owner obstruction of the commission was equally problematic.[112] In the aftermath of these failed negotiations, industrialists from across Mexico united to form the National Council of Textile Industry Entrepreneurs (Consejo Nacional de Empresarios de la Industria Textil).

However, as some labor leaders in the cotton textile industry began to collaborate in studying the possibilities for new machinery in the mid-1940s, they found themselves in a tenuous position. Amid the fierce labor struggles that persisted between the CROM, the CTM, and the FROC in the industry, they were careful not to appear soft on modernization for fear that they might lose adherents. As part of this battle, they sought to protect their legally conferred powers over the production process and workforce. Therefore, they contested what they argued was a desire among employers to pursue modernization in order to weaken unions and reassert a more direct, paternal relationship between management and individual workers. As evidence, they pointed to employers' insistence that modern machinery necessitated giving owners rights over hiring and firing and the distribution of personnel, as well as access to a more flexible salary schedule.[113] In this light, labor leaders opposed investing in new machinery because its impact on jobs would threaten their authority by shrinking their membership base and by deskilling previously skilled jobs.[114] The resulting labor surplus and job uncertainty would further impede their attempts to build worker unity within unions. Moreover, since unions had won the contractual right to maintain the size of the textile workforce, any decline signified a loss of union position both in relation to the state and to labor.

The introduction of more modern machinery would have admitted a new factor into contract negotiations over job skills and the wage rates

---

112. Coalición Nacional Obrera de la Industria Textil to Alemán, May 5, 1949, and July 13, 1948, MAV/AGN, exp. 111/4010; "La actitud patronal disgusta a los trabajadores del ramo de textiles," *El Nacional*, June 14, 1950; Consejo Nacional de Empresarios de la Industria Textil to Alemán, May 6, 1948, MAV/AGN, exp. 111/4010; "Memorándum sobre modernización de la industria textil del algodón, para el Señor Presidente de la República," September 21, 1949, MAV/AGN, exp. 151.3/241; "El problema de la modernización textil," *Excélsior*, September 13, 1950.

113. "Dictamen que formula la Comisión Técnica Textil Mexicana," 32; Comisión Mixta Especial de Modernización de la Industria Textil del Algodón y sus Mixturas to STPS, letter and report, August 15, 1947, IM.

114. Federación de Trabajadores de la Region de Orizaba to Alemán, January 21, 1949, MAV/AGN, 111/4010; Sindicato de Obreros Progresistas de La Estrella, Parras de la Fuente, Coahuila to Alemán, August 4, 1949, DGI/AGN, v. 130, 391/332.1/-28.

attached to them. It therefore would potentially undermine the power that union leaders had attained in determining the wage schedule. The contract for the cotton textile industry contained hundreds of distinct wage rates based on highly technical arguments about job skills, primary materials, and knowledge of the old machinery, each of which resulted from extensive wrangling between employers and labor leaders during the negotiations. Only a few people understood the technical aspects of these jobs, and these were mostly union leaders who were able to draw on the knowledge of their members during wage talks. For example, during contract negotiations in the late 1930s, labor leader Martín Torres took command of the discussion over wages for the different jobs. Employers had little to offer in return, and, worn down by Torres's knowledgeable and extensive arguments, they gave up in frustration.[115] Union leaders therefore understood that linking wage rates to the productivity of the new machinery, as opposed to skills defined by union bosses, would inevitably diminish the forms of knowledge that ensured their authority.[116] Additionally, it would usurp the ability of the state to intervene in contract negotiations between workers and employers.

Unions argued that employers also sought to invest in new machinery in order to undercut the authority that workers had over the production process. Historically, worker knowledge of and power over their machines in Mexico's antiquated cotton textile industry were integral to the working class's success in negotiating managerial authority. Yet, as David Montgomery has argued, allowing machines to define the production process would shift the knowledge and authority over the factory floor from union leaders to management.[117] According to unions, machinery catalogues, and even industrialists themselves, modern machinery would turn workers into specialized machine operators who understood little about the production process. But, as one government study reported, workers knew very well that most employers had very little appreciation for the complexity of work processes and therefore were ill-prepared to administer them in a more rational or modern way.[118] Labor leaders capitalized on this to seek governmental support in their negotiations with industrialists over the introduction of more modern machinery. For instance, the CTM stated that since industrialists were motivated only by profit, allowing them to control more facets

115. Bortz, "Genesis," 57; Bortz, "Legal and Contractual Limits," 281.
116. On managerial control and knowledge of work processes, see Braverman, *Labor and Monopoly Capital*, 109–18.
117. Montgomery, *Fall of the House of Labor*, 44–46, chapter 3.
118. Miguel Quintana and Fernando Pruneda, "Estudio sobre la modernización de la industria nacional textil del algodón para la Comisión Federal de Planificación Económica," April 27, 1943, GR/AGN, c. 76, exp. 9, pp. 89–90.

of the production process would lead to poor management and exacerbate inefficiency in the industry. In contrast, the organization lauded its workers for putting production ahead of labor demands during the war, despite poor working conditions and bad management. As a solution, the CTM recommended that modernization be grounded in improved technical and administrative processes, and occur under the guidance of a tripartite commission that included the state.[119]

No doubt inspired by Taylorism and the promises of scientific management to expand the power of management over production, some employers dabbled with the idea of reclassifying job functions based on the results of detailed time and productivity analyses.[120] Although some also touched on industrial hygiene programs that coupled new work processes with better social services and working conditions, most employers were more attracted by what industrial rationalization could mean in terms of restraining unions.[121] Detailed time and motion studies would enable them to appropriate knowledge about the production process from workers who had gained it over generations of work with the old machinery.[122] This not only would hurt union authority, but it would also address perceived problems of worker commitment and initiative. As David Montgomery claims for the U.S. context, managers assumed that these studies would lead to a worker who was "so carefully instructed and supervised, it would no longer be necessary for him to possess a broad understanding of the processes in which he was engaged."[123] Each production process could be overseen by one skilled worker, who then would assign tasks to a group of unskilled laborers who had little autonomy over or mental engagement with their work.[124] Thus, employer efforts to invest in new machinery constituted a serious assault on the knowledge and authority of union leaders and would subvert union solidarity by increasing distinctions between skilled and unskilled labor.

119. Fidel Velázquez, Blas Chumacero, and Sindicato de Trabajadores de la Industria Textil y Similares de la República Mexicana to Ávila Camacho, November 30, 1944, MAC/AGN, 523/116, pp. 6–7, 13–15.
120. For a classic Marxist analysis of the role of Taylorism in expanding managerial control over labor, see Braverman, *Labor and Monopoly Capital*, 87–107. Similarly, Daniel James examines the use of rationalization by Argentine factory owners as part of an effort to transform the "balance of forces" in factories. James, "Rationalisation and Working Class Response," 375–402. See also Farnsworth-Alvear, *Dulcinea in the Factory*.
121. For example, see Schmidhuber Martínez, "Plan general de higiene industrial."
122. Montgomery, *Workers' Control in America*, 115.
123. Montgomery, *Fall of the House of Labor*, 56, 223.
124. Braverman, *Labor and Monopoly Capital*, 113–18.

The reorganization of work processes according to the dictates of machinery or of time and motion studies would also undercut the social aspects of production that were central to union authority on the shop floor. Union leaders manipulated this to foster fears among the workforce about the introduction of new machinery. The Federation of Pueblan Workers (Federación de Trabajadores de Puebla, an affiliate of the CTM) inflamed sentiments against new technologies by comparing workers to modern machines. The union argued that the newer machines could do repetitive jobs consistently, perfectly, and without interruption, so they would soon displace many workers. This comparison between worker and machine also played on the relationship between labor control of the factory and mastery over the machinery. In a certain sense, Puebla's workers had attained skills with the old machinery after years of working with it, and they took pride in their ability to repair and cajole it in order to keep it producing.[125] The introduction of modern machinery would invert this relationship by making the machine the master of the workers and by increasing worker dependence on employers.

Unions proposed their own methods for modernizing work processes. Like employers, they focused on the technical use of primary materials, the rational organization of work, and even job specialization. However, better factory conditions and protections for workers were central to their proposals. Significantly, rather than allowing the new machinery to determine the pace of work, they would define productivity based on worker fatigue and include limits on the number and speed of machines. They added that changes should include minimum base salaries, extra pay for excess production, and salaries on a par with the workers' U.S. counterparts. Finally, workers displaced by machinery should have priority in getting other jobs in the industry or in receiving training in new fields, rather than being laid off and given Social Security, as industrialists proposed. If no job could be found, workers who were older than fifty years of age should receive their full pension, while those below fifty should receive 75 percent of their salary for six years.[126]

During the mid- to late 1940s, the agreement between employers, unions, and the state that had protected jobs and profits at the expense of

---

125. On the union's comparison of machinery to workers, see CTM to Alemán, May 25, 1949, MAV/AGN, exp. 111/4010; *Acción*, June 21, 1941. This argument persisted into at least the 1950s. See "Máquinas que trabajan solas en la Fábrica Santa Lucia," *La Opinión*, February 13, 1956. On the issue of worker pride and mastery of the machinery, see Gauss, "Working Class Masculinity."

126. Comisión Mixta Especial de Modernización de la Industria Textil del Algodón y sus Mixturas to STPS, letter and report, August 15, 1947, IM; "La modernización de las máquinas es la clave," *La Opinión*, January 29, 1949.

modernization and efficiency since the late 1920s gave way in the face of economic crisis. For many of Puebla's industrialists, investment in new machinery was at the heart of their proposals to revive the industry. Some advanced efficiency as their prime motivation, and they sincerely tried to update machinery and work processes. Others, however, were not actively planning to invest in new machinery, but they still emphasized the importance of doing that, because it would enable them to reassert their place in the state's industrial project while curbing what they viewed as the excesses of state-backed union authority. Though not united in their support for modernization, some labor unions saw the advantages of modernization. However, this support likely had a lot to do with demonstrating their compliance with the state or with assuming control of a modernizing process that they may have seen as inevitable. Regardless of their motives, their recommendations for modernization almost uniformly countered industrialists' proposals, by emphasizing the protection of workers' jobs and of union authority and by insisting on the presence of the state in determining the process.

The Limits of Owner Paternalism

The textile industry in Puebla was at a crossroads after the war. Persistent union violence, postwar economic decline, and many industrialists' intransigent opposition to corporatist labor relations complicated efforts to resolve crises in this economically vital industry. It was evident that the future of the industry necessitated investment in machinery. Yet when faced with the prospective impact on the region's workforce, President Alemán chose to shore up state-labor relations at the expense of industry modernization and local authority.

Both Presidents Ávila Camacho and Alemán expressed concern about the textile industry's inefficiency and poor worker productivity. They pointed out that the industry lagged behind most of Mexico's other manufacturing industries in terms of the ratio of worker output to production costs; in a comparison of twenty-four manufacturing sectors, textiles were fourth from the bottom in terms of worker productivity.[127] This was despite labor productivity in the cotton textile industry having grown steadily, with

127. Miguel Quintana and Fernando Pruneda, "Estudio sobre la modernización de la industria nacional textil del algodón para la Comisión Federal de Planificación Económica," April 27, 1943, GR/AGN, c. 76, exp. 9, pp. 40–44; Pruneda R., "La industria textil," 7–9.

average annual growth ranging from 2.2 percent to 3.4 percent between 1850 and 1933.[128] Both administrations also stated their wish to overcome the inconsistent standards for quality, production, costs, and salaries that continued to prevent the industry from matching efficiency levels in countries with more advanced textile sectors, such as England and the United States. The Ávila Camacho administration even cited the industry's importance in the industrial revolutions of Europe to lament Mexico's inability to capitalize on the textile industry as a basis for advanced industrial growth.[129]

Both governments committed resources to studying the industry, including through the OII, NAFINSA, and other government agencies. A central concern that emerged from these studies was the disequilibrium between production and consumption, and its potential to cause inflation, factory closures, and labor-employer strife. The economic instability of the 1940s and early 1950s contributed to problems with matching production and demand. For example, during the war, the concern was the impact of weak consumer buying power on the ability of Mexico's industry to diversify beyond its concentration in low-grade, cheap textiles, such as manta.[130] By 1951, however, the OII declared that one of its new goals was to address the incapacity of Mexico's industry to meet the growing demand for cheap textiles.[131]

The need for industry modernization was a point most agreed on. Studies most often concluded that modernization through both the rationalization of work processes and investment in new machinery was necessary to increase productivity and make Mexico's textile industry more competitive.[132] For example, in 1946, the Armour Research Foundation stated that, along with modern equipment, technical advances in the textile industry must include the use of high-quality yarns and cloth, humidity control, suitable sizing materials, standardization of the production process, and product inspection. Following this, however, the Alemán administration failed to take coherent, concerted action to update machinery. Instead, his government

128. Razo and Haber, "Rate of Growth," 496–501, 516.
129. Cue Cánovas, "Economía de emergencia," 305–6.
130. Pruneda R., "La industria textil," 10–13.
131. Manuel Sánchez Sarto, OII, "Modernización de la industria textil," July 4, 1952, GR/AGN, c. 76, exp. 14.
132. Camiro, "La industria textil," 70; *Conferencias de Mesa Redonda*, 23; Héctor Argüero Ramírez (Departamento de Inspección, STPS) to Ávila Camacho, study, August 4, 1944, MAC/AGN, exp. 523/116; Manuel Sánchez Sarto, OII, "Modernización de la industria textil," July 4, 1952, GR/AGN, c. 76, exp. 14; "Notas para un memorándum sobre el grupo textil," April 2, 1948, GR/AGN, c. 76, exp. 11; Manuel Bravo Jiménez to Gonzalo Robles, memorandum, September 29, 1949, GR/AGN, c. 76, exp. 13.

vaguely implored industrialists to improve efficiency by lowering costs, improving quality, satisfying markets, and sustaining the labor force.[133]

One possibility for expanding the industry's access to new machinery was to produce it domestically, though the government did not begin to vigorously support these efforts until the 1950s. Some workshops had begun to build a limited amount of rudimentary machinery during the war. In 1948, Mexico's first major manufacturer of textile machinery, Tecnotex, initiated operations in association with the English company, Casablancas High Draft Co. Ltd. Controlled by Fernando Casablancas, a naturalized Mexican citizen, Tecnotex sought to build textile machinery to replace English imports. However, its immediate impact was minimal. For example, in 1948, the company built about 10,000 spindles for an industry that already had approximately 1,200,000 installed.[134] Toyoda de México, Mexico's first full-scale textile machinery manufacturer, opened in 1951, as a mixed capital venture funded largely by Toyoda Automatic Looms of Japan but with some minority public-sector involvement. However, it did not begin to produce machinery until 1956.[135]

Regardless of the availability of domestically produced machinery, in the late 1940s, the Alemán administration resisted the demands by Puebla's industrialists for machinery import permits. This was not done solely to direct machinery to more modern textile ventures. Labor conflicts in this politically important state made investment in new technology and the consequent renegotiation of collective contracts untenable. The layoffs that would attend the renegotiation of textile industry contracts in Puebla would inevitably have a huge impact in a state where, in 1945, roughly 59 percent of the workforce labored in the textile industry. Of those, about 86 percent were in cotton textile production.[136] Layoffs would exacerbate labor strife in the state at a time when the federal government was using the Cold War milieu to justify its crackdown on labor radicalism and to foster compliant labor federations. The CTM demonstrated that it understood the Alemán

---

133. Interview form, Banco de México, February 1942, GR/AGN, c. 75, exp. 4; OII, "Datos que deberá obtener el Departamento de Textiles para el estudio de modernización," March 6, 1951, GR/AGN, c. 76, exp. 8; OII, "El problema de la modernización de la industria textil del algodón," May 26, 1952, GR/AGN, c. 76, exp. 14; Miguel Quintana and Fernando Pruneda, "Estudio sobre la modernización de la industria nacional textil del algodón para la Comisión Federal de Planificación Económica," April 27, 1943, GR/AGN, c. 76, exp. 9, pp. 69, 117, 119–29; Godwin, Nelson, and Villaseñor, *Technological Audit*, 79.

134. Fernando Casablancas, Tecnotex, S.A. to NAFINSA, letter and memorandum, January–February 1949, GR/AGN, c. 76, exp. 14.

135. "The New Prosperity," *Time*, July 2, 1956.

136. Gamboa Ojeda, "Los últimos años de predominio," 308.

administration's commitment to quiescent labor sectors when its leaders Fernando Amilpa, Fidel Velázquez, and Blas Chumacero asserted that the organization did not oppose modernization but wanted the state, rather than employers, to regulate it. By proposing that the state expand its regulation of the industry, the CTM was expressing its desire to ally with the state to guarantee the protection of workers, to curb employer authority, and to ensure its own political future.[137]

The Alemán administration consequently rejected most pleas for machinery import permits based in part on concerns about the political fallout of the short-term displacement of workers, as well as what it claimed was the potential impact of worker indemnities on industry costs.[138] Textile industrialists received some tax-exempt machinery imports in 1945, though the number of permits granted in that year and throughout the 1940s was extremely low. As a result, by 1949, ECLA characterized machinery in the industry as "antiquated." Though it provided no criteria for its figures, it estimated that only about 6 percent of looms and 14.5 percent of spindles in Mexico were modern.[139] The U.S. machinery export policy in the 1940s complemented the Alemán administration's sluggishness in granting import permits. During the war, the United States argued that wartime demands made machinery exports impossible. After the war, the United States continued to resist shipping machinery abroad, arguably in order to undermine the development of foreign production.[140]

Moreover, when machinery did begin to arrive, Puebla's industrialists received an amount disproportionately less than the region's total contribution to national production. This most likely was because the Alemán administration favored large, modern factories and new textile manufacturers who were exempt from the industrywide collective contract.[141] Consequently, in 1950, in Mexico City's cotton textile mills, 26 percent of the carding machines, about 56 percent of the looms, and 49 percent of the

---

137. Fidel Velázquez, Blas Chumacero, and Sindicato de Trabajadores de la Industria Textil y Similares de la República Mexicana to Ávila Camacho, November 30, 1944, MAC/AGN, 523/116; Fernando Amilpa to Alemán, May 25, 1949, MAV/AGN, exp. 111/4010.

138. For example, see factory visit guidelines for Departamento de Textiles, Banco de México, March 6, 1951, GR/AGN, c. 76, exp. 8; Carlos Quintana, "Puntos de partida para la resolución del problema textil," April 7, 1948, GR/AGN, c. 76, exp. 8; Víctor Urquidi, "Mexican Industry, a Descriptive Survey—Its Recent Evolution," January 1943, GR/AGN, c. 23 exp. 17 and c. 22, exp. 54.

139. CEPAL, "El desarrollo económico de México," 168.

140. In December 1950, the United States allegedly once again prohibited new requests for textile machinery and requests already in process were frozen. "No será modernizada la industria textil," *El Universal*, December 30, 1950.

141. Gómez Galvarriato, "Political Economy of Protectionism," 396.

warping machines had been manufactured after 1945. The same figures for those mills in the Estado de México were 56 percent, 48 percent, and 50 percent, respectively. However, the figures for Puebla's cotton textile mills were only 6 percent, 10 percent, and 23 percent.[142]

According to Aurora Gómez Galvarriato, the opposition to modernization by traditional industrialists and state-backed unions, both of whom chose the security of protectionism over the uncertainty of innovation, ensured that relative productivity in the textile industry would continue to fall further behind as the twentieth century progressed.[143] Although she is largely correct based on outcomes, a widening swath of textile producers lobbied for machinery imports after the war, despite its lack of availability, which points to another facet of the story. Using machinery as a means to try to compel a revision of collective contracts demonstrates the willingness of Puebla's textile industrialists to upset the institutional arrangements underpinning the industry since the late 1920s in order to reassert authority over their factories and in the project for statist industrialism. For the Alemán administration, however, the state-labor alliance in Puebla took precedence over resolving persistent inefficiency in the industry, thereby narrowing employers' options for reestablishing authority over their factories.

Conclusion

At a December 1949 meeting of the AETPT, President José Pellón Mediavilla requested that the organization approve the use of funds to pursue industry modernization without the knowledge of labor. His goal, he claimed, was to investigate the issue while avoiding having to grant salary increases or other advantages to workers in collective contract negotiations. The members passed the motion unanimously.[144] This is significant because it shows that despite machinery being virtually impossible to obtain, Pueblan textile industrialists still considered this investment to be vital to the

---

142. Barajas Manzano, *Aspectos de la industria,* 155–74. See note 76 in this chapter.

143. According to Gómez Galvarriato, when rules for the modernization of the industry were finally agreed upon in 1951 and appended to the wage list, they actually hurt the modern producers because most of the input in designing the rules had come from traditional industrialists. Therefore, the rules served to hamper the development of modernized mills. Gómez Galvarriato, "Political Economy of Protectionism," 397–98; Gómez Galvarriato, "Impact of Revolution," 592–98; Gómez Galvarriato, "Measuring the Impact," 315–16; Bortz, "Genesis," 62–63.

144. Asamblea General, AETPT, meeting minutes, December 10, 1949, CITPT, F-VI/LAAG-3.

future of the industry. Efficiency certainly was a motive, but these industrialists also conceived of machinery as a means to unseat state-sanctioned union authority at the factory level by forcing a renegotiation of collective contracts. If it were possible to buy modern machinery and implement the principles of scientific management, employers would be able to displace thousands of workers, creating a more dependent and pliable workforce. In the process, they hoped to recover local authority by curbing the power of state-backed unions while propelling their regional industry to the forefront of national industrialism. In this case, employers chose technical modernization in order to reassert authority over their factories.

The response of textile unions varied. Some tentatively supported the idea of investment in new machinery, but they tempered that support with an insistence that the state control machine imports and protect labor. More commonly, unions opposed it, influenced by the knowledge that the introduction of new machinery and the principles of scientific management would result in a loss of union power in factories, over the production process, and in the state's industrial project. The institutionalization of regional politics within the avilacamachista cacicazgo, which prevented regional politicians from intervening in meaningful ways in defense of employers, in some ways aided unions. Therefore, despite enjoying good relations with regional political leaders, Puebla's textile industrialists continued to struggle against their political and economic exclusion at the national level. In Puebla, the Alemán administration used industrial policy, in this case, machinery import policy, to marginalize ambivalent and sometimes even antagonistic regional industrialists. As it faced the challenges of deteriorating terms of trade, postwar inflation, declining living standards, and Cold War pressures, the administration chose to shore up corporatist labor relations to the detriment of regional political authority.

THE POLITICS OF NATIONALIST DEVELOPMENT IN POSTWAR MEXICO CITY

Though President Alemán took office with a pledge to promote industry through a combination of tax exemptions and tariff modifications, within seven months he had abandoned that pledge in favor of trade controls.[1] This decision was controversial, since tariffs merely deterred imports and exports, while trade quotas prohibited them. President Alemán turned to these controls in part to redress the mounting postwar trade deficit and diminishing monetary reserves. Yet, a range of political and social factors was also critical in his decision to adopt trade controls. This included a surge of economic nationalism in the wake of U.S. efforts to dominate postwar trade and loan agreements and the ruling party's ongoing struggles to secure its relationship with labor and business. In this light, a favorable domestic political climate coupled with an apparently new, more predatory stage in U.S. imperialism—committed to postwar reconstruction and Cold War objectives—jointly encouraged the maturation of protectionism into a comprehensive program that culminated in midcentury ISI.

After World War II, the United States redoubled pressure on Mexico to commit to free trade and raw material production. This heightened concerns among many industrialists, technocrats, and politicians about continued dependence. It also fostered resentments due to Mexico's recent sacrifices in support of the war effort. U.S. pressure therefore provoked a sharp nationalist response that entailed treaty, tariff, and loan conflicts between the two countries from 1944 to 1948. As Mexican discontent took on new nationalist overtones directed at the United States, it fed popular support for protected industrialization.

1. *Conferencias de Mesa Redonda*, xxvii.

Amid this rising nationalist tide, the CTM and CANACINTRA became more vocal in campaigning for protectionist policies. They did so presumably to defend the jobs and factories on which their constituents' economic security rested. For CANACINTRA, collaboration with the state became a strategy to gain the financing, subsidies, and protection enjoyed by many large-scale industrialists, some of whom had leveraged their political influence and personal connections to obtain concessions in the 1940s.[2] Yet, by uniting around statist development, each also hoped that an alliance with the ruling party would ensure their long-term national authority. In doing so, they shed their earlier ambivalence about state economic intervention, including concerns about its potential to contribute to corruption, inefficiency, and rent seeking. Ultimately, though projected as national, this alliance encouraged the concentration of industry and political power in Mexico City.

Remarkably, the postwar deterioration of trade terms also prompted CONCAMIN and COPARMEX to back limited, temporary protection. Each saw tariffs and even some trade controls as a stopgap to slow the loss of postwar reserves. Industrialist consensus around protectionism did not translate into unity behind state economic intervention, however. Rather, it set off a new round of clashes among industrialists over the rights of private enterprise in the face of the growing authority of the state. Amid these battles, both CANACINTRA and its more conservative counterparts tied economic nationalism to the unfolding Cold War, yet each drew on distinct definitions of class struggle to propose different resolutions to dependency. CANACINTRA linked nationalism to class collaboration and cooperation with the state, around statist industrialism. COPARMEX and CONCAMIN, by contrast, continued to espouse freer trade and the rights of private enterprise. They defended themselves with arguments about the advantages of stronger global trade ties in countering dependency and fostering economic growth. Significantly, this postwar debate between CANACINTRA and industrialists in COPARMEX and CONCAMIN reveals the contingent nature of the mid-twentieth-century association between economic nationalism and protected industrialization. It also reveals how the Cold War milieu and the prominence of protectionist policies in ECLA-promoted structuralist programs secured that correlation.[3]

Despite opposition to state economic intervention that persisted through Mexico's midcentury economic "miracle," wider acceptance of tariffs was

---

2. Shadlen, *Democratization Without Representation*, 32.
3. For more, see Gauss, "Politics of Economic Nationalism."

an important step in enabling the consolidation of ISI into an enduring project underpinning the state and ruling-party authority. That acceptance became the foundation for an alliance between the CTM, CANACINTRA, and the PRI that augmented the state's capacity to resolve postwar labor discord and industrialist discontent.[4] By successfully tying nationalism to class collaboration and cooperation with the state, CANACINTRA and the CTM helped to define a project for protected industrialism that justified the role of the state in the economy, as well as their own authority within that project.

The Politics of Industrial Centralization

Though CANACINTRA was a political creation of the state, its transformation into an organization representing small industry reflected the evolution of urban industrialization in Mexico City after the Revolution.[5] Yet, internal divisions within the organization and tensions with industrialists outside of it compromised its ability to represent its members' interests. Moreover, these divisions and tensions complicated state efforts to institutionalize its relationship with urban industrialists.

By 1950, 38 percent of total manufacturing production nationwide was located in Mexico City, up from 27 percent in 1930.[6] Production in Mexico City was diverse, with both consumer and capital goods playing a prominent role in the city's growth. Some of the causes of this industrial surge were common to other industrializing areas of Mexico in the 1940s, including better access to credit, state fiscal incentives, and international factors, such as war and tourism.[7] However, Mexico City was different in some important ways. For example, it had disproportionately high investment in public works, infrastructure, utilities, and communications.[8] It also departed from other industrial cities in the scale of its demographic boom after the Revolution. Not only did Mexico City's population grow, but it did so at a rate much faster than many of the country's other major industrial centers. For example, in 1930, Mexico City had 5.8 times the population of Guadalajara, but by 1950, that figure had grown to 7.2 times larger.[9]

4. Carr, *Marxism and Communism*, 154.
5. Davis, *Urban Leviathan*.
6. Reynolds, *Mexican Economy*, 169.
7. Garza Villarreal, *El proceso de industrialización*, 154, 157.
8. Davis, *Urban Leviathan*, 103.
9. Monterrey was an exception. Garza Villarreal, *La urbanización de México*, appendix A-1.

With this growth, CANACINTRA evolved into a representative of small industry, especially of that located in Mexico City. The reasons for this transformation are numerous. Larger industrialists tended to seek political representation by way of informal channels or sector-specific chambers, which they felt could represent their interests more effectively than could an industrial chamber with a broad membership. Some of these sector-specific chambers formed in fast-growing areas, such as paper and pulp, steel and iron, and pharmaceuticals, which siphoned away some of CANACINTRA's most dynamic industries. Changes in voting procedures reinforced this specialization of industrial chambers. For example, in the late 1940s, CONCAMIN instituted a policy that weighted voting according to each member's financial contribution, thus favoring larger firms. About the same time, CANACINTRA implemented a policy that gave one vote to each member, therefore giving smaller companies an incentive to join. Moreover, CANACINTRA's location in Mexico City enhanced the authority of the capital's manufacturers in the organization, even as it remained a representative for all national manufacturers. CANACINTRA unsuccessfully resisted the creation of regional manufacturing chambers in Jalisco and Nuevo León, but that merely intensified Mexico City manufacturers' hold over the chamber in Mexico's capital.[10] By 1945, 4,585 of CANACINTRA's 6,925 members were located in Mexico City.[11]

As the organization grew, internecine conflicts began to emerge. One of the more serious disputes erupted between those who sought an alliance with the state and those who viewed the costs of collaboration, including the loss of autonomy and ability to publicly criticize the state, as too high. For example, in 1947, CANACINTRA commissioned a series of public lectures designed to promote the role of industry in resolving Mexico's economic crisis. As part of the series guidelines, the chamber requested that all lecturers abstain from disparaging public functionaries.[12] Yet, in a June 3 lecture, former CANACINTRA president José R. Colín attacked the Secretariat of the Economy. The next day, CANACINTRA president Joaquín de la Peña shot off an apologetic letter to the secretariat's head, Antonio Ruiz Galindo. In the letter, he disavowed any personal or organizational connection to the lecture. He then issued a statement to the press rebuking any lecturers whose speeches might jeopardize CANACINTRA's relationship with the government. Moreover, at his own lecture in early July, de la

---

10. Shadlen, *Democratization Without Representation*, 40–42.
11. Lavín, *Actividades durante el año de 1945*, 24–25.
12. Shadlen, *Democratization Without Representation*, 48, 60.

Peña once again censured Colín.¹³ In doing so, he made clear that the chamber's priority was to establish a conciliatory relationship with the Alemán administration, despite conflicts that such a compromise with federal officials might engender within the organization.

CANACINTRA nevertheless struggled to gain favors from and forge ties with government officials. Throughout the Alemán administration, CANACINTRA complained of a bias against small-scale industry, including in credit opportunities that were skewed toward infrastructure and large-scale ventures in the electric, cement, steel, fertilizer, and railroad car industries.¹⁴ Between 1949 and 1950, 80 percent of NAFINSA's investment went to just fourteen projects.¹⁵ Even tax exemptions demonstrated a trend toward "giantism" by the 1950s. Between 1940 and 1950, the average initial capital of firms benefiting from tax exemptions was Mex$1.2 million; between 1951 and 1955, it rose to Mex$2.04 million; and between 1956 and 1961 to Mex$9 million.¹⁶

Even more troubling for CANACINTRA were the cozy personal and business relationships between ruling-party officials and large-scale manufacturers, which gave them a status within the party that eluded most CANACINTRA members. For example, in October 1945, a large deputation of government and business leaders attended the Mexican-American Conference on Industrial Research in Chicago. They arrived at the conference in style, having flown on two chartered Braniff Airways planes. Sponsored by the Armour Research Foundation of the Illinois Institute of Technology, the conference brought together a select group of Mexican and U.S. leaders in politics, banking, and industry to discuss industrial and technical coordination and development. Attending the conference were Gustavo Serrano, head of the SEN at that time, and Eduardo Villaseñor, general director of the Banco de México. Other attendees included past and future CONCAMIN presidents Evaristo Araiza, José Cruz y Celis, and Pedro Chapa; conservative banker Luis Legorreta; and important industrial leaders from Monterrey, such as Araiza, Roberto Garza Sada, Joel Rocha, and Enrique

13. Joaquín de la Peña to Antonio Ruiz Galindo, June 4, 1947, MAV/AGN, exp. 565.4/19; Roberto Palacios M. to D. Roberto Amorós G., June 19, 1947, MAV/AGN, exp. 565.4/19.
14. Cypher, *State and Capital in Mexico,* 44. NAFINSA's focus on these industries was likely influenced by the fact that the Export-Import Bank and other international lenders that favored investment in infrastructure were an important source of its funding. Blair, "Nacional Financiera," 211–25; Torres, *Hacia la utopía industrial,* 180–85.
15. Ramírez, *Development Banking in Mexico,* 73; Aubey, *Nacional Financiera and Mexican Industry,* 45–46.
16. Shadlen, *Democratization Without Representation,* 35; de Navarrete, *Los incentivos fiscales,* 21–23.

Sarro.[17] Current representatives of CANACINTRA were noticeably absent.

Under President Alemán, prominent industrialists attained new levels of political influence. For example, he included important business leaders, such as Antonio Ruiz Galindo, in his administration. Also commonplace during the late 1940s were joint public-private commissions composed of a select group of government and business representatives who advised the president on monetary, fiscal, and developmental issues. Finally, large-scale business owners formed voluntary organizations to advise or lobby the government about specific issues. For example, the Mexican Association of Roads (Asociación Mexicana de Caminos), which informally advised the Alemán administration on road construction, included owners from the Fundidora de Hierro y Acero de Monterrey, Ford, GM, and Chrysler, as well as banker Agustín Legorreta and former government official and sugar magnate Aarón Sáenz. Notably, President Alemán substantially increased funding for road building during his administration.[18]

CANACINTRA was alarmed by the growing influence of these prominent industrialists. José R. Colín declared, "The large isolated industries that do not benefit the people in general, which channel riches into a few hands, which create castes and worsen the poverty of the masses" threatened the future of the Mexican nation and undercut efforts to "elevate the material, cultural, hygienic, and ethical levels of [the Mexican] people."[19] CANACINTRA president José Domingo Lavín (1945) agreed, and he condemned the large-scale business interests that had organized into the "nefarious employers' organizations" to the detriment of industrial chambers.[20] Lavín's ire was fueled by what he saw as the failure of CONCAMIN to grant CANACINTRA members equitable representation within the larger organization.[21] Consequently, though the two organizations shared office space and even a president at one time (José Cruz y Celis, 1941–43), by the early 1950s, they had grown apart.[22] They confirmed this when each modified its voting procedures in the late 1940s.

---

17. Eduardo Suárez and conservative banker Luis Montes de Oca were invited, though Montes de Oca could not attend due to illness. Paul D. Herman, "Mexican-American Conference on Industrial Research," October 1945, in Godwin, Nelson, and Villaseñor, *Technological Audit*; "Junta celebrada en la Secretaría de la Economía Nacional el día 15 de noviembre de 1945, por las personas que asistieron a la Conferencia Mexicana-Norteamericana de Investigación Industrial," GR/AGN, c. 23, exp. 19.

18. Zabludovsky, "Proposiciones para el estudio," 23–24.

19. Colín, *Requisitos fundamentales*, 39–43.

20. Lavín, "Dos conferencias," 24–25.

21. Lavín, *Actividades durante el año de 1945*, 23–24.

22. Shadlen, *Democratization Without Representation*, 42; Gracida Romo, *El programa industrial*, 84–86.

Yet, CANACINTRA also struggled to expand its influence among the small-scale industrialists who constituted its base. As we have seen in chapter 2, small industries regularly took advantage of the clause in the 1941 chambers law that allowed them to form sectorally and often regionally specific industrial chambers. As a result, the number of chambers in CONCAMIN multiplied from five in 1941, including CANACINTRA, to thirty-six in 1946.[23] CANACINTRA spokesmen protested that these new chambers prevented it from amassing the members, budget, and resources needed to defend industry interests. To curb their formation, CANACINTRA lobbied the government to raise the number of industrialists needed to petition for a special chamber from twenty-five to one hundred. It also asked the government to punish any company that did not join CANACINTRA and pay its membership fee, as industries of a certain size were legally obligated to do.[24] The owners of small industries retorted that the chamber was trying to undermine the representative gains they had made, as well as enforce payments that were onerous to small business.[25]

By the end of World War II, CANACINTRA was internally divided and arrayed against both older, established industries and newer, smaller, often regional ones. While enhancing the authority of Mexico City industrialists in the organization, these conflicts undercut CANACINTRA's effectiveness in representing industry interests. It therefore struggled to exploit its size to gain national political influence. For the ruling party, the question of how to build a state-business alliance to support statist industrialization and political consolidation continued to be a challenge. Ultimately, postwar economic shifts and industrialist reaction to U.S. imperialism provided the context for the ruling party to resolve this problem.

From Collaboration to Dissent: Mexico-U.S. Trade Conflicts in the Postwar Years

Wartime cooperation between the United States and Mexico, exemplified in the 1942 Reciprocal Trade Agreement, buoyed economic growth in

---

23. Shafer, *Mexican Business Organizations*, 57.
24. CANACINTRA, Saltillo to Alemán, February 1, 1951, and CANACINTRA, Durango to Alemán, January 25, 1951, both in MAV/AGN, exp. 411/12909; Jorge Heyser (CANACINTRA) to Alemán, telegram, August 24, 1948, Hector Barona (CANACINTRA) to Alemán, telegram, April 20, 1949, and Agustín Fouque (CANACINTRA) to Alemán, telegram, July 21, 1949, all in MAV/AGN, exp. 545.22/211; CANACINTRA to Alemán, memorandum, 1947, MAV/AGN, exp. 545.3/35.
25. Organizations of small business and Cámaras de Comercio in Puebla, Chiapas, Chihuahua, et al. to Alemán, January 13, 1949, MAV/AGN, exp. 545.3/35. For CANACINTRA's response, see Jorge M. Heyser, memorandum, July 22, 1948, MAV/AGN, exp. 545.3/35.

Mexico. It also fed hopes within Mexico that U.S. investment, trade, machinery, and technical assistance would be channeled toward the development of industry after the war. Instead, the United States stepped up pressure on Mexico to enter into free trade arrangements that would have deepened Mexico's dependence on global markets and its comparative advantage in raw material production. These postwar U.S. attitudes toward Mexico caught the Ávila Camacho administration off guard. As recently as 1944, officials in the United States and Mexico had touted their exceptional relationship. Therefore, when the United States made foreign aid and loans contingent on Mexico's engaging in free trade, it sparked resentment among many Mexican industrialists, technocrats, and politicians. As postwar financing and assistance failed to materialize, a critique of Mexican dependence on the United States dominated national debates about development. Steven Sanderson summed up the postwar dilemma faced by developing countries: "Latin America viewed global trade through a development lens, whereas the United States viewed global development through a trade lens."[26]

The 1942 Reciprocal Trade Agreement aimed to guarantee supplies needed for wartime production in the United States and to diminish scarcities and inflation in basic items in Mexico. The trade agreement froze or reduced tariffs on 203 categories of goods.[27] The United States promised markets for an array of Mexican products, including rubber, henequen, garbanzos, pineapples, bananas, salt, and fish. In return, Mexico pledged to supply at reduced prices the primary materials, especially minerals, needed for war production. The Ávila Camacho administration welcomed the 1942 trade agreement as a stimulus to the economy, even though it tied Mexico more tightly to the United States. In 1937, slightly more than 56 percent of Mexican exports went to the United States, but by 1946, that figure had surpassed 71 percent. During that same period, Mexico's U.S. imports grew from about 62 percent of Mexico's total imports to close to 84 percent.[28] Notably, import scarcities during the war helped to contribute to a trade imbalance that led Mexican monetary reserves to surge to US$372.7 million by 1945.[29]

U.S. officials encouraged the idea that this wartime alliance would lead to trade and credit concessions for Mexican industry after the war. For example, at the 1942 Third Meeting of Foreign Ministers in Rio de Janeiro,

26. Sanderson, *Politics of Trade*, 56.
27. CANACINTRA, *El Tratado Comercial*, 15–17.
28. Urquidi, *Otro siglo perdido*, 134–35. Blanca Torres cites slightly higher figures. Torres, *México en la segunda guerra mundial*, 156–63, 195.
29. Cárdenas, *La hacienda pública*, table A.21; Thorp, "Reappraisal," 186–88.

Undersecretary of State Sumner Welles reiterated the intention of the United States to promote economic development, including industry, in Latin America at the conclusion of the war.[30] Members of the joint Mexican-American Commission for Economic Cooperation, formed after two days of meetings between President Ávila Camacho and President Roosevelt in 1943, agreed. They urged the United States to foster Mexican industry after the war by providing machinery, equipment, primary materials, and replacement parts for Mexico's electric, transportation, iron, steel, sugar, alcohol, textile, pulp, paper, rubber, and cement industries.[31]

President Ávila Camacho believed that by assisting the war effort with supply commitments negotiated directly with the United States, his administration was securing Mexico's prominence in postwar global reconstruction. For many Mexicans, the president's two days of meetings with Roosevelt, which took place in Monterrey, Nuevo León, and Corpus Christi, Texas, confirmed this rising status. In 1944, a confident President Ávila Camacho even created the National Commission for Peace Planning (Comisión Nacional de Planeación para la Paz) to map Mexico's participation in postwar international planning. The commission emphasized that rather than leaving the negotiations of the terms of postwar peace to "two or three great powers," all independent nations had the right to participate.[32]

Despite the surge of economic nationalism sparked by the oil expropriation in 1938, many agreed that collaborating with the United States should remain a part of Mexico's long-term economic strategy. In 1943, Eduardo Suárez, secretary of the Treasury and Public Credit, argued that the solution to Mexico's price and supply problems lay in working more closely with the international community, especially the United States.[33] Throughout 1944, Mexican newspapers emphasized the benefits that this would bring to both countries.[34] In effect, Suárez and others embraced the belief that Mexico's future economic development lay in global cooperation. At the same

30. Rabe, "Elusive Conference," 279.
31. Comisión México-Norteamericano de Cooperación Económica, report, July 10, 1943, GR/AGN, c. 33, exp. 5; Stiller, *George S. Messersmith,* 196–97.
32. "Temario de la Comisión Nacional de Planeación para la Paz," July 1944, AMGM, v. 367, exp. 1263, pp. 3–5.
33. Eduardo Suárez to Ávila Camacho, memorandum, May 26, 1943, MAC/AGN, exp. 550/44-2.
34. "Bases de cooperación entre México y EEUU," *El Nacional,* July 13, 1944; "El Licenciado Padilla regresa con el cuerno de la abundancia," *Excélsior,* July 12, 1944; "La industrialización de México promueve oportunidades de prosperidad recíproca," *El Nacional,* July 20, 1944; "Las entidades y sus planes industriales," *El Nacional,* April 3, 1944; "Industrialización de México en 1944 y 1945," *Novedades,* April 8, 1944.

time, they were maneuvering to establish Mexico as a significant and *equal* member of the international postwar community.

But, as the war progressed, it became clear that collaboration with the United States came at a cost. In particular, a growing number of politicians, industrialists, labor leaders, and technocrats perceived that U.S. efforts to shape Mexican production to meet wartime demands had left little room to address the needs of Mexican consumers. Many blamed U.S. export limits for scarcities and high prices and condemned its policies as a threat to Mexico's fledgling industries.[35] President Ávila Camacho had tried to obtain more imports from the United States. For example, in 1942, he sent Ramón Beteta, undersecretary of the Treasury and Public Credit, to Washington to facilitate export permits for goods needed for manufacturing. Yet, the U.S. Board of Economic Warfare fixed export limits on a range of items during the war, especially equipment, machinery, primary materials, and replacement parts. Its goal was to funnel supplies to industries that contributed to the war effort. Thus, even when Mexico tried to obtain equipment and machinery needed to develop industries critical to the domestic economy, including the electric industry, the United States refused its requests.[36] These rejections soon generated discontent in Mexico. For example, the United States refused to export articles necessary for the production of steel furniture in Mexico, stating that its production had already been suppressed domestically because it was not a war industry. In this instance, the rebuff was notable, since the owner of the rejected factory, Antonio Ruiz Galindo, was a friend of President Ávila Camacho, and the president had intervened directly to appeal the U.S. decision. In response, Ruiz Galindo's defenders countered that Mexico had no war industries, and that in terms of industrial priorities, "the American government and the Mexican government do not share the same point of view."[37] As industrialist criticism of U.S. quotas grew, Suárez perceptively stated that, in effect, industries could only be developed with the approval of the United States during the war.[38]

35. Tripartite commission of the STPS, report, November 12, 1941, MAC/AGN, exp. 523/30.

36. John H. Nelson (Chief of Projects Division, Requirements and Supply Branch of the Foreign Economic Administration, Bureau of Supplies) to Ebasco International Corporation, April 10, 1945, DGI/AGN, v. 27, exp. 391/300 (03)/-1–16, letra N.

37. Ávila Camacho, Antonio Ruiz Galindo, F. Javier Gaxiola, Jr., and Francisco Castillo Najera (Mexican Ambassador to the U.S.), correspondence, June 26, 1941, to October 28, 1942, MAC/AGN, exp. 564.2/27.

38. Eduardo Suárez to Ávila Camacho, memorandum, May 26, 1943, MAC/AGN, exp. 550/44–2.

Moreover, as the war drew to a close, the promise of postwar assistance dimmed. The yawning gap between First World and Third World expectations for the postwar period became evident at the 1944 Bretton Woods conference. While there, the Mexican delegation proposed an amendment to the agreement that would put postwar "'reconstruction' and 'development' . . . on the same footing." In principle, the international community concurred, and representatives included a phrase to the effect that reconstruction and development would be given equitable consideration in funding decisions. In practice, however, as Víctor Urquidi later recalled, "the concept of development was practically absent" at the conference.[39]

By 1945, President Ávila Camacho realized that his plan to parlay wartime collaboration into postwar assistance for Mexican industry was failing under the weight of U.S. demands on Mexico to commit to free trade and raw material production. Intersecting political, economic, and security concerns drove U.S. desires for Mexico to remain a supplier of primary materials. Foremost was U.S. interest in rebuilding Europe in order to create a bulwark against the spread of communism. To achieve that, it needed countries like Mexico to continue to supply raw materials. The United States also sought guaranteed raw materials in the face of the buildup of Soviet resources.[40] Finally, the United States wanted to ensure that Mexico would remain a long-term supplier of raw materials for American industries. U.S. industrial interests, including the privately funded U.S. Council on Foreign Relations, put heavy pressure on the U.S. government to expand access to foreign markets and raw materials.[41] Some even brought this campaign to the Mexican press. In 1949, the Foreign Trade Council, a U.S. organization of businesspeople seeking to facilitate global free trade, published a statement in *El Universal* denouncing protectionist policies that supported "artificial industries" and hindered foreign investment to the detriment of Mexico's economy. In response, Mexico's business community accused the council of trying to convert Mexico into a country of tourism, agriculture, and mining.[42] When Mexico's business community sensed that foreign investors in vital industries, such as electricity, were only interested in profits and had little concern for national development, it only fueled the resentment.[43] Moreover, the United States remained reluctant to ship

39. Urquidi, "Reconstruction vs. Development," 41.
40. Rosenberg, *Spreading the American Dream*, 196.
41. O'Brien, *Century of U.S. Capitalism*, 105–6.
42. Zabludovsky, "Antecedentes," 76–83.
43. Wionczek, *El nacionalismo mexicano*, 6–11.

machinery and equipment abroad after the war ended. Some in Mexico even speculated that vertical trusts in the United States were controlling their access to modern machinery.[44] Along with others in Latin America, Mexican officials and businesspeople were frustrated by apparent U.S. efforts to undermine industry in the region in order to shape their economies into tools to help rebuild Europe and support U.S. industrial expansion.[45]

The rapid decline in monetary reserves after the war heightened the suspicions held by Mexico's politicians, technocrats, and industrialists. As early as 1944, the United States began to increase the export of items that lacked a specified fixed price in the 1942 trade agreement. It thereby introduced the transition to a peacetime economy earlier than Mexicans had expected.[46] Postwar imports continued their ascent, driven by large wartime reserves in Mexico, an overvalued peso, an increase in domestic demand, and a lack of trade restrictions on key U.S. exports. By 1947, the value of imports was 93 percent higher than it had been just two years earlier. At the same time, the value of Mexican exports continued to drop, due in part to price ceilings in the 1942 trade agreement. As Mexico's trade deficit grew, its monetary reserves plummeted from US$372.7 million in 1945 to US$122.6 million in 1948.[47]

The onset of postwar economic difficulties amid U.S. efforts to have Mexico focus on free trade and raw material production provoked a series of treaty, tariff, and loan conflicts. Most Mexicans homed in on the 1942 trade agreement and pressed for its renegotiation. As it stood, the trade agreement narrowed Mexico's options for responding to postwar crises because it limited the tariffs that Mexico could place on an array of goods. Some of these were already being produced in Mexico in 1942, while the production of others was initiated during the war to offset the drop in imports. Included were industries critical to the Mexican economy, such as segments of the textile industry, the iron and steel industry, the paper industry, the food industry, machinery manufacturing, medicines, and paints and varnishes. In 1944, when the United States resumed exports of some goods that competed with Mexican manufactures, Mexican producers began to push for a revision of the 1942 agreement.[48]

As early as December 1943, the Mexican government made its first attempt to alter trade terms by proposing to raise tariffs on a number of goods

44. "La industrialización y la planeación," mid-1940s, GR/AGN, c. 84, exp. 5.
45. Roxborough, "Labor Control," 254.
46. *Conferencias de Mesa Redonda*, xviii.
47. Cárdenas, *La hacienda pública*, table A.21.
48. CANACINTRA, *El Tratado Comercial*, 21–22, 24–25.

not covered by the 1942 agreement.⁴⁹ The United States responded with its first of many complaints against Mexican attempts to change the terms of trade. But as the war's end neared, the clamor for higher levels of protection in Mexico mounted.⁵⁰ As Eduardo Suárez declared, many increasingly saw trade regulation as the only way for Mexico to shed its agricultural past and pursue its manufacturing future. However, Suárez, who was a moderate protectionist, sensed that postwar anxieties would lead to poorly planned and politically motivated protectionism, which had already deformed past industrialization in Mexico.⁵¹ Similarly, Víctor Urquidi warned against allowing postwar fears and transitory crises to drive irrational policy, especially the costly mistake of seeing "any little wartime factory as our economic salvation."⁵² Some U.S. officials also recognized the right of Mexico to protect its economy in the face of the crisis, even as the United States sustained its formal opposition to trade controls. For example, William Clayton, head of the U.S. delegation to the Chapultepec conference (1945), acknowledged that Latin American countries would be justified in manipulating exchange rates in order to ensure that nonessential trade did not drain wartime monetary reserves.⁵³ Furthermore, though he sought to spread free trade across the Americas, Ambassador George Messersmith implored the U.S. State Department to remain open to protectionism, at the very least to show the countries of the region that the United States "valued their well-being more than ideological orthodoxy."⁵⁴

Following its first aborted attempt at revising controls in 1943, on February 19, 1944, the Mexican government issued a decree authorizing the SHCP to prepare a list of imports it recommended for licensing. Initially, the list was quite short, and the decree foundered under the weight of U.S. opposition. Again, in September 1945, the SHCP attempted to revise the list of regulated imports, only to be met, once more, by resistance from U.S. officials.⁵⁵ During the next year and a half, U.S. and Mexican officials continued their tense negotiations over trade controls, with the latter repeatedly tightening import restrictions only to retreat in the face of U.S.

49. Torres, *México en la segunda guerra mundial*, 165–72, 185–92.
50. Comisión de Asuntos Generales, "Reglamentación de importaciones y exportaciones," July 12, 1946, MAC/AGN, exp. 527/22.
51. "Sección editorial—El programa proteccionista," *El Universal*, December 21, 1945.
52. Urquidi, "Espejismos económicos actuales," 27.
53. Cosío Villegas, "Chapultepec Conference," 193.
54. Stiller, *George S. Messersmith*, 214–15.
55. Interview with Ramón Beteta, in Wilkie and Monzón de Wilkie, *México visto en el siglo XX*, 47; CANACINTRA to Ávila Camacho, telegram, December 29, 1945, MAC/AGN, exp. 545.22/262.

objections. With each round, however, the list of regulated imports grew slightly.⁵⁶

The 1944 decree, and subsequent negotiations over trade controls, anticipated important trends that emerged to shape postwar trade relations. First, it introduced stricter government revision of compliance with import and export controls. Second, issued under an emergency war powers act, the 1944 decree gave the president unlimited power to control imports. When the war powers act expired, President Ávila Camacho included this right in his list of emergency powers he wished to have extended. Congress granted his request, and executive oversight of trade grew. Third, the 1944 decree was issued without consulting U.S. officials. It therefore augured a new independence in Mexico's trade relationship with the United States.⁵⁷ Mexico confirmed this new independence at a series of three inter-American conferences in the mid-1940s: the Chapultepec conference, the Rio conference (August 1947), and the Bogotá conference (April 1948). Despite U.S. pressure on Mexico and other Latin American nations to lower tariff barriers and sign the General Agreement on Tariffs and Trade, most refused, including Mexico.⁵⁸

Loans and credit to develop industry and infrastructure also became points of contention between Mexico and the United States after the war. Throughout the 1940s, CANACINTRA and CONCAMIN urged the Ávila Camacho and Alemán administrations to improve medium- and long-term credit opportunities for industry.⁵⁹ Therefore, they delighted at President Alemán's success at getting loans from the United States and the Export-Import Bank right after he took office, believing it to be a sign of Mexico's global importance and of a new era in U.S.-Mexico cooperation.⁶⁰ This included a US$100 million loan to be used for building roads to link the two countries, granted after President Alemán's celebrated nine-day visit to the United States in April–May 1947.⁶¹

---

56. Torres, *México en la segunda guerra mundial,* 191.

57. Mosk, *Industrial Revolution in Mexico,* 77–78; "Limitación de exportaciones," *El Universal,* October 16, 1943; Secretaría de Gobernación, *Seis años de actividad nacional,* 371–72.

58. Rabe, "Elusive Conference," 281–82.

59. Gustavo Serrano (presidente, Comisión General del Consejo Nacional de Economía), July 12, 1946, MAC/AGN, exp. 527/22; CANACINTRA, "Memorandums que dirige al Sr. Presidente de la República, Lic. Miguel Alemán, el Presidente de la Cámara Nacional de la Industria de Transformación," 1947, MAV/AGN, exp. 433/99; Lavín, "Dos conferencias," 46; Guillermo Guajardo Davis (presidente, CONCAMIN) to Alemán, September 20, 1948, AMGM, v. 237, exp. 768; Mosk, *Industrial Revolution in Mexico,* 44–45, 235.

60. Torres, *Hacia la utopía industrial,* 180–85.

61. Aguayo, *Myths and [Mis]Perceptions,* 48–53.

It soon became apparent, however, that little had changed. Indeed, many of the loans that did arrive came with controversial conditions attached, including U.S. oversight of funded projects, pressure to back U.S. diplomatic objectives in Latin America, and the mandate that Mexico maintain a fixed exchange rate.[62] Much-sought-after loans from the International Bank for Reconstruction and Development (the first institution of the World Bank) did not begin to flow into Mexico until 1949. Once they did, they too were contingent on the satisfactory completion of a study of national industry, once again provoking frustration about foreign, and especially U.S., oversight of the Mexican economy.[63] Additionally, between 1949 and 1952, U.S. officials stated that no aid would be forthcoming for any Latin American country that did not also welcome foreign direct investment (FDI).[64] Given this Hobson's choice, President Alemán courted these investments, but CANACINTRA vociferously opposed them. The organization argued that a 1944 law limiting foreign ownership of many key industries was too weak and would allow FDI to deform the Mexican economy and impoverish the nation.[65] President Alemán responded by creating the Intersecretarial Commission on Foreign Capital Investment Rules (Comisión Intersecretarial de Coordinación de Normas sobre Inversiones de Capital Extranjero) to ensure that foreign investors who sought exemptions to the 1944 law did not compete with local industry.[66] However, when his administration produced a list of industries ineligible for the exemption, it included only radio broadcasting; motion pictures; domestic air travel; urban and suburban transport; fishing; publishing; and the bottling, distribution, and sale of carbonated beverages. This short list narrowed the law's nationalist potential.

After Bretton Woods, Latin America entertained little hope of receiving aid on a par with Europe. However, Mexicans did not anticipate the wholesale abandonment by the international lending community that they would see with the announcement of the Marshall Plan in 1948. In that same year, Antonio Carrillo Flores, general director of NAFINSA, echoed Víctor

62. Niblo, *Mexico in the 1940s*, 171; Rosenberg, *Spreading the American Dream*, 182.
63. Héctor Martínez d'Meza (Banco de México) to Antonio Ruiz Galindo, August 8, 1947, DGI/AGN, v. 26, 391/300 (03)/-1-11, letra J; Rosenberg, *Spreading the American Dream*, 194.
64. Rabe, "Elusive Conference," 290–91.
65. Joaquín de la Peña, "La penetración de capitales extranjeros y el desplazamiento de industrias nacionales," July 8, 1947, MAV/AGN, exp. 565.4/19, pp. 10–13; Comisión de Planeación Industrial de la CANACINTRA, *Proceso ocupacional*, 106–12, 203–5; López-Portillo Tostado, *Estado e ideología empresarial*, 179–80.
66. José H. López Alcar (Comisión Intersecretarial de Coordinación de Normas sobre Inversiones de Capital Extranjero) to general director of Industrias de Transformación, SEN, September 5, 1947, DGI/AGN, v. 26, 391/300 (03)/-1-11, letra J.

Urquidi's reflections about Bretton Woods when he stated that the development of the Americas needed to be given the same level of importance as the reconstruction of Europe.[67] Just two years later, in 1950, Gonzalo Robles astutely pointed out the disadvantages for the United States of disregarding industrialization in the developing world, including missed opportunities to create consumer markets and fostering global inequalities that encouraged political upheaval and economic nationalism.[68] Nevertheless, by 1951, Latin America remained the only region of the world not covered by a U.S. aid program. Between 1945 and 1950, less than 2 percent of U.S. foreign aid went to Latin America.[69] As European countries, designated as esteemed allies of the United States, benefited from the Marshall Plan, Mexico learned that, despite its wartime collaboration, it would remain less equal, less powerful, and less entitled.[70] Conflicts over the terms and conditions attached to available loans contributed to a further deterioration of U.S.-Mexico relations, worsening Mexico's alienation from an international lending community focused on European reconstruction. To many Mexican officials, technocrats, and industrialists, a renewed commitment to the principles of comparative advantage would only exacerbate Mexico's dependence on international markets, undermine its industrial aspirations, and foster underdevelopment.

Nationalist Collaboration and State Economic Intervention

Suspicions about U.S. long-term goals for Mexican industrial development prompted a surge of postwar economic nationalism in defense of Mexico's autonomy. Solutions proffered by industrialists ranged widely. Predictably, protectionists turned to state economic intervention to curb U.S. aggressions. By contrast, advocates of the rights of private enterprise presented free trade as the best means to limit dependency, though many now also began to support limited, temporary tariffs to slow the postwar loss of reserves. Yet rather than bringing unity, broader backing for tariffs exacerbated tensions between CANACINTRA and conservative business groups. The latter questioned the state's authority, attained as it expanded

67. *El Mercado de Valores* 8, no. 6 (February 9, 1948).
68. Robles, "Los pueblos atrasados," 55–56.
69. Rabe, "Elusive Conference," 292–93; Pollard, *Economic Security,* 213.
70. For more on the postwar construction of development and underdevelopment, see Arndt, *Economic Development*; Leys, *Rise and Fall*; Ramírez-Faria, *Origins of Economic Inequality.*

its regulation of industry at the expense of private enterprise. To strengthen its position in these debates, CANACINTRA forged a tighter alliance with the CTM, while insisting that the only way to lessen dependency was through class collaboration and cooperation with the state. To challenge this alliance and defend their own nationalist credentials, CONCAMIN and COPARMEX condemned CANACINTRA's leaders as communist sympathizers.

CANACINTRA set its nationalist sights on the 1942 trade agreement, contending that the Mexican state should not be bound by limits on the actions that it could take to protect industry. It argued that the 1942 agreement had inequalities built into it that compelled Mexico to remain an exporter of low-priced primary materials and an importer of relatively higher-priced manufactured goods.[71] Nevertheless, in the early years after the war, CANACINTRA stated that tariffs should be implemented as far as allowable *within the limits* of the 1942 agreement.[72] Only in 1947, as the postwar economic crisis deepened, did CANACINTRA become more aggressive in pressing for a revision of the agreement. At that time, it blamed the United States for exploiting the wartime treaty to impede the development of new industries in Mexico in order to protect its postwar access to Mexican markets.[73] CANACINTRA added that if Latin America were to adopt free trade, as the United States was pressing it to do, it would remain semi-colonial, with its industry disappearing as it fell back into historic patterns of exporting primary materials and importing manufactured goods.[74] Even though it opposed free trade agreements like the General Agreement on Tariffs and Trade, however, CANACINTRA still sought trade with the United States.[75] But as Joaquín de la Peña averred,

71. Lavín, "La industria química nacional"; Joaquín de la Peña, "La penetración de capitales extranjeros y el desplazamiento de industrias nacionales," July 8, 1947, MAV/AGN, exp. 565.4/19; José R. Colín, "El actual desajuste económico en México y sus consecuencias," June 3, 1947, MAV/AGN, 565.4/19; Joaquín de la Peña, speech, Primer Congreso Nacional, CANACINTRA, April 1947, MAV/AGN, exp. 433/99; CANACINTRA, *El Tratado Comercial*; Lavín and Hector Barona to Ávila Camacho, telegram, December 20, 1945, MAC/AGN, exp. 545.22/262. For an exposition of CANACINTRA's position on trade treaties between Mexico and the United States in the 1940s, see Fouque, *El Tratado de Comercio*.
72. CANACINTRA to Alemán, December 18, 1946, MAV/AGN, exp. 564.2/4.
73. CANACINTRA, "Memorandums que dirige al Sr. Presidente de la República, Lic. Miguel Alemán el Presidente de la Cámara Nacional de la Industria de Transformación," 1947, MAV/AGN, exp. 433/99.
74. Joaquín de la Peña, speech, Primer Congreso Nacional, CANACINTRA, 1947, MAV/AGN, exp. 433/99.
75. Antonio Ruiz Galindo to Ávila Camacho, February 10, 1945, and February 28, 1945, MAC/AGN, exp. 545.22/262; Víctor Urquidi, pers. comm., September 4, 1998; Mosk, *Industrial Revolution in Mexico*, 22. For a discussion of CANACINTRA's opposition to the General Agree-

in working together, the United States and Mexico did not need to adhere to universal rules.[76]

The revisions proposed by CANACINTRA included the implementation of ad valorem tariffs, or tariffs assessed on the value of an item rather than the unit of merchandise. In the past, Mexico had generally applied specific tariffs, which had proven to be vulnerable to shifts in currency values that often eroded effective rates of protection. CANACINTRA added that the state should set official minimum prices so that merchants could not circumvent tariffs by artificially depressing the value of imports. Finally, it recommended that tariffs favor industries that used domestic primary materials or where labor was the largest cost of production. To those who complained that tariffs would lead to higher prices and lower quality, José R. Colín responded only that they were necessary in order to impede imports that could displace nationally produced goods, even if it occurred at a cost to consumers. He added, "The entire nation needs to pay for our industrial backwardness."[77]

A range of labor groups also supported tariffs and trade controls as the best way to save factories, protect jobs, and avert scarcities.[78] For example, one union suggested that it was criminal for the government to allow imports to flood Mexican markets, since they would eventually undermine national industry and lead to job losses.[79] The CROM also complained of the invasion of low-priced foreign manufactures, which it labeled an "illicit competition for national production."[80] Along with various textile unions, it requested tariffs and suggested trade limits on products commonly produced in Mexico, such as cotton textiles.[81]

It was amid this growing clamor for government action that the CTM joined more tightly with CANACINTRA in support of statist industrialization. Their alliance grew out of their opposition to U.S. free trade pressures

---

ment on Tariffs and Trade, see Reyes Heroles, *La Carta de la Habana*. For CONCANACO support for the General Agreement on Tariffs and Trade, see CONCANACO, *Problemas derivados de la intervención*, 7.

76. Joaquín de la Peña, speech, Primer Congreso Nacional, CANACINTRA, 1947, MAV/AGN, exp. 433/99; *Tiempo*, April 21, 1947.

77. Colín, *Requisitos fundamentales*, 25–26; Lavín, "Dos conferencias," 48–50; Lavín, *Actividades durante el año de 1945*, 21–22.

78. Liga de Pequeños Industriales del Distrito Federal, January 13, 1947, MAV/AGN, exp. 523/12. For labor opposition to excessive exports, see "Precisa un regimen que impida que las exportaciones sean excesivas y perjudiciales," *El Nacional*, October 14, 1946.

79. Unión Nacional de Trabajadores to Alemán, telegrams, June 11, 1947, MAV/AGN, exp. 564.2/4.

80. "Verdadera invasión de artículos extranjeros," *El Universal*, May 13, 1946.

81. Form letters sent by textile unions and labor federations, MAV/AGN, exp. 564.2/12 and MAV/AGN, exp. 705.2/1.

at the Chapultepec conference, which prompted them to convert their budding wartime collaboration into the Worker-Employer Pact (Pacto Obrero-Patronal) signed in April 1945. Along with a few other labor groups, they pledged to work together toward economic development and independence.[82] CANACINTRA and the CTM garnered notable public support for the pact, as when editors at *El Popular* lauded their spirit of unity and rejection of "sterile protest" and "rhetorical disagreements," which should be eschewed in favor of confronting the problems of hunger and poverty.[83]

The CTM hoped that collaboration would also signal a new phase in its relations with the state. As seen in chapter 3, the state had intentionally worked to lessen the power of CTM labor leaders in the early 1940s by fostering the rise of competing labor groups. Therefore, by the mid-1940s, the CTM was weaker than it had ever been since its founding. During the war, moreover, an internal schism between conservatives and radicals further enfeebled the organization. Moderates in the CTM could do little to control the wave of politicized strike activity that unfolded after the war under the guidance of its more radical unions, including in the oil and railway industries. Soon thereafter, these radical unions broke away from the CTM, and by the end of 1947, its membership had fallen to just 100,000 workers. Many were concentrated in small company- and plant-level unions, especially in Mexico City.[84] Amid this organizational instability, the pact helped to advance the power of conservative leaders, such as Fernando Amilpa y Rivera and Fidel Velázquez, over the CTM, and it ensured the organization's commitment to labor peace and collaborationist politics.

As support for protectionism mounted, and in defiance of the "export pessimism" that seemed to be taking hold, merchants along with a small but vocal group of industrialists and officials maintained that a positive trade balance would best be secured by recommitting to Mexico's comparative advantage in the export of primary materials.[85] For example, Secretary of Foreign Relations Jaime Torres Bodet (Secretario de Relaciones Exteriores, 1946–48) declared that the Marshall Plan could actually help Mexico, since

---

82. Carr, *Marxism and Communism*, 154–55; Gracida Romo, *El programa industrial*, 59–82.
83. "Sección editorial—Consejo Nacional de Economía," *El Popular*, July 5, 1946.
84. L. Medina, *Civilismo y modernización*, 152–56; Azaola, *La clase obrera*, 45; Roxborough, "Mexico," 202–5, 209; Carr, *Marxism and Communism*, 146, 164; Middlebrook, *Paradox of Revolution*, 108–9, 111–17, 214–15.
85. For more on "export pessimism," see Bulmer-Thomas, *Economic History of Latin America*, 263–64.

the recovery of Europe would provide the country with permanent markets for its primary materials.[86] Similarly, a few industrialists, including owners of subsidiaries, companies with significant foreign ownership, or companies that produced for export, stated that no tariff revisions were necessary, since current levels of protection were sufficient to protect viable Mexican industries.[87] An advisor to the Banco de México, Miguel Gleason Álvarez, also backed outward-oriented development and urged Mexico to respect international treaties that called for free trade, such as the Havana Charter. He added that only industries that could reasonably compete against foreign producers deserved protection.[88]

But free trade advocates in Mexico found themselves increasingly isolated after World War II, as CONCAMIN and even COPARMEX took a protectionist turn. Since its inception in 1917, CONCAMIN had pressed for targeted tariffs to protect specific industries, though its support was generally narrow and expressed privately. By the early 1940s, however, its position had matured to include a critique of global inequalities, as it advocated the need for underdeveloped countries to use protectionist policies due to the extraordinary economic power of more developed regions. Like CANACINTRA, it said protectionism was the price that the collective had to pay in order to diversify the economy and minimize dependence.[89] The postwar deterioration in the terms of trade and U.S. refusals to modify the 1942 trade agreement broadened CONCAMIN support for tariffs even further. The organization began to speak more publicly and forcefully in favor of tariffs while criticizing the 1942 agreement for the limits it placed on Mexico.[90] CONCAMIN remained chary of direct controls, however, as it sought to retain access to the foreign primary materials on which its members disproportionately relied. Moreover, it argued that tariffs and controls should be temporary and that they should be abandoned once a company could compete freely.[91] Like CANACINTRA, CONCAMIN rejected

---

86. *El Mercado de Valores* 8, no. 4 (January 26, 1948).

87. Mexican Pineapple Co., S.A. to Secretaría de Relaciones Exteriores, January 4, 1947, DGI/AGN, v. 26, exp. 24/300 (03)/-1-15 letra M; William G. Kane, "Memorandum to the Bank of Mexico," June 12, 1945, GR/AGN, c. 20, exp. 2; Niblo, *War, Diplomacy, and Development*, 186.

88. Miguel Gleason Álvarez, "Estudio de industrias. Carta de Comercio." 1948, GR/AGN, v. 84, exp. 10; *El Mercado de Valores* 8, no. 13 (March 29, 1948).

89. "Descansa la industria en la protección arancelaria," *El Universal*, August 6, 1943.

90. CONCAMIN, "Nuestra campaña de Acción Social en el año de 1949," MAV/AGN, exp. 704/615; CONCAMIN to Alemán, August 11, 1947, MAV/AGN, exp. 708.1/5–8.

91. Guillermo Guajardo Davis (presidente, CONCAMIN), speech at the Congreso de Derecho del Trabajo, July 19, 1949, DGI/AGN, v. 23, exp. 391/300 (03)/1–3.

neoclassical economics, contending instead that a more flexible, renegotiable treaty that reflected differences between the economic capacity of Mexico and that of the United States would be ideal.[92]

After the war, even COPARMEX began to publicly, albeit tentatively, espouse support for tariffs. The turning point for the confederation came at the Chapultepec conference, when the U.S. insistence on free trade across the Americas sharpened worries about the penetration of Mexican markets by foreign producers. In response, COPARMEX proposed protectionism to curb U.S. influence over the Mexican economy and reverse the swelling trade deficit. But its backing remained confined to limited, temporary tariffs aimed at hindering the influx of luxury and superfluous imports while enhancing access to machinery and primary materials. Like CONCAMIN, it contended that this could be accomplished with a minimal modification of the 1942 trade agreement to make it more reciprocal.[93]

Despite their support for protectionism, however, COPARMEX and CONCAMIN continued to denounce state intervention in the economy.[94] Their concern, they claimed, was the growing tendency of the state to act as an industrial entrepreneur. As evidence, they pointed to the expansion of state-owned, state-regulated, or state-financed enterprises from the 1930s through the 1950s, including in steel, petrochemicals, railways, electrical power, fertilizers, paper, cement, and sugar.[95] They urged the state to refrain from entrepreneurial activity and to limit its investment to infrastructure and to areas where the private sector could not or would not invest.[96] Global competitiveness, and thus economic independence and collective welfare, they maintained, relied on efficiency that could only be attained with free enterprise and the protection of private property and individual rights. They

---

92. *Confederación: Boletín Quincenal de la CONCAMIN*, no. 4 (January 1, 1949); *Confederación: Boletín Quincenal de la CONCAMIN*, no. 5 (February 1, 1949); *Confederación: Boletín Quincenal de la CONCAMIN*, no. 7 (February 15, 1949); Guillermo Guajardo Davis (presidente, CONCAMIN) and Alfonso Noriega, Jr. (gerente, CONCAMIN) to Alemán, September 20, 1948, AMGM, v. 237, exp. 768.

93. "Protección a la industrial," *Actividad,* January 1, 1946; Gustavo Serrano (presidente, Comisión General del Consejo Nacional de Economía), July 12, 1946, MAC/AGN, exp. 527/22; López-Portillo Tostado, *Estado e ideología empresarial,* 228–30.

94. "Empresa libre-Iniciativa privada," *Actividad,* October 15, 1946; CONCAMIN to Alemán, August 11, 1947, MAV/AGN, exp. 708.1/5–8. See also CONCAMIN to Ávila Camacho, September 14, 1944, and Ávila Camacho to CONCAMIN, September 26, 1944, and October 31, 1944, all in MAC/AGN, exp. 545.22/262. The tone and content of these three letters suggest a tension between President Ávila Camacho and CONCAMIN.

95. NAFINSA, *La política industrial,* 222–29, 283–85.

96. Alcazar, *Las agrupaciones patronales,* 55–56.

even reconceived of protectionist legislation as that which provided individual investors with protection from excessive and arbitrary state authority.[97]

COPARMEX and CONCAMIN censured CANACINTRA and the CTM for encouraging state economic intervention. As mentioned earlier, both CANACINTRA and the CTM argued that the state could play a vital role in overcoming dependency and promoting growth in underdeveloped countries, a position shared by structuralists. To defend this position, they linked nationalism to class collaboration and cooperation with the state, as evidenced in the Worker-Employer Pact. Their alliance sparked broad condemnation from both workers and employers, however. Some organizations contended that the alliance was sheer opportunism. For example, the National Proletarian Confederation (Confederación Proletaria Nacional, CPN), a labor organization founded in 1942 by CTM dissidents and others who opposed Vicente Lombardo Toledano, accused the CTM of strengthening its relationship with employers to offset the "constant desertion" of its members. The CPN added that a recent banquet with "thirty employers and thirty workers was . . . a political maneuver by CTM leaders and . . . [an] aristocratic conviviality between millionaires and rich [labor] leaders."[98]

More commonly, labor and employer groups used the Cold War to frame their hostility toward the alliance. They vilified collaboration as indicative of Soviet influence and therefore emblematic of the CTM's and CANACINTRA's betrayal of both their class and nation. The CPN even asserted that the pact stemmed from accords developed by the Communist Party in Moscow.[99] The CROM also joined in, branding its longtime enemy "Lombardoff Toledanoff" and charging the CTM with having communist leanings and abandoning the working class.[100] Similarly, COPARMEX alleged that the leaders of CANACINTRA were traitors as well, characterizing its members as "pseudo-employers" who purportedly had allied with Marxist extremists in support of a command economy that would eliminate

---

97. Guillermo Guajardo Davis, "Discurso pronunciado en el Primer Congreso de la Industria Eléctrica," May 1948, and Guillermo Guajardo Davis, "Discurso pronunciado en la Inauguración de la XIV Convención Ordinaria de Centros Patronales," September 1948, both in *Recopilación de los más importantes discursos pronunciados y artículos publicados por el señor Guillermo Guajardo Davis, como Presidente de la Confederación de Cámaras Industriales*, April 1948–March 1950, MAV/AGN, 704/439.

98. CPN to Ávila Camacho, April 10, 1945, and CPN, declaration, April 8, 1945, both in MAC/AGN, exp. 437.3/165. For more on the CPN, see Loyo, "La Confederación Proletaria Nacional," 85–108.

99. CPN to Ávila Camacho, April 10, 1945, and CPN, declaration, April 8, 1945, both in MAC/AGN, exp. 437.3/165.

100. "La medalla a Lombardoff Toledanoff . . . Puro camouflage cetalista," *Germinal*, January 5, 1946.

free enterprise.¹⁰¹ The Monterrey Group singled out CANACINTRA presidents José Domingo Lavín and José R. Colín, dubbing them opportunistic "pseudo-Communists" whose Soviet orientation made them sympathize with the "fundamentals of Leninism." The evidence was Lavín's and Colín's association with Vicente Lombardo Toledano, their participation in the Worker-Employer Pact, and their defense of communism, albeit a tepid one, in public statements.¹⁰² Even some pharmaceutical and chemical producers who were members of CANACINTRA criticized Lavín's and Colín's purported communistic tendencies.¹⁰³

Although the assertions of Soviet direction are far-fetched, Communists did tout the special relationship they shared with CANACINTRA, including their joint campaigns against the peso devaluation, scarcities, and inflation. For his part, José R. Colín questioned the Cold War battles over communism, claiming that having the world's most powerful capitalist nation as a neighbor precluded Mexico from even having a choice in the matter. He further accused conservatives of exploiting the Cold War to pursue their individual interests and the rollback of revolutionary reforms. He presciently concluded that while communism was a potential threat, the more immediate danger lay in the postwar anticommunist campaign.¹⁰⁴

To counter their detractors, CANACINTRA and the CTM held up the Worker-Employer Pact as a rebuttal to Cold War ideologues. Initially, some of Mexico's most prominent industrialists and labor leaders had joined in the pact. This included the presidents of CONCAMIN and CONCANACO, as well as communist and conservative unionists. However, most quickly backed out.¹⁰⁵ As CANACINTRA took the initiative to keep the pact alive, it emphasized that the agreement did not indicate an abandonment of class struggle or an attack on capitalism. Rather, along with the CTM, it portrayed the pact as an effort to manage class struggle by fostering cooperation among industrialists, labor, and the state in pursuit of independent industrial growth. Together, they lauded the accomplishments of the labor and employer signatories of the pact in managing labor conflict free from bureaucratic and political interference.¹⁰⁶ They concluded that this was

101. "Empresa libre-Iniciativa privada," *Actividad,* October 15, 1946.
102. "Patrones comunistas," *Actividad,* December 1, 1946; Joaquín de la Peña to Rogerio de la Selva (Secretaría de la Presidencia de la República), March 12, 1947, and to Mariano Suarez (presidente, COPARMEX), March 10, 1947, MAV/AGN, exp. 432/115.
103. Gracida Romo, *El programa industrial,* 85–86.
104. Campa, *Mi testimonio,* 182, 200; Colín, *Hacia dónde vamos?* 53–57; Lavín, *Actividades durante el año de 1945,* 18, 33–34.
105. Lavín, *Actividades durante el año de 1945,* 15–16; Colín, *Hacia dónde vamos?* 52.
106. Lavín, "Dos conferencias," 22–23.

the only means to counter the ideological allure of communism, defend Mexico's autonomy, and overcome U.S. dominance of the Mexican economy.

The alliance between CANACINTRA and the CTM did not portend a radical shift in labor-employer relations nor was it simply an example of opportunistic perfidy. It was fleeting and shallow, but it fit the complex political and economic imperatives of Cold War conservative consolidation and economic nationalism aimed against the United States. The ruling party, for its part, cultivated the pact's message of collaboration between industrialists, labor, and the state, if at the very least to expand its political base as it faced mounting domestic and international opposition to its pursuit of nationalist protected development.

The Meanings of Economic Nationalism

Both protectionists and liberals portrayed themselves as nationalist proponents of modernization and a front against U.S. imperialism. In fact, the postwar period was the first occasion during which such a broad range of industrialists joined to express their interests in terms of economic nationalism.[107] Yet, though both portrayed their projects as compatible with revolutionary aims to improve living standards, only CANACINTRA linked dependence on the United States to domestic poverty and inequality. The durability of the mid-twentieth-century association of ISI and economic nationalism, and the depiction of free trade as a betrayal of Mexico's revolutionary nationalist goals, rests heavily on the protectionists' emphasis on the links between dependency and poverty.

Nationalist reaction against the Porfiriato's self-imposed subjugation to foreign interests had helped to set off the Revolution. Yet, it was not until the 1920s and 1930s, when the United States resisted Mexico's revolutionary reforms, that political patriotism became associated with economic nationalism and a critique of underdevelopment. The 1938 oil conflict cemented this transformation and gave economic nationalism mass appeal for the first time.[108] Therefore, when Mexican officials faced free-trade pressures after the war, they could draw on commonly understood and well-articulated ideas of economic nationalism identified with opposition to dependence on the United States. For example, former government official

---

107. Knight, *U.S.-Mexican Relations*, 72.
108. Knight, "Peculiarities of Mexican History," 128; Knight, *U.S.-Mexican Relations*, 31–36; Knight, "Political Economy," 294.

Josué Sáenz, along with the ardently pro-protectionist Ramón Beteta, secretary of the Treasury and Public Credit (1946–52), averred that the postwar period was the time for Mexico to think less of integration with stronger economies and more about industrialization. Ricardo Torres Gaitán, a director at NAFINSA, added that U.S. opulence relied on the poverty of the rest of the world. Along with NAFINSA general director Antonio Carrillo Flores, he insisted that autonomy was critical if Mexico wanted to limit U.S. influence over the Mexican economy.[109]

Trade controls and tariffs presented an obvious challenge to foreign economic penetration. Therefore, CANACINTRA and its supporters easily promoted protective policies as nationalist.[110] Yet COPARMEX and CONCAMIN also were justified in touting outward-oriented growth and limited protection as nationalist. Historically, ties to external trade and capital drove economic growth in Latin America, including in Mexico, while protectionism was linked to slower rates of growth.[111] Despite concerns that Mexico was falling behind its neighbor to the north, the largest economies of Latin America had been expanding at rates similar to the United States during the export age since 1870.[112] Moreover, as we have seen in chapter 1, the dichotomy between orthodox liberalism and protectionism had long been more of an intellectual and political division than a material one. Since the nineteenth century, liberals had expressed a pragmatic appreciation of the role that tariffs, taxation, and even some state regulation and nationalization could play in developing industry and curbing dependency.

After World War II, CANACINTRA was distinguished from its more economically liberal opponents by its portrayal of protectionism as a means to build a more diverse, dynamic manufacturing sector aimed explicitly at satisfying domestic demand. It was backed by structuralists, who argued that economic nationalism, as characterized by the use of tariffs, exchange controls, taxes, subsidies, and even the confiscation of foreign investment, "implied a rejection . . . of foreign, especially American, trade and

---

109. *El Mercado de Valores* 8, no. 24 (June 14, 1948); *El Mercado de Valores* 8, no. 11 (March 15, 1948); *El Mercado de Valores* 8, no. 14 (April 5, 1948); Ricardo Torres Gaitán to Gonzalo Robles, November 8, 1947, GR/AGN, c. 34, exp. 9.

110. Antonio Ruiz Galindo to Ávila Camacho, February 10, 1945, MAC/AGN, exp. 545.22/262; Hernández Rodríguez, "Antonio Ruiz Galindo," 37.

111. Coatsworth and Williamson, "Always Protectionist?" 214–15; Coatsworth, "Mexico," 504. See also Taylor, "On the Costs of Inward-Looking Development."

112. Coatsworth, "Economic and Institutional Trajectories," 44. Coatsworth draws this conclusion from the comprehensive analysis of global GDP by Angus Maddison, *The World Economy: Historical Statistics* (Paris: OECD, 2003). He further critiques and commends this work in Coatsworth, "Structures, Endowments, and Institutions," 127–29.

investment. . . . [And it] was based on the belief that Mexico should abandon or amend its previous policy of export-led growth (*desarrollo hacia afuera*), which accorded a high priority to both exports and foreign investments, and should instead strive for a more autarkic, nationally based, and (in most versions) industrial model of development (*desarrollo hacia adentro*)."[113]

More important, postrevolutionary protectionists promised what nineteenth-century liberals had failed to deliver: development. Much of the substance behind the association of protectionism with economic nationalism rests with this distinction. CANACINTRA did not only contend that strong external economic ties would hurt Mexico's chances for sustained economic development, an assertion whose validity was contradicted by past growth rates and the organization's later alliances with foreign investors. Rather, like structuralists in ECLA, CANACINTRA also maintained that ending dependence on the United States through protected industrialization would allow Mexico to achieve the revolutionary goals of tackling endemic poverty and inequality. In doing so, CANACINTRA, in alliance with the CTM and the ruling party, capitalized on postwar suspicions and revolutionary aspirations to argue that dependence on the United States, which would only deepen with free trade, was largely to blame for underdevelopment.[114]

Licensed to Trade: From Tariffs to Quotas

Before 1947, the Mexican government largely disregarded trade controls in favor of using tax exemptions, tariffs, and other measures to promote and protect industry. Therefore, when President Alemán implemented trade controls that year, it marked a departure from prior industrial policy. The president's decision stemmed from a number of factors, including the anti-U.S. backlash, the legislative and administrative ease of implementing trade barriers, and the alliance between CANACINTRA and the CTM in support of state intervention. While intended to stem the postwar decline of reserves and to counter dependency, the decision satisfied an array of

---

113. Knight, *U.S.-Mexican Relations*, 53.

114. Similarly, Valpy FitzGerald extrapolates from Joyce Appleby's study of the seventeenth-century English ruling class to suggest that the "persistence of nonorthodox economic ideas" may be explained by the "moral or ethical" dimension of politics, "whereas the free-traders had no equivalent political vision." FitzGerald, "Conflict of Economic Doctrines," 109. See Appleby, *Economic Thought*, 277–78.

industrialist and labor groups, confirmed the ruling party's revolutionary nationalist credentials, and increased the regulatory capacity of the state. It thereby aided President Alemán in resolving persistent social and political conflicts while fostering forms of industrial growth and industrial politics in Mexico City.

The Ávila Camacho and Alemán administrations considered a host of ways to meet the postwar economic crisis. In 1946, President Ávila Camacho revised the 1941 federal tax-exemption law to exclude export taxes in order to deter exports and guarantee domestic supplies.[115] The resulting Law on the Promotion of Manufacturing Industries (Ley de Fomento de Industrias de Transformación) also narrowed the breadth of industries that qualified for an exemption in an attempt to plan industrial development more precisely. Like its 1941 predecessor, however, the 1946 law was vague and its impact in stimulating industry negligible.[116] Other proposals, such as expanding primary materials exports, were not viable due to labor unrest, political opposition, or international trade and diplomatic conditions. The Alemán administration even contemplated devaluing the peso, which was a popular option among conservative businesspeople organized in CONCAMIN and COPARMEX.[117] Though the overvalued peso facilitated the postwar flood of U.S. imports, devaluation seemed politically untenable owing to worries about inflation and its potential effect on labor unrest.[118]

With the United States refusing to renegotiate the 1942 trade agreement, trade controls appeared as a remedy for balance-of-payment difficulties, plunging monetary reserves, scarcities, and growing employment problems. Trade controls were also appealing simply because they defied the United States in a way that tax exemptions and tariffs did not. Unlike credit and trade agreements, the Mexican government could enact trade controls by unilateral decree, without depending on the cooperation of another government. Moreover, trade controls allowed Mexico to legally exclude, rather than merely deter, the import of specific goods, implying an independence that challenged U.S. assumptions about its collaborative relationship with Mexico. Finally, the 1944 promulgation of legislation that allowed the state to tighten regulations on imports and exports meant that the expansion of trade controls could occur with relative ease.

115. Mosk, *Industrial Revolution in Mexico*, 65.
116. Ross and Christensen, *Tax Incentives for Industry in Mexico*, 49–54; de Navarrete, *Los incentivos fiscales*, 21–22; Torres, *México en la segunda guerra mundial*, 291.
117. CONCAMIN to Alemán, September 20, 1948, AMGM, v. 237, exp. 768; *El Mercado de Valores* 8, no. 32 (August 9, 1948).
118. Interview with Ramón Beteta, in Wilkie and Monzón de Wilkie, *México visto en el siglo XX*, 47–48.

In July 1947, the government indefinitely suspended the importation of more than 120 articles defined as luxuries and seen as draining reserves, none of which were covered by the 1942 trade agreement. These controls affected 18 percent of total imports in 1946. Included on the list were obvious luxury items, such as furs, pianos, diamonds, and jewelry. However, items like clothing, carpets, and Kraft paper were also blocked.[119] Notably, the list included finished metal furniture, the very industry that Antonio Ruiz Galindo had wanted to develop but could not because the United States blocked his attempts to obtain primary materials during the war.

In November 1947, the Alemán administration enacted the first major tariff overhaul since 1930. The revision applied to five thousand articles not included in the trade agreement. For the first time in Mexico's history, and at the urging of CANACINTRA, the government adopted a compounded tariff system that included both specific and ad valorem tariffs based on official minimum prices. It applied ad valorem tariffs in part due to the erosion of effective rates of protection since 1930.[120] The 1947 tariff revision therefore reestablished higher rates of protection for already covered items, and it incorporated some previously unprotected industries into the tariff schedule.

Industrialists reacted with ambivalence to the tightening of controls and tariff revisions. Both CONCAMIN and CANACINTRA were troubled that certain key industries remained exposed, including clothing, footwear, food products, some chemical products, and the paint and dye industries. These industries had been excluded from further tariffs because they were already regulated by the 1942 trade agreement. CANACINTRA, in response, drew up a list of 134 articles, or two-thirds of the products controlled by the trade agreement, which it argued were in immediate need of more protection. Among the items listed were approximately thirty-five food-related products; sixteen textile and clothing products; some footwear; a significant number of chemical, paint, and dye products; and ten types of autos or auto parts.[121]

The United States condemned the 1947 expansion of trade controls and tariffs. President Alemán predicted this reaction. As recently as April 1947,

---

119. Cabral, "Industrialización y política económica," 95–96; de Navarrete, *Los incentivos fiscales*, 116; Torres, *Hacia la utopía industrial*, 96–97; Mosk, *Industrial Revolution in Mexico*, 80–82.

120. Esquivel and Márquez Colín, "Some Economic Effects," 336–38; Villarreal, *Industrialización, deuda y desequilibrio externo*, 39, 50–53, 57; Reynolds, *Mexican Economy*, 221; Cárdenas, *La industrialización mexicana*, 107.

121. For the complete list, see CANACINTRA, *El Tratado Comercial*, 35–47.

his government had informally agreed with U.S. officials to augment Mexican exports rather than curb imports in order to stem the loss of reserves.[122] Therefore, to ease opposition both at home and abroad, President Alemán avowed that modifications to licensing and tariffs were temporary and would apply only to luxury imports.[123] Like President Ávila Camacho, he also assured the business community that trade controls and tariffs were being used solely to plan industrialization and benefit industrialists, not to raise revenue for the state.[124] To avoid angering the United States, however, President Alemán resisted labeling trade controls as protectionist. He contended that licensing was a fiscal measure aimed at putting an end to balance-of-payment problems. He denied that his goal was to protect Mexican industries from dumping and unfair competition or a political move designed to generate domestic favor.[125]

Despite the initial U.S. opposition, by December 1947, pressure from the Mexican government forced the U.S. State Department to concede to trade controls on the original 120 luxury items. In return, the Mexican government expanded the list in early 1948. By the end of that year, the Alemán administration authorized the Secretariat of the Economy to amend the list of controlled articles at its own discretion. It needed the approval of the SHCP only in cases where national revenue would potentially be affected. Therefore, by 1948, import and export controls were entrenched in President Alemán's protectionist program, and on December 31, 1950, Mexico and the United States finally abrogated the 1942 trade agreement. In subsequent years, the Mexican government regularly modified tariffs and trade controls in reaction to shifting economic, social, and political conditions, including when it temporarily eased controls during the Korean War amid fears about scarcities.[126] In general, however, trade controls grew during the next ten to fifteen years. In 1947, just 1 percent of the categories of imports were subject to controls, but by 1956, that figure had risen to 28 percent.[127] By 1964, that figure had grown to more than 65 percent. At that time, 99.9 percent of beverages and tobacco imports required licenses,

122. Niblo, *Mexico in the 1940s*, 175, 182.
123. *Conferencias de Mesa Redonda*, xi.
124. Secretaría de Gobernación, *Seis años de actividad nacional*, 311. For industrialist opposition to the imposition of trade controls for fiscal ends, see CANACINTRA, "Memorandums que dirige al Sr. Presidente de la República, Lic. Miguel Alemán, el Presidente de la Cámara Nacional de la Industria de Transformación," 1947, MAV/AGN, exp. 433/99.
125. Mosk, *Industrial Revolution in Mexico*, 75, 80–81.
126. Izquierdo, "Protectionism in Mexico," 265, 269; Torres, *Hacia la utopía industrial*, 96–99.
127. Solís, *La realidad económica mexicana*, 225.

although less than 50 percent of manufactured goods and arms and munitions did.[128]

Scholars generally concur that in the early easy phase of import substitution, from the late 1940s through the 1950s, protectionist policies favored consumer goods industries, such as food products, clothing, shoes, and textiles. In 1939, imports of capital goods made up 50 percent of all imports, while consumer goods and intermediate goods each were about 25 percent. By 1958, consumer goods made up less than 10 percent of manufactured imports, while intermediate goods surged to make up 33 percent and capital goods grew to 59 percent of the total, typical of an economy trying to develop its consumer goods industries.[129] Significantly, Mexico's reliance on its consumer goods industries did not deepen during these years. In 1935, consumer goods made up 77 percent of Mexican industry, but by 1955, they had slipped to just about 52 percent. During that same time, intermediate goods as a percentage of total Mexican industry climbed from roughly 12 percent to about 21 percent, and capital goods went from 11 percent to more than 27 percent.[130]

The regional impact of postwar protectionism is unclear, partly due to the variety of factors in addition to policy that spur industrial change. Although the contribution of consumer goods to Mexico City's economy held steady at roughly 75 percent between 1940 and 1960, Mexico City's contribution to total national production of consumer goods grew in those years from almost 31 percent in 1940 to 52 percent in 1960. To illustrate the dramatic concentration of consumer manufacturing there, by 1955, Mexico City was responsible for producing more than one-half of the national production value of pharmaceuticals, knitwear, soaps and detergents, matches, crackers and pastas, wheels and tires, silk and rayon textiles, cigars and cigarettes, and auto assembly. It had a strong presence in numerous other industries as well.[131] This occurred at a time when Mexico City's contribution to the national production of capital goods dropped from approximately 63 percent in 1930 to under 55 percent in 1960. For intermediate goods, its share of national production dropped from about 37 percent in 1940 to 33 percent in 1960. Therefore, as the federal government pursued a form of protectionism that focused in its early stages on the substitution of imported

128. Esquivel and Márquez Colín, "Some Economic Effects," 340–41.
129. Ibid., 341–44; Villarreal, *Industrialización, deuda y desequilibrio externo*, 70–73, 271–72.
130. Story, *Industry*, 23–25.
131. López Malo, *Ensayo sobre localización*, 113.

consumer manufactures, Mexico City's contribution to total national production of that type of industry grew relative to other industrial sectors.[132] Although suggestive, the role of tariffs and trade controls in creating this concentration of consumer goods production in Mexico City remains uncertain. Other factors also encouraged this trend, including the city's rapid population growth and heavy investment in transportation, infrastructure, and public services.

Trade controls and tariffs ultimately fostered state centralization by expanding the federal government's regulatory capacity. Unlike tariffs and tax exemptions, which applied uniformly to all relevant industries or products, the federal government made decisions about quantitative controls on a case-by-case basis. Once an import or export quota was established for a particular product, individual companies had to apply for permits that apportioned a part of that quota to them. As a result, during their attempts to receive import or export licenses, industrialists had regular and individual contact with the federal government.[133] In order to be granted a license, companies had to comply with state-defined production standards and official oversight. For example, companies that imported controlled products had to send regular reports to the Manufacturing Industries Affairs Office (Dirección General de Industrias de Transformación, part of the Secretariat of the Economy) about factors such as primary material usage. Moreover, the secretariat inspected machinery, labor-code compliance, primary material consumption, and production so that it could make decisions about establishing or modifying an import quota. If a company failed to comply with government standards, it could lose its rights to import or export. Therefore, licensing gave the state a useful tool to compel industrialists to meet state-defined developmental priorities.

Even though the process of granting licenses normally took four to eight weeks, industrialists maintained that this increased vigilance delayed production. Many first had to prove that the desired import was not available domestically, and then primary materials often languished in ports because of a lack of coordination between customs officials and government agencies. For instance, the rug manufacturer Tapetes Luxor initiated a request for wool imports in mid-1950. It first had to prove that the desired wool was not available from national producers. After the company received an

---

132. Gustavo Garza Villarreal makes a similar observation. Garza Villarreal, *El proceso de industrialización*, 149–54, 171.

133. Izquierdo, "Protectionism in Mexico," 254.

approval, Port of Veracruz customs officials refused to release the wool until the Secretariat of the Economy specified the permissible amount that could enter the country.[134] Other manufacturers protested that materials were rotting as they waited to pass through customs and that warehousing costs and production stoppages resulted from these sorts of delays.[135]

Also purportedly slowing production was the program of Compensated Exchange (*trueques*), which required companies that desired an imported good to seek an exchange with the foreign exporter so that Mexico's balance of payments would not be affected.[136] Arranged through the Banco Nacional de Comercio Exterior, this exchange at times went smoothly. For example, Beijer Continental set up an exchange with Switzerland that allowed it to import artificial fibers in exchange for Mexican exports of zinc oxide, produced by the Compañía Comercial Azteca.[137] Others contended that the exchange program slowed imports, however, since some exporting countries, including the United States, refused to participate.[138]

Industrialists also complained that they had too little input in decisions about tariffs and quotas. CONCAMIN, CANACINTRA, and other business organizations lobbied for more representation on tariff and trade commissions, arguing their knowledge about production was critical if the government was to make informed and equitable decisions.[139] As an example, CONCAMIN pointed out that the SHCP had approved export permits for animal skins without considering the ramifications for Mexico's tanning industry.[140]

Nevertheless, when the Alemán administration reconstituted the General Tariff Commission (Comisión General de Aranceles) in 1949, it excluded

---

134. Tapetes Luxor, S.A., Secretaría de Economía, and SHCP, correspondence, August 21, 1950–June 9, 1951, DGI/AGN, v. 131, exp. 391/332.1/-40.

135. For example, see La Purisima, Aguascalientes to Dirección General de Industrias, July 16, 1947, DGI/AGN, v. 130, exp. 391/332.1/-28.

136. King, *Mexico: Industrialization and Trade*, 80–81.

137. Beijar Continental, S.A., to Dirección General de Industrias, November 27, 1950, DGI/AGN, v. 130, exp. 391/332.1/-28.

138. Alfombras Mohawk de México, S.A. de C.V., to SEN, Dirección General de Industrias, Oficina de Registro y Control Industrial de la Industria Textil, memorandum, February 16, 1951, DGI/AGN, v. 130, exp. 391/332.1/-28.

139. Guillermo Guajardo Davis (presidente, CONCAMIN) to Alemán, September 20, 1948, AMGM, v. 237, exp. 768; CANACINTRA, "Memorandums que dirige al Sr. Presidente de la República, Lic. Miguel Alemán, el Presidente de la Cámara Nacional de la Industria de Transformación," 1947, MAV/AGN, exp. 433/99; "Informe del Señor Edmundo J. Phelan, a la Asamblea General Ordinaria, durante el ejercicio social de 1951–1952," in CONCAMIN, *La Confederación de Cámaras Industriales*, 2:402–3; Cámara Regional de la Industria de Aceites, Jabones, Grasas, y Similares de Occidente to Secretario de Economía Nacional, June 24, 1947, AMGM, v. 302, exp. 1050.

140. CONCAMIN to Alemán, February 20, 1947, and August 25, 1947, MAV/AGN, 564.2/16.

industrialists from the important tariff committees. Although they retained their representation on advisory boards, they were shut out of decision-making committees.[141] Despite the protests of both CONCAMIN and CANACINTRA, when the Alemán administration created the Import and Export Commission (Comisión de Importaciones y Exportaciones) in March 1950, industrialists once again found themselves on the outside. They responded that they were willing to settle for one nonvoting member.[142] But the Alemán administration rebuffed them, and the commissions remained staunchly bureaucratic. Moreover, many decisions about controls and tariffs were opaque, with the decisions handed down without possibility of appeal.[143] The creation of the Compañía Exportadora e Importadora Mexicana, S.A. (CEIMSA) in 1949, which had a monopoly over granting licenses for some controlled basic goods, also angered industrialists. A redefinition of the regulations governing it in early 1950 seemed to assuage CONCAMIN.[144] Yet, when the government passed the Law on Federal Executive Powers in Economic Matters (Ley sobre Atribuciones del Ejecutivo Federal en Materia Económica) in 1950, it once again met opposition. The law extended executive oversight of prices, production and distribution, imports and exports, protectionist policies, and supplies. CANACINTRA cautiously supported it as a necessary measure to defend the economy in the face of global uncertainties stemming from the Korean War. But CONCAMIN, COPARMEX, and CONCANACO protested the new law on the grounds that regulation was historically ineffective, contrary to the "principles of liberty" recognized by the 1917 Constitution, and evidence of the state's push to build a planned economy.[145] Critically, by excluding the private sector from anything but, at best, an advisory role in policy making, state efforts at regulating production and consumption never gained broad popular legitimacy.

141. Izquierdo, "Protectionism in Mexico," 267.
142. Sesión Ordinaria de Consejo Nacional de Empresarios de la Industria Textil, Acta no. 128, March 20, 1950, Archivo de la Compañía Industrial de Guadalajara, S.A. (CIGSA)/Universidad Iberoamericana (UI), c. 136.
143. Shadlen, *Democratization Without Representation*, 34–36.
144. CEIMSA had the authority to intervene in the pricing and distribution of primary necessities in order to "maintain just prices," though the parastate company was often accused of operating more in its own interests. Azpeitia Gómez, *Compañía Exportadora*, 52–56.
145. Quote from the "Informe del Señor Edmundo J. Phelan, a la Asamblea General Ordinaria del 12 de marzo de 1951, sobre el ejercicio social de 1950–1951," in CONCAMIN, *La Confederación de Cámaras Industriales*, 2:397; Zabludovsky, "Proposiciones para el estudio," 25–26. More than ten years later, some were still asserting that the law was unconstitutional. See Isla González de Cosío, "Estudio de la Ley."

According to Vivek Chibber, industrialists' reaction to state regulation was common in many industrializing countries of the developing world in the middle of the twentieth century. Even in Mexico, where planning was never comprehensive, government officials regularly promoted their industrial policies by referencing the benefits of economic planning. They often portrayed import-substituting protectionist policies and state regulations as complementary planning tools. But although industrialists welcomed tariffs, subsidies, and loans that could enhance profits, many often rejected the discipline of state economic management. Therefore, rather than uniting industrialists and state officials, the concurrent expansion of protection and regulation instead led to tensions.[146] Chibber emphasizes the opposition to planning by owners who benefited from ISI, but state officials were also to blame for the weak links between protectionism and planning in Mexico in the early 1950s. Although licensing had the potential to inject rigor into industrial planning, the breadth of items subject to controls and the ease with which industrialists gained licenses meant that the evaluation of individual controls became simpler and less exact, and it could not take price, quality, and costs fully into account.[147] Industrialists seeking to receive or modify permits pressured the state, either individually or through industrialist chambers rather than through formal channels, which exacerbated this.[148] Moreover, different government agencies were involved in administering tariffs and licenses, and there was only limited coordination between them.[149] For some, the government seemed to make decisions about tariffs and controls with little concern for industrial planning, even as the government continued to tout its planning initiatives. For instance, some tariff increases occurred across the board and did not discriminate among product groups, such as the 1954 modification that raised all tariffs by 25 percent.[150] Finally, since it introduced a particularist and discretionary aspect into the

---

146. Chibber argues that state planners used "'soft'" incentives, such as tariffs and subsidies, to encourage industrialists to invest in capitalist ventures. They then issued regulatory measures to assure that public monies went not only into profits, but also into investments, ensuring long-term growth and development. Chibber, "Reviving the Developmental State?" 5–7.

147. NAFINSA, *La política industrial*, 152–53.

148. For example, in 1951, CANACINTRA intervened to help members with eighty-eight import permits and fifteen export permits. Cardoso, *Informe*, 67–68, 73–74. Also Guillermo Guajardo Davis, "Discurso pronunciado en la Convención Anual de la Asociación de Banqueros de México," April 1949, in *Recopilación de los más importantes discursos pronunciados y artículos publicados por el señor Guillermo Guajardo Davis, como Presidente de la Confederación de Cámaras Industriales,* April 1948–March 1950, MAV/AGN, 704/439.

149. Bueno, "Structure of Protection in Mexico," 181.

150. Esquivel and Márquez Colín, "Some Economic Effects," 339–44; Mosk, *Industrial Revolution in Mexico*, 75–76.

regulatory structure, the process of apportioning licenses based on quotas opened the government up to accusations of coercion, corruption, incompetence, and favoritism.[151]

Conclusion

Two events beginning in 1948 demonstrate the immediate domestic impact of the adoption of trade controls and tariff increases. First, despite broad opposition from industrialist and labor groups, the Alemán administration allowed the peso to float. By June 1949, it had depreciated by about 80 percent.[152] Second, with the CTM's backing, President Alemán initiated the *charrazo*, a crackdown on leftist labor leaders. By the early 1950s, his administration had dismantled and rebuilt the railway, oil, and mining unions, using force, arrests, and anticommunist rhetoric. In the process, he destroyed the left's position within the official labor movement, secured the role of corrupt, PRI-allied union leaders at the head of national unions, and severely weakened alternative unions. Though the CTM continued to struggle into the 1950s to rebuild its membership, it consolidated its hold over national labor with the PRI's assistance.[153]

The peso devaluation is important because it hints at the ambivalent economic outcomes of the expansion of trade controls and tariffs, which had failed to adequately stem the loss of reserves, at least in the short term, leading to the devaluation. Yet manufacturing continued its steady climb as a percentage of total national production, growing from 18 percent in 1940 to more than 20 percent by 1950, and 23 percent by 1960.[154] As a project to lessen economic dependence, the results of protectionism were even hazier. Although total U.S. investment in manufacturing grew during the 1950s, the overall U.S. investment in Mexican manufacturing dropped from almost 10 percent in 1950 to about 8 percent in 1960. However, the influx of subsidiaries from the late 1940s presented new nationalist complications, as U.S. companies jumped over trade barriers to take advantage of protectionist policies.[155]

151. Wallace, "Policies of Protection," 48–49; Cardoso, *Informe*, 12–17; Alcazar, *Las agrupaciones patronales*, 51–52, 119–23; Cordero H., *Concentración industrial*, 9.

152. Cárdenas, "Process of Accelerated Industrialization," 186.

153. For more on the impact of the Cold War on labor politics, see Carr, *Marxism and Communism*, 153–56, 168–76; Middlebrook, *Paradox of Revolution*, 135–41; L. Medina, *Civilismo y modernización*, 15, 112; Gómez Tagle and Miquet, "Integración o democracia sindical," 156–57.

154. Reynolds, *Mexican Economy*, 61.

155. Ibid., 190–91; Cárdenas, "Process of Accelerated Industrialization," 187–89; L. Meyer, "Historical Roots of the Authoritarian State in Mexico," 17.

The political legacy of protectionism, as evidenced over the short run in the devaluation and the charrazo, was more categorical. The expansion of protectionism fostered the consolidation of the CTM and CANACINTRA, thereby improving the state's relationship with industrialists and labor. This enabled the Alemán administration to pursue policies, such as the devaluation, which previously had been politically untenable. It also allowed the president to repress remaining labor opposition and drive down real wages. In Mexico City alone, the minimum wage remained fixed during the late 1940s, despite a cumulative inflation of more than 41 percent for 1946–47 and 1948–49.[156]

Protectionism also became the foundation for a new version of revolutionary nationalism rooted in statist, urban industrialism. It provided the material means for the PRI to forge the crony arrangements that underpinned its enduring authority. CANACINTRA seemed to be the favored child of statist industrialism. Yet, by the late 1940s, the chamber's political sheen had begun to tarnish, and not just because José R. Colín broke with the organization and condemned the PRI for its oligarchic tendencies.[157] Despite its political prominence, the organization faced the bigger challenge of a bias toward large-scale industry. Moreover, even as protectionists in alliance with the ruling party captured the nationalist card, in organizations like COPARMEX and the PAN, economic liberalism survived and thrived through the halcyon days of ISI. The members of conservative industrial and business chambers continued to defend revolutionary principles, economic independence, and market forces even as they profited from state assistance and personal connections to high-ranking members of the PRI. Consequently, even at the height of midcentury industrial protectionism, opposition to state economic intervention remained strong and continued to express itself in nationalist terms.

---

156. Bortz and Aguila, "Earning a Living," 125–29. Although standards of living did not decline as rapidly under President Alemán as they had during World War II, the period from 1946 to 1952 saw a steady drop in the real minimum daily wage. Middlebrook, *Paradox of Revolution*, 214–15. This occurred not due to inflation, but because the Alemán administration held the minimum daily wage steady from 1946 through 1951.

157. Colín, *Hacia dónde vamos?*; Shadlen, *Democratization Without Representation*, 50.

6

RECENTERING THE NATION

Industrial Liberty in Postrevolutionary Monterrey

In February 1946, Monterrey business leaders cautioned, "Currently, there is a divorce between the state government and the 'active forces' in the city of Monterrey." This followed comments by the ruling-party governor Arturo de la Garza (1944–49) that condemned the "rich" businesspeople of the city.[1] The contretemps occurred a mere two months after a contentious December 1945 municipal election, in which the PRM, the PAN, and the Partido Liberal had fronted candidates. To challenge the PRM-backed Félix González Salinas, who happened to be the brother-in-law of Governor de la Garza, the Monterrey business community had supported local businessman Manuel L. Barragán in the election. Rather than allowing the election to decide the outcome, however, Governor de la Garza had intervened and illegally installed his brother-in-law in office, over the protests of the business community.[2] Soon after, local business leaders had launched a campaign to stop paying municipal taxes and pressured the ruling party to recognize that González Salinas had lost the election.[3]

By the 1940s, Monterrey's business elites were well versed in political exclusion, having experienced more than twenty years of turbulent dealings with revolutionary leaders. Still, the 1945 municipal election was in some ways surprising. In 1939, the Monterrey Group had forged a pact with the Ávila Camacho campaign to support his presidential bid in exchange for influence in selecting local leaders. Additionally, conflicts between the Monterrey Group and the ruling party had waned in the early 1940s, as the

---

1. "El gobierno del estado y la comunidad," *Actividad*, February 15, 1946; López-Portillo Tostado, *Estado e ideología empresarial*, 223–24.
2. Niblo, *Mexico in the 1940s*, 150–51.
3. Shafer, *Mexican Business Organizations*, 142–44.

PRM became more moderate and as personal and business connections between national politicians and Monterrey industrialists grew stronger. Under President Alemán, relations further improved, fueled by the government's extensive support for Monterrey industries, labor repression, and the president's close ties to the so-called *regiomontano,* or Monterrey, elites. Nevertheless, the Monterrey Group continued to challenge the ruling party, as well as the efforts of the central government to extend its influence over Nuevo León at the expense of the business community's historic regional authority.

The Cold War and President Alemán's 1947 decision to expand trade controls provided an opportunity for the Monterrey Group to express this opposition while preserving the benefits of collaboration with ruling-party officials. On the one hand, the region's industrialists denounced corporatist labor politics, singling out the CTM for allegedly facilitating the communist infiltration of Mexico. In its place, they embraced scientific management as a way to discipline workers to the rhythms of capitalist production and reassert paternal authority over their factories while displacing state-backed unions.[4] On the other hand, they modified their liberal opposition to state economic intervention by accommodating broader protectionist policies, which they had long supported for their own industries. However, they continued to stridently oppose state regulation seen as impinging on the rights of private enterprise, such as distribution controls or state oversight of production.[5]

Like Antioqueño industrialists in Colombia and Paulistas in Brazil, Monterrey's industrialists advanced their vision of economic development by crafting an identity for themselves as leaders of a form of nationalist modernization rooted in their region's distinct social relations and industrial growth.[6] The Monterrey Group reinscribed regiomontano identity to contest corporatism and statist industrialism and thereby challenge assertions of the revolutionary state as the guarantor of economic development and defender of the Mexican nation. Monterrey's elites did not define their economic liberalism in ideological terms. Instead, it was an outgrowth of the region's rugged frontier past, where individual hard work, thrift, sobriety, ingenuity, commitment, and cooperation were responsible for the city's industrial modernity. They contrasted this with Mexico City, where they charged that the

---

4. Similarly, Brazilian industrialists redefined themselves according to understandings of rationalization and scientific management in an attempt to gain national authority. Weinstein, *For Social Peace.*

5. Melgar Palacios, "Economic Development in Monterrey," 68–71.

6. Weinstein, *For Social Peace*; Farnsworth-Alvear, *Dulcinea in the Factory.*

indiscipline of corporatist labor politics and state intervention had replaced the discipline of production, to the detriment of both employers and workers. Regiomontano businesspeople thereby created a durable image of Monterrey as the "'moral capital'" of Mexico, where an identity built on social conservatism, paternalism, and cross-class collaboration had engendered the region's remarkable industrial modernization, a situation similar to that of nineteenth-century Milan, as described by Adrian Lyttelton. They therefore conceived of Monterrey as an alternative and opposing center of power to Mexico City, a place, they charged, where the revolutionary excesses of ruling-party-directed statist development had bred immorality and national degradation.[7]

From Frontier to Center

Monterrey's business leaders saw themselves as having a singular responsibility to the Mexican people to free their nation from the "lethargic, submissive, economically backward societies" of central Mexico.[8] Although reading like an apocryphal tale of redemption and glory, the story of their city's identity nevertheless gained traction due to Monterrey's location, its relatively recent and rapid industrial growth, and the middle-class origins of many of its most prominent business leaders, including the Garza Sada family.[9] This provincialism was sustained by the strong financial, social, and familial ties among the region's elites, as well as by the cross-class collaboration to which most employers, as well as many workers, subscribed. In turn, it encouraged an independent, even rebellious, reaction to the corporatist and centralizing politics of the 1920s and 1930s.[10]

Monterrey was at the epicenter of one of Mexico's most economically and politically independent regions. During the colonial and early post-Independence periods, it remained a regional outpost that survived on agriculture and trade with the surrounding mining regions. The early stages of its transformation into a northern industrial city came with the rise to power of Governor Santiago Vidaurri (1855–64). Governor Vidaurri implemented

7. Lyttelton, "Shifting Identities," 45, 48.
8. Snodgrass, *Deference and Defiance*, 9. Snodgrass provides an excellent analysis of the historically contingent and strategic nature of this identity. Snodgrass, *Deference and Defiance*, 8–13. Others have been less critical in reproducing these representations, including Fuentes Mares, *Monterrey: Una ciudad creadora*.
9. Walton, *Elites and Economic Development*, 48.
10. Abraham Nuncio termed this a "spirit of obstruction." Nuncio, *El Grupo Monterrey*, 66.

policies to support regional trade and the start-up of the local sugar and textile industries, while securing relative peace amid the midcentury liberal-conservative upheavals. Monterrey also benefited from the recent loss of northern territory to the United States in the 1846–48 war, which effectively moved the city closer to U.S. markets. Furthermore, the American Civil War boosted trade through the region, since a northern blockade forced the Confederate States to trade via northeastern Mexico. Therefore, under Governor Vidaurri, Monterrey became a customs-control center and trading entrepôt for the northern ports and frontier, while also exercising considerable economic and politico-military influence over Chihuahua, San Luis Potosí, Zacatecas, and Durango. But the return of liberal-conservative fighting after the fall of Governor Vidaurri once again slowed the region's industrial advances.[11]

The Pax Porfiriana finally brought lasting peace to this part of Mexico, as it shook loose regionally rooted cacicazgos and expanded central authority by imposing loyal local governments.[12] Governor Bernardo Reyes (1889–1909) embodied the extension of Porfirian authority over the north, as he balanced his loyalty to the Porfiriato with his promotion and protection of regional economic interests. He soon forged strong ties with the region's diverse merchants, who used their capital from decades of trade and their political connections to initiate large-scale industry during this era of social peace.[13] By 1900, these owners had become Mexico's most tightly knit business group, united with each other through family and capital. Among them were the extended families of foreign-born businesspeople, such as Patricio Milmo, the Hernández-Mendirichaga family, and Valentín Rivero, as well as sons of immigrants and native-born entrepreneurs, such as Evaristo Madero and Francisco Sada y Garza. Together, they constituted a closely integrated regional bourgeoisie that fueled Porfirian economic growth and dominated northeastern politics and society.[14] Their success at generating capital from regional mining, agricultural, and commercial ventures distinguished them from businesspeople in other states. Along with national and foreign capital, they used this local capital to finance industrial

---

11. Cerutti, "Monterrey and Its *Ámbito Regional*," 152–53; Mora-Torres, *Making of the Mexican Border*, 36, 46–48; Walton, *Elites and Economic Development*, 44–45; Vizcaya Canales, *Los orígenes de la industrialización*, 31–41; Montemayor Hernández, *Historia de Monterrey*, 149–96.

12. Montemayor Hernández, *Historia de Monterrey*, 236–41, 252.

13. Alba Vega, "Las regiones industriales," 114–16; Vellinga, "*Regiomontana* Bourgeoisie," 200–205.

14. For two examples of the rise and connections of these families, see Cerutti, "Patricio Milmo, empresario regiomontano del siglo XIX," 231–66; Hernández Elizondo, "Comercio e industria textil en Nuevo León," 267–86.

expansion. The region's business community also heavily invested in the creation of regional banking institutions, such as the powerful Banco de Nuevo León in 1892 and the Banco Mercantil de Monterrey in 1899, further facilitating their access to local capital.[15] Moreover, by taking advantage of two new commercial codes issued in 1884 and 1887, which governed the creation and function of corporations, they formed a range of joint stock ventures wherein Monterrey's most prominent fifteen to twenty families invested in each other's businesses. In one study of ten prominent late nineteenth-century regiomontano families, three companies counted members of each of those families among their investors.[16] From its outset, however, local industry demonstrated some important internal differences. The Cervecería Cuauhtémoc, for example, relied largely on local capital and business ties. By contrast, the Fundidora de Hierro y Acero de Monterrey, Mexico's first modern iron and steel factory, actively courted investors from Mexico City. Moreover, early on it received federal subsidies, tariffs, and exemptions that were critical to its survival. Nevertheless, access to local capital and the tendency to use joint stock ventures helped to mute potential rivalries and gave the region considerable economic independence.

The federal and regional governments played a prominent role in encouraging Monterrey's industry in the late 1800s. For example, the abolishment of internal excise taxes (*alcabalas*) and the narrowing of the Border Free Trade Zone in 1896 improved regiomontano access to national markets. The federal and regional governments also provided protection, improved taxation, invested in infrastructure, and encouraged railroad building that tied Monterrey to both the United States and the rest of Mexico. Monterrey's proximity to U.S. capital, raw materials, machinery, and markets, in turn, helped to spur its unique growth. The implementation of the McKinley tariff in 1890, for example, critically influenced regional industry. By limiting Mexican mining exports to the United States, it induced Mexican and U.S. entrepreneurs to invest in smelting facilities in Mexico.[17] In 1890 alone, local investors initiated production of two goods, steel and beer, which would become the cornerstone of local industry. In the next ten

15. Mora-Torres, *Making of the Mexican Border*, 97–98; Saragoza, *Monterrey Elite*, 33–34, 43–51.
16. The three companies were the Compañía Fundidora de Hierro y Acero de Monterrey, S.A., the Compañía Carbonífera de Monterrey, S.A., and the Fábrica de Vidrios y Cristales de Monterrey, S.A. Cerutti, "Producción capitalista," 30. Cerutti discusses these families more extensively in Cerutti, *Burguesía, capitales e industria*, chapter 5. On the commercial codes, see Beato and Sindico, "Beginning of Industrialization," 503–7.
17. Mora-Torres, *Making of the Mexican Border*, 89–90, 93; Vizcaya Canales, *Los orígenes de la industrialización*, 77.

years, the number of enterprises in Nuevo León grew to 101, and the state established itself as the center of metallurgy by generating roughly one-quarter of the national production of metals.[18] During these years, the anchor companies of Monterrey's two most important business groups emerged, including the Cervecería Cuauhtémoc, created in 1891 by the Sada and Garza Sada families, and the Fundidora, which was founded in 1903. The Cuauhtémoc group soon began to vertically integrate production by setting up bottling, bottle cap, and cardboard factories.[19]

By 1910, Nuevo León was Mexico's largest regional contributor to national industrial production, generating almost 14 percent of the nation's total industrial production. It had a presence in both consumer goods and heavy industry. Mexico City and the Estado de México were close behind at almost 12 percent and slightly more than 11 percent, respectively. Puebla, with its dominance of Mexico's textile industry, trailed at not quite 8 percent. Monterrey, in particular, experienced remarkable growth during the Porfiriato. Of the almost Mex$40 million invested in registered industries in Nuevo León in 1906, roughly Mex$36 million were in Monterrey companies. Moreover, between 1883 and 1910, the city's population grew by 112 percent, constituting close to one-quarter of the state's population by the eve of the Revolution.[20] Consequently, during its era of "great industry" between 1890 and 1910, Monterrey transformed itself from a struggling frontier city into one of Mexico's industrial centers.[21]

The Revolution disrupted the patterns of economic and social life in Monterrey and brought major fighting and a Constitutionalist occupation to the region. Business leaders became the targets of extortion, confiscations, and even imprisonment. Some, like the Garza Sadas, fled into exile in the United States. They returned only in 1916, when they were able to recover the Cervecería Cuauhtémoc from the Constitutionalist forces who had seized it, reportedly as punishment for the Cuauhtémoc group's support of Victoriano Huerta.[22] Industry rebounded after the Revolution, though not uniformly. A flush of new firms emerged in the 1920s, and many older companies recovered and expanded into new areas. For example, the Cervecería Cuauhtémoc grew rapidly in the mid-1920s, even without major government assistance. The Fundidora faltered, but federal contracts and

18. Vellinga, *Industrialización, burguesía, y clase obrera*, 90; Cerutti, *Burguesía, capitales e industria*, 178.
19. Gómez Galvarriato, "El desempeño de la Fundidora," 201–10.
20. Cerutti, "Producción capitalista," 22–23; Montemayor Hernández, *Historia de Monterrey*, 277; Walton, *Elites and Economic Development*, 48–49.
21. Vizcaya Canales, *Los orígenes de la industrialización*, 75.
22. Vellinga, *Industrialización, burguesía, y clase obrera*, 110.

protection ensured its survival. Recognizing how critical this federal support was to the Fundidora's future, its general director, Adolfo Prieto, lived in Mexico City.[23]

Political peace did not accompany this economic recovery, however. In contrast to the *reyista* period, regional governments in the 1920s proved too unstable to provide local industrialists with consistent protection or guarantees. Political instability also created a climate that enabled some governors, such as Porfirio G. González (1920–21, 1923–25), to treat Nuevo León like a personal fiefdom. Tax hikes, graft, and extortion of the local business community were rampant. Moreover, Monterrey's industrialists found that due to their support of Porfirio Díaz and Victoriano Huerta, they had gone from being favored political insiders to being viewed with suspicion by the Revolution's victors. This only deepened when Monterrey's business leaders offered to mediate a settlement between the government and rebels during the 1923 Adolfo de la Huerta revolt. President Obregón suspected that their offer was simply opportunistic meddling intended to mask their backing of de la Huerta. He therefore rebuffed them.[24] This political disorder and exclusion during the 1920s fostered enduring antipathy among the Monterrey Group toward the Revolution's victors, and ultimately toward the ruling party when it emerged at the end of that decade.[25]

Not until the rise to power of Jerónimo Siller (1925–27) and especially Nuevo León-native Aarón Sáenz (1927, 1929–31) did the Monterrey business community have governors more amenable to their interests. Governor Sáenz integrated the Monterrey Group into regional commissions charged with studying and revising industrial and commercial policy, infrastructure, and local taxation. He also called on local business to help devise an economic plan for the state. The appointment of Juan Andreu Almazán to regional military commander confirmed the pro-business turn in regional politics. Almazán quickly embedded himself in the region's social and economic life, and he used his authority to bring political peace, labor repression, and funding and infrastructure to the state. However, when Calles refused to designate Sáenz as the PNR's candidate for the presidency in 1929, Monterrey's business community once again found itself excluded from national politics.[26]

23. Saragoza, *Monterrey Elite*, 126–28.
24. Collado Herrera, *Empresarios y políticos*, 151–53.
25. Vellinga, "*Regiomontana* Bourgeoisie," 205.
26. Saragoza, *Monterrey Elite*, 122–25. For more on the antagonism of regiomontano business owners to the PNR and their backing of Governor Sáenz, see Daniel García Cerda (Casa de la Estufa, Monterrey) to Portes Gil, June 9, 1929, Fondo Emilio Portes Gil (EPG)/AGN, 672, v. 18.

Further frustrating the Monterrey Group were callista efforts to expand state regulation of production and consumption, as we have seen in chapter 1. Though posited by the federal government as a way to foster economic recovery from the Great Depression and achieve nationalist economic development, regulation also extended the authority of the callista-controlled state over the private sphere. Regiomontano elites therefore criticized federal legislation aimed at regulating trade and industry, including the 1930 Tariff Code and the 1931 Federal Labor Law. Monterrey businessman Joel Rocha even scoffed at the code by arguing that trade barriers were nonsensical, since all civilized countries depended in some measure on goods produced abroad.[27]

The Monterrey Group countered the federal government by promoting its own version of industrialism that emphasized the function of the market, rather than state regulation, in bringing about class harmony and nationalist development. It focused, in particular, on the consumption of nationally produced goods, which it affirmed would improve living standards and undermine class warfare.[28] For the Monterrey Group, the most critical factor in the struggle to achieve nationalist development was winning over the hearts and minds of Mexico's consumers.[29] The federal government agreed that propaganda could help to reverse attitudes favoring foreign over domestic goods, and it sponsored special events to promote the purchase of nationally produced clothing and shoes.[30] Although the regiomontano business community initially had been slow to join the movement to "buy Mexican" in the late 1920s, it soon dominated national efforts to build pride in Mexican-made goods.[31] For example, it spearheaded the National Prosperity Campaign (Campaña de Prosperidad Nacional) in early 1931. The Monterrey Group drew from many suggestions made by the federal government about ways to encourage the consumption of domestically produced goods.[32] For example, it sent letters to business groups across the

27. *Boletín Semanal,* no. 81, SICT, Dirección de Publicaciones y Propaganda, February 2, 1931, IC/AGENL, c. 4.

28. "Declaraciones del C. Gobernador Constitucional Interino, Lic. José Benítez, relativas a la Campaña de Prosperidad Nacional," November 22, 1930, IC/AGENL, c. 4; "Fue integrada la Junta Constitutiva del Comité Pro-Campaña de Prosperidad Nacional," *Boletín Semanal,* no. 77, SICT, Dirección de Publicaciones y Propaganda, January 5, 1931, DF/SSICT/AGENL, c. 5; editorial, *Excélsior,* December 16, 1930.

29. *Boletín Semanal,* no. 81, SICT, Dirección de Publicaciones y Propaganda, February 2, 1931, IC/AGENL, c. 4.

30. "Notas sobre las actividades del estado en materia de fomento industrial," 1939, GR/AGN, c. 84, exp. 5; "Sugestiones del público," Campaña de Prosperidad Nacional, Cámara Nacional del Comercio, Industria, y Minería del Estado de Nuevo León, February 25, 1931, IC/AGENL, c. 4; SEN, February 23, 1933, AHJ, Ramo Fomento, F-9–933, 10, 729.

31. Saragoza, *Monterrey Elite,* 145–46, 237; Vellinga, "*Regiomontana* Bourgeoisie," 208.

32. Jefe, Departamento de Industrias, SICT to Oficial Mayor, February 1927, DT/AGN, c. 1211, exp. 7.

country urging them to support domestic consumption as a way to reverse the worst effects of the Great Depression.³³ It also ran an aggressive national media campaign on the radio, in newspapers, and at movie theaters, which linked religion, family, and nation in one grand effort to "buy Mexican." Additionally, the Monterrey Group urged the Archbishop of Monterrey to order priests in his diocese to publicize the campaign in their sermons. It also provided elementary schoolchildren with slogans and data that they could use to convince family members to buy Mexican-made products, and teachers were urged to visit students' homes to talk up the campaign.³⁴ This all culminated in the National Consumption Week (Semana del Consumo Nacional) from May 3 to 10, 1931, a week that included celebrations for the Cinco de Mayo and Mother's Day. During it, Monterrey's business leaders tied nation and family to nationalist development by averring, "The sincerity of our homages to the heroes that gave us our fatherland and to the mothers who give us life will be proven by our cooperation during National Consumption Week."³⁵

Economic growth and social conservatism, along with strong personal and business ties among local business elites cemented Monterrey's transition from a hardscrabble frontier outpost into a regional center of production and power. The Monterrey Group constructed an identity to fit this transition, which emphasized the moral, upright, hardworking character and harmonious social relations of regiomontanos, as proven by the modern, capitalist city they had created. This identity became critical in the 1920s and early 1930s, as they parried ruling-party political and economic intervention by imagining a sense of exceptionalism that conferred on Monterrey and its inhabitants a unique mission to lead the nation and protect the working class. But they remained frustrated during the 1920s as what they perceived to be a feckless revolutionary ruling class continued to exclude them politically. This frustration would be transformed into outright opposition under President Cárdenas, as his corporatist labor reforms threatened the paternalism that underpinned employer authority at the regional level.

33. "Declaraciones del C. Gobernador Constitucional Interino, Lic. José Benítez, relativas a la Campaña de Prosperidad Nacional," November 22, 1930, IC/AGENL, c. 4; "Fue integrada la Junta Constitutiva del Comité Pro-Campaña de Prosperidad Nacional," *Boletín Semanal*, no. 77, SICT, Dirección de Publicaciones y Propaganda, January 5, 1931, DF/SSICT/AGENL c. 5.

34. Dirección General de Instrucción Pública, Gobierno del Estado de Nuevo León to directors of state schools, November 22, 1930, IC/AGENL, c. 4; *Boletín Semanal*, no. 116, SICT, Dirección de Publicaciones y Propaganda, September 17, 1931, DF/SSICT/AGENL, c. 5.

35. Cámara Nacional de Comercio, Industria, y Minería del Estado de Nuevo León to Cámara Nacional de Comercio, April 20, 1931, IC/AGENL, c. 4.

The Discipline of Production Against the Indiscipline of Revolution

The Monterrey Group appeared remarkably united when faced with the vicissitudes of postrevolutionary reconstruction. This unity cut across class lines, as both workers and employers espoused the idea of a unique regional character that fostered collaboration in pursuit of modern industrialization.[36] Elites undoubtedly propagated this vision of cross-class harmony more heartily than did the working class. But it proved to be a forceful countercurrent to cardenista reforms, as it masked workers' subordination within paternalist relations that balanced material rewards and loyalty. Therefore, when the cardenista state and the CTM began to make serious inroads in Nuevo León in the mid-1930s, they represented their intervention as an emancipation of the working class from the regional fealties that subordinated workers and prevented them from allying along class lines. Although some industrialists accepted national labor organizing in their factories, many remained intransigent in the face of state intervention in labor affairs. In turn, the rift between the Monterrey Group and the national ruling party deepened, as the regiomontano employers depicted corporatist labor relations as a form of state-managed class conflict that politicized the working class in order to advance the cardenista hold over Nuevo León.

Monterrey's employers reflected nostalgically on the class harmony that they claimed had characterized labor-employer relations during the Porfiriato.[37] Yet this emphasis on harmony belies the inequality that had ensured employer prerogative during that time. The federal government had supported employer authority by providing workers with few guarantees, which helped to impede efforts at labor organizing in the region. Four of the largest companies in Monterrey had provided work for more than one-half of the city's labor force, which facilitated employer unity in the face of independent organizing drives. Thus, workers generally had settled for mutual aid societies, many of which doubled as pro-Reyes political clubs. In this climate, many workers felt their best option was to accept paternalism, with its incentives, bonuses, and coercion.[38]

As elsewhere in Mexico, however, by the eve of Revolution, Monterrey's workers began to tap into national opposition movements in order to demand better wages and challenge employer abuses. Though workers and

---

36. Snodgrass, *Deference and Defiance*, 26.

37. Studies that reproduce notions of class harmony and employer benevolence include Fuentes Mares, *Monterrey: Una ciudad creadora*; Montemayor Hernández, *Historia de Monterrey*.

38. Rojas Sandoval, *Monterrey: Poder político*, 89–97; Saragoza, *Monterrey Elite*, 92–93; Snodgrass, *Deference and Defiance*, 27–29.

employers often allied to defend their factories from revolutionists, each also recognized that the Revolution nevertheless transformed labor relations in the state. As labor organizing and strike activity took on new proportions in the early 1920s, employers sought novel strategies to stem independent organizing. At times, they collaborated with local union leaders to militate against work actions, and they participated in regional labor boards to try to manage their employees. But employer paternalism backed by coercion remained the most prominent and potent means to mute the appeal of militants. Industrialists therefore began to offer a range of social services and subsidies to workers in exchange for loyalty and quiescence.[39] Some scholars have suggested that Catholic social action teachings, which emphasized mutual responsibility and respect as the foundations of class harmony, shaped employers' conceptions of company paternalism.[40] However, Michael Snodgrass argues that Monterrey was quite secular, especially when compared to places like Jalisco, and employers' Catholic faith did not significantly impact their regional identity or labor relations. Moreover, Catholic unions made no inroads in organizing in the region. Instead, company paternalism "developed as an institutionalized system of labor relations after the Revolution" rather than as an outcome of late nineteenth-century Vatican teachings.[41] In fact, scientific management played a much more defining role in employer efforts to manage labor. Some of Monterrey's elites, including Roberto Garza Sada and Luis Garza Sada, had been exposed to Taylorism during their studies abroad in the United States, and the Fundidora paid to have Frederick W. Taylor's work on scientific management published in Spanish. During the 1920s, then, owners of companies such as the Cervecería Cuauhtémoc and the Fundidora employed a mix of collaborative unionism, paternalism, and repression to forestall labor militancy. Local labor leaders likely saw the authority and wealth that might accrue to them if they allied with employers, and they also identified collaboration as indicative of Monterrey's modernity and progress.[42]

By the end of the 1920s and in the 1930s, however, for some workers, company paternalism and collaborationist unions began to lose their appeal. The effects of the Great Depression and surviving labor militancy fueled this disillusion. Workers subsequently were emboldened when the cardenista

---

39. Snodgrass, *Deference and Defiance*, 29–30, 45, 49–52; Saragoza, *Monterrey Elite*, 111–13, 129–35.

40. Sherman, *Mexican Right*, 6. For more on Catholic social doctrine in the Mexican business community, see Sánchez Navarro, "La ética del empresariado mexicano."

41. Snodgrass, *Deference and Defiance*, 56–57, 131.

42. Ibid., 54–55, 83–86, 99, 117, 131, 143–44, 212; Saragoza, *Monterrey Elite*, 90–92.

state began to empower sympathetic regional governors, such as Interim Governor Pablo Quiroga (1933–35), to take on company unions (alternatively referred to as employers' unions or *sindicatos blancos*) and craft labor boards to favor militants. As the state interceded more vigorously in defense of labor and national labor organizations made progress in the state, the brewing conflict between Monterrey elites and the federal government over state intervention in labor-employer relations came to a head.[43]

The conflict dated back to the late 1920s, when President Portes Gil barred employers from participating in federal efforts to codify article 123 of the Constitution, and Calles refused to nominate Governor Sáenz as the ruling-party presidential candidate.[44] All of this heightened regiomontano rancor at the blatant assertion of callista authority. Although many industrialists in Monterrey and beyond supported the federalization of labor law, they insisted that industrialists should help to craft it. Consequently, CONCAMIN, CONCANACO, the Association of Industrial and Commercial Businesses, and later COPARMEX formed an employers' group to press the Portes Gil government to include business input. In particular, it sought to amend perceived pro-labor biases in the draft law, which it argued would frighten investors, foster radicalism, and generate unemployment and poverty.[45] After the draft failed to become law, the group spent the next two years lobbying for a revision that would preserve employer authority over production and their workforces.[46]

COPARMEX took an especially hard line against the government over the federalization of labor law and the rights of private enterprise. The Monterrey Group dominated COPARMEX both ideologically and financially.[47] At its founding in 1929, its mission was defined as limiting the state's mediation of labor-employer relations, though it soon expanded to include curbing state economic intervention more broadly.[48] The Monterrey Group

43. Snodgrass, *Deference and Defiance*, 97–99, 107–9, 118, 174.
44. The following discussion about the shift in labor-employer relations, the codification of labor legislation, and the founding of COPARMEX was drawn from Saragoza, *Monterrey Elite*, 151–69; Juárez González, "Una década en la organización," 268–70; Camp, *Entrepreneurs and Politics*, 163; Schneider, "Why Is Mexican Business So Organized?" 86; Córdova, *La Revolución en crisis*, 258–59; Shafer, *Mexican Business Organizations*, 36–43, 201; Vellinga, "*Regiomontana* Bourgeoisie," 205; and Jesús Rivero Quijano (CONCAMIN) to Manuel Gómez Morin, August 2, 1930, AMGM, v. 442, exp. 1443.
45. Cámara Nacional de Comercio, Industria, y Minería del Estado de Nuevo León to Aarón Sáenz, November 8, 1930, IC/AGENL, c. 4.
46. Shafer, *Mexican Business Organizations*, 36–38; Alcazar, *Las agrupaciones patronales*, 114–16; annual reports for 1928–29 and 1929–30, in CONCAMIN, *La Confederación de Cámaras Industriales*, vol. 1.
47. Nuncio, *El Grupo Monterrey*, 59.
48. "Acta constitutiva de la COPARMEX," 1929–30, AMGM, v. 442, exp. 1443.

wanted to use COPARMEX to challenge what it saw as the destructive conciliatory politics between the country's "weak and timid" business organizations and the state. It thus intended the confederation to be an intersectoral and interregional business organization that pooled the economic resources and the political weight of entrepreneurs from all over Mexico to provide them with independent representation.[49]

In 1931, the government finally passed the Federal Labor Law. COPARMEX immediately denounced it for demonstrating a clear bias toward labor and claimed the government had passed it without sincerely consulting with employers.[50] The SICT issued an immediate rejoinder, asserting that collective contracts and state intervention in labor-employer relations were essential for guaranteeing labor rights. Questioning COPARMEX's motives, it argued that the 1931 Federal Labor Law would counteract individualists who took on an "appearance of liberty" that in the end enabled the strong to impose their will on the weak.[51] Monterrey's industrialists soon perceived the significance of the changes wrought by the law. Although affirming their support for labor rights and collective contracts, they redoubled their efforts to build so-called independent or employers' unions.[52]

The rising tide of militancy in the 1930s, now buoyed by the Federal Labor Law and cardenista reformism, put the Monterrey Group and the Cárdenas administration on a collision course. Viewing Cárdenas as another lackey of Calles, Monterrey's business elites had refused to support his presidential campaign and had persistently obstructed attempts to organize national unions in the state. Moreover, in 1935, there was a heated clash over the president's efforts to impose a cardenista governor in Nuevo León.

The conflict between President Cárdenas and traditional sectors of the Monterrey Group peaked in a 1936 labor conflict at the Vidriera de Monterrey, the large glass factory belonging to the prominent Garza Sada family. Tensions were already high in the region due to a rift between employers and local steel workers, who recently had broken with the Independent Unions of Nuevo León in favor of the national Miner-Metalworkers Union. Soon after, on February 1, 1936, workers at the Vidriera struck to protest their employer's refusal to recognize their union, which was an affiliate of the predecessor to the CTM. Over the objections of employers,

---

49. Shafer, *Mexican Business Organizations*, 39–40.
50. Ibid., 41.
51. *Boletín Semanal*, no. 93, SICT, Dirección de Publicaciones y Propaganda, May 18, 1931, DF/SSICT/AGENL, c. 5.
52. León, "Cárdenas en el poder," 230; Nuncio, *El Grupo Monterrey*, 129; Martínez Nava, *Conflicto estado empresarios*, 88–89.

the JCCA declared the strike legal. In response, and in a dramatic display of the ability of the Monterrey Group to mount broad cross-class support, business leaders led a protest demonstration of fifty thousand bankers, industrialists, merchants, large landowners, agricultural laborers, members of the fascist Gold Shirts, and unionists who opposed the CTM, including members of employers' unions and of the CGT. Employers followed the demonstration with a lockout on February 5 and 6, which virtually shut down the city. They also fronted a national media campaign that charged the Cárdenas administration with having a communist orientation. Interim cardenista governor Gregorio Morales Sánchez (1935–36) soon intervened by defending the rights of workers to organize independently. He also rebuked the business leaders for fostering public opinion against workers by, among other things, making false allegations that workers were planning to seize factories. The CTM, for its part, declared that workers who supported employers lacked class consciousness. Strikes, lockouts, and even shootings ensued.[53]

The situation became a referendum on the authority of President Cárdenas in the state. On February 7, President Cárdenas traveled to Monterrey to intervene personally. After meeting with local representatives, he proclaimed his fourteen points, in which he reaffirmed labor's right to organize independently of employers and to elect their own leaders. He also reiterated that the state had the right to intervene in labor-employer relations, and he warned industrialists against politicizing labor issues. He concluded that should employers tire of social struggle, they could turn their factories over to their workers or to the state.[54]

The state's heavy-handed mediation of the conflict incensed industrialists. Alarmed at the escalating opposition, both President Cárdenas and CTM leader Vicente Lombardo Toledano abandoned their efforts to organize more CTM-allied unions in Monterrey for fear of losing gains already made in the region. The retreat by President Cárdenas was short-lived, however. About five weeks later, under threat of state expropriation, the owners of the Vidriera agreed to a collective contract with workers organized in the United Glass Workers Union.[55] Soon thereafter, in April 1936, ruling-party candidate Anacleto Guerrero emerged from the gubernatorial

53. Gobernador Gregorio Morales Sánchez, declaration, February 6, 1936, Fondo Secretaría General de Gobierno (SGG)/Serie Secretaría General de Gobierno (SSGG)/AGENL, c. 29; Llinás Álvarez, *Vida y obra de Ramón Beteta*, 20; Snodgrass, *Deference and Defiance*, 210–13.
54. Martínez Nava, *Conflicto estado empresarios*, 91–93.
55. Snodgrass, *Deference and Defiance*, 218–19.

elections as the state's new leader over the Monterrey Group's widely supported candidate, Fortunato Zuazua. Before he left office, Governor Morales Sánchez once again castigated employers for harassing workers.[56]

Though cardenistas extended the authority of the federal government and national labor organizations in Nuevo León, they did not wholly transform labor-employer relations during the remaining years of the Cárdenas presidency. To be sure, state-backed unions were now an entrenched feature of local labor relations. The CTM carried on with its organizing efforts in the state through the Federation of Workers of Nuevo León (Federación de Trabajadores de Nuevo León), which targeted sindicatos blancos in industries such as steel, railroads, smelting, textiles, construction, furniture, apparel, and electric power. But the 1936 strike and the advance of corporatist labor relations also galvanized cross-class conservative interests. This was manifest in the persistent commitment of some workers to company paternalism and its realization in sindicatos blancos. Although technically fulfilling the legal mandates of labor organizing, these company unions sustained the region's cross-class alliances, which were under threat by the cardenista state. In the months after the Vidriera strike, employers underscored how these alliances were critical to the region's industrial progress, social peace, and collective welfare. They contrasted this with what they contended was the state's communistic politicization of class relations and nurturing of indiscipline to the detriment of the nation, production, and the working class. Business leaders also formed the precursor to the PAN, Nationalist Civic Action (Acción Cívica Nacionalista), a cross-class conservative organization whose stated goal was the defense of class harmony, family, patria, and progress. The Gold Shirts also began to operate in the state in early 1936, though President Cárdenas repressed them and Civic Action by the end of that year.[57]

The moderation of cardenismo in the late 1930s also augured well for industrialist authority in the region. Even though Governor Guerrero continued to blame employers for using their influence over company unions to foster factional labor strife, he reached out to employers and checked labor militants.[58] In subsequent years, employers successfully curbed union

56. Gobernador Gregorio Morales Sánchez, declaration, Monterrey, April 3, 1936, SGG/SSGG/AGENL, c. 29.
57. Snodgrass, *Deference and Defiance*, 2, 217–23, 251; León, "Cárdenas en el poder," 231; Saragoza, *Monterrey Elite*, 180, 186; Sherman, *Mexican Right*, 61.
58. "Informe que rinde el C. Gral. de Brigada Anacleto Guerrero, Gobernador Constitucional del Estado de Nuevo León, a la XLVII Legislatura del mismo sobre la situación general de dicha entidad federativa y los trabajos desarrollados por su gobierno durante el año 1937–38," Monterrey, September 16, 1938, Biblioteca del Congreso del Estado de Nuevo León (BCENL).

rights over hiring and firing and used local labor boards to decertify Communist-led unions.[59] Indeed, industry and banking in Nuevo León thrived under President Cárdenas. In the late 1930s, Monterrey's businesspeople created a series of new credit institutions and financial associations designed to pool local resources. They joined with national investors in an array of joint stock ventures as well. In 1936, the Garza Sada interests underwent a major reorganization, splitting the management of their numerous companies between the Cuauhtémoc and Vidriera groups. They also formed the Compañía General de Aceptaciones, which facilitated the sharing of financial resources among the various businesses of the two groups. Additionally, in 1938, the Garza Sada family created Valores Industriales, S.A. (VISA), which became the holding group of the various firms associated with the Cervecería Cuauhtémoc. Ultimately, these financial institutions and associations facilitated access to capital, coordinated production, and protected investors.[60] Along with the moderation of cardenista reforms, this industrial growth and modernization softened regiomontano opposition to the extension of state authority over labor-employer relations. Nevertheless, the Monterrey Group remained staunchly against the regulation of industry and the statist assault on the rights of private enterprise.

Liberals and Structuralism in Midcentury Mexico

As seen in chapter 5, COPARMEX had modified its defense of free trade after World War II to accommodate temporary, limited tariffs aimed at slowing U.S. imports and reversing the surging trade deficit. Yet, the state had coupled protectionism with aggressive forms of regulation that together aimed to achieve nationalist industrial development. Thus, mid-twentieth-century statist industrialization in reality was much more than an advance of protectionist trends that had existed since the nineteenth century. To the Monterrey Group, it constituted an assault on individual property rights. Consequently, as structuralism became embedded in the ideological project of the left, industrial politics became more polarized.

The Monterrey Group was among Mexico's most ardent proponents of economic liberalism. The group insisted that protectionism inhibited capitalist industrial development by eliminating free and fair competition and

---

59. Snodgrass, *Deference and Defiance*, 230–35.
60. Hamilton, *Limits of State Autonomy*, appendix B, 325–29.

abrogating the individual rights of private property owners. Together, these led to higher-priced, lower-quality goods that could not compete with foreign manufactures.[61] Yet, since the mid-nineteenth century, the Monterrey Group had also accepted that targeted protection could play a role in advancing industrialization. They even regularly applied for regional and federal tax exemptions and pressed for tariffs that could benefit their own industries.

During the Porfiriato, Monterrey's industrialists received a steady stream of state-level tax exemptions. In 1888, the Nuevo León government promulgated its first law to promote regional industry. It provided seven-year exemptions from state and municipal taxes for all types of industries established within two years of its enactment and whose capital exceeded Mex$1,000, excepting industries dedicated to producing spirits. By 1889, another law extended twenty-year exemptions to industries deemed to be of public utility.[62] These laws were amended by new legislation in 1907 and 1911. Between 1888 and 1910, 146 companies received state-level exemptions. The biggest beneficiaries were food, beverages, and tobacco, which jointly received close to 24 percent of all the exemptions granted in the state. Nonmetallic construction materials, such as cement, bricks, artificial stone, glass, and tiles, received roughly 14 percent of the total, and chemical products received slightly more than 12 percent. Other industries to benefit were textiles, cotton, paper, basic metals, furniture, soap, steel, a cold storage plant, and a tourist spa.[63] Federal officials also supported regiomontano industry with tariffs, tax exemptions, and subsidies, though they claimed to favor production that could substitute for imports in areas like steel, iron, and cement. The troubled Fundidora was a prime recipient of assistance from both the state and federal governments, in part owing to lobbying by its general director, Vicente Ferrara. Indeed, steady tariff increases and other measures deliberately designed to protect the steel industry between 1901 and 1911 enabled the Fundidora to increase its sales during that decade, despite repeated threats of shutdowns.[64]

Monterrey industrialists continued to receive state and federal backing in the 1920s and 1930s, though the capacity of postrevolutionary regional governments to intervene to assist industry varied due to fiscal crises, political upheavals, and popular pressure. In the late 1920s, however, the Nuevo

    61. Cámara Nacional de Comercio, Industria, y Minería del Estado de Nuevo León to Aarón Sáenz, November 8, 1930, IC/AGENL, c. 4; Córdova, *La ideología de la Revolución*, 319.
    62. Vizcaya Canales, *Los orígenes de la industrialización*, 78.
    63. Ortega Ridaura, "Política fiscal," 100; Garduña Garcia, "Nuevo León," 43.
    64. Gómez Galvarriato, "El desempeño de la Fundidora," 207, 215–18.

León government began to take a more active role in promoting industry and collaborating with local industrialists. This included joint public-private propaganda campaigns that aimed to attract new industries to the state by emphasizing the low costs of doing business in Monterrey because of its cheap labor, tax exemptions, inexpensive electricity, and good labor-employer relations.[65] Some governors also began to represent the interests of local industry at the national level more aggressively. For example, Governor José Benítez (1928) protested an increase in duties on wood imports, which he stated would possibly paralyze the furniture industry in Monterrey. To back his complaint, he emphasized that despite its use of foreign primary materials, Monterrey's furniture industry was a completely Mexican industry since all of its workers and managers were Mexican.[66] Governor Benítez also contacted no fewer than three federal secretariats as he helped local cement producers obtain higher federal duties on foreign cement.[67] Official intervention did not guarantee success, however. When Governor Sáenz interceded on behalf of J. Cram y Compañía to request tariff reductions on inputs needed for the production of hinges and related metal products, the SHCP rejected him on legal grounds.[68] Nevertheless, business-state collaboration resurged during this period as being integral to perceptions of the region's progress and civilization, an association that originally emerged under Governor Reyes. Business leaders even contrasted Nuevo León with other states, where they argued that political radicalism and obstructionist officials were hurting the development of business.[69]

On November 30, 1927, the Nuevo León government issued a new tax exemption law for industry. In contrast to Porfirian laws, it offered exemptions not just to new industries of "public utility," but also to existing ones

---

65. Gobernador, Nuevo León to Jefes de las Industrias Locales, December 10, 1928, IC/AGENL, c. 3; Secretario General de Gobierno, Int., Nuevo León to presidente, Cámara Nacional de Comercio, Industria, y Minería del Estado de Nuevo León, November 19, 1925, IC/AGENL, c. 3; Cámara Nacional de Comercio, Industria, y Minería del Estado de Nuevo León to Gobernador General Porfirio G. González, December 28, 1923, IC/AGENL, c. 3; gobernador de Nuevo León and Cámara Nacional de Comercio, Industria, y Minería del Estado de Nuevo León to Crane Company, RCA Victor Co., San Francisco Mines of Mexico, Ltd., and Compañía Manufacturera de Cigarros El Aguila, S.A., April–July 1930, IC/AGENL, c. 4.

66. Gobernador Benítez to Secretario de Industria, Comercio, y Trabajo, Distrito Federal, May 9, 1930, IC/AGENL, c. 4.

67. Cementos Portland Monterrey, S.A., Cementos Hidalgo, S.A., SICT, SHCP, Secretaría de Comunicaciones y Obras Públicas, and Gobernador Benítez, correspondence, September 19, 1928–March 8, 1929, IC/AGENL, c. 3.

68. J. Cram y Cía., request and correspondence, August 12–October 9, 1930, MF/MH/AGENL, c. 38.

69. Cámara Nacional de Comercio, Industria, y Minería del Estado de Nuevo León to Aarón Sáenz, November 8, 1930, IC/AGENL, c. 4.

seeking to restart production or expand their capital or workforce. The definition of new industries was broad and took into account factors such as the proposed product, production efficiency, number of employees, and primary materials usage. Between 1927 and 1939, the state granted 158 concessions. Over 90 percent went to industries in Monterrey, although company owners came from across the state, nation, and even abroad. A range of industries received these exemptions, but the dominant recipients remained foodstuffs, textiles, and clothing. Also benefiting were intermediate and capital goods, such as chemical products, electric products, and various construction materials.[70]

Many industrialists supported their applications by proposing that their improvements in efficiency would generate lower-cost, higher-quality goods for consumers.[71] Others cited their contributions to the creation of jobs and national welfare.[72] In one case, Alberto Escamilla, owner of an underwear factory, had to defend his application against a competitor who accused him of having stolen his workforce. Escamilla countered his accuser, H. F. Goldhamer, by pointing to the latter's poor treatment of his workers, as reported to Escamilla by Goldhamer's former employees. Escamilla received the exemption, though the state government emphasized that it was because he produced a larger range of higher-quality items, employed more workers, and invested more capital than did Goldhamer.[73]

Applicants also framed production to address concerns about economic nationalism. They often projected Monterrey's distinct industrial culture as Mexico's best option for achieving national sovereignty. They expediently lauded its pro-industry state government for realizing the "patriotic and nationalist" import-substituting efforts urged by the federal government.[74]

---

70. Ortega Ridaura, "Política fiscal," 107–12; Garduña Garcia, "Nuevo León," 47–48. For an example of a foreign applicant, see National Carbon Company, Inc. to Aarón Sáenz, August 26, 1931, Fondo Concesiones (CON)/AGENL, c. 40, exp. 7.

71. For example, see Garza Hermanos y Cía., correspondence, October 31, 1930–February 3, 1931, CON/AGENL, c. 41, exp. 3; Virgilio Garza Jr., application, July 31, 1931, CON/AGENL, c. 40, exp. 7; Arturo Garza, application, October 16, 1933, CON/AGENL, c. 42, exp. 42/12; Manuel M. Garcia, application, January 7, 1935, CON/AGENL, c. 45, exp. 45/5; Abastecedora del Norte, Fábrica de Calzada, exemption, May 13, 1931, CON/AGENL, c. 40, exp. 40/3.

72. Ruperto Flores, Flores Hermanos, application, April 20, 1936, CON/AGENL, c. 40, exp. 40/4; Garza Hermanos y Cía., correspondence, October 31, 1930–February 3, 1931, CON/AGENL, c. 41, exp. 3; Vidriera Monterrey, S.A., application, February 7, 1933, CON/AGENL, c. 42, exp. 7; Arturo Garza, application, October 16, 1933, CON/AGENL, c. 42, exp. 42/12; Gustavo Treviño, pronouncement, January 8, 1937, CON/AGENL, c. 48, exp. 48/2.

73. Alberto Escamilla, correspondence, April 28, 1932–September 5, 1932, CON/AGENL, c. 41, exp. 11.

74. Arturo Garza, Garza Hermanos y Cía. to Gobernador Benítez, December 13, 1930, CON/AGENL, c. 41, exp. 3; Ruperto A. Flores, Flores Hermanos, application, February 19, 1931, CON/

Invoking the predominant regiomontano conception of progress, they used the term "industrial liberty" to signify not just the liberal ethos of private property but also freedom from foreign markets and products.[75] But the conflicts between producers that often arose during the application process revealed that Monterrey was as vulnerable to self-interest and divisiveness as were other regions. For instance, Gregorio Treviño received an exemption for the production of safety matches by declaring that a competitor who opposed his application, the Fábrica de Fósforos y Cerillos El Fénix, was in fact importing matches from other regions and marking them as having been manufactured in Monterrey. Treviño characterized the owners of El Fénix as engaging in "immoral" and "prejudicial" activity detrimental to regional industry and workers. Treviño went on to name his factory the Fábrica de Cerillos La Regiomontana.[76] In another case, when Ramón Ruiz sought an exemption to begin the manufacture of beer and ice, he garnered the opposition of none other than Roberto Garza, lawyer and representative of the formidable Cervecería Cuauhtémoc. Garza marshaled an array of arguments to contest Ruiz's application, asserting that Cuauhtémoc's production already exceeded local demand and used the most efficient methods. He suggested that by reducing Cuauhtémoc's sales and possibly even driving the brewery to ruin, any new producer would hurt the state treasury. Ruiz responded by meeting Garza point for point, stating that he was proposing to use better production methods and would employ higher standards for worker hygiene and safety. He added that the small 25 percent reduction of state taxes that he sought would hardly be prejudicial to the Cervecería Cuauhtémoc. He concluded by noting that because Cuauhtémoc was a monopoly, the introduction of competition would benefit consumers. He received the exemption.[77]

In 1940, the Nuevo León government promulgated new tax-exemption legislation to promote industry. The definitions of new industry and new methods were similar to the preceding law in design though not always in degree. The law also sought to standardize and speed the process for evaluating tax-exemption requests. The government even created a special agency

---

AGENL, c. 40, exp. 40/4; Jesús González Montemayor to gobernador, Nuevo León, April 20, 1931, CON/AGENL, c. 40, exp. 40/6.

75. Cía. Industrial Fundidora y Minera Mexicana, S.A., correspondence, September 26, 1932–March 1, 1933, CON/AGENL, c. 48, exp. 4.

76. Gregorio Treviño, correspondence, July 7–September 13, 1932, CON/AGENL, c. 41, exp. 41/12.

77. Ramón Ruiz, correspondence, January 9–February 27, 1931, CON/AGENL, c. 41, exp. 1.

(the Departamento de Fomento), whose task was to research the applications. Between 1940 and 1960, the state government granted 252 tax exemptions. Manufacturers of consumer goods, such as foodstuffs and textiles, remained prominent recipients. However, in comparison to the period between 1927 and 1939, their share of the number of exemptions granted and the total capitalization of the recipient companies dropped significantly. Intermediate and capital goods, by contrast, received more support relative to the previous period. Exemptions between 1940 and 1960 also favored the continued concentration of industry in Monterrey and its metropolitan area. Regiomontano industrialists simultaneously lobbied the federal government for tax exemptions. Between 1940 and 1960, industries from Nuevo León received eighty-eight of the 1,041 federal tax exemptions granted, or about 8.5 percent of the total. The only other two entities to receive more were Mexico City and the Estado de México.[78]

By the 1940s, new concerns began to shape state-level exemption requests. Most notable were an increased emphasis on investment in new machinery and modern production methods and the efforts to meet supply shortfalls caused by World War II.[79] For example, Enrique Barragán L. testified that his factory, Equipos Camiones Monterrey, would be among the most technically advanced in Latin America.[80] By contrast, the issues of jobs and wages disappeared from most state-level applications during the 1940s or industrialists mentioned them only briefly. Although, as in the case of Roberto González's 1947 application for an exemption for his ice manufacturing plant, providing employment to a large number of workers was sufficient reason to receive an exemption.[81]

When Nuevo León promulgated its exemption law in 1940, the Banco de México and the federal government had already begun to press states to

78. Ortega Ridaura, "Política fiscal," 83, 117; Garduña Garcia, "Nuevo León," 55, 79–80.
79. Manufacturas de Acero Monterrey, S.A., application, April 16, 1945, CON/AGENL, c. 68, exp. 7; Lavanderías Generales, application, November 21, 1945, and pronouncement, March 8, 1946, CON/AGENL, c. 70, exp. 70/1; Canada Dry de Monterrey, S.A., application, March 6, 1946, CON/AGENL, c. 70, exp. 70/3; Artefactos de Metal Laminado El Aguila, S.A., correspondence, March 27–August 5, 1947, CON/AGENL, c. 72, exp. 8; Fábrica de Alpargatas La Unión, S. de R.L., February 21, 1948, CON/AGENL, c. 75, exp. 75/5; CUPRUM, S. de R.L., December 1, 1950, CON/AGENL, c. 80, exp. 80/7. For concerns about the impact of war on production and supplies, see Maria de la Luz, Alicia y Elsa Perez, Mario Cartez, and Gerardo Treviño Lozano, application, February 3, 1940, CON/AGENL, c. 52, exp. 52/1.
80. Enrique Barragán L., application, November 29, 1945, CON/AGENL, c. 70, exp. 5.
81. Roberto González, correspondence and decrees, February 20, 1947, through mid-1947, CON/AGENL, c. 72, exp. 4.

pass tax-exemption legislation that adhered more closely to federal exemption laws and that contributed to national, rather than regional, development. However, applications for state-level exemptions reveal that Monterrey's industrialists felt an acute sense of competition with producers from other regions, and they wanted to preserve local protection that would help them compete with outsiders. They pointed to tax-exemption legislation and lower wages in other states to justify regional legislation crafted specifically to enhance the competitiveness of locally made products.[82]

The impact of tax exemptions on industry is difficult to assess. Other factors likely had a more significant effect, including the expansion of domestic and foreign markets, new sources of labor and technical assistance, state investment in infrastructure and public utilities, tariffs and trade controls, the greater availability of credit, labor repression, the recovery from the Great Depression, and the stimulus of World War II. Between 1937 and 1946 alone, Monterrey grew from having 438 industries capitalized at Mex$153 million to having 650 industries capitalized at Mex$409 million.[83] The emergence and growth of large-scale industry was a significant part of this development, including the Cuauhtémoc group's founding of the first major chemical company (Celulosa y Derivados, or CYDSA) and a new steel company (Hojalata y Lámina, or HYLSA). The Fundidora, for its part, doubled its capacity during World War II in response to foreign demand and a drop-off in imports. Although retaining their presence in consumer goods production, the region's industrialists moved boldly into capital and especially intermediate goods in the 1940s, including chemicals and secondary petrochemicals, basic metals, nonmetallic minerals, and metallic products.[84] For example, by 1955, Nuevo León produced more than one-third of the total national production value of steel and was responsible for a remarkable three-quarters of total national production of glass and related items.[85] Tax exemptions reflected this growth. Of the eighty-eight federal exemptions given to industries in Nuevo León between 1940 and 1960, roughly 91 percent went to intermediate and capital goods industries. By comparison, intermediate and capital goods industries received just about 73 percent of the exemptions granted to Mexico City, and about 67 percent to Jalisco and Puebla. The national average for intermediate and capital

82. Gustavo Treviño, Hulera Monterrey, S.A. to gobernador, May 8, 1941, CON/AGENL, c. 48, exp. 48/2; Artículos de Celuloide, S.A., application, July 15, 1948, CON/AGENL, exp. 75/10.
83. Montemayor Hernández, *Historia de Monterrey*, 374.
84. Ortega Ridaura, "Política fiscal," 54–64.
85. López Malo, *Ensayo sobre localización*, appendix V.

goods industries during those two decades was slightly more than 68 percent.[86]

Between 1940 and 1960, both federal and regional protectionist policies favored larger industries in Nuevo León. The policies also led to the concentration of capital in the hands of a few family groups.[87] At the state level, these industries obtained a higher share of tax exemptions in that period, 21 percent, compared to slightly more than 11 percent in the 1927–39 period. These industries made up about 26 percent of the capital of all of the companies that received exemptions in the earlier period, but almost 61 percent for the 1940–60 period. During this time, of the federal exemptions granted to Nuevo León industries, close to 30 percent benefited large industrial groups.[88] This was due in part to changes in the 1941 federal exemption law that favored established companies that had the potential to invest great sums of capital, though undoubtedly the political influence of some industrialists allowed them to lobby for exemptions more effectively. Roberto Garza Sada, who took over as head of the Cuauhtémoc group in the 1930s, recognized that using his personal connections could speed requests for concessions and tax breaks for HYLSA, since "the normal procedures are absolutely ineffective to obtain fast results in an issue of this nature." Manuel Gómez Morin agreed, though he added that speaking directly with the president would facilitate the process even more.[89] Nineteen companies related to the Cuauhtémoc group received state exemptions, eleven of which also received federal exemptions. Moreover, in 1934, the government in Nuevo León enacted a new law that offered a reduction in the fee to register an industry in the Public Property Record. Though available to all, in practice, it helped only those who could mobilize the capital to create corporations. Therefore, in 1936, the majority of these reduced fees went to businesses created by the Cuauhtémoc group.[90]

After the Revolution, Monterrey's business leaders consistently professed their social conservatism and economic liberalism. At most, they saw the state as an adjunct to private enterprise that should assist with infrastructure, financing, and other benefits.[91] Perhaps opportunistically, they availed

86. Ortega Ridaura, "Política fiscal," 86.
87. Morado Macías, *Concesiones*, 4.
88. Ortega Ridaura, "Política fiscal," 90–93, 134–38.
89. Roberto Garza Sada and Manuel Gómez Morin, correspondence, July–August 1942, AMGM, v. 234, exp. 747.
90. Ortega Ridaura, "Política fiscal," 137–45.
91. "Razón y derecho de los hombres de empresa para criticar al gobierno," *Actividad*, November 1, 1945; "El Lic. Gómez Morin habla de la intervención estatal," *Excélsior*, February 15, 1945; López-Portillo Tostado, *Estado e ideología empresarial*, 244, 260–63; "Convención Patronal," *Activi-*

themselves of state incentives and protection, such as tax exemptions, tariffs, subsidies, and loans. But they distinguished this aid from state regulation, which grew rapidly during World War II. Sometimes conservatives succeeded in weakening regulations, as when they petitioned to have distribution controls loosened in 1942.[92] And in 1948, in conjunction with CONCAMIN, COPARMEX successfully lobbied for a peso devaluation, despite ongoing opposition from labor and other industrialist groups. In doing so, it argued that monetary controls had a draconian effect on imports and exports, undermined confidence in the Mexican economy, and fed state economic intervention.[93] However, in the end, pressure by Monterrey industrialists had little impact on the proliferation of new regulations. Despite opposition, laws expanding government agency oversight of the economy, production, and business organizations grew significantly in the 1940s and 1950s, as did the creation of new agencies like CEIMSA, all vital to the consolidation of statist industrialization.[94]

Monterrey's business community acclaimed the region's cross-class respect for individualism and private property as the foundation of its unique industrial culture, economic progress, and social peace. Moreover, its opposition to regulations persisted, as regiomontanos argued that measures like trade controls and state mediation of labor relations constituted an assault on private property rights. They maintained that when the state acted as a private enterprise and thus competed with owners, it could not be an "authentic expression of the Nation and insurer of the National Good."[95] By the late 1940s, then, the Monterrey Group specifically identified regulation as emblematic of federal corruption, and it accused ruling-party politicians of using industrial policy to serve their personal and political objectives to the detriment of industry, working-class welfare, and the nation.

Sentinels for Conservatism

In 1939, when ruling-party candidate General Bonifacio Salinas Leal won a tense, violent gubernatorial election over longtime railway worker and

---

dad, July 15, 1945; "La Confederación Patronal de la República Mexicana ante el momento actual," *Actividad*, October 15, 1946; Vellinga, "*Regiomontana* Bourgeoisie," 208.

92. Shafer, *Mexican Business Organizations*, 140.

93. *El Mercado de Valores* 8, no. 32 (August 9, 1948), 2.

94. For opposition to a 1947 law granting more power to the SHCP over companies and a 1948 law giving the Secretaría de Economía more oversight of business organizations, see "¿Somos todavía una República?" *Actividad*, March 15, 1948; "Planificación sin plan (La nueva Ley de Cámaras de Comercio y de Industria)," *Actividad*, August 15, 1948; "Editorial-Secretaría de Abastos," *Actividad*, October 1, 1948.

95. "El estado-empresario," *Actividad*, March 15, 1945.

radical labor leader Juan Gutiérrez, it seemed to mark the renascence of public-private collaboration in Nuevo León. In the aftermath, Monterrey's industrialists achieved a new level of personal and business collaboration with ruling-party officials, tempering the antagonism that had characterized their relationship during the early Cárdenas years. This rapprochement resulted in part from the more moderate, pro-business climate of the Ávila Camacho and Alemán administrations. By the late 1940s, a number of Monterrey industrialists had even attained positions in the national government. Some scholars have consequently characterized regiomontano elites as being part of an "alliance for profits" that united ruling-party officials and the private sector in defense of their common political and economic interests.[96]

On closer inspection, however, the relationship between the ruling party and the Monterrey Group appears much more complicated and erratic. To be sure, some benefited immensely from their close ties to ruling-party officials at the federal and regional level, including the directors of the Fundidora. Others, however, approached the federal government much more cautiously. For example, the Cuauhtémoc group, a more insular, regional business family, never relied as intimately on federal contacts as the Fundidora did.[97] Moreover, even as the PRI marginalized its leftist currents under President Alemán, members of the Monterrey Group continued to oppose corporatist labor relations and state economic intervention. In the late 1940s, they recast this opposition to take advantage of the Cold War milieu by reinvigorating their historic antagonism to communism and tying it to the ruling party's class politics and statist aggressions against private property. They also modified company paternalism by redefining it to incorporate the modernization of labor-employer relations through the technical organization of work processes.

The Monterrey business community was among the biggest supporters of the PAN in its early days. Their conservatism and close relationship with the PAN's founder, Manuel Gómez Morin, the lawyer for many regiomontano businesspeople, help to explain their attraction to the party. With the formation of the PAN in 1939, the Monterrey Group became more actively involved in opposition politics, and it helped to finance the campaign of the PAN presidential candidate, Juan Andreu Almazán. As the 1940 presidential election neared, however, the working and poorer classes began supporting Almazán more vigorously, which alarmed the Monterrey Group. It soon

96. Reynolds, *Mexican Economy*, 185–91.
97. De León Garza, *Monterrey: Un vistazo*, 80; Vellinga, *Industrialización, burguesía, y clase obrera*, 9; Saragoza, *Monterrey Elite*, 8–10, 62–71.

made a pact with Miguel Alemán, the campaign manager for Ávila Camacho, wherein it agreed to withdraw support for Almazán in return for influence in deciding the region's PRM mayoral and gubernatorial candidates. President Cárdenas's overtures to support industry with five-year tax exemptions and Ávila Camacho's five visits to Monterrey during his campaign also encouraged the Monterrey Group to back the ruling-party candidate.[98] Almazán lost the fraudulent and violent election, after which regiomontano support and funding for the PAN waned. As the PAN focused on doctrinal issues over the next decade and failed to elaborate a project for industrial development, its relevance for the Monterrey Group diminished, even though a number of regiomontano elites remained members. In the 1952 presidential elections, the PAN candidate took almost 10 percent of the vote in Nuevo León. However, this paled in comparison to Jalisco and Michoacán, both of which polled more than 20 percent for the PAN candidate.[99]

Ariel José Contreras contends that the negotiations between Alemán and the Monterrey Group were a turning point in the elections, and the moment in which Monterrey's business leaders and ruling-party insiders formed a "hegemonic pact."[100] Their deal making possibly affected the outcome of the 1940 elections. Moreover, early in the Ávila Camacho administration, the government pressed for a number of measures that aided industry and moderated class politics. President Ávila Camacho also invited more participation by Monterrey industrialists in his administration. For example, he appointed Evaristo Araiza, the general manager of the Fundidora, to be the representative to the Mexico-U.S. Commission responsible for studying trade relations. Later, Araiza would become the president's close advisor.[101] Moreover, President Ávila Camacho visited Monterrey again in 1943, furthering reconciliation between the ruling party and the northern entrepreneurs.

Despite this postelection improvement in relations between the PRM and Monterrey industrialists, the Monterrey Group continued to chafe at the efforts of the national ruling party to extend its authority over the state. As recounted at the outset of this chapter, in the 1945 municipal elections, the ruling party once again imposed its candidate on Monterrey, despite the

---

98. Puga, "Las elecciones de 1940," 281–82; Hamilton, *Limits of State Autonomy*, 261–69; Contreras, *México 1940*, 137, 154–57, 167–68; Camp, *Entrepreneurs and Politics*, 212; Sherman, *Mexican Right*, 117–31; Cockcroft, *Mexico's Hope*, 134–35; Vellinga, *Industrialización, burguesía, y clase obrera*, 111. Some authors contend that the Monterrey Group judiciously supported both presidential candidates. See Saragoza, *Monterrey Elite*, 192–98.

99. Mabry, *Mexico's Acción Nacional*, 51–52, 136, 174–75.

100. Contreras, *México 1940*, 169–70.

101. Niblo, *War, Diplomacy, and Development*, 107.

opposition of local elites and the pact they had made with Alemán going into the 1940 presidential election. And PRM governor Arturo de la Garza shared a troubled relationship with the region's business community.[102] In 1947, local business leaders denounced Governor de la Garza for operating on the margins of legality and in flagrant violation of the Constitution. Accusing him of not understanding the gravity of his position, they added that he had regularly rebuffed employers when they offered him their assistance, showed bias in favor of labor, and vacillated in his decision making.[103]

In this light, the notion of a "hegemonic pact" overstates the amity that emerged between the Monterrey Group and the ruling party by the late 1940s. Moreover, it fails to recognize that their accord stemmed from more than opportunism or clientelism. It also reflected shifting global currents. As the international community moved from Popular Front politics to the Cold War, anticommunism moved from the conservative margins to mainstream politics in Mexico. Since its formation, the national ruling party had had a turbulent relationship with communism, at times collaborating with communist elements and at other times repressing them. Although Alemán courted the left during his candidacy, he began to condemn Communists soon after his election. Partly in an effort to consolidate conservative control of the PRI and entice U.S. investment, he rejected all overtures by the Mexican Communist Party (Partido Comunista Mexicano, PCM) for its incorporation into the ruling party, even though moderate Browderist forces dominated the PCM by then. The PRI then became more publicly anticommunist and purged suspected Communists from its membership rolls.[104] Cold War anticommunism brought the ruling party and the Monterrey Group closer together.

President Alemán's pro-business orientation and personal ties with regiomontano elites also helped to heal the rift between the ruling party and the Monterrey Group. One writer captured the spirit of the times when he stated, "In truth, one could talk business with President Alemán."[105] His crackdown on labor militants, heavy investment in infrastructure, and tax exemptions and loans for large-scale industry augured well for industrialists in Monterrey. Moreover, with the end of the de la Garza governorship in 1949, regiomontano elites successfully pressed for a governor more attuned to local business interests than the candidate initially proposed by the ruling

---

102. "Arbitrios y autonomía del municipio," *Actividad,* January 1, 1945.
103. Cámara Nacional de Comercio de Monterrey, Centro Patronal de Nuevo León, Cámara de la Industria de Transformación, et al. to Gobernador Arturo de la Garza, February 6, 1947, SGG/SSGG/AGENL, c. 43.
104. Carr, *Marxism and Communism,* 106–41, 147–53.
105. Nuncio, *El Grupo Monterrey,* 61–62.

party. The new governor, Ignacio Morones Prieto (1949–52), implemented tax exemptions and other policies to promote industry, and he also provided the Monterrey Group with more effective access to Mexico City politics. This facilitated the ability of regiomontano businesspeople to express dissent and apply pressure on government administrations through the party apparatus, rather than working against it. Governor Morones Prieto also fostered better communication between the regional government and the Monterrey business community. During this time, Manuel L. Barragán, head of the Topo Chico bottling company, became a key connection between the state's governors and the Monterrey Group.[106] Though Morones Prieto's appointment to head a federal agency in 1952 cut short this relationship, Governor Raúl Rangel Frías (1955–61) reestablished it.[107]

But even with the closer ideological alignment brought about by the Cold War and the pro-business climate of the Alemán presidency, the relationship between regiomontano elites and national officials remained complicated. This was underscored when President Alemán adapted nationalist industrial growth to signal state economic intervention. His use of "Hecho en México" embodied this shift, as it implied the state's right to compel producers to submit to regulation. In fact, alluding to the 1930s National Prosperity Campaign, President Alemán initiated the Campaign for Economic Recovery. Instead of focusing solely on propaganda to modify consumer attitudes, however, the economic recovery campaign targeted producers themselves and the role the ruling party believed they should play in achieving protected import-substituting industrialization. In turn, President Alemán redefined mexicanidad to refer to the unity of producers and consumers within a revolutionary nationalist project for development oriented around statist, urban industrialism.[108] By portraying the PRI-dominated state as the legitimate protector of nationalist development, President Alemán attempted to undermine the salience of members of the Monterrey Group as leaders of national progress and modernization.

106. De León Garza, *Monterrey: Un vistazo*, 81–82.
107. Vellinga, *Industrialización, burguesía, y clase obrera*, 111–12.
108. "Acotaciones al Primer Mensaje del Presidente Lic. Alemán," *Actividad*, December 15, 1946; various letters to Alemán, early 1947, MAV/AGN, exp. 708.1/5 and exp. 708.1/5–8; SEN, memorandum, early 1947, MAV/AGN, exp. 708.1/5; Jesús Leal Carrillo, "Se cristalizan los deseos del c. Presidente de la República al establecerse una nueva industria en la Baja California," December 7, 1947, DGI/AGN, v. 25, 391/300 (03)/-1–9, letra H; Secretaría de Economía, "El esfuerzo económico de México," December 8, 1947, MAV/AGN, exp. 523/1; Secretario General de Gobierno de Jalisco Carlos G. Guzmán to municipal presidents, circular, March 22, 1947, MGSGG, correspondencia, 1-02-48.

Even the Alemán administration's crackdown on labor radicals was only tepidly received by the Monterrey Group. Monterrey's industrialists undoubtedly appreciated the increasingly pro-employer bias of the JCCA and the resolution of strikes in their favor, including ones at Camiones Círculo Azul, Artefactos Metálicos Monterrey, and the momentous conflicts at Cristalería and the Fundidora. But though some employers learned to work with state-backed unions in their factories, many of Monterrey's industrialists still condemned state intervention in labor-employer affairs. For example, in the year before President Alemán took office, industrialists concluded that the government's intervention in a local transport strike had been "absurd," even though it had settled the strike in the employers' favor.[109] The Cuauhtémoc-Vidriera group in particular sustained its challenges to national unions. It countered these unions through a combination of company paternalism and repression. Some workers, for their part, continued to prefer company unions because they often did better with them.[110]

The Cold War provided the context for the Monterrey Group to reframe its opposition to its loss of local authority while preserving its collaboration with PRI officials. It pursued this in part by targeting the two organizations that represented the state's interventionist and corporatist strains: CANACINTRA and the CTM. As we have seen in chapter 5, the Monterrey Group opposed CANACINTRA's pressure on the Alemán administration to increase trade controls, derided its members for politicizing private enterprise, and even censured it for involving itself in labor issues that it maintained were the province of COPARMEX.[111] The Monterrey Group exploited the growing Cold War panic to foster industrialist opposition toward CANACINTRA by accusing it of allying with Marxists in support of a command economy that would eventually eliminate free enterprise.[112] It also criticized industrialists, such as those in CANACINTRA, who looked to the state to defend their interests rather than to other business organizations.[113]

The CTM, for its part, had been a target of regiomontano ire since its founding due to its efforts to undercut company unions in Nuevo León.

109. "Consecuencias nefastas de un absurdo intervencionismo de estado," *Actividad,* February 15, 1946.
110. Snodgrass, *Deference and Defiance,* 297–98.
111. "Los problemas de trabajo y las cámaras de industria," *Actividad,* July 1, 1945.
112. "Empresa libre-Iniciativa privada," *Actividad,* October 15, 1946; "Patrones comunistas," *Actividad,* December 1, 1946.
113. COPARMEX, *Modernización de las relaciones de trabajo,* 17–19, 28–29, 48–49.

Throughout the 1940s, Monterrey's business community continued to denounce the CTM's leaders for political opportunism that fostered Marxist-inspired class warfare and undermined labor-employer cooperation to the detriment of the working class.[114] It even drew parallels between the wave of strike activity taking place across Mexico during 1946 and 1947 and the Russian experience in 1917, concluding that it could be the first step toward a bloody liquidation of Mexico's middle class.[115] Into the mid-1940s, the PCM, Lombardo Toledano, and the CTM insisted that class struggle was integral to their efforts to improve workers' living standards. For many, however, that argument merely justified the Monterrey Group's accusations, even though the CTM eventually eschewed class struggle in favor of conciliation.[116]

The Monterrey Group also drew on its region's history of social conservatism, economic modernization, and cross-class collaboration to accuse the ruling party of having betrayed the revolutionary goals of national progress, economic independence, and collective welfare. Perhaps ironically, Monterrey industrialists questioned how Mexico could aspire to achieve social justice and morality if the revolutionary family now consisted of an oligarchy that had amassed millions in shameful business dealings. The northern entrepreneurs blamed these revolutionary parvenus for supporting rabid leftism and the mindless pursuit of wealth at the expense of human values and the collective well-being. They urged the government to clean up its personnel and end the favoritism that enriched revolutionary insiders.[117]

Additionally, supporters of the Monterrey Group assailed the state for failing to protect the working class from the excesses of capitalism. They averred that the state had subverted worker dignity by empowering unions that extorted and enslaved workers through their use of exclusion clauses and subjected workers to humiliating coercion.[118] As evidence, the Monterrey Group pointed to union violence and disorder to demonstrate the moral and material abyss into which the working class had fallen under the

---

114. *Voz Patronal*, July 9, 1949; "Aclarando conceptos," *Actividad*, March 15, 1945; "Memorándum que someten a la consideración del Señor Presidente de la República las organizaciones representativas de los hombres de negocios," *Actividad*, November 1, 1945; "El sindicalismo político," *Actividad*, August 1, 1945; "Hacia la anarquía," *Actividad*, June 15, 1946; "Convención Patronal," *Actividad*, July 15, 1945; "La Confederación Patronal de la República Mexicana ante el momento actual," *Actividad*, October 15, 1946; López-Portillo Tostado, *Estado e ideología empresarial*, 261.

115. "La destrucción de la clase media," *Actividad*, December 1, 1946.

116. Carr, *Marxism and Communism*, 127.

117. "La Revolución Mexicana," *Actividad*, January 1, 1948; "Editorial-Secretaría de Abastos," *Actividad*, October 1, 1948; "El epílogo de la paz social," *Actividad*, August 15, 1949.

118. CONCANACO, *Problemas derivados de la intervención*, 47–56.

state's tutelage. It insinuated that unions were merely eroding workers' rights with their political activities and *pistolerismo*. Monterrey industrialists then asked the state to abstain from providing workers with absurd and immoral privileges and to defend workers and employers equally.[119] In effect, and reflecting their paternalistic view of the working class, they alleged that state-backed unions were incapable of fulfilling the responsibilities to the working class that the state had delegated to those unions. Similarly, conservative employers from across the country contended that state-backed union authority was not just an assault on private property rights but also curbed workers' rights to free association, dignity, and even their livelihoods. This, they argued, had enervated the working class, damaged national production, and threatened to radically alter the social organization of Mexican society. In turn, they demanded "rectitude and morality" in state intervention in labor-employer relations and the creation of labor organizations that worked to procure the economic, social, and moral benefit of workers through "authentic representation."[120]

By denying the existence of a legitimate revolutionary family, Monterrey business leaders presented themselves as the moral guardians of the nation. They juxtaposed the discipline of production against the indiscipline of revolutionary politics to show that employers themselves could best serve as the moral vanguard against the excesses of capitalism. They stated that businesspeople needed to step into the purported lacuna of morality created by the state, so that they could "intervene directly in the indispensable social reform that the country . . . needed."[121] Monterrey's industrialists concurrently lauded local workers for their unique and selfless desire to guarantee social order and national progress. For example, they contrasted the opportunism of self-interested union leaders who made outrageous demands with the example of the pragmatic accommodation by workers at Hulera Monterrey who, seeing their company struggle, agreed to salary reductions in order

---

119. "Datos y juicios de la Confederación de la República Mexicana," *Actividad*, January 1, 1945. For examples of the Monterrey Group calling for legislation to protect the working class from the abuses of unions, see "Puntos resolutivos de la Confederación Patronal," *Actividad*, October 1, 1945; "Industrializar a México," *Actividad*, November 15, 1946; COPARMEX, *Modernización de las relaciones de trabajo*, 17–21, 28–29, 48–49.

120. CONCANACO, *Problemas derivados de la intervención*, 47–56, 113–18; Guillermo Guajardo Davis, "Discurso pronunciado en el Primer Congreso de la Industria Eléctrica," Distrito Federal, May 1948, and Guillermo Guajardo Davis, "Discurso pronunciado en la inauguración de la XIV Convención Ordinaria de Centros Patronales," September 1948, both in *Recopilación de los más importantes discursos pronunciados y artículos publicados por el señor Guillermo Guajardo Davis, como Presidente de la Confederación de Cámaras Industriales*, April 1948–March 1950, MAV/AGN, 704/439.

121. "La justicia social y las relaciones obrero-patronales," *Actividad*, October 1, 1945; "Factores de la producción," *Actividad*, December 1, 1948; "Conceptos de alto significación económica y social," *Actividad*, June 1, 1948; "Principios de acción social," *Actividad*, February 1, 1952.

to keep the factory open.[122] In return for this loyalty, the Monterrey Group added that employers had an obligation to care for their workers.[123]

In some ways, company paternalism that balanced incentives and control appeared remarkably similar to what employers had initiated in the 1920s. In an effort to build loyalty to the company, mitigate potential unrest, and nurture discipline, many employers paid a family wage and provided benefits for their workers that included education, housing, higher wages, vacations, legal services, loans, health and pension plans, and subsidies.[124] They portrayed the company as a family whose members could achieve class harmony through fulfillment of their natural familial obligations.[125] Accordingly, the factory and private property were not a means to exploit workers but rather to advance social welfare and the common good.[126] In Monterrey, the almost complete dependence of workers on employer benevolence and the prevalence of company unions assured worker quiescence, despite the high levels of abuse that persisted in some factories.[127] Since the 1930s, the Cervecería Cuauhtémoc was well-known for its success in asserting company paternalism as the dominant means to manage labor-employer relations. Though it used regulations and oversight to ensure labor peace, workers often supported this style of shop floor relations because it allowed workers to defend their regional practices and families from "the destructive designs of the 'Communist government' and its labor allies."[128] By the late 1940s, most regiomontano workers were reconciled to paternalism, and employers' unions organized within the National Federation of

---

122. COPARMEX, *Boletín Confidencial*, no. 13 (August 30, 1941), AMGM, v. 442, exp. 1442.
123. López-Portillo Tostado, *Estado e ideología empresarial*, 239–41.
124. Snodgrass, *Deference and Defiance*, 4, 25–26; Garduña Garcia, "Nuevo León," 86–87; "La justicia social y las relaciones obrero-patronales," *Actividad*, October 1, 1945; "Factores de la producción," *Actividad*, December 1, 1948; "Conceptos de alto significación económica y social," *Actividad*, June 1, 1948; "Principios de acción social," *Actividad*, February 1, 1952. For interpretations of the use of social action in determining a family wage, see "Memorandum sobre los trabajos de las Comisiones del Salario Mínimo," November 19, 1932, Archivo Municipal de Monterrey (AMM), Colección: Contemporáneo, c. 583, exp. 13. For labor-employer conflicts over calculating a family wage, see various employers and the Comité de Salario Mínimo, Monterrey, correspondence, September 1933, AMM, Colección: Civil, v. 592, exp. 45; Comisión Especial del Salario Mínimo, Municipio de Monterrey, and the Comisión Mixta del Salario Mínimo, Municipio de Monterrey, correspondence, October–November 1937, AMM, Colección: Contemporáneo, c. 326, exp. 8; Comisión del Salario Mínimo, Municipio de Monterrey, correspondence, November 1941, AMM, Colección: Contemporáneo, c. 327, exp. 1.
125. Vellinga, "*Regiomontana* Bourgeoisie," 207–9.
126. "Convención Patronal," *Actividad*, July 15, 1945; "La Confederación Patronal de la República Mexicana ante el momento actual," *Actividad*, October 15, 1946.
127. Vellinga, "*Regiomontana* Bourgeoisie," 210.
128. Snodgrass, *Deference and Defiance*, 253–60, quote from 256. See also Vellinga, *Industrialización, burguesía, y clase obrera*, 124–35.

Independent Unions. Even the directors of the Fundidora, whose workers eschewed company unions in favor of national affiliations, learned to balance company paternalism with respect for union authority. Consequently, both militant unionism and class conciliation became part of the factory's labor-employer relations.[129]

But even as some employers sustained their objections to state intervention in labor affairs, COPARMEX adapted its liberal vision of class relations to accommodate a limited state role. As early as 1945, Monterrey industrialists recognized that "modern man" accepted the positive role of limited state intervention that did not compete with private enterprise or undermine employers' rights.[130] At the same time, the Monterrey Group proposed technological modernization as one way to stave off both the "vices of liberal capitalism" and "totalitarian absorption by the state."[131] Indeed, by the late 1940s, it increasingly posited the technical organization of work processes as a means to achieve workforce discipline, autonomous from employer or state intervention. It consequently initiated a spate of activities geared toward enhancing technical education and expertise in the region. For example, led by the Cuauhtémoc group's Eugenio Garza Sada, Monterrey's business leaders created the Monterrey Institute of Technology and Higher Education (Instituto Tecnológico y de Estudios Superiores de Monterrey) in 1943 as an alternative to what they considered the left-wing tendencies of public universities.[132] In 1950, they expanded the school by adding the Institute of Industrial Research (Instituto de Investigaciones Industriales), to investigate solutions to the region's unique industrial problems. It collaborated with the Southwest Research Institute in Texas to study problems relating to manufacturing, product improvement, and efficiency. Additionally, many large companies, including the Fundidora and the Fábrica de Ladrillos Industriales y Refractarios, started their own research departments to develop new products, improve efficiency, and enhance quality control. The Cuauhtémoc group even established a separate company, the Técnica Industrial, which employed more than six hundred workers and technicians dedicated solely to supporting its affiliated industries. Moreover, many companies seeking to improve their production hired foreign technicians as

---

129. Snodgrass, *Deference and Defiance*, 265–81, 291–94.
130. "Estatismo contra iniciativa privada," *Actividad,* August 15, 1945; "El intervencionismo de estado," *Actividad,* December 1, 1950.
131. "Empresa libre-Iniciativa privada," *Actividad,* October 15, 1946.
132. "El indispensable tecnicismo," *Actividad,* September 1, 1945; COPARMEX, *Modernización de las relaciones de trabajo,* 26–31; Babb, *Managing Mexico,* 70–71; D. C. Levy, *Higher Education and the State in Latin America,* 121.

consultants. The region's businesspeople also sent their children abroad to study in fields that would support the family business and some also trained their workers' children to be future technicians.[133]

In the late 1940s, COPARMEX drew on the appeal of technological modernization to turn its efforts to improving labor-employer relations through the technical organization of work processes.[134] Thus, Monterrey industrialists ceded some aspects of paternalistic labor control to forms of control offered by factory modernization.[135] In 1949, COPARMEX President Mariano Suárez contended that the organization of work and production processes in most factories was backwards. He called for a new mentality among employers and workers founded on a faith in the technical organization of work to resolve labor problems. To organize work technically, Suárez advocated a revision of salary systems based on qualifications rather than seniority or union influence and a change to the personnel-selection process. He also supported incentives to increase worker production, methods to improve product quality and factory conditions, and the freedom of factory managers to move workers between jobs. At the same time, Suárez pressed employers to continue paying family wages and to improve social services, subsidies, savings plans, daycare, and other services.[136] As did his counterparts in Puebla, Suárez reasoned that the revision of collective contracts would create the conditions necessary to achieve these production shifts.[137]

COPARMEX proposed investment in new machinery and rational work processes as the "modern way to take advantage of social and collective forces."[138] The effect would be to reestablish industrialist authority by curbing union prerogatives over production. Its proposals, not surprisingly, often met with resistance. For example, to save the steel industry, employers argued that they needed to invest in new machinery and to modernize work processes, which would necessitate a revision of hiring practices, wages, and production methods, over which unions exercised significant control. In

133. Garduña Garcia, "Nuevo León," 87–88.
134. COPARMEX, *Modernización de las relaciones de trabajo*, 22; Alcazar, *Las agrupaciones patronales*, 45–46.
135. Ann Farnsworth-Alvear argues similarly that industrialists in mid-twentieth-century Medellín, Colombia sought to blend "an older paternalistic tradition with the progressive adoption of imported technology." Farnsworth-Alvear, *Dulcinea in the Factory*, 17.
136. COPARMEX, *Modernización de las relaciones de trabajo*, 22, 28–31, 35–41.
137. COPARMEX, *El contrato colectivo de trabajo*.
138. COPARMEX, *Modernización de las relaciones de trabajo*, 25.

contrast, to save Monterrey's industries, labor representatives endorsed protectionism and state intervention to prevent dumping through better licensing of U.S. goods.[139]

Conclusion

During the 1940s and early 1950s, the regulatory and corporatist facets of statist industrialism and ruling party consolidation aggravated industrialists in Monterrey. In response, regiomontano elites adapted liberalism to assert Monterrey as an alternative center of power, consciously constructed against the political practices and social relations that dominated in Mexico City. Although accommodating the positive role that limited state intervention could have in developing the economy, they stridently opposed the expansion of state authority through the regulation of private enterprise. Moreover, they eschewed dogmatic liberal renderings of labor-employer relations in favor of framing class collaboration as the historical outcome of the region's rugged, frontier individualism. They contrasted this with what they depicted as the laziness, irresponsibility, immorality, and opportunism that had resulted from the rise of corporatist labor relations and the politicization of the working class by the ruling party since the late 1920s.

Therefore, as Mexico City's growth outpaced Monterrey's and political power became concentrated in the capital, regiomontano elites identified the orderly, modern, and harmonious nature of Monterrey's development as a counterpoint to what they portrayed as the indiscipline of revolutionary politics and its detrimental impact on the working-class and nationalist progress. Monterrey's industrialists declared that only employer-controlled production, rather than an activist state, could overcome the excesses of capitalism by disciplining workers to the rhythms of industrial production and educating them in the values of modern life. Regiomontanos propagated a vision of the nation defined by the class collaboration, conservative values, and modern production that constituted their regional identity. They also projected Monterrey as a moral capital that embodied the collective welfare of the Mexican nation and its modern industrial future. The PRI's ability to marginalize this alternative nationalist project while incorporating its proponents underscores the powerful appeal of Mexico's mid-century economic miracle and its critical role in legitimizing Mexico's

139. *Conferencias de Mesa Redonda*, 87–97.

permeable postrevolutionary state. The post-1940s period, in this light, points not to the creation of a "hegemonic pact" between a national bourgeoisie and a Leviathan state, but rather to the ability of the ruling party to forge compromises with antagonistic sectors of Mexico's varied industrialists, even as the latter opposed the state's interventionist and corporatist practices.

CONCLUSION

We need sources of work for our people, both campesinos and workers. It is necessary to give them work in order to lift them out of the state of being pariahs in which they find themselves, lift them out of vice and bad living in order to make them worthy of the land of their elders. It is necessary to create industries, it is necessary to produce what we need. This fully reflects the great plans that your Government has outlined for the aggrandizement and prosperity of our Mexico.
—*Comité Pro-Industrialización de Progreso, Yucatán*

By the early 1950s, statist industrialism promised to deliver not just industrial development but also cultural sovereignty, political unity, economic independence, and social change. By adapting the revolutionary possibilities of mexicanidad, President Alemán affirmed the legitimacy of ruling-party claims to be leading this regeneration of the Mexican nation through statist industrialism. Therefore, as demonstrated in the epigraph from an entreaty sent to President Alemán on May 31, 1950, many Mexicans looked to the state to achieve revolutionary vindication by fostering industry in their own communities.[1] In response to the plea, the Alemán administration ordered Yucatec officials to initiate a study of industrial potential in the region. However, more than three years later, local groups were still requesting federal support to develop a comprehensive plan for local industry. Their enthusiasm soon melted into disillusion. One youth group finally pointedly remarked, "When we find out that Mexico contributes fabulous quantities for the growth of other less developed countries, we think that an injustice is being committed against the people of Progreso, Yucatán."[2]

1. Comité Pro-Industrialización de Progreso, Yucatán to Alemán, May 31, 1950, DGI/AGN, v. 23, 391/300 (03)/-1–3, leg. 3.
2. Alianza Juvenil Yucateca Siempre Adelante to Adolfo Ruiz Cortines, December 28, 1953, DGI/AGN, v. 23, 20/300 (03)/1–1.

This episode points to the material promises, revolutionary attachments, and nationalist import of statist industrialism while also highlighting the problems of viewing industry in national terms. The 1950s may have marked the take-off of the Mexican "miracle" and the aspirations associated with it, but it also exposed the anxieties of a diverse country undergoing rapid urbanization, industrialization, and social change. These anxieties became apparent in the response to the 1950 publications of Frank Tannenbaum's well-known work *Mexico: The Struggle for Peace and Bread* and Sanford A. Mosk's *Industrial Revolution in Mexico*.³ Published in 1951 in *Problemas agrícolas e industriales de México,* these books sparked retorts from no fewer than twenty-five prominent Mexican business, labor, and political leaders.

Reactions to Tannenbaum were especially critical, due largely to his conclusion that Mexico should forgo its industrial ambitions and return to its rural, agricultural roots. Many who objected to Tannenbaum's thesis drew attention to his factual errors, but the most serious critiques focused on his imperialist essentialization of the Mexican national character. One of the most fervid rejoinders came from protectionist Manuel Germán Parra Gutiérrez, who had been an undersecretary in the Secretariat of the Economy from 1946 to 1948. Parra Gutiérrez disputed Tannenbaum's complementary arguments that Mexico could best prosper by fostering rural agricultural development and that industrialization would rob Mexico of its true nature. He asserted that Tannenbaum's vision for this "bucolic utopia" in Mexico revealed his "romantic prejudice." Parra Gutiérrez then went on to provide an array of data aimed at proving that Mexico's material and cultural improvement could best be achieved through industrial development.⁴

The reaction to Tannenbaum underscores the breadth of statist industrialism as a nationalist political project for economic growth, cultural sovereignty, and social change. However, many Mexicans treated Tannenbaum's ideas seriously, which reflects the uncertainties and tensions arising from the dramatic dislocations that statist industrialism had wrought. Indeed, although more muted, the responses to Mosk's book demonstrated the inability of statist industrialism to overcome frictions among its principal beneficiaries, Mexico's political and economic elites. While noting Mosk's

---

3. Tannenbaum, *Mexico: The Struggle for Peace and Bread*; Mosk, *Industrial Revolution in Mexico.*

4. Parra Gutiérrez, "México: La lucha por la independencia económica," 231. Parra Gutiérrez went on to publish a book-length rebuttal of Tannenbaum. See Parra Gutiérrez, *La industrialización de México.*

omissions and exaggerations, many agreed with much of his analysis of Mexico's industrial circumstances and potential. However, many also took exception to his characterization of Mexico's industrialists, specifically, his emphasis on the New Group, which he associated with CANACINTRA and to which he attributed Mexico's recent industrial expansion. For example, Manuel Gómez Morin denounced Mosk's interpretation as biased and narrow, though he and others generally refrained from attacking CANACINTRA outright.[5] By contrast, former CANACINTRA president José Domingo Lavín supported Mosk. Additionally, in his reply to the book, he took the opportunity once again to condemn CONCAMIN and COPARMEX as enemies of the goals of the Mexican Revolution.[6]

The postwar economic crisis brought a range of industry and political leaders into closer accord about the need for protectionist policies. Moreover, the conservative pro-industry turn in ruling-party politics in the 1940s benefited many of Mexico's elites with its relatively high levels of protection, subsidies, loans, infrastructure investment, repression of labor radicalism, and even opportunities for graft. Yet distinct class affiliations, political proclivities, regional identities, and personal rivalries continued to divide Mexico's industrialists and profoundly affect how they experienced and responded to statist industrialism. Consequently, the notion of a national bourgeoisie colluding with a Leviathan state in pursuit of their overlapping economic and political interests seems narrow, if not crude. Rather, Mexico's path to statist, protected development was contested and erratic, which indicates the permeability of Mexico's midcentury state.

Even groups that strongly supported statist industrialism as a panacea for revolutionary upheaval, economic stagnation, and Catholic provincialism remained divided over the best means to achieve capitalist industrial growth. For example, technocrats in the OII supported the role of the state in overcoming obstacles to industrialization unique to developing countries. Nevertheless, they continued to promote industrial planning as a means to curb the intrusion of politics into economic decision making. They appealed to rationalist arguments that gained legitimacy from their pretensions to scientific objectivity. However, Mexico's fractured technocratic elites were dispersed across a range of state agencies, and so they struggled to coordinate

---

5. *Problemas agrícolas e industriales de México* 3, no. 2 (April–June 1951). Manuel Gómez Morin also critiqued Mosk's book in a four article series in *Excélsior*, August 27–30, 1951. For more on these debates, see López-Portillo Tostado, *Estado e ideología empresarial*, 104–25.

6. Lavín, "Notas sobre los capítulos II y III."

their efforts, especially when facing economic crisis, dependency, and the regular sexennial transitions in federal administrations that often subordinated planning to politics. These factors precluded designing or implementing a comprehensive economic plan, which some technocrats argued was essential for achieving long-term development. CANACINTRA, by contrast, favored an activist state, limited only by the demands of industrialists themselves. Moreover, at least until the 1960s, CANACINTRA seemed to hold the nationalist card with the backing of Latin American structuralists, many of whom celebrated the potential of an alliance of the state with the national bourgeoisie to overcome the problems of dependency. In the end, however, CANACINTRA leaders never obtained the level of influence in the state apparatus that they had sought. Its members may have profited from the implementation of trade controls and tariffs that favored the types of industry that dominated in Mexico City, but the nationalist political alliance of CANACINTRA, the CTM, and the PRI was partial and temporary.

Regional industrialists adapted to new postrevolutionary forms of political authority and statist industrialism, though in ways that evolved out of their rival visions of local rule and modern social relations. For example, the national ruling party and Puebla's textile industrialists steered a course between exclusion and accommodation in negotiating the role that textile production and textile industrialists, themselves, would play in state consolidation and industrial modernization. The Alemán administration refused to grant machinery import permits to most traditional textile industrialists in that state, many of whom sought the machinery as a means to weaken collective contracts and reassert their authority within local labor regimes. This refusal stemmed from his government's emphasis on modern industry and the limited availability of machinery during and after World War II, among other factors. However, it also signaled the ruling party's capacity to use industrial policy to protect corporatist labor relations at the expense of traditional forms of industrialist authority. In the end, the state continued to provide traditional textile producers with tariff protection, due in part to the importance of the industry to the national economy. However, this merely reinforced the mechanical backwardness of Puebla's textile industry and the industry's image as a relic of Mexico's early capitalist adventures. As the textile industry in Puebla stagnated, owners' recalcitrance to corporatist populism grew.

In contrast, and despite heavy support for the PAN in Jalisco, industrialists in Guadalajara successfully balanced cooperation with the central government with local forms of regional authority. Regional elites there contested state intervention with geographically and culturally based assertions of identity founded on a defense of small-scale, regional industry and local class relations. Even as Jaliscan industrialists ceded on issues of labor authority, they continued to create local industrial organizations and to protect types of local industries that were at odds with national political and industrial priorities. Local political leaders mediated tensions over these issues by committing to regional industrial growth while remaining loyal to the ruling party. Nationalist, state-sponsored industrialism, in turn, evolved to accommodate identities and practices derived from concepts of the distinct nature of Jalisco's industries. Ultimately, Guadalajaran industrialists were drawn into an archetypal, accommodationist pact with the ruling party, even as many continued to condemn the state's partiality toward large-scale, modern industries and its negative impact on small- and medium-sized producers.[7]

By comparison, accommodation between the national ruling party and the Monterrey Group was both deeper and more frangible. By the 1940s, political influence and personal connections between Monterrey's business leaders and ruling-party officials dimmed the former's bitter memories of political exclusion and labor intervention during the 1920s and 1930s. However, Monterrey's industrialists continued to adamantly oppose state regulations that they perceived to be an infringement on private property rights and prejudicial to access to the foreign supplies and markets on which they disproportionately relied. Moreover, they censured corporatist labor politics for undermining the social conservatism, paternalism, and cross-class collaboration that they identified as responsible for the region's industrial modernization. Though their midcentury experiments with opposition politics were short-lived, Monterrey's business leaders nevertheless contested the central government by fostering an image of Monterrey as the moral capital and nationalist vanguard of Mexico in opposition to what they argued were the revolutionary excesses of ruling-party-directed statist development concentrated in Mexico City. In doing so, they projected their regional class and productive relations as a nationalist project that epitomized Mexico's modern industrial future.

Despite broader support for tariffs after the war, the legacy of statist industrialization is rife with ambivalences. Even as it matured into a full-fledged program of import substitution in the 1950s, it never gained universal national support. By the beginning of that decade, CONCAMIN was

---

7. Herrera Rossi, "Defensa de la pequeña industria."

already pressuring the state to abandon both its narrow focus on imports and the price controls that were hurting exports.[8] However, the economic "miracle" of the 1950s and 1960s helped to lessen both popular and conservative opposition to ISI. Many soon became enamored of Mexico's sustained high average annual growth rates, which brought both urban opportunities and an overall decline in poverty. Moreover, many welcomed political stability under the PRI, which managed to maintain power with only a minimum of blatant electoral fraud in the 1950s, in contrast to political leaders in other Latin American industrializing countries.

However, statist industrialization also brought with it redistributive problems that appeared to many to be a betrayal of the ruling party's commitment to revolutionary reformism. Mexicans were wealthier and had improved access to education and work opportunities, but the 1940s marked the beginning of steadily widening disparities between rich and poor. As rural Mexicans streamed into cities in search of jobs, they soon learned the limits of ISI's manufacturing miracle. Some privileged working-class sectors benefited from government wage protection, even though at the loss of union autonomy. Other people, however, were forced to eke out a living in the informal sector, fighting at the edge of poverty to take part in Mexico's growth. By the 1970s, ISI's nationalist and revolutionary virtues had fallen victim to economic and political crises. Some blamed the flawed nature of Mexico's industrialization, emphasizing its inefficiency and unsustainability. Additionally, one of ISI's biggest promises—independence from the United States—was soon overwhelmed by the flood of direct foreign investment that poured into Mexico after the late 1940s.[9] Conservative businesspeople with ties to U.S. markets and capital courted that investment. For instance, in response to the U.S. Foreign Trade Council's 1949 denunciation of Mexican protectionism (see chapter 5), CONCAMIN urged the council's members to collaborate with Mexico's industrialists. This outreach was partially responsible for the 1951 creation of the Mexican-American Committee of Businessmen (Comité México-Norteamericano de Hombres de Negocios), whose principles included a desire to end state economic intervention, which was seen as retarding economic development.[10] Even

---

8. "Informe del Señor Edmundo J. Phelan, a la Asamblea General Ordinaria, durante el ejercicio social de 1951–1952," in CONCAMIN, *La Confederación de Cámaras Industriales*, 2:403–4.

9. A joint U.S.-Mexico commission was formed in the early 1950s to study Mexico's capacity to continue absorbing foreign investment. Combined Mexican Working Party, *Economic Development of Mexico*.

10. Zabludovsky, "Antecedentes," 76–88; "Informe del Señor Edmundo J. Phelan, a la Asamblea General Ordinaria, durante el ejercicio social de 1951–1952," in CONCAMIN, *La Confederación de Cámaras Industriales*, 2:431–32.

members of CANACINTRA, who continued to oppose high levels of foreign investment that fostered dependency, began to build ties with foreign investors. These alliances, in turn, proved to be a profitable way for U.S. investors to skirt nationalist legislation and gain security for their capital.

In the end, though nationalist industrial policy helped to change the structure of U.S. investment in Mexico, its impact on dependence is less categorical.[11] On the one hand, imports as a percentage of Mexico's GDP dropped from 11.3 percent between 1946 and 1955 to 7.6 percent between 1956 and 1970, although this decline cannot be ascribed to protectionist policies alone.[12] On the other hand, ISI relied on the continuous infusion of foreign investment. Moreover, many U.S. companies simply jumped over trade barriers by building subsidiaries in Mexico, a practice that, in turn, led some U.S. businesspeople to oppose the abandonment of protection decades later.[13] Indeed, despite the prevalent postwar rhetoric of freer trade, in practice the U.S. government and international lending institutions like the World Bank tacitly supported the adoption of protectionist policies in the developing areas of the world in the 1950s and, especially, the 1960s. The reasons for the pro-ISI bias are complex but related to the highly circumscribed lending possibilities for international banks in the 1950s and credit policies that ended up, on occasion, favoring ISI-related projects. It also stemmed from Cold War security concerns in the 1960s; pressure from transnational companies benefiting from trade protection; and the acknowledgment that continuing protectionist pressures at home diminished the ability of the U.S. government to lower its own tariffs after World War II, which inhibited developing countries from turning to export-oriented growth models. In essence, pragmatism outweighed free-trade ideology in shaping the tolerance and even support for ISI by the United States and the international lending community during the middle of the twentieth century.[14]

---

11. Some U.S. investors demonstrated a deft understanding of the factors affecting the new nationalist economic policies in Latin America, including the desire of Latin American leaders to develop rapidly in part by building currency reserves. They noted that a return to the pre–World War I model of "colonial" foreign investment was no longer possible. The securities firm Hayden Stone and Company added, "The future of American industry beyond its natural borders seems to lie rather in partnerships with foreign interests in foreign markets than in increased exports." Marcel Aubry, Hayden Stone & Co., memorandum, January 22, 1957, AMGM, v. 404, exp. 1351.

12. Moreno-Brid and Ros, *Development and Growth*, 101.

13. Coatsworth, "United States and Democracy," 147–48.

14. Maxfield and Nolt, "Protectionism and the Internationalization of Capital"; Webb, "Influence of International Financial Institutions on ISI," 98–113. John H. Coatsworth agreed that by the 1950s, the U.S. more broadly "supported, promoted, and pressured for the adoption of ISI policies throughout the less-developed world," though it continued to oppose state planning. Coatsworth, "Structures, Endowments, and Institutions," 133.

Moreover, though accusations of corruption and ruling-party betrayal of the Revolution were decades old by the 1960s, the crisis of 1968 prompted the Mexican left to develop a more comprehensive critique of the PRI.[15] The significance of the politics of statist industrialization for understanding ruling-party authority becomes apparent when we see how the PRI weathered this crisis, even as ISI was running out of steam. The capacity of industrialism to contribute to ruling-party legitimacy lay in its agility in the face of the competing claims by regional industrialists, in part because it never demanded that they fully submit to the state's corporatist arrangements. Industrialism therefore neither displaced nor superseded regional identities. Rather, regional identities rooted in distinct social and political relations were reproduced amid the midcentury process of conflict and reconciliation over industrialization. Consequently, statist industrialism evolved as a flexible, nationalist, political project that reflected the ruling party's ambition to create a stable political system that could accommodate, or at least tolerate, enduring social and political opposition. This included allowing ambivalent or even hostile industrialists to maintain a regionally grounded preserve of local power, thereby balancing the tensions between twentieth-century consolidating growth and Mexico's deep legacies of regional authority.

---

15. In 1947, Daniel Cosío Villegas blamed ruling party leaders for the state's authoritarian turn, which he said stemmed from their tendency to act in their immediate, pecuniary, and corrupt interests. Cosío Villegas, "Mexico's Crisis." At the time, politicians and intellectuals almost universally condemned Cosío Villegas's statements, regardless of their political affiliation. Márquez Colín, "Daniel Cosío Villegas," 893; Cosío Villegas, *Ensayos y notas*, 1:369–71.

Bibliography

ARCHIVES CONSULTED

Mexico City
AGN   Archivo General de la Nación
- DGI   Fondo Dirección General de Industrias
- DT   Fondo Departamento del Trabajo
- EPG   Ramo Presidencial, Fondo Emilio Portes Gil
- GR   Fondo Gonzalo Robles
- LC   Ramo Presidencial, Fondo Lázaro Cárdenas del Río
- MAC   Ramo Presidencial, Fondo Manuel Ávila Camacho
- MAV   Ramo Presidencial, Fondo Miguel Alemán Valdés
- OC   Ramo Presidencial, Fondo Álvaro Obregón-Plutarco Elías Calles
- POR   Ramo Presidencial, Fondo Pascual Ortiz Rubio

AMGM   Archivo Manuel Gómez Morin, Instituto Tecnológico Autónomo de México
CEHM   Centro de Estudios de Historia de México Carso
HN   Hemeroteca Nacional de México, UNAM
IM   Instituto de Investigaciones Dr. José María Luis Mora
LTAE   Biblioteca Miguel Lerdo de Tejada, Archivos Económicos
UI   Universidad Iberoamericana, Biblioteca Francisco Xavier Clavigero
- CIGSA   Archivo de la Compañía Industrial de Guadalajara, S.A.

Guadalajara, Jalisco
AHJ   Archivo Histórico del Estado de Jalisco
CRIT-J   Cámara Regional de la Industria de Transformación del Estado de Jalisco
MGSGG   Archivo Municipal de Guadalajara Salvador Gómez García
VGF   Biblioteca del Congreso Valentín Gómez Farías

Monterrey, Nuevo León
AGENL   Archivo General del Estado de Nuevo León
- CON   Fondo Concesiones
- DF/SSICT   Fondo Dependencia Federal, Serie Secretaría de Industria, Comercio, y Trabajo
- IC   Fondo Industria y Comercio

MF/MH	Fondo Correspondencia Ministerios Federales, Serie Correspondencia Ministerio de Hacienda
SGG/SSGG	Fondo Secretaría General de Gobierno, Serie Secretaría General de Gobierno
AMM	Archivo Municipal de Monterrey
BCENL	Biblioteca del Congreso del Estado de Nuevo León

Puebla, Puebla
CITPT   Archivo de la Cámara de la Industria Textil de Puebla y Tlaxcala

JOURNALS AND NEWSPAPERS

Acción (Mexico City)
Actividad (Monterrey)
Carta Semanal (Mexico City)
Confederación: Boletín Quincenal de la CONCAMIN (Mexico City)
Excélsior (Mexico City)
Germinal (Puebla)
El Mercado de Valores (Mexico City)
Mexican Labor News (Mexico City)
El Nacional (Mexico City)
Novedades (Mexico City)
La Opinión (Puebla)
Periódico Oficial, El Estado de Jalisco (Jalisco)
Planificación Económica (Mexico City)
El Popular (Mexico City)
La Prensa (Puebla)
Tiempo (Mexico City)
El Universal (Mexico City)
Voz Patronal (Mexico City)

BOOKS, ARTICLES, PUBLISHED PRIMARY MATERIALS, AND THESES

Aboites Aguilar, Luis. *Excepciones y privilegios: Modernización tributaria y centralización en México, 1922–1972*. Mexico City: El Colegio de México, 2003.

Adler Lomnitz, Larissa, and Marisol Pérez-Lizaur. *A Mexican Elite Family, 1820–1980: Kinship, Class, and Culture*. Translated by Cinna Lomnitz. Princeton: Princeton University Press, 1987.

Aguayo, Sergio. *Myths and [Mis]Perceptions: Changing U.S. Elite Visions of Mexico*. Translated by Julián Brody. La Jolla: Center for U.S.-Mexican Studies, University of California, San Diego, 1998.

Aguirre Anaya, María del Carmen. *El horizonte tecnológico de México bajo la mirada de Jesús Rivero Quijano*. Mexico City: Instituto de Ciencias Sociales y Humanidades, Benemérita Universidad Autónoma de Puebla, 1999.

Alba Vega, Carlos. "Las regiones industriales y los empresarios de México." In *Los empresarios mexicanos: Ayer y hoy*, edited by Cristina Puga and Ricardo Tirado. Mexico City: Ediciones El Caballito, 1992.

Alba Vega, Carlos, and Dirk Kruijt. "La burguesía industrial de Guadalajara." In *Las empresas y los empresarios en el México contemporáneo*, edited by Ricardo Pozas and Matilde Luna. Mexico City: Editorial Grijalbo, 1991.

———. *Los empresarios y la industria de Guadalajara*. Guadalajara: El Colegio de Jalisco, 1988.

———. "Urban *Hacendados*: The Industrial Bourgeoisie of Guadalajara." In *Region, State, and Capitalism in Mexico: Nineteenth and Twentieth Centuries*, edited by Wil Pansters and Arij Ouweneel. Amsterdam: Centro de Estudios y Documentación Latinoamericanos, 1989.

Alcazar, Marco Antonio. "Las agrupaciones patronales en México." *Jornadas* (El Colegio de México) 66 (1970).

Aldana Rendón, Mario. "El derrumbe del Porfiriato." In *Jalisco desde la Revolución*, vol. 1, *Del reyismo al nuevo orden constitucional, 1910–1917*. Guadalajara: Gobierno del Estado de Jalisco and the Universidad de Guadalajara, 1987.

———. *Desarrollo económico de Jalisco, 1821–1940*. Guadalajara: Instituto de Estudios Sociales, Universidad de Guadalajara, 1979.

Anderson, Charles W. "Bankers as Revolutionaries: Politics and Development Banking in Mexico." In *The Political Economy of Mexico*, two studies by William Glade and Charles W. Anderson. Madison: University of Wisconsin Press, 1968.

Anderson, Rodney. *Outcasts in Their Own Land: Mexican Industrial Workers, 1906–1911*. DeKalb: Northern Illinois University Press, 1976.

Appleby, Joyce Oldham. *Economic Thought and Ideology in Seventeenth-Century England*. Princeton: Princeton University Press, 1978.

Applegate, Celia. "A Europe of Regions: Reflections on the Historiography of Sub-National Places in Modern Times." *American Historical Review* 104, no. 4 (1999): 1157–82.

Arias, Patricia. *Fuentes para el estudio de la industrialización en Jalisco: Siglo XX*. Mexico City: Cuadernos de la Casa Chata, 1983.

———. "La industria en perspectiva." In *Guadalajara: La gran ciudad de la pequeña industria*, edited by Patricia Arias. Michoacán: El Colegio de Michoacán, 1985.

———. "Presentación." In *Guadalajara: La gran ciudad de la pequeña industria*, edited by Patricia Arias. Michoacán: El Colegio de Michoacán, 1985.

———. "El proceso de industrialización: Siglo XX." In *Industria y comercio*, edited by José María Muriá and Jaime Olveda. Vol. 5 of *Lecturas históricas de Guadalajara*. Mexico City: Instituto Nacional de Antropología e Historia, 1993.

———. "Talleres, comerciantes e industriales: Una trilogía persistente." In *Guadalajara: La gran ciudad de la pequeña industria*, edited by Patricia Arias. Michoacán: El Colegio de Michoacán, 1985.

Arndt, H. W. *Economic Development: The History of an Idea*. Chicago: University of Chicago Press, 1987.

Arroio Junior, Raimundo. "El proceso de industrialización y la pauperización del proletariado mexicano: 1940–1950." In *Desarrollo y crisis de la economía mexicana: Ensayos de interpretación histórica*, edited by Rolando Cordera. Mexico City: Fondo de Cultura Económica, 1981.

Ashby, Joe C. *Organized Labor and the Mexican Revolution Under Lázaro Cárdenas*. Chapel Hill: University of North Carolina Press, 1963.

Aubey, Robert T. *Nacional Financiera and Mexican Industry*. Los Angeles: Latin American Center, University of California, 1966.

Ayers, Edward L., and Peter S. Onuf. "Introduction." In *All Over the Map: Rethinking American Regions*, by Edward L. Ayers, Patricia Nelson Limerick, Stephen Nissenbaum, and Peter S. Onuf. Baltimore: Johns Hopkins University Press, 1996.

Azaola, Elena. *La clase obrera como sujeto de estudio en México (1940–1980)*. Mexico City: Cuadernos de la Casa Chata, 1984.

Azpeitia Gómez, Hugo. *Compañía Exportadora e Importadora Mexicana, S. A. (1949–59): Conflicto y abasto alimentario*. Mexico City: Centro de Investigaciones y Estudios Superiores en Antropología Social, 1994.

Babb, Sarah. *Managing Mexico: Economists from Nationalism to Neoliberalism*. Princeton: Princeton University Press, 2001.

Bailey, David C. *Viva Cristo Rey! The Cristero Rebellion and the Church-State Conflict in Mexico*. Austin: University of Texas Press, 1974.

Banco de México, Departamento de Investigaciones Industriales. *Directorio de empresas industriales beneficiadas con exenciones fiscales, 1940–1960*. Mexico City: Banco de México, 1961.

Barajas Manzano, Javier. *Aspectos de la industria textil de algodón en México*. Mexico City: Instituto Mexicano de Investigaciones Económicas, 1959.

Barba González, Silvano. *Informe que el C. Gobernador Constitucional del Estado, Lic. Silvano Barba González, rindió ante la XXXV Legislatura de Jalisco, en el tercer año de su gestión administrativa* (1942). In Vol. 4 of *Jalisco: Testimonio de sus gobernantes (1940–1959)*, edited by Aída Urzúa Orozco and Gilberto Hernández Z. Guadalajara: Unidad Editorial and the Gobierno del Estado de Jalisco, 1989.

Bassols Batalla, Angel. *México: Formación de regiones económicas: Influencias, factores, y sistemas*. Mexico City: UNAM, 1992.

Beato, Guillermo, and Domenico Sindico. "The Beginning of Industrialization in Northeast Mexico." *Americas* 39, no. 4 (1983): 499–518.

Beatty, Edward. *Institutions and Investment: The Political Basis of Industrialization Before 1911*. Stanford: Stanford University Press, 2001.

Becerra, René A. "Recordando a Robles." In *Economía e industrialización: Ensayos y testimonios, Homenaje a Gonzalo Robles*. Mexico City: Fondo de Cultura Económica, 1982.

Becker, Marjorie. *Setting the Virgin on Fire: Lázaro Cárdenas, Michoacán Peasants, and the Redemption of the Mexican Revolution*. Berkeley and Los Angeles: University of California Press, 1995.

Benjamin, Thomas. "Laboratories of the New State, 1920–1929: Regional Social Reform and Experiments in Mass Politics." In *Provinces of the Revolution: Essays on Regional Mexican History, 1910–1929*, edited by Thomas Benjamin and Mark Wasserman. Albuquerque: University of New Mexico Press, 1990.

Bennett, Douglas, and Kenneth Sharpe. "The State as Banker and Entrepreneur: The Last-Resort Character of the Mexican State's Economic Intervention, 1917–1976." *Comparative Politics* 12, no. 2 (1980): 165–89.

Berins Collier, Ruth, and David Collier. *Shaping the Political Arena: Critical Junctures, the Labor Movement, and Regime Dynamics in Latin America*. Princeton: Princeton University Press, 1991.

Bernal Tavares, Luis. *Vicente Lombardo Toledano y Miguel Alemán: Una bifurcación en la Revolución Mexicana*. Mexico City: Centro de Estudios e Investigación para el Desarrollo Social, Facultad de Filosofía y Letras, UNAM, 1994.

Blair, Calvin P. "Nacional Financiera: Entrepreneurship in a Mixed Economy." In *Public Policy and Private Enterprise in Mexico*, edited by Raymond Vernon. Cambridge: Harvard University Press, 1964.

Bortz, Jeffrey. "The Genesis of the Mexican Labor Relations System: Federal Labor Policy and the Textile Industry 1925–1940." *Americas* 52, no. 1 (1995): 43–69.

———. "The Legal and Contractual Limits to Private Property Rights in Mexican Industry During the Revolution." In *The Mexican Economy, 1870–1930: Essays on the Economic History of Institutions, Revolution, and Growth*, edited by Jeffrey Bortz and Stephen H. Haber. Stanford: Stanford University Press, 2002.

———. *Revolution Within the Revolution: Cotton Textile Workers and the Mexican Labor Regime, 1910–1923*. Stanford: Stanford University Press, 2008.

Bortz, Jeffrey, and Marcos Aguila. "Earning a Living: A History of Real Wage Studies in Twentieth-Century Mexico." *Latin American Research Review* 41, no. 2 (2006): 112–38.

Boyer, Christopher R. *Vanishing Woods: Community, Forest, and Scientific Management in Mexico, 1880–2000*. Durham: Duke University Press, forthcoming.

Brady, Robert A. "The Meaning of Rationalization: An Analysis of the Literature." *Quarterly Journal of Economics* 46, no. 3 (1932): 526–40.

———. *The Rationalization Movement in German Industry: A Study in the Evolution of Economic Planning*. New York: Howard Fertig, 1933, 1974.

Brandenburg, Frank R. *The Making of Modern Mexico*. Englewood Cliffs, N.J.: Prentice-Hall, 1964.

———. "Organized Business in Mexico." *Inter-American Economic Affairs* 12, no. 3 (1958): 26–52.

Braverman, Harry. *Labor and Monopoly Capital: The Degradation of Work in the Twentieth Century*. New York: Monthly Review Press, 1974.

Bravo Jiménez, Manuel. "Con Gonzalo Robles." In *Economía e industrialización: Ensayos y testimonios, Homenaje a Gonzalo Robles*. Mexico City: Fondo de Cultura Económica, 1982.

———. *Planeación industrial en México: Notas sobre ensayos y experiencias*. Mexico City: Investigaciones Industriales, Banco de México, 1949.

Broers, Michael. "The Myth and Reality of Italian Regionalism: A Historical Geography of Napoleonic Italy, 1801–1814." *American Historical Review* 108, no. 3 (2003): 688–709.

Buchenau, Jürgen. *Plutarco Elías Calles and the Mexican Revolution*. Lanham, Md.: Rowman and Littlefield, 2007.

Bueno, Gerardo. "The Structure of Protection in Mexico." In *The Structure of Protection in Developing Countries*. Baltimore: Johns Hopkins Press, for the International Bank for Reconstruction and Development and the Inter-American Development Bank, 1971.

Bullejos, José. *Índice bibliográfico de obras y estudios especiales*. Mexico City: Departamento de Investigaciones Industriales, Banco de México, 1955.

Bulmer-Thomas, Victor. *The Economic History of Latin America Since Independence*. Cambridge: Cambridge University Press, 1994.

Cabral, Roberto. "Industrialización y política económica." In *Desarrollo y crisis de la economía mexicana*, edited by Rolando Cordera. Mexico City: Fondo de Cultura Económica, 1981.

Camiro, Max. "La industria textil de México y la política económica del estado de 1933 a 1943. La situación en 1944. Las perspectivas. Cuestiones industriales de México." *Jornadas* (El Colegio de México) 48 (1945).

———. "Ponencia de la Asociación Nacional de Empresarios de la Industria Textil." In *Segunda Convención Mexicana de Empresarios Textiles: Rama del algodón*. Mexico City: Consejo Nacional de Empresarios de la Industria Textil, 1948.

Camp, Roderic Ai. *Entrepreneurs and Politics in Twentieth-Century Mexico*. New York: Oxford University Press, 1989.

———. *Mexican Political Biographies, 1935–1993*. Austin: University of Texas Press, 1995.

———. "The National School of Economics and Public Life in Mexico." *Latin American Research Review* 10, no. 3 (1975): 137–51.

Campa, Valentín. *Mi testimonio: Memorias de un comunista mexicano.* 2nd ed. Mexico City: Ediciones de Cultura Popular, 1985.
CANACINTRA. *Conclusiones sobre los puntos del temario del Tercer Congreso Nacional de Industriales.* Mexico City: CANACINTRA, 1945.
———. *El Tratado Comercial con los Estados Unidos.* Mexico City: CANACINTRA, 1947.
Cárdenas, Enrique. "The Great Depression and Industrialisation: The Case of Mexico." In *Latin America in the 1930s: The Role of the Periphery in World Crisis,* edited by Rosemary Thorp. Vol. 2 of *An Economic History of Twentieth-Century Latin America,* edited by Enrique Cárdenas, José Antonio Ocampo, and Rosemary Thorp. Basingstoke, Hampshire: Palgrave, in association with St. Antony's College, Oxford, 1984, 2000.
———. *La hacienda pública y la política económica, 1929–1958.* Mexico City: El Colegio de México and the Fondo de Cultura Económica, 1994.
———. *La industrialización mexicana durante la Gran Depresión.* Mexico City: El Colegio de México, 1987.
———. "The Process of Accelerated Industrialization in Mexico, 1929–82." In *Industrialization and the State in Latin America: The Postwar Years,* edited by Enrique Cárdenas, José Antonio Ocampo, and Rosemary Thorp. Vol. 3 of *An Economic History of Twentieth-Century Latin America,* edited by Enrique Cárdenas, José Antonio Ocampo, and Rosemary Thorp. Basingstoke, Hampshire: Palgrave, in association with St. Antony's College, Oxford, 2000.
Cardoso, Alfonso. *Informe que presenta el Señor Alfonso Cardoso, Presidente de la CANACINTRA, a la XI Asamblea General Ordinaria.* Mexico City: Editorial Cultura, 1951.
Carr, Barry. *Marxism and Communism in Twentieth-Century Mexico.* Lincoln: University of Nebraska Press, 1992.
———. "Recent Regional Studies of the Mexican Revolution." *Latin American Research Review* 15, no. 1 (1980): 3–14.
Cavazos Lerma, Manuel. "Cincuenta años de política monetaria." In *Cincuenta años de banca central: Ensayos conmemorativos, 1925–1975.* Mexico City: Banco de México and the Fondo de Cultura Económica, 1976.
Ceceña Cervantes, José Luis. *La planificación económica nacional en los países atrasados de orientación capitalista (El caso de México).* Mexico City: UNAM, 1983.
Centro de Información y Estudios Nacionales, A.C. "La Cámara Nacional de la Industria de Transformación y la economía nacional." *Análisis Mensual.* Mexico City: Centro de Información y Estudios Nacionales, A.C., 1981.
CEPAL. "El desarrollo económico de México." *Problemas agrícolas e industriales de México* 3 (1951): 116–72.
Cerutti, Mario. *Burguesía, capitales e industria en el norte de México: Monterrey y su ámbito regional (1850–1910).* Mexico City: Alianza Editorial and the Facultad de Filosofía y Letras de la Universidad Autónoma de Nuevo León, 1992.
———. "Monterrey and Its *Ámbito Regional,* 1850–1910: Historical Context and Methodological Recommendations." In *Mexico's Regions: Comparative History and Development,* edited by Eric Van Young. La Jolla: Center for U.S.-Mexican Studies, University of California, San Diego, 1992.
———. "Patricio Milmo, empresario regiomontano del siglo XIX: En torno a la acumulación de capitales en Monterrey (1845–1890)." In *Formación y desarrollo de la burguesía en México, siglo XIX,* edited by Ciro F. S. Cardoso. Mexico City: Siglo XXI Editores, 1978.
———. "Producción capitalista y articulación del empresariado en Monterrey (1890–1910)." In *Grupos económicos y organizaciones empresariales en México,* edited by Julio Labastida. Mexico City: UNAM and Alianza Editorial Mexicana, 1986.

Chibber, Vivek. *Locked in Place: State-Building and Late Industrialization in India.* Princeton: Princeton University Press, 2003.
———. "Reviving the Developmental State? The Myth of the National Bourgeoisie." Theory and Research in Comparative Social Analysis Series, Department of Sociology, University of California, Los Angeles, Paper 20 (October 14, 2004). Available at http://repositories.cdlib.org/uclasoc/trcsa/20.
Chilcote, Ronald H. "Dependency: A Critical Synthesis of the Literature." *Latin American Perspectives* 1, no. 1, "Dependency Theory: A Reassessment" (1974): 4–29.
Cleaves, Peter S. *Professions and the State: The Mexican Case.* Tucson: University of Arizona Press, 1987.
Coatsworth, John H. "Economic and Institutional Trajectories in Nineteenth-Century Latin America." In *Latin America and the World Economy Since 1800,* edited by John H. Coatsworth and Alan M. Taylor. Cambridge: Harvard University Press, 1998.
———. "Mexico." In *The Oxford Encyclopedia of Economic History.* Vol. 3, edited by Joel Mokyr. Oxford: Oxford University Press, 2003.
———. "Structures, Endowments, and Institutions in the Economic History of Latin America." *Latin American Research Review* 40, no. 3 (2005): 126–44.
———. "The United States and Democracy in Mexico." In *The United States and Latin America: The New Agenda,* edited by Victor Bulmer-Thomas and James Dunkerley. London: Institute of Latin American Studies, University of London and David Rockefeller Center for Latin American Studies, Harvard University, 1999.
Coatsworth, John H., and Jeffrey G. Williamson. "Always Protectionist? Latin American Tariffs from Independence to Great Depression." *Journal of Latin American Studies* 36, no. 2 (May 2004): 205–32.
Cockcroft, James. *Mexico's Hope: An Encounter with Politics and History.* New York: Monthly Review Press, 1998.
Colín, José R. *Hacia dónde vamos?* Mexico City: CANACINTRA, November 14, 1946.
———. *Requisitos fundamentales para la industrialización de México.* Mexico City: CANACINTRA, October 1945.
Collado Herrera, María del Carmen. *Empresarios y políticos: Entre la Restauración y la Revolución, 1920–1924.* Mexico City: Instituto Nacional de Estudios Históricos de la Revolución Mexicana, 1996.
Combined Mexican Working Party. *The Economic Development of Mexico.* Baltimore: Johns Hopkins Press and the International Bank for Reconstruction and Development, 1953.
Comisión de Planeación Industrial de la CANACINTRA. *Proceso ocupacional (Un análisis del proceso en México).* Mexico City: Editorial América Nueva, 1956.
CONCAMIN. *La Confederación de Cámaras Industriales de los Estados Unidos Mexicanos a través de los informes anuales rendidos por sus presidentes a las Asambleas Generales Ordinarias, 1919–1969.* Vols. 1 and 2. Mexico City: CONCAMIN, 1970.
CONCANACO. *Problemas derivados de la intervención del estado en la economía pública.* Mexico City: CONCANACO, January 1946.
Conferencias de Mesa Redonda presididas durante su campaña electoral por el Licenciado Miguel Alemán, 27 de agosto de 1945–17 de junio de 1946. Mexico City: Talleres Gráficos de la Nación, 1949.
Contreras, Ariel José. *México 1940: Industrialización y crisis política: Estado y sociedad civil en las elecciones presidenciales.* Mexico City: Siglo XXI Editores, 1977.
COPARMEX. *El contrato colectivo de trabajo: Su significado económico-social.* Mexico City: COPARMEX, 1949.
———. *Modernización de las relaciones de trabajo: Aspectos de una nueva conciencia patronal.* Mexico City: COPARMEX, 1949.

Cordero H., Salvador. *Concentración industrial y poder económico en México*. Mexico City: Centro de Estudios Sociológicos, El Colegio de México, 1977.

Córdova, Arnaldo. *La formación del poder político en México*. Mexico City: Ediciones Era, 1971.

———. *La ideología de la Revolución Mexicana: La formación del nuevo régimen*. 10th ed. Mexico City: Instituto de Investigaciones Sociales, UNAM and Ediciones Era, 1973, 1982.

———. *La Revolución en crisis: La aventura del Maximato*. Mexico City: Cal y Arena, 1995.

Cornelius, Wayne A., Jr. "Contemporary Mexico: A Structural Analysis of Urban Caciquismo." In *The Caciques: Oligarchical Politics and the System of Caciquismo in the Luso-Hispanic World*, edited by Robert Kern. Albuquerque: University of New Mexico Press, 1973.

———. *Politics and the Migrant Poor in Mexico City*. Stanford: Stanford University Press, 1975.

Cosío Villegas, Daniel. "The Chapultepec Conference (February 21–March 8, 1945)." In *American Extremes*. Translated by Américo Paredes. Austin: University of Texas Press, 1964.

———. *La cuestión arancelaria en México*. Vol. 3 of *Historia de la política aduanal*. Mexico City: Mijares y Hermano, 1932.

———. *Ensayos y notas*. Vol. 1. Mexico City: Editorial Hermes, 1966.

———. "Mexico's Crisis." In *American Extremes*. Translated by Américo Paredes. Austin: University of Texas Press, 1964. Originally published as "La crisis de México." *Cuadernos americanos* 6, no. 2 (1947): 29–51.

———. "La riqueza legendaria de México." *El trimestre económico* 6 (1939): 58–83.

Crider, Greg. "Material Struggles: Workers' Strategies During the 'Institutionalization of the Revolution' in Atlixco, Puebla, Mexico, 1930–1942." PhD diss., University of Wisconsin, Madison, 1996.

Cue Cánovas, Augustín. "Economía de emergencia e industria." In *Seis años de actividad nacional*. Mexico City: Secretaría de Gobernación, 1946.

Cuervo, Raimundo. "Evolución tecnológica e industrialización racional." *Jornadas* (El Colegio de México) 48 (1945).

Cypher, James M. *State and Capital in Mexico: Development Policy Since 1940*. Boulder: Westview Press, 1990.

Dahms, Harry F. "From Creative Action to the Social Rationalization of the Economy: Joseph A. Schumpeter's Social Theory." *Sociological Theory* 13, no. 1 (1995): 1–13.

Davis, Diane E. *Discipline and Development: Middle Classes and Prosperity in East Asia and Latin America*. Cambridge: Cambridge University Press, 2004.

———. "Uncommon Democracy in Mexico: Middle Classes and the Military in the Consolidation of One-Party Rule, 1936–1946." In *The Social Construction of Democracy, 1870–1990*, edited by George Reid Andrews and Herrick Chapman. New York: New York University Press, 1995.

———. *Urban Leviathan: Mexico City in the Twentieth Century*. Philadelphia: Temple University Press, 1994.

Dean, Warren. *The Industrialization of São Paulo, 1880–1945*. Austin: University of Texas Press, 1969.

de la Peña, Guillermo. "Populism, Regional Power, and Political Mediation: Southern Jalisco, 1900–1980." In *Mexico's Regions: Comparative History and Development*, edited by Eric Van Young. La Jolla: Center for U.S.-Mexican Studies, University of California, San Diego, 1992.

de la Peña, M. T. *La industria textil de algodón: Crisis-salarios-contratación.* Mexico City: Sindicato Nacional de Economistas, 1938.
De León Garza, Máximo. *Monterrey: Un vistazo a sus entrañas.* Monterrey: Talleres Imp. Linotipográfica, 1968.
De Navarrete, Ifigenia M. *Los incentivos fiscales y el desarrollo económico de México.* Mexico City: Instituto de Investigaciones Económicas, UNAM, 1967.
De Oliveira, Orlandina. *Migración y absorción de mano de obra en la Ciudad de México: 1930–1970.* Mexico City: Centro de Estudios Sociológicos, El Colegio de México, 1976.
Derossi, Flavia. *The Mexican Entrepreneur.* Paris: OECD, 1971.
Díaz-Cayeros, Alberto. *Federalism, Fiscal Authority, and Centralization in Latin America.* Cambridge: Cambridge University Press, 2006.
"Dictamen que formula la Comisión Técnica Textil Mexicana como resultado del viaje de estudio a las fábricas textiles de los Estados Unidos, que le encomendó la Convención Revisora del Contrato Colectivo de Trabajo de la Industria Textil del Algodón." Mexico City: Consejo Nacional de Empresarios de la Industria Textil, 1947.
Drake, Paul W. "Mexican Regionalism Revisited." *Journal of Interamerican Studies and World Affairs* 12, no. 3 (1970): 401–15.
Duara, Prasenjit. *Rescuing History from the Nation: Questioning Narratives of Modern China.* Chicago: University of Chicago Press, 1995.
Durand, Jorge. "Siglo y medio en el camino de la industrialización." In *Guadalajara: La gran ciudad de la pequeña industria,* edited by Patricia Arias. Michoacán: El Colegio de Michoacán, 1985.
Eakin, Marshall C. *Tropical Capitalism: The Industrialization of Belo Horizonte, Brazil.* New York: Palgrave, 2001.
Eckstein, Susan. *The Poverty of Revolution: The State and the Urban Poor in Mexico.* Princeton: Princeton University Press, 1977.
Enríquez Perea, Alberto. "Gilberto Bosques, revolucionario de siempre: La disputa por la gobernatura de Puebla en 1936." In *Perspectivas sobre el cardenismo: Ensayos sobre economía, trabajo, política y cultura en los años treinta,* edited by Marcos Tonatiuh Aguila M. and Alberto Enríquez Perea. Mexico City: Universidad Autónoma Metropolitana, Azcapotzalco, 1996.
Esquivel, Gerardo, and Graciela Márquez Colín. "Some Economic Effects of Closing the Economy: The Mexican Experience in the Mid-Twentieth Century." In *The Decline of Latin American Economies: Growth, Institutions, and Crises,* edited by Sebastian Edwards, Gerardo Esquivel, and Graciela Márquez Colín. Chicago: University of Chicago Press, 2007.
Estrada Urroz, Rosalina. *Del telar a la cadena de montaje: La condición obrera en Puebla, 1940–1976.* Puebla: Benemérita Universidad Autónoma de Puebla, 1997.
———. "El poder de compra de la clase obrera en Puebla de 1940–1960." In *Memorias del Encuentro Sobre Historia del Movimiento Obrero.* Puebla: Universidad Autónoma de Puebla, 1980.
Evans, Peter. *Dependent Development: The Alliance of Multinational, State, and Local Capital in Brazil.* Princeton: Princeton University Press, 1979.
———. *Embedded Autonomy: States and Industrial Transformation.* Princeton: Princeton University Press, 1995.
Farnsworth-Alvear, Ann. *Dulcinea in the Factory: Myths, Morals, Men, and Women in Colombia's Industrial Experiment, 1905–1960.* Durham: Duke University Press, 2000.
Fernández Aceves, María Teresa. "En-gendering *Caciquismo:* Guadalupe Martínez, Heliodoro Hernández Loza, and the Politics of Organized Labor in Jalisco." In *Caciquismo in Twentieth-Century Mexico,* edited by Alan Knight and Wil Pansters.

London: Institute for the Study of the Americas, School of Advanced Study, University of London, 2005.

———. "José Guadalupe Zuno Hernández and the Revolutionary Process in Jalisco." In *State Governors in the Mexican Revolution, 1910–1952: Portraits in Conflict, Courage, and Corruption,* edited by Jürgen Buchenau and William H. Beezley. Lanham, Md.: Rowman and Littlefield, 2009.

Fishlow, Albert. "Origins and Consequences of Import Substitution in Brazil." In *International Economics and Development: Essays in Honor of Raúl Prebisch,* edited by Luis Eugenio Di Marco. New York: Academic Press, 1972.

FitzGerald, E. V. K. "The Conflict of Economic Doctrines in Latin America." In *Economic Doctrines in Latin America: Origins, Embedding, and Evolution,* edited by E. V. K. FitzGerald and Rosemary Thorp. Basingstoke, Hampshire: Palgrave Macmillan, in association with St. Antony's College, Oxford, 2005.

———. "Restructuring through the Depression: The State and Capital Accumulation in Mexico, 1925–40." In *Latin America in the 1930s: The Role of the Periphery in World Crisis,* edited by Rosemary Thorp. Vol. 2 of *An Economic History of Twentieth-Century Latin America,* edited by Enrique Cárdenas, José Antonio Ocampo, and Rosemary Thorp. Basingstoke, Hampshire: Palgrave, in association with St. Antony's College, Oxford, 2000.

Fouque, Agustín. *El Tratado de Comercio México-Americano (Guión para una revisión equitativa).* Mexico City: Edición y Distribución Ibero Americana de Publicaciones, 1949.

Franco, Fernando. "Labor Law and the Labor Movement in Mexico." In *Unions, Workers, and the State in Mexico,* edited by Kevin J. Middlebrook. La Jolla: Center for U.S.-Mexican Studies, University of California, San Diego, 1991.

Friedrich, Paul. "The Legitimacy of a Cacique." In *Local-Level Politics: Social and Cultural Perspectives,* edited by Marc J. Swartz. Chicago: Aldine, 1968.

Fuentes Mares, José. *Monterrey: Una ciudad creadora y sus capitanes.* Mexico City: Editorial Jus, 1976.

Gabayet Ortega, Luisa. "Diferenciación social y formación de clase obrera: Análisis comparativo de tres casos jaliscienses." In *Cambio regional, mercado de trabajo y vida obrera en Jalisco,* edited by Guillermo de la Peña and Agustín Escobar. Guadalajara: El Colegio de Jalisco, 1986.

———. "La industria textil." In *Industria y comercio,* edited by José María Muriá and Jaime Olveda. Vol. 5 of *Lecturas históricas de Guadalajara.* Mexico City: Instituto Nacional de Antropología e Historia, 1993.

Gamboa Ojeda, Leticia. *Los empresarios de ayer: El grupo dominante en la industria textil de Puebla, 1906–1929.* Puebla: Editorial Universidad Autónoma de Puebla, 1985.

———. "El mundo empresarial en la industria textil de Puebla: Las primeras tres décadas del siglo XX." In *Las empresas y los empresarios en el México contemporáneo,* edited by Ricardo Pozas and Matilde Luna. Mexico City: Editorial Grijalbo, 1989.

———. *El perfil organizativo del Centro Industrial Mexicano, 1906–1936.* Puebla: Instituto de Ciencias Sociales y Humanidades, Universidad Autónoma de Puebla, 1995.

———. "La trayectoria de una familia empresarial de la industria textil de Puebla: Los Quijano-Rivero, 1864–1921." In *Grupos económicos y organizaciones empresariales en México,* edited by Julio Labastida. Mexico City: UNAM and the Alianza Editorial Mexicana, 1986.

———. "Los últimos años de predominio de la industria textil en Puebla." In *Memoria del Primer Coloquio Regional de Historia Obrera.* Mexico City: Centro de Estudios Históricos del Movimiento Obrero Mexicano, 1977.

———. *La urdimbre y la trama: Historia social de los obreros textiles de Atlixco, 1899–1924.* Mexico City: Fondo de Cultura Económica and the Benemérita Universidad Autónoma de Puebla, 2001.

Garduña Garcia, Horacio. "Nuevo León: Un ejemplo de protección a la industria de transformación." Undergraduate thesis, Escuela Nacional de Economía, UNAM, 1958.

Garrido, Luis Javier. *El partido de la revolución institucionalizada: La formación del nuevo estado en México (1928–1945).* Mexico City: Siglo XXI Editores, 1982.

Garza Villarreal, Gustavo. "Desarrollo económico, urbanización, y políticas urbano-regionales en México (1900–1982)." *Demografía y economía* 18 (1983): 157–80.

———. *El proceso de industrialización en la ciudad de México, 1821–1970.* Mexico City: El Colegio de México, 1985.

———. *La urbanización de México en el siglo XX.* Mexico City: El Colegio de México, 2003.

Gauss, Susan M. "The Politics of Economic Nationalism in Postrevolutionary Mexico." *History Compass* 4, Issue 3 (2006): 567–77. Available at www.history-compass.com.

———. "Working Class Masculinity and the Rationalized Sex: Gender and Industrial Modernization in the Textile Industry in Postrevolutionary Puebla." In *Sex in Revolution: Gender, Politics, and Power in Modern Mexico,* edited by Jocelyn Olcott, Mary Kay Vaughan, and Gabriela Cano. Durham: Duke University Press, 2006.

Gerschenkron, Alexander. *Economic Backwardness in Historical Perspective.* Cambridge: Harvard University Press, 1962.

Glade, William P., Jr. "Party-Led Development." In *Politics, Policies, and Economic Development in Latin America,* edited by Robert Wesson. Stanford: Hoover Institution Press, Stanford University, 1984.

———. "Revolution and Economic Development: A Mexican Reprise." In *The Political Economy of Mexico,* two studies by William P. Glade and Charles W. Anderson. Madison: University of Wisconsin Press, 1968.

Godwin, Frances, Milton E. Nelson, and Roberto Villaseñor. *Technological Audit of Selected Mexican Industries with Industrial Research Recommendations.* Chicago: Armour Research Foundation of the Illinois Institute of Technology, 1946.

Goldstein, Judith. *Ideas, Interests, and American Trade Policy.* Ithaca: Cornell University Press, 1993.

Gómez, Alicia. "Una burguesía en ciernes." In *Jalisco desde la Revolución,* vol. 5, *Movimientos sociales, 1929–1940,* edited by Laura Patricia Romero. Guadalajara: Gobierno del Estado de Jalisco and the Universidad de Guadalajara, 1988.

———. "Los empresarios y el estado en Jalisco, 1929–1940." In *Los empresarios mexicanos: Ayer y hoy,* edited by Cristina Puga and Ricardo Tirado. Mexico City: Ediciones El Caballito, 1992.

Gómez Fregoso, J. Jesús. "Los orígenes del sindicato de panaderos." In *Industria y comercio,* edited by José María Muriá and Jaime Olveda. Vol. 5 of *Lecturas históricas de Guadalajara.* Mexico City: Instituto Nacional de Antropología e Historia, 1993.

Gómez Galvarriato, Aurora. "El desempeño de la Fundidora de Hierro y Acero de Monterrey durante el Porfiriato: Acerca de los obstáculos a la industrialización en México." In *Historia de las grandes empresas en México, 1850–1930,* edited by Carlos Marichal and Mario Cerutti. Mexico City: Universidad Autónoma de Nuevo León and the Fondo de Cultura Económica, 1997.

———. "The Impact of Revolution: Business and Labor in the Mexican Textile Industry, Orizaba, Veracruz, 1900–1930." PhD diss., Harvard University, 1999.

———, ed. *La industria textil en México.* Mexico City: Instituto Mora, 1999.
———. "Measuring the Impact of Institutional Change in Capital-Labor Relations in the Mexican Textile Industry." In *The Mexican Economy, 1870–1930: Essays on the Economic History of Institutions, Revolution, and Growth,* edited by Jeffrey Bortz and Stephen H. Haber. Stanford: Stanford University Press, 2002.
———. "Networks and Entrepreneurship: The Modernization of the Textile Business in Porfirian Mexico." *Business History Review* 82 (2008): 475–502.
———. "The Political Economy of Protectionism: The Mexican Textile Industry, 1900–1950." In *The Decline of Latin American Economies: Growth, Institutions, and Crises,* edited by Sebastian Edwards, Gerardo Esquivel, and Graciela Márquez Colín. Chicago: University of Chicago Press, 2007.
Gómez Morin, Manuel. *La nación y el régimen.* Mexico City: Biblioteca de Acción Nacional, 1939.
Gómez Tagle, Silvia, and Marcelo Miquet. "Integración o democracia sindical: El caso de los electricistas." In "Tres estudios sobre el movimiento obrero en México," special issue, *Jornadas* (El Colegio de México) 80 (1976).
González, Luis. *Los días del Presidente Cárdenas.* Vol. 15 of *Historia de la Revolución Mexicana, 1934–1940.* Mexico City: El Colegio de México, 1981.
González Casanova, Pablo. *Sociología de la explotación.* Mexico City: Siglo XXI Editores, 1969.
González González, Fernando, and Carlos Alba Vega. *Cúpulas empresariales y poderes regionales en Jalisco.* Guadalajara: Universidad de Guadalajara, 1989.
González Navarro, Moisés. "Masones y cristeros en Jalisco." *Jornadas* (El Colegio de México) 131 (2000).
Gootenberg, Paul. "*Hijos* of Dr. Gerschenkron? The Strange Case of 'Late-Comer' Conceptions in Latin American Economic History." In *The Other Mirror: Social Theory and Latin America,* edited by Miguel Centeno and Fernando López-Alves. Princeton: Princeton University Press, 2000.
———. *Imagining Development: Economic Ideas in Peru's "Fictitious Prosperity" of Guano, 1840–1880.* Berkeley and Los Angeles: University of California Press, 1993.
Gracida Romo, Elsa Margarita. *El programa industrial de la Revolución.* Mexico City: Facultad de Economía, Instituto de Investigaciones Económicas, UNAM, 1994.
Gramsci, Antonio. *Selections from the Prison Notebooks.* Edited and translated by Quintin Hoare and Geoffrey Nowell Smith. London: Lawrence and Wishart, 1971.
Granovetter, Mark. "Economic Action and Social Structure: The Problem of Embeddedness." *American Journal of Sociology* 91, no. 3 (1985): 481–510.
Gruening, Ernest. *Mexico and Its Heritage.* New York: D. Appleton-Century Company, 1934.
Guillén, Arturo. *Planificación económica a la mexicana.* Mexico City: Editorial Nuestro Tiempo, 1971.
Gutiérrez Álvarez, Coralia. *Experiencias contrastadas: Industrialización y conflictos en los textiles del centro-oriente de México, 1884–1917.* Mexico City: Centro de Estudios Históricos, El Colegio de México, and the Instituto de Ciencias Sociales y Humanidades, Benemérita Universidad Autónoma de Puebla, 2000.
Haber, Stephen H. *Industry and Underdevelopment: The Industrialization of Mexico, 1890–1940.* Stanford: Stanford University Press, 1989.
Haber, Stephen H., Noel Maurer, and Armando Razo. "Sustaining Economic Performance Under Political Stability: Political Integration in Revolutionary Mexico." In *Crony Capitalism and Economic Growth in Latin America: Theory and Evidence,* edited by Stephen H. Haber. Stanford: Hoover Institution Press, Stanford University, 2002.

Haber, Stephen H., Armando Razo, and Noel Maurer. *The Politics of Property Rights: Political Instability, Credible Commitments, and Economic Growth in Mexico, 1876–1929*. Cambridge: Cambridge University Press, 2003.
Haggard, Stephan. *Pathways from the Periphery: The Politics of Growth in Newly Industrializing Countries*. Ithaca: Cornell University Press, 1990.
Hale, Charles A. *The Transformation of Liberalism in Late Nineteenth-Century Mexico*. Princeton: Princeton University Press, 1989.
Hall, Peter A. "Conclusion: The Politics of Keynesian Ideas." In *The Political Power of Economic Ideas: Keynesianism across Nations*, edited by Peter A. Hall. Princeton: Princeton University Press, 1989.
Halperín-Donghi, Tulio. *Politics, Economics, and Society in Argentina in the Revolutionary Period*. Translated by Richard Southern. Cambridge: Cambridge University Press, 1975.
Hamilton, Nora. *The Limits of State Autonomy: Post-Revolutionary Mexico*. Princeton: Princeton University Press, 1982.
Hansen, Roger D. *The Politics of Mexican Development*. Baltimore: Johns Hopkins Press, 1971.
Harding, Timothy F. "Maoism: An Alternative to Dependency Theory?" *Latin American Perspectives* 1, no. 1, "Dependency Theory: A Reassessment" (1974): 62–65.
Hart, John M. *Anarchism and the Mexican Working Class, 1860–1931*. Austin: University of Texas Press, 1978.
Haynes, Keith Allen. "*Orden y Progreso:* The Revolutionary Ideology of Alberto J. Pani." In *Intellectuals and Power in Mexico*, edited by Roderic Ai Camp, Charles Hale, and Josefina Vázquez. Los Angeles: UCLA Latin American Center Publications, 1991.
Heath, Hilarie J. "British Merchant Houses in Mexico, 1821–1860: Conforming Business Practices and Ethics." *Hispanic American Historical Review* 73, no. 2 (1993): 261–90.
Heilbroner, Robert, and William Milberg. *The Crisis of Vision in Modern Economic Thought*. Cambridge: Cambridge University Press, 1995.
Henderson, Timothy, and David LaFrance. "Maximino Ávila Camacho of Puebla." In *State Governors in the Mexican Revolution, 1910–1952: Portraits in Conflict, Courage, and Corruption*, edited by Jürgen Buchenau and William H. Beezley. Lanham, Md.: Rowman and Littlefield, 2009.
Hernández Delgado, José. *The Contribution of Nacional Financiera to the Industrialization of Mexico*. Mexico City: Nacional Financiera, 1961.
———. "El pensamiento pragmático de Don Gonzalo Robles." In *Economía e industrialización: Ensayos y testimonios, Homenaje a Gonzalo Robles*. Mexico City: Fondo de Cultura Económica, 1982.
Hernández Elizondo, Roberto C. "Comercio e industria textil en Nuevo León, 1852–1890, un empresario: Valentín Rivero." In *Formación y desarrollo de la burguesía en México, siglo XIX*, edited by Ciro F. S. Cardoso. Mexico City: Siglo XXI Editores, 1978.
Herrera Rossi, José. "Defensa de la pequeña industria." Mexico City: Editorial Jus, 1954.
Herrigel, Gary. *Industrial Constructions: The Sources of German Industrial Power*. London: Cambridge University Press, 1996.
Higgins Industries, Inc. *Estudio sobre México: Economía-transportes-navegación*. Vols. 1 and 2 and commentaries. Mexico City: Banco de México, 1949.
Hirschman, Albert O. "Economic Policy in Underdeveloped Countries." *Economic Development and Cultural Change* 5 (1958): 362–70. Reprinted in Hirschman, *A Bias for Hope: Essays on Development and Latin America*. New Haven: Yale University Press, 1971.

———. "The Political Economy of Import-Substituting Industrialization in Latin America." *Quarterly Journal of Economics* 82 (1968): 2–32. Reprinted in Hirschman, *A Bias for Hope: Essays on Development and Latin America*. New Haven: Yale University Press, 1971.
Hudson, Pat, ed. *Regions and Industries: A Perspective on the Industrial Revolution in Britain*. Cambridge: Cambridge University Press, 1989.
INEGI. *Estadísticas históricas de México*. Vol. 2. Mexico City: INEGI, the Instituto Nacional de Antropología e Historia, and the Secretaría de Educación Pública, 1985.
Isla González de Cosío, Manuel. "Estudio de la Ley Sobre Atribuciones del Ejecutivo Federal en Materia Económica y de otras disposiciones relativas." Undergraduate law thesis, Escuela Libre de Derecho, 1963.
Izquierdo, Rafael. "Protectionism in Mexico." In *Public Policy and Private Enterprise in Mexico*, edited by Raymond Vernon. Cambridge: Harvard University Press, 1964.
James, Daniel. "Rationalisation and Working Class Response: The Context and Limits of Factory Floor Activity in Argentina." *Journal of Latin American Studies* 13, no. 2 (1981): 375–402.
Johnson, Chalmers. *MITI and the Japanese Miracle: The Growth of Industrial Policy, 1925–1975*. Stanford: Stanford University Press, 1982.
Joseph, Gilbert M., and Daniel Nugent, eds. *Everyday Forms of State Formation: Revolution and the Negotiation of Rule in Modern Mexico*. Durham: Duke University Press, 1994.
Juárez González, Leticia. "Una década en la organización y participación empresarial: 1928–1938." In *Las empresas y los empresarios en el México contemporáneo*, edited by Ricardo Pozas and Matilde Luna. Mexico City: Editorial Grijalbo, 1989.
Kalberg, Stephen. "Max Weber's Types of Rationality: Cornerstones for the Analysis of Rationalization Processes in History." *American Journal of Sociology* 85, no. 5 (1980): 1145–79.
Kandell, Jonathan. *La Capital: The Biography of Mexico City*. New York: Random House, 1988.
Kane, N. Stephen. "Bankers and Diplomats: The Diplomacy of the Dollar in Mexico, 1921–1924." *Business History Review* 47, no. 3 (1973): 335–52.
Kate, Adriaan ten, and Robert Bruce Wallace. *Protection and Economic Development in Mexico*. New York: St. Martin's Press, 1980.
Kaufman, Robert R. "How Societies Change Developmental Models or Keep Them: Reflections on the Latin American Experience in the 1930s and the Postwar World." In *Manufacturing Miracles: Paths of Industrialization in Latin America and East Asia*, edited by Gary Gereffi and Donald L. Wyman. Princeton: Princeton University Press, 1990.
Kemper, Robert V. *Migration and Adaptation: Tzintzuntzan Peasants in Mexico City*. Beverly Hills: SAGE Publications, 1977.
Kenny, Michael, Virginia García Acosta, Carmen Icazuriaga, Clara Elena Suárez Argüello, and Gloria Artís Espriu. *Inmigrantes y refugiados españoles en México (siglo XX)*. Ediciones de la Casa Chata. Mexico City: Centro de Investigaciones Superiores del Instituto Nacional de Antropología e Historia, 1979.
Keremitsis, Dawn. "La doble jornada de la mujer, 1910–1940." In *Industria y comercio*, edited by José María Muriá and Jaime Olveda. Vol. 5 of *Lecturas históricas de Guadalajara*. Mexico City: Instituto Nacional de Antropología e Historia, 1993.
King, Timothy. *Mexico: Industrialization and Trade Policies Since 1940*. London: Oxford University Press, 1970.
Kirsch, Henry W. *Industrial Development in a Traditional Society: The Conflict of Entrepreneurship and Modernization in Chile*. Gainesville: University Presses of Florida, 1977.

Knight, Alan. "*Caciquismo* in Twentieth-Century Mexico." In *Caciquismo in Twentieth-Century Mexico*, edited by Alan Knight and Wil Pansters. London: Institute for the Study of the Americas, School of Advanced Study, University of London, 2005.

———. "Cardenismo: Juggernaut or Jalopy?" *Journal of Latin American Studies* 26, no. 1 (1994): 73–107.

———. "Export-Led Growth in Mexico, c. 1900–30." In *The Export Age: The Latin American Economies in the Late Nineteenth and Early Twentieth Centuries*, edited by Enrique Cárdenas, José Antonio Ocampo, and Rosemary Thorp. Vol. 1 of *An Economic History of Twentieth-Century Latin America*, edited by Enrique Cárdenas, José Antonio Ocampo, and Rosemary Thorp. Basingstoke, Hampshire: Palgrave, in association with St. Antony's College, Oxford, 2000.

———. "El liberalismo desde la Reforma hasta la Revolución (Una interpretación)." *Historia mexicana* 35, no. 1 (1985): 59–91.

———. *The Mexican Revolution*. Vol. 2, *Counter-revolution and Reconstruction*. Cambridge: Cambridge University Press, 1986.

———. "The Mexican Revolution: Bourgeois? Nationalist? Or Just a 'Great Rebellion'?" *Bulletin of Latin American Research* 4, no. 2 (1985): 1–37.

———. "The Peculiarities of Mexican History: Mexico Compared to Latin America, 1821–1991." *Journal of Latin American Studies* 24, "Quincentenary Supplement" (1992): 99–144.

———. "The Political Economy of Revolutionary Mexico, 1900–1940." In *Latin America, Economic Imperialism, and the State: The Political Economy of the External Connection from Independence to the Present*, edited by Christopher Abel and Colin M. Lewis. London: Athlone Press, 1985.

———. "Popular Culture and the Revolutionary State in Mexico, 1910–1940." *Hispanic American Historical Review* 74, no. 3 (1994): 393–444.

———. "Revolutionary Project, Recalcitrant People: Mexico, 1910–40." In *The Revolutionary Process in Mexico: Essays on Political and Social Change, 1880–1940*, edited by Jaime E. Rodríguez O. Los Angeles: UCLA Latin American Center Publications, 1990.

———. "The Rise and Fall of Cardenismo, c. 1930–c. 1946." In *Mexico Since Independence*, edited by Leslie Bethell. Cambridge: Cambridge University Press, 1991.

———. "Subalterns, Signifiers, and Statistics: Perspectives on Mexican Historiography." *Latin American Research Review* 37, no. 2 (2002): 136–58.

———. *U.S.-Mexican Relations, 1910–1940: An Interpretation*. La Jolla: Center for U.S.-Mexican Studies, University of California, San Diego, 1987.

Krauze, Enrique. *Caudillos culturales en la Revolución Mexicana*. Mexico City: Siglo XXI Editores, 1976.

———. *La reconstrucción económica*. Vol. 10 of *Historia de la Revolución Mexicana, 1924–1928*. Mexico City: El Colegio de México, 1977.

Kuisel, Richard F. *Capitalism and the State in Modern France: Renovation and Economic Management in the Twentieth Century*. Cambridge: Cambridge University Press, 1981.

Kuntz Ficker, Sandra. "The Export Boom of the Mexican Revolution: Characteristics and Contributing Factors." *Journal of Latin American Studies* 36, no. 2 (2004): 267–96.

LaFrance, David G. *Revolution in Mexico's Heartland: Politics, War, and State Building in Puebla, 1913–1920*. Lanham, Md.: Rowman and Littlefield, 2003.

Lailson, Silvia. "De mercaderes a industriales." In *Guadalajara: La gran ciudad de la pequeña industria*, edited by Patricia Arias. Michoacán: El Colegio de Michoacán, 1985.

Langton, John. "The Industrial Revolution and the Regional Geography of England." *Transactions of the Institute of British Geographers*, n.s., 9, no. 2 (1984): 145–67.

Larroa Torres, Rosa María. "Cárdenas y la doble vía del desarrollo agrario." In *Perspectivas sobre el cardenismo: Ensayos sobre economía, trabajo, política y cultura en los años treinta*, edited by Marcos Tonatiuh Aguila M. and Alberto Enríquez Perea. Mexico City: Universidad Autónoma Metropolitana, Azcapotzalco, 1996.

Lavín, José Domingo. *Actividades durante el año de 1945 bajo la presidencia del Sr. Ingeniero Don José Domingo Lavín*. Mexico City: CANACINTRA, 1946.

———. "Dos conferencias sustentadas en los cursos de invierno de la Escuela Nacional de Economía de la Universidad Autónoma de México." Mexico City: CANACINTRA, 1946.

———. "La industria química nacional." *Jornadas* (El Colegio de México) 48 (1945).

———. "Notas sobre los capítulos II y III del libro 'La revolución industrial en México.'" *Problemas agrícolas e industriales de México* 3, no. 2 (1951): 239–41.

———. *Plan inmediato de industrialización en México*. Mexico City: CANACINTRA, July 3, 1945.

———. "Relaciones obrero-patronales." In *En la brecha mexicana (Temas económicos para México y Latinoamérica)*. Mexico City: Edición y Distribución Ibero Americana de Publicaciones, 1948.

Leal, Juan Felipe. *Del estado liberal al estado interventor en México*. Mexico City: Ediciones El Caballito, 1991.

Leff, Nathaniel H. *Economic Policy-Making and Development in Brazil, 1947–1964*. New York: John Wiley and Sons, 1968.

León, Samuel. "Cárdenas en el poder (I)." In *Evolución del estado mexicano: Reestructuración, 1910–1940*. Vol. 2. Mexico City: Ediciones El Caballito, 1991.

Levy, Carl, ed. *Italian Regionalism: History, Identity, and Politics*. Oxford: Berg, 1996.

Levy, Daniel C. *Higher Education and the State in Latin America: Private Challenges to Public Dominance*. Chicago and London: University of Chicago Press, 1986.

Lewis, Stephen E. "The Nation, Education and the 'Indian Problem' in Mexico, 1920–1940." In *The Eagle and the Virgin: Nation and Cultural Revolution in Mexico, 1920–1940*, edited by Mary Kay Vaughan and Stephen E. Lewis. Durham: Duke University Press, 2006.

Leys, Colin. *The Rise and Fall of Development Theory*. 2nd ed. London: James Currey, 1996.

Lindley, Richard B. *Haciendas and Economic Development: Guadalajara, Mexico, at Independence*. Austin: University of Texas Press, 1983.

Llinás Álvarez, Edgar. *Vida y obra de Ramón Beteta*. Mexico City: Libros del Umbral, 1996.

Loaeza, Soledad. *El Partido Acción Nacional: La larga marcha, 1939–1994. Oposición leal y partido de protesta*. Mexico City: Fondo de Cultura Económica, 1999.

Lomnitz-Adler, Claudio. *Exits from the Labyrinth: Culture and Ideology in the Mexican National Space*. Berkeley and Los Angeles: University of California Press, 1992.

López Malo, Ernesto. *Ensayo sobre localización de la industria en México*. Mexico City: Dirección General de Publicaciones, UNAM, 1960.

López-Portillo Tostado, Felícitas. *Estado e ideología empresarial en el gobierno alemanista*. Mexico City: UNAM, 1995.

Lorwin, Lewis L. "Some Political Aspects of Economic Planning." *American Political Science Review* 26, no. 4 (1932): 723–27.

Love, Joseph L. "Institutional Foundations of Economic Ideas in Latin America, 1914–1950." In *Economic Doctrines in Latin America: Origins, Embedding, and Evolution*, edited by E. V. K. FitzGerald and Rosemary Thorp. Basingstoke, Hampshire: Palgrave Macmillan, in association with St. Antony's College, Oxford, 2005.

———. "The Rise and Fall of Economic Structuralism in Latin America: New Dimensions." *Latin American Research Review* 40, no. 3 (2005): 100–125.

———. "The Rise and Fall of Structuralism." In *Economic Doctrines in Latin America: Origins, Embedding, and Evolution,* edited by E. V. K. FitzGerald and Rosemary Thorp. Basingstoke, Hampshire: Palgrave Macmillan, in association with St. Antony's College, Oxford, 2005.

Love, Joseph L., and Nils Jacobsen, eds. *Guiding the Invisible Hand: Economic Liberalism and the State in Latin American History.* New York: Praeger, 1988.

Loyo, Aurora. "La Confederación Proletaria Nacional: Un primer intento de quebrar la hegemonía de la CTM." In *Entre la guerra y la estabilidad política: El México de los 40,* edited by Rafael Loyola. Mexico City: Editorial Grijalbo, 1986.

Loyola Díaz, Rafael. *Una mirada a México:* El Nacional, *1940–1952.* Mexico City: Instituto de Investigaciones Sociales, UNAM, 1996.

Lütke-Entrup, Monika. "Business, Labour, and the State in Mexican Industrial Development: The Political Economy of Unidad Nacional." DPhil thesis, University of Oxford, 2000.

Lynch, Frances M. B. "Resolving the Paradox of the Monnet Plan: National and International Planning in French Reconstruction." *Economic History Review,* n.s., 37, no. 2 (1984): 229–43.

Lyttelton, Adrian. "Shifting Identities: Nation, Region, and City." In *Italian Regionalism: History, Identity, and Politics,* edited by Carl Levy. Oxford: Berg, 1996.

Mabry, Donald J. *Mexico's Acción Nacional: A Catholic Alternative to Revolution.* Syracuse: Syracuse University Press, 1973.

Maier, Charles S. "Between Taylorism and Technocracy: European Ideologies and the Vision of Industrial Productivity in the 1920s." *Journal of Contemporary History* 5, no. 2 (1970): 27–61.

Malpica Uribe, Samuel. "La derrota de la FROC en Atlixco, 1931–1939." In *Memorias del Encuentro Sobre Historia del Movimiento Obrero.* Puebla: Universidad Autónoma de Puebla, 1984.

Márquez Colín, Graciela. "Daniel Cosío Villegas: Sus años como economista." *El trimestre económico* 71 (4), no. 284 (2004): 877–907.

———. "The Political Economy of Mexican Protectionism, 1886–1911." PhD diss., Harvard University, 2002.

———. "Protección y cambio institucional en México (1910–1929)." In *México y España: Historias económicas paralelas?* Edited by Rafael Dobado, Aurora Gómez Galvarriato, and Graciela Márquez Colín. Mexico City: Fondo de Cultura Económica, 2007.

Martínez Nava, Juan. *Conflicto estado empresarios en los gobiernos de Cárdenas, López Mateos, y Echeverría.* Mexico City: Editorial Nueva Imagen, 1984.

Maurer, Noel. "Banks and Entrepreneurs in Porfirian Mexico: Inside Exploitation or Sound Business Strategy?" *Journal of Latin American Studies* 31, no. 2 (1999): 331–61.

———. *The Power and the Money: The Mexican Financial System, 1876–1932.* Stanford: Stanford University Press, 2002.

Maxfield, Sylvia, and James H. Nolt. "Protectionism and the Internationalization of Capital: U.S. Sponsorship of Import Substitution Industrialization in the Philippines, Turkey, and Argentina." *International Studies Quarterly* 34, no. 1 (1990): 49–81.

Maxfield, Sylvia, and Ben Ross Schneider, eds. *Business and the State in Developing Countries*. Ithaca: Cornell University Press, 1997.

Meakin, Walter. *The New Industrial Revolution: A Study for the General Reader of Rationalisation and Post-War Tendencies of Capitalism and Labor*. London: Victor Gollancz, 1928.

Medina, Ignacio. "Un dinamismo frustrado: La industria metal-mecánica." In *Industria y comercio*, edited by José María Muriá and Jaime Olveda. Vol. 5 of *Lecturas históricas de Guadalajara*. Mexico City: Instituto Nacional de Antropología e Historia, 1993.

Medina, Luis. *Civilismo y modernización del autoritarismo*. Vol. 20 of *Historia de la Revolución Mexicana, 1940–1952*. Mexico City: El Colegio de México, 1979.

———. *Del cardenismo al avilacamachismo*. Vol. 18 of *Historia de la Revolución Mexicana, 1940–1952*. Mexico City: El Colegio de México, 1978.

Melgar Palacios, María de Lourdes. "Economic Development in Monterrey: Competing Ideas and Strategies in Mexico." PhD diss., Massachusetts Institute of Technology, 1992.

Meyer, Jean. *The Cristero Rebellion: The Mexican People Between Church and State, 1926–1929*. Cambridge: Cambridge University Press, 1976.

———. *Estado y sociedad con Calles*. Vol. 11 of *Historia de la Revolución Mexicana, 1924–1928*. Mexico City: El Colegio de México, 1977.

———. "An Idea of Mexico: Catholics in the Revolution." In *The Eagle and the Virgin: Nation and Cultural Revolution in Mexico, 1920–1940*, edited by Mary Kay Vaughan and Stephen E. Lewis. Durham: Duke University Press, 2006.

———. "Revolution and Reconstruction in the 1920s." In *Mexico Since Independence*, edited by Leslie Bethell. Cambridge: Cambridge University Press, 1991.

Meyer, Lorenzo. *El conflicto social y los gobiernos del Maximato*. Vol. 13 of *Historia de la Revolución Mexicana, 1928–1934*. Mexico City: El Colegio de México, 1978.

———. "Historical Roots of the Authoritarian State in Mexico." In *Authoritarianism in Mexico*, edited by José Luis Reyna and Richard S. Weinert. Philadelphia: Institute for the Study of Human Issues, 1977.

Middlebrook, Kevin J. *The Paradox of Revolution: Labor, the State, and Authoritarianism in Mexico*. Baltimore: Johns Hopkins University Press, 1995.

Miller, Simon. "Social Dislocation and Bourgeois Production on the Mexican *Hacienda*: Querétaro and Jalisco." In *Region, State, and Capitalism in Mexico: Nineteenth and Twentieth Centuries*, edited by Wil Pansters and Arij Ouweneel. Amsterdam: Centro de Estudios y Documentación Latinoamericanos, 1989.

Montemayor Hernández, Andrés. *Historia de Monterrey*. Monterrey: Asociación de Editores y Libreros de Monterrey, 1971.

Montgomery, David. *The Fall of the House of Labor: The Workplace, the State, and American Labor Activism, 1865–1925*. Cambridge: Cambridge University Press, 1987.

———. *Workers' Control in America*. Cambridge: Cambridge University Press, 1979.

Morado Macías, César. *Concesiones: Política de fomento industrial, 1886–1950*. Monterrey: AGENL, 1991.

Mora-Torres, Juan. *The Making of the Mexican Border: The State, Capitalism, and Society in Nuevo León, 1848–1910*. Austin: University of Texas Press, 2001.

Moreno, Alejandro, and Manuel Sánchez-Castro. "A Lost Decade? László Radványi and the Origins of Public Opinion Research in Mexico, 1941–1952." *International Journal of Public Opinion Research* 21, no. 1 (2009): 3–24.

Moreno, Julio. *Yankee Don't Go Home! Mexican Nationalism, American Business Culture, and the Shaping of Modern Mexico, 1920–1950*. Chapel Hill: University of North Carolina Press, 2003.

Moreno-Brid, Juan Carlos, and Jaime Ros. *Development and Growth in the Mexican Economy: A Historical Perspective*. New York: Oxford University Press, 2009.

Mosk, Sanford A. *Industrial Revolution in Mexico*. Berkeley and Los Angeles: University of California Press, 1950.

Movimiento Económico Nacional. *México y su evolución económica*. Mexico City: Editorial Arquitectura y lo Demás, 1952.

———. "3 conferencias a técnicos, hombres de empresa, y dirigentes obreros por una mejor producción y un mayor consumo de artículos nacionales." Mexico City: Movimiento Económico Nacional, 1950.

Muñoz, Humberto, Orlandina de Oliveira, and Claudio Stern. *Mexico City: Industrialization, Migration, and the Labour Force, 1930–1970*. France: UNESCO, 1982.

Muriá, José María. *Breve historia de Jalisco*. Guadalajara: Colección La Feria, Universidad de Guadalajara, 1988. An updated and abridged version of this publication appears as José María Muriá. *Breve historia de Jalisco*. 2nd ed. Mexico City: El Colegio de México, the Fideicomiso Historia de las Américas, and the Fondo de Cultura Económica, 2000.

Myrdal, Gunnar. *The Political Element in the Development of Economic Theory*. Translated by Paul Streeten. Cambridge: Harvard University Press, 1961.

NAFINSA. *50 años de Revolución Mexicana en cifras*. Mexico City: Nacional Financiera, S.A., 1963.

———. *La política industrial en el desarrollo de México*. Mexico City: NAFINSA and CEPAL, 1971.

Niblo, Stephen R. *Mexico in the 1940s: Modernity, Politics, and Corruption*. Wilmington, Del.: Scholarly Resources, 1999.

———. *War, Diplomacy, and Development: The United States and Mexico, 1938–1954*. Wilmington, Del.: Scholarly Resources, 1995.

Nolan, Mary. *Visions of Modernity: American Business and the Modernization of Germany*. New York: Oxford University Press, 1994.

Novoa, Carlos. "Planeación económica de México." Mexico City: Sociedad Mexicana de Geografía y Estadística, 1951.

Nuncio, Abraham. *El Grupo Monterrey*. Mexico City: Editorial Nueva Imagen, 1982.

O'Brien, Thomas. *The Century of U.S. Capitalism in Latin America*. Albuquerque: University of New Mexico Press, 1999.

O'Donnell, Guillermo A. *Bureaucratic Authoritarianism: Argentina, 1966–1973, in Comparative Perspective*. 2nd ed. Berkeley and Los Angeles: University of California Press, 1988.

Olveda, Jaime. "Banca y banqueros de Guadalajara." In *La banca regional en México (1870–1930)*, edited by Mario Cerutti and Carlos Marichal. Mexico City: El Colegio de México and the Fondo de Cultura Económica, 2003.

———. *Guadalajara: Abasto, religión y empresarios*. Guadalajara: El Colegio de Jalisco and the H. Ayuntamiento de Guadalajara, 2000.

Oñate, Abdiel. "La batalla por el banco central: Las negociaciones de México con los banqueros internacionales, 1920–1925." *Historia mexicana* 49, no. 4 (2000): 631–72.

Ortega Ridaura, Isabel. "Política fiscal e industria en Monterrey (1940–1960)." Master's thesis, Universidad Autónoma de Nuevo León, 2000.

Padgett, L. Vincent. *The Mexican Political System*. Boston: Houghton Mifflin Company, 1966.

Palma, Gabriel. "From an Export-Led to an Import-Substituting Economy: Chile 1914–39." In *Latin America in the 1930s: The Role of the Periphery in World Crisis*, edited by Rosemary Thorp. Vol. 2 of *An Economic History of Twentieth-Century Latin America*, edited by Enrique Cárdenas, José Antonio Ocampo, and Rosemary Thorp. Basingstoke, Hampshire: Palgrave, in association with St. Antony's College, Oxford, 1984, 2000.

Pani, Alberto. *Apuntes autobiográficos*. Vols. 1 and 2. Mexico City: Manuel Porrúa, 1950.

———. *La política hacendaria y la Revolución*. Mexico City: Editorial Cultura, 1926.

Pansters, Wil. "Building a *Cacicazgo* in a Neoliberal University." In *Caciquismo in Twentieth-Century Mexico*, edited by Alan Knight and Wil Pansters. London: Institute for the Study of the Americas, School of Advanced Study, University of London, 2005.

———. "Paradoxes of Regional Power in Post-Revolutionary Mexico: The Rise of *Avilacamachismo* in Puebla, 1935–1940." In *Region, State, and Capitalism in Mexico: Nineteenth and Twentieth Centuries*, edited by Wil Pansters and Arij Ouweneel. Amsterdam: Centro de Estudios y Documentación Latinoamericanos, 1989. Reprinted in Wil Pansters, *Politics and Power in Puebla: The Political History of a Mexican State, 1937–1987*. Amsterdam: Centro de Estudios y Documentación Latinoamericanos, 1990.

———. *Politics and Power in Puebla: The Political History of a Mexican State, 1937–1987*. Amsterdam: Centro de Estudios y Documentación Latinoamericanos, 1990.

Pardo, María del Carmen. *La modernización administrativa en México: Propuesta para explicar los cambios en la estructura de la administración pública, 1940–1990*. Mexico City: El Colegio de México, 1991.

Parra Gutiérrez, Manuel Germán. *La industrialización de México*. Mexico City: Imprenta Universitaria, 1954.

———. "México: La lucha por la independencia económica." *Problemas agrícolas e industriales de México* 3, no. 4 (1951).

Partido de la Revolución Mexicana (PRM). *Segundo plan sexenal, 1941–1946*. Mexico City: PRM, 1939.

Partido Nacional Revolucionario (PNR). *Plan sexenal del PNR*. Mexico City: PNR, 1934.

Partido Revolucionario Institucional (PRI). *Programa de acción para 1947*. Mexico City: PRI, 1947.

Passananti, Thomas P. "'Nada de Papeluchos!' Managing Globalization in Early Porfirian Mexico." *Latin American Research Review* 42, no. 3 (2007): 101–28.

Pichardo Pagaza, Ignacio. *10 años de planificación y administración pública en México: Ensayos*. Mexico City: Instituto de Administración Pública, 1972.

Pick, James B., and Edgar W. Butler. *Mexico Megacity*. Boulder: Westview Press, 1997.

Pollard, Robert A. *Economic Security and the Origins of the Cold War, 1945–1950*. New York: Columbia University Press, 1985.

Potash, Robert A. *Mexican Government and Industrial Development in the Early Republic: The Banco de Avío*. Amherst: University of Massachusetts Press, 1959, 1983.

Pozas, Ricardo, and Matilde Luna, eds. *Las empresas y los empresarios en el México contemporáneo*. Mexico City: Editorial Grijalbo, 1989.

Primera Convención para el Estudio de Problemas Económicos de México. *Escasez y carestía: Memoria de los trabajos aprobados*. Mexico City: n.p., 1946.

Pruneda R., Fernando. "La industria textil del algodón en México." Mexico City: Comisión de Aranceles, SHCP, 1942.

Puga, Cristina. "La Confederación de Cámaras Industriales (1917–1924)." *Trimestre político* 1 (1976): 103–31.

———. "Las elecciones de 1940: El difícil tránsito." In *Evolución del estado mexicano: Reestructuración, 1910–1940*. Vol. 2. Mexico City: Ediciones El Caballito, 1991.

Purcell, John F. H., and Susan Kaufman Purcell. "Mexican Business and Public Policy." In *Authoritarianism and Corporatism in Latin America,* edited by James M. Malloy. Pittsburgh: University of Pittsburgh Press, 1977.

Purcell, Susan Kaufman. *The Mexican Profit-Sharing Decision: Politics in an Authoritarian Regime.* Berkeley and Los Angeles: University of California Press, 1975.

———. "Mexico: Clientelism, Corporatism, and Political Stability." In *Political Clientelism: Patronage and Development,* edited by S. N. Eisenstadt and René Lemarchand. Beverly Hills: SAGE Publications, 1981.

Quintana, Carlos. "Problemas fundamentales de la industrialización de México." *Jornadas* (El Colegio de México) 48 (1945).

Rabe, Stephen G. "The Elusive Conference: United States Economic Relations with Latin America, 1945–1952." *Diplomatic History* 2, no. 3 (1978): 279–94.

Radványi, László. "Planeación del desarrollo económico." *Investigación económica* 12, no. 2 (1952): 125–39.

Ramírez, Miguel D. *Development Banking in Mexico: The Case of Nacional Financiera, S.A.* New York: Praeger, 1986.

Ramírez-Faria, Carlos. *The Origins of Economic Inequality Between Nations: A Critique of Western Theories on Development and Underdevelopment.* London: Unwin Hyman, 1991.

Ramírez Rancaño, Mario. *La burguesía industrial: Revelaciones de una encuesta.* Mexico City: Instituto de Investigaciones Sociales, UNAM, and the Editorial Nuestro Tiempo, 1974.

———. *Burguesía textil y política en la Revolución Mexicana.* Mexico City: Instituto de Investigaciones Sociales, UNAM, 1987.

———. "Un frente patronal a principios del siglo XX: El Centro Industrial Mexicano de Puebla." *Revista mexicana de sociología* 44, no. 4 (1982): 1351–78. Reprinted in Salvador Cordero H. and Ricardo Tirado, eds. *Clases dominantes y estado en México.* Mexico City: Instituto de Investigaciones Sociales, UNAM, 1984.

———. "El Primer Congreso de Industriales y la constitución política." In *Grupos económicos y organizaciones empresariales en México,* edited by Julio Labastida. Mexico City: UNAM and the Alianza Editorial Mexicana, 1986.

Razo, Armando, and Stephen H. Haber. "The Rate of Growth of Productivity in Mexico, 1850–1933: Evidence from the Cotton Textile Industry." *Journal of Latin American Studies* 30, no. 3 (1998): 481–517.

Recio Cavazos, María Gabriela. "El abogado y la empresa: Una mirada al despacho de Manuel Gómez Morin, 1920–1940." PhD diss., Centro de Estudios Históricos, El Colegio de México, 2008.

"Resoluciones y acuerdos adoptados por la Convención." In *Memoria de la Primera Convención Mexicana de Empresarios Textiles (Rama del algodón).* Mexico City: National Advertising Service, 1945.

Reyes Heroles, Jesús. *La Carta de la Habana: Comentarios y digresiones.* Mexico City: Edición y Distribución Ibero Americana de Publicaciones, 1948.

Reynolds, Clark. *The Mexican Economy: Twentieth-Century Structure and Growth.* New Haven: Yale University Press, 1970.

Ritzer, George. "Professionalization, Bureaucratization, and Rationalization: The Views of Max Weber." *Social Forces* 53, no. 4 (1975): 627–34.

Rivero Quijano, Jesús. *La revolución industrial y la industria textil en México.* Vol. 2. Mexico City: Joaquín Porrúa Editores, 1990.

Robles, Gonzalo. "Obstáculos a la industrialización de los paises latinoamericanos." In *Ensayos sobre el desarrollo de México.* Mexico City: Banco de México and the Fondo de Cultura Económica, 1982.

———. "Los pueblos atrasados: Sus problemas y su planeación económica." In *Ensayos sobre el desarrollo de México*. Mexico City: Banco de México and the Fondo de Cultura Económica, 1982.

Robredo, José. "Cuarta ponencia de la Asociación de Empresarios Textiles de Puebla y Tlaxcala. Tema: Modernización de la industria textil del algodón." In *Memoria de la Primera Convención Mexicana de Empresarios Textiles (Rama del algodón)*. Mexico City: National Advertising Service, 1945.

Rodríguez Garza, Francisco Javier. "Cambio institucional y pensamiento económico en el México de entre-guerras (1920–1946)." PhD diss., Centro de Estudios Históricos, El Colegio de México, 1996.

Rojas Sandoval, Javier. *Monterrey: Poder político, obreros y empresarios en la coyuntura revolucionario*. Monterrey: Facultad de Filosofía y Letras de la Universidad Autónoma de Nuevo León and the Fundación Cultural Alfonso Reyes Aurrecoechea, 1992.

Romero, Laura. "El movimiento obrero en Jalisco, 1927–29." In *El movimiento obrero jalisciense y la crisis del '29: La última batalla de los rojos*, edited by Jaime Tamayo. Guadalajara: Instituto de Estudios Sociales, Universidad de Guadalajara, 1986.

———. *El Partido Nacional Revolucionario en Jalisco*. Guadalajara: Universidad de Guadalajara, 1995.

Romero Kolbeck, Gustavo, and Víctor L. Urquidi. *La exención fiscal en el Distrito Federal como instrumento de atracción de industrias*. Mexico City: Departamento del Distrito Federal, 1952.

Rosenberg, Emily S. *Spreading the American Dream: American Economic and Cultural Expansion, 1890–1945*. New York: Hill and Wang, 1982.

Ross, Stanford G., and John B. Christensen. *Tax Incentives for Industry in Mexico: A Report of a Study Carried Out in Mexico During the Summer of 1958*. Cambridge: Law School of Harvard University, 1959.

Rovzar, Eugenio F. "Alberto J. Pani: Un capitalista revolucionario." *Investigación económica* 145 (1978): 205–40.

Roxborough, Ian. "Labor Control and the Postwar Growth Model in Latin America." In *Latin America in the 1940s: War and Postwar Transitions*, edited by David Rock. Berkeley and Los Angeles: University of California Press, 1994.

———. "Mexico." In *Latin America Between the Second World War and the Cold War, 1944–1948*, edited by Leslie Bethell and Ian Roxborough. Cambridge: Cambridge University Press, 1992.

Rubin, Jeffrey W. *Decentering the Regime: Ethnicity, Radicalism, and Democracy in Juchitán, Mexico*. Durham: Duke University Press, 1997.

Ruiz, Ramón Eduardo. *Labor and the Ambivalent Revolutionaries: Mexico, 1911–1923*. Baltimore: Johns Hopkins University Press, 1976.

Salinas Cantú, Hernán. *Biografía del Gral. Bonifacio Salinas Leal: Último gobernador de Nuevo León de procedencia militar y con duración de cuatro años*. Monterrey: H. Salinas Cantú, 2002.

Salmerón Sanginés, Pedro. "El mito de la riqueza de México: Variaciones sobre un tema de Cosío Villegas." *Estudios de historia moderna y contemporánea de México* 26 (2003): 127–52.

Salvucci, Richard J., Linda K. Salvucci, and Aslán Cohen. "The Politics of Protection: Interpreting Commercial Policy in Late Bourbon and Early National Mexico." In *The Political Economy of Spanish America in the Age of Revolution, 1750–1850*, edited by Kenneth J. Andrien and Lyman L. Johnson. Albuquerque: University of New Mexico Press, 1994.

Sánchez Navarro, Juan. "La ética del empresariado mexicano y la doctrina social de la iglesia." In *El pensamiento social de los católicos mexicanos*, edited by Roberto J. Blancarte. Mexico City: Fondo de Cultura Económica, 1996.

Sanderson, Steven E. *The Politics of Trade in Latin American Development*. Stanford: Stanford University Press, 1992.
Saragoza, Alex M. *The Monterrey Elite and the Mexican State, 1880–1940*. Austin: University of Texas Press, 1988.
Schmidhuber Martínez, Guillermo. "Plan general de higiene industrial." Puebla: Atoyac Textil, S.A., 1946.
Schmidt, Henry C. *The Roots of "Lo Mexicano": Self and Society in Mexican Thought, 1900–1934*. College Station: Texas A&M University Press, 1978.
Schneider, Ben Ross. *Business Politics and the State in Twentieth Century Latin America*. Cambridge: Cambridge University Press, 2004.
———. "Why is Mexican Business So Organized?" *Latin American Research Review* 37, no. 1 (2002): 77–118.
Schoppa, R. Keith. "Province and Nation: The Chekiang Provincial Autonomy Movement, 1917–1927." *Journal of Asian Studies* 36, no. 4 (1977): 661–74.
Schumpeter, Joseph A. "The Communist Manifesto in Sociology and Economics." *Journal of Political Economy* 57, no. 3 (1949): 199–212.
———. *The Theory of Economic Development: An Inquiry into Profits, Capital, Credit, Interest, and the Business Cycle*. New Brunswick, N.J.: Transaction Books, 1911, 1983.
Secretaría de Economía, Dirección General de Estadística. *Cuarto censo industrial de los Estados Unidos Mexicanos: 1945, Resumen general*. Mexico City: Secretaría de Economía, 1953.
Secretaría de Economía, Dirección General de Estudios Económicos. *Industrialización y planeación regional de México*. Mexico City: Secretaría de Economía, 1950.
Secretaría de Gobernación. *Seis años de actividad nacional*. Mexico City: Secretaría de Gobernación, 1946.
Secretaría de Programación y Presupuesto. *Los primeros intentos de planeación en México (1917–1946)*. Vol. 1 of the *Antología de la planeación en México (1917–1985)*. Mexico City: Secretaría de Programación y Presupuesto and the Fondo de Cultura Económica, 1985.
———. *La programación de la inversión pública y la planeación regional por cuencas hidrológicas (1947–1958)*. Vol. 2 of the *Antología de la planeación en México (1917–1985)*. Mexico City: Secretaría de Programación y Presupuesto and the Fondo de Cultura Económica, 1985.
SEN (Secretaría de la Economía Nacional), Departamento de Estudios Económicos. *La industria textil en México: El problema obrero y los problemas económicos*. Mexico City: SEN, 1934.
SEN (Secretaría de la Economía Nacional), Dirección General de Estadística. *Compendio estadístico*. Mexico City: SEN, 1947.
———. *Primer censo industrial de 1930*. Vol. 1, *Resumenes generales*. Mexico City: SEN, 1933.
———. *Segundo censo industrial 1935*. Mexico City: SEN, 1937.
———. *Segundo censo industrial 1935*. Vol. 3, book 1, *Hilados y tejidos de algodón*. Mexico City: SEN, 1936.
SEN (Secretaría de la Economía Nacional), Oficina de Barómetros Económicos. *El desarrollo de la economía nacional bajo la influencia de la guerra, 1939–1946*. Mexico City: SEN, 1946.
Serrano, Gustavo P. *Centralización o descentralización de la industria*. Mexico City: CONCAMIN, 1945.
Servín, Elisa. *Ruptura y oposición: El movimiento henriquista, 1945–1954*. Mexico City: Cal y Arena, 2001.

Shadlen, Kenneth C. *Democratization Without Representation: The Politics of Small Industry in Mexico*. University Park: Pennsylvania State University Press, 2004.

Shafer, Robert J. *Mexican Business Organizations: History and Analysis*. Syracuse: Syracuse University Press, 1973.

Shearer, J. Ronald. "The Reichskuratorium für Wirtschaftlichkeit: Fordism and Organized Capitalism in Germany, 1918–1945." *Business History Review* 71, no. 4 (1997): 569–602.

Shelton, David H. "The Banking System: Money and the Goal of Growth." In *Public Policy and Private Enterprise in Mexico*, edited by Raymond Vernon. Cambridge: Harvard University Press, 1964.

Sherman, John W. *The Mexican Right: The End of Revolutionary Reform, 1929–1940*. Westport, Conn.: Praeger, 1997.

SICT (Secretaría de Industria, Comercio, y Trabajo). *La industria, el comercio y el trabajo en México durante la gestión administrativa del Señor General Plutarco Elías Calles, 1925–1927*. Vol. 1, *Ramo Industrial*. Mexico City: Tip. Galas, 1928.

———. *Memoria de los trabajos realizados por la Secretaría de Industria, Comercio y Trabajo durante la gestión administrativa del Señor Lic. Emilio Portes Gil*. Mexico City: Talleres Gráficos Editorial and the *Diario Oficial*, 1929.

Sikkink, Kathryn. *Ideas and Institutions: Developmentalism in Brazil and Argentina*. Ithaca: Cornell University Press, 1991.

Silva, Eduardo. "The Import-Substitution Model: Chile in Comparative Perspective." *Latin American Perspectives* 34, no. 3 (2007): 67–90.

Silva Herzog, Jesús. *Nueve estudios mexicanos*. Mexico City: Imprenta Universitaria, 1953.

———. *El pensamiento económico, social y político de México, 1810–1964*. Mexico City: Instituto Mexicano de Investigaciones Económicas, 1967.

Simpson, Eyler N. *The Ejido: Mexico's Way Out*. Chapel Hill: University of North Carolina Press, 1937.

Smithies, Arthur. "Schumpeter and Keynes." *Review of Economics and Statistics* 33, no. 2 (1951): 163–69.

Snodgrass, Michael. *Deference and Defiance in Monterrey: Workers, Paternalism, and Revolution in Mexico, 1890–1950*. Cambridge: Cambridge University Press, 2003.

Solís, Leopoldo. *Planes de desarrollo económico y social en México*. Mexico City: SepSetentas, 1975.

———. *La realidad económica mexicana: Retrovisión y perspectivas*. Mexico City: Siglo XXI Editores, 1970.

Stavenhagen, Rodolfo. *Las clases sociales en las sociedades agrarias*. Mexico City: Siglo XXI Editores, 1969.

Sternberg, Marvin. "Dependency, Imperialism, and the Relations of Production." *Latin American Perspectives* 1, no. 1, "Dependency Theory: A Reassessment" (1974): 75–86.

Stiller, Jesse H. *George S. Messersmith: Diplomat of Democracy*. Chapel Hill: University of North Carolina Press, 1987.

Story, Dale. "Industrial Elites in Mexico: Political Ideology and Influence." *Journal of Interamerican Studies and World Affairs* 25, no. 3 (1983): 351–76.

———. *Industry, the State, and Public Policy in Mexico*. Austin: University of Texas Press, 1986.

Suárez, Eduardo. *Comentarios y recuerdos (1926–1946)*. Mexico City: Editorial Porrúa, 1977.

Talavera Aldana, Luis Fernando. "Organizaciones sindicales obreras de la rama textil: 1935–1970." *Revista mexicana de ciencias políticas y sociales* 21, no. 83 (1976): 227–99.

Tamayo, Jaime. "La aurora roja en Jalisco." In *Anarquismo, socialismo, y sindicalismo en las regiones,* edited by Jaime Tamayo and Patricia Valles. Guadalajara: Centro de Investigaciones Sobre los Movimientos Sociales, Universidad de Guadalajara, 1993.

———. "La Confederación Obrera de Jalisco: Un proyecto comunista de sindicalismo." In *El movimiento obrero jalisciense y la crisis del '29: La última batalla de los rojos,* edited by Jaime Tamayo. Guadalajara: Instituto de Estudios Sociales, Universidad de Guadalajara, 1986.

———. "Movimiento obrero y lucha sindical." In *Guadalajara: La gran ciudad de la pequeña industria,* edited by Patricia Arias. Michoacán: El Colegio de Michoacán, 1985.

———. "Los obreros." In *Jalisco desde la Revolución,* vol. 5, *Movimientos sociales, 1929–1940,* edited by Laura Patricia Romero. Guadalajara: Gobierno del Estado de Jalisco and the Universidad de Guadalajara, 1988.

Tannenbaum, Frank. *Mexico: The Struggle for Peace and Bread.* New York: Alfred A. Knopf, 1950.

Tarrow, Sidney. *Between Center and Periphery: Grassroots Politicians in Italy and France.* New Haven: Yale University Press, 1977.

Taylor, Alan. "On the Costs of Inward-Looking Development: Price Distortions, Growth, and Divergence in Latin America." *Journal of Economic History* 58, no. 1 (1998): 1–28.

Tenorio-Trillo, Mauricio. *Mexico at the World's Fairs: Crafting a Modern Nation.* Berkeley and Los Angeles: University of California Press, 1996.

Thomson, Guy P. C. "Protectionism and Industrialization in Mexico, 1821–1854: The Case of Puebla." In *Latin America, Economic Imperialism, and the State: The Political Economy of the External Connection from Independence to the Present,* edited by Christopher Abel and Colin M. Lewis. London: Athlone Press, 1985.

Thorp, Rosemary. "A Reappraisal of the Origins of Import-Substituting Industrialisation, 1930–1950." *Journal of Latin American Studies* 24 (1992): 181–95.

Tobler, Hans Werner. "Peasants and the Shaping of the Revolutionary State, 1910–1940." In *Riot, Rebellion, and Revolution: Rural Social Conflict in Mexico,* edited by Friedrich Katz. Princeton: Princeton University Press, 1988.

Topik, Steven. "Karl Polanyi and the Creation of the 'Market Society.'" In *The Other Mirror: Social Theory and Latin America,* edited by Miguel Centeno and Fernando López-Alves. Princeton: Princeton University Press, 2000.

———. *The Political Economy of the Brazilian State, 1889–1930.* Austin: University of Texas Press, 1987.

———. "La revolución, el estado y el desarrollo económico en México." *Historia mexicana* 40, no. 1 (1990): 79–144.

Torres, Blanca. *Hacia la utopía industrial.* Vol. 21 of *Historia de la Revolución Mexicana, 1940–1952.* Mexico City: El Colegio de México, 1984.

———. *México en la segunda guerra mundial.* Vol. 19 of *Historia de la Revolución Mexicana, 1940–1952.* Mexico City: El Colegio de México, 1979.

Torres Mejía, David. *Proteccionismo político en México, 1946–1977.* Mexico City: UNAM, 2001.

Tuck, Jim. *The Holy War in Los Altos: A Regional Analysis of Mexico's Cristero Rebellion.* Tucson: University of Arizona Press, 1982.

Urquidi, Víctor. "Espejismos económicos actuales." *Revista de economía* 7, nos. 11 and 12 (1944): 26–27.

———. "El impuesto sobre la renta en el desarrollo económico de México." *El trimestre económico* 23, no. 4 (1956): 424–37.

———. *Otro siglo perdido: Las políticas de desarrollo en América Latina (1930–2005)*. Mexico City: El Colegio de México, the Fideicomiso Historia de las Américas, and the Fondo de Cultura Económica, 2005.

———. "Reconstruction vs. Development: The IMF and the World Bank." In *The Bretton Woods-GATT System: Retrospect and Prospect After Fifty Years*, edited by Orin Kirshner. London: M. E. Sharpe, 1996.

Valencia Castrejón, Sergio. *Poder regional y política nacional en México: El gobierno de Maximino Ávila Camacho en Puebla (1937–1941)*. Mexico City: Instituto Nacional de Estudios Históricos de la Revolución Mexicana, 1996.

Van Young, Eric. *Hacienda and Market in Eighteenth-Century Mexico: The Rural Economy of the Guadalajara Region, 1675–1820*. Berkeley and Los Angeles: University of California Press, 1981.

———. "Introduction: Are Regions Good to Think?" In *Mexico's Regions: Comparative History and Development*, edited by Eric Van Young. La Jolla: Center for U.S.-Mexican Studies, University of California, San Diego, 1992.

Vaughan, Mary Kay. *Cultural Politics in Revolution: Teachers, Peasants, and Schools in Mexico, 1930–1940*. Tucson: University of Arizona Press, 1997.

———. *The State, Education, and Social Class in Mexico, 1880–1928*. DeKalb: Northern Illinois University Press, 1982.

Velasco, Leticia. "La vicepresidencia municipal de Guadalajara." In *Miscelánea jalisciense*, edited by José María Muriá. Zapopan: El Colegio de Jalisco, 1997.

Vellinga, Menno. *Industrialización, burguesía, y clase obrera en México: El caso de Monterrey*. Mexico City: Siglo XXI Editores, 1979.

———. "The *Regiomontana* Bourgeoisie and the State." In *Region, State, and Capitalism in Mexico: Nineteenth and Twentieth Centuries*, edited by Wil Pansters and Arij Ouweneel. Amsterdam: Centro de Estudios y Documentación Latinoamericanos, 1989.

Ventura Rodríguez, María Teresa. "La FROC en Puebla, 1942–1952." In *Memorias del Encuentro Sobre Historia del Movimiento Obrero*. Puebla: Universidad Autónoma de Puebla, 1984.

Vernon, Raymond. *The Dilemma of Mexico's Development: The Roles of the Private and Public Sectors*. Cambridge: Harvard University Press, 1963.

Villarreal, René. *Industrialización, deuda y desequilibrio externo en México: Un enfoque neoestructuralista (1929–1988)*. 2nd ed. Mexico City: Fondo de Cultura Económica, 1988.

Vizcaya Canales, Isidro. *Los orígenes de la industrialización de Monterrey: Una historia económica y social desde la caída del Segundo Imperio hasta el fin de la Revolución (1867–1920)*. Monterrey: AGENL, 2001.

Waisman, Carlos H. *Reversal of Development in Argentina: Postwar Counterrevolutionary Policies, and Their Structural Consequences*. Princeton: Princeton University Press, 1987.

Walker, David W. *Kinship, Business, and Politics: The Martínez del Río Family in Mexico, 1824–1867*. Austin: University of Texas Press, 1986.

Wallace, Robert Bruce. "Policies of Protection in Mexico." In *Protection and Economic Development in Mexico*, edited by Adriaan ten Kate and Robert Bruce Wallace. New York: St. Martin's Press, 1980.

Walton, John. *Elites and Economic Development: Comparative Studies on the Political Economy of Latin American Cities*. Austin: Institute of Latin American Studies, University of Texas at Austin, 1977.

Ward, Peter M. *Mexico City: The Production and Reproduction of an Urban Environment*. Boston: G. K. Hall, 1990.

Wasserman, Mark. *Persistent Oligarchs: Elites and Politics in Chihuahua, Mexico, 1910–1940.* Durham: Duke University Press, 1993.

Webb, Richard. "The Influence of International Financial Institutions on ISI." In *Industrialization and the State in Latin America: The Postwar Years,* edited by Enrique Cárdenas, José Antonio Ocampo, and Rosemary Thorp. Vol. 3 of *An Economic History of Twentieth-Century Latin America,* edited by Enrique Cárdenas, José Antonio Ocampo, and Rosemary Thorp. Basingstoke, Hampshire: Palgrave, in association with St. Antony's College, Oxford, 2000.

Weiner, Richard. "El declive económico de México en el siglo XIX: Una perspectiva cultural." *Signos históricos* 12 (2004): 68–93.

———. "Economic Thought and Culture in Revolutionary Mexico: Carlos Díaz Dufoo's Critique of the Humboldtian Idea of Mexico's Legendary Wealth." *História e economia* 2, no. 1 (2006): 13–31.

———. *Race, Nation, and Market: Economic Culture in Porfirian Mexico.* Tucson: University of Arizona Press, 2004.

Weinstein, Barbara. "The Discourse of Technical Competence: Strategies of Authority and Power in Industrializing Brazil." *Political Power and Social Theory* 12 (1998): 141–79.

———. *For Social Peace in Brazil: Industrialists and the Remaking of the Working Class in São Paulo, 1920–1964.* Chapel Hill: University of North Carolina Press, 1996.

Wigen, Kären. "Culture, Power, and Place: The New Landscapes of East Asian Regionalism." *American Historical Review* 104, no. 4 (1999): 1183–1201.

Wilkie, James W. *The Mexican Revolution: Federal Expenditure and Social Change Since 1910.* Berkeley and Los Angeles: University of California Press, 1967.

Wilkie, James W., and Edna Monzón de Wilkie. *México visto en el siglo XX.* Mexico City: Instituto Mexicano de Investigaciones Económicas, 1969.

Winn, Peter. *Weavers of Revolution: The Yarur Workers and Chile's Road to Socialism.* New York: Oxford University Press, 1986.

Wionczek, Miguel S. *El nacionalismo mexicano y la inversión extranjera.* Mexico City: Siglo XXI Editores, 1967.

Wirth, John D. *The Politics of Brazilian Development, 1930–1954.* Stanford: Stanford University Press, 1970.

Womack, John, Jr. "The Mexican Economy During the Revolution, 1910–1920: Historiography and Analysis." *Marxist Perspectives* 1, no. 4 (1978): 80–123.

Zabludovsky, Gina. "Antecedentes del Comité México-Norteamericano de Hombres de Negocios." In *Clases dominantes y estado en México,* edited by Salvador Cordero H. and Ricardo Tirado. Mexico City: Instituto de Investigaciones Sociales, UNAM, 1984.

———. "Proposiciones para el estudio de las relaciones entre estado y empresarios durante el período presidencial de Miguel Alemán." *Estudios políticos: Revista del Centro de Estudios Políticos,* UNAM 3, no. 1 (1984): 22–27.

Zapata, Francisco. "Afiliación y organización sindical en México." In "Tres estudios sobre el movimiento obrero en México," special issue, *Jornadas* (El Colegio de México) 89 (1976).

Zebadúa, Emilio. *Banqueros y revolucionarios: La soberanía financiera de México, 1914–1929.* Mexico City: El Colegio de México, the Fideicomiso Historia de las Américas, and the Fondo de Cultura Económica, 1994.

Index

Acción Cívica Nacionalista. *See* Nationalist Civic Action
Aceites, Grasas, y Derivados, 84
AETPT. *See* Association of Textile Entrepreneurs of Puebla and Tlaxcala
agrarian reform
   agraristas, 20, 25, 59, 104–7, 108
   and capitalist growth, 109–10
   and industry, 11, 40, 57, 61, 106
   limits of, 4–5, 94, 103–7, 109
   political uses of, 8, 13
   and urbanization, 57, 88
agraristas. *See* agrarian reform
Agricultural Chamber of Puebla (Cámara Agrícola de Puebla), 134
Alanis Patiño, Emilio, 107, 116, 122
Alemán, Miguel
   Campaign for Economic Recovery, 2–3, 232
   on economic planning, 95, 125
   "Hecho en México," 1, 2, 232
   industrial protection under, 23, 85, 169, 194–97
   and labor, 203–4, 233
   large industry ties, 173, 174
   and Mexican Communist Party, 231
   on *mexicanidad*, 3, 4, 17–18, 232
   and Monterrey Group, 206, 229, 230, 231, 232–33
   peso devaluation under, 195, 203, 204
   and statist economic intervention, 2, 3, 200–201, 241
   and textile industry, 10, 22, 132, 149–51, 163, 164–68, 244
   U.S.-Mexican relations under, 182–83
Allende, Sebastián, 65–66, 81, 87
Almazán, Juan Andreu, 70–71, 99, 211, 229–30
Almazán, Leonides Andreu, 140
Amilpa (y Rivera), Fernando, 165–66, 187
anarchism, 61
Ancona, Hernando, 78–79
Ancona-Ederer, 78
Andreu Almazán, Juan. *See* Almazán, Juan Andreu
Andreu Almazán, Leonides. *See* Almazán, Leonides Andreu
Anisz, Enrique, 53, 79

anticlericalism, 8, 70, 71, 109
Araiza, Evaristo, 173–74, 230
Arbitration Commission (Comisión Arbitral), 158–59. *See also* Joint Review Convention for the Cotton Textile Industry
Arias, Patricia, 82, 84 n. 114, 88 n. 134
Armour Research Foundation, 127, 156, 164, 173
Asociación de Empresarios Textiles de Puebla y Tlaxcala. *See* Association of Textile Entrepreneurs of Puebla and Tlaxcala
Asociación de Empresas Industriales y Comerciales. *See* Association of Industrial and Commercial Businesses
Asociación Mexicana de Caminos. *See* Mexican Association of Roads
Asociación Mexicana de Planificación Económica. *See* Mexican Economic Planning Association
Association of Industrial and Commercial Businesses (Asociación de Empresas Industriales y Comerciales), 69, 216
Association of Textile Entrepreneurs of Puebla and Tlaxcala (AETPT; Asociación de Empresarios Textiles de Puebla y Tlaxcala), 131, 134, 142–43, 145, 146, 154, 167
Atlixco, Puebla, 140, 152, 157
autonomy
   fiscal, of state, 27, 30–32
   industrialist, 8–9, 36, 48–49, 62, 69, 71–72, 74–75, 100, 172
   labor, 161, 246
   regional, 20, 60, 66, 124
   state, 8, 12, 17, 21, 33
   textile industrialists, 132, 133–40, 147
   from U.S., 184, 192, 193
Ávila Camacho, Manuel
   1940 election of, 70–71, 205
   and business chambers, 71–72
   on economic planning, 95, 112, 130
   industrial protection under, 79, 85, 151, 182, 195
   and labor, 79, 94, 143
   and Monterrey Group, 205, 229, 230
   National Unity, 102, 103
   and textile industry, 150, 151, 163–64

U.S.-Mexican relations under, 101, 150, 176–79
Ávila Camacho, Maximino
  avilacamachista cacicazgo, 132, 140, 142, 143, 144, 168
  and labor, 142, 143
  rise to power, 141–42
  and textile industrialists, 142

Banco de México
  clientelism in, 33
  origins, 21, 30–32, 33
  role in economic planning, 114, 127, 152
  role in tax exemptions, 77, 78, 225
  weaknesses of, 51
Banco de Nuevo León, 209
Banco Mercantil de Monterrey, 209
Banco Nacional de Comercio Exterior, 128, 200
Banco Nacional de México, 28, 30, 53
Barba González, Silvano, 80–81, 82–83
Barcelonnettes, 19, 56
Barragán, Enrique L., 225
Barragán, Manuel L., 205, 232
basic industry, 95 147, 151
  OII research and opinion about, 95, 96, 98, 124, 125, 127–30
Bassols, Narciso, 98
Bautista Castillo, Gonzalo, 142–43, 144
Beatty, Edward, 7
Beijer Continental, 200
Benítez, José, 44, 222
Betancourt, Carlos, 142–43, 144
Beteta, Ramón, 178, 193
Bogotá conference, 182
Border Free Trade Zone, 209
Bortz, Jeffrey, 61 n. 27, 138
Brady, Robert A., 113, 119
Bravo Jiménez, Manuel, 107, 109, 117, 127
Bretton Woods conference, 179, 183–84
Bucareli Accords, 31
Budapest Sunday Circle, 125 n. 132

cacique, 132, 208
  avilacamachista cacicazgo, 132, 140, 142–44, 147, 168
  caciquismo, limits on, 140, 144, 144 n. 44, 147
Calles, Plutarco Elías
  crony capitalism under, 25
  industrial protection under, 21, 35, 36, 38–39, 41, 43, 45
  and labor, 62, 141
  and Monterrey Group, 211, 216
  on state economic intervention, 21, 26, 36, 45–47, 52
  on state fiscal autonomy, 27, 32
  U.S.-Mexican relations under, 41
Cámara de Comercio de Jalisco. *See* Jalisco Chamber of Commerce
Cámara de Comercio de Puebla. *See* Puebla Chamber of Commerce
Cámara de la Industria Textil de Puebla y Tlaxcala. *See* Puebla and Tlaxcala Chamber of the Textile Industry
Cámara de Mezcaleros de Jalisco. *See* Chamber of Mezcal Producers of Jalisco
Cámara de Propietarios. *See* Chamber of Owners
Cámara Española de Comercio de Puebla. *See* Spanish Chamber of Commerce of Puebla
Cámara Nacional de Comercio, Industria, y Minería de Jalisco. *See* National Chamber of Commerce, Industry, and Mining of Jalisco
Cámara Nacional de la Industria de Transformación. *See* National Chamber of Manufacturing Industry
Cámara Regional de la Industria de Aceites, Jabones, Grasas, y Similares de Occidente. *See* Western Regional Chamber of Oils, Soaps, Fats, and Similar Products
Camisas Doradas. *See* Gold Shirts
Campaign for Economic Recovery (Campaña de Recuperación Económica), 2, 3, 232
Campaña de Prosperidad Nacional. *See* National Prosperity Campaign
Campaña de Recuperación Económica. *See* Campaign for Economic Recovery
CANACINTRA. *See* National Chamber of Manufacturing Industry
CAOLJ. *See* Confederation of Libertarian Workers Groups of Jalisco
capital goods, 7 n. 20, 59, 171, 198, 223, 225, 226
Cárdenas, Enrique, 6, 42, 45 n. 87
Cárdenas, Lázaro
  agrarian reform under, 57, 104–5, 107
  business relations under, 53, 57, 69–70, 145
  cardenismo, 8, 13, 219
  cardenistas, 66, 219
  on economic planning, 112
  and labor, 67, 72, 100, 141, 155, 213, 217–18
  and Maximino Ávila Camacho, 141–42, 143, 144
  and Monterrey Group, 217–19, 220, 229, 230
  tax exemptions under, 82
Cardoso, Fernando Henrique, 14
Carranza, Venustiano, 26, 28, 34, 37, 39, 42

Carrillo Flores, Antonio, 183–84, 193
Casablancas, Fernando, 165
Casablancas High Draft Co. Ltd., 165
catholicism
    beliefs about class relations, 10, 29, 54, 55–56, 60–62
    Catholic Church, 106, 106 n. 45
    conservatism, 55, 60, 92
    cristeros, 61, 61 n. 25
    Monterrey Group and, 215
    National Action Party and, 70
    provincialism, 5, 105, 243
    Social Action, 54, 55–56, 89
CEIMSA. *See* Compañía Exportadora e Importadora Mexicana, S.A.
Celanese Mexicana, 53, 151
Celulosa y Derivados (CYDSA), 226
census
    census-taking, 49
    critique of industrial census, 58 n. 14
Central Board of Conciliation and Arbitration (JCCA; Junta Central de Conciliación y Arbitraje), 64, 67, 137–38, 218, 233
Centro Empresarial de Jalisco, 62
Centro Industrial de México, 137
Centro Industrial Mexicano. *See* Mexican Industrial Center
Cervecería Cuauhtémoc
    labor relations, 215, 233, 236
    origins and early years, 210
    protection of, 224, 227
    use of local capital, 209, 220, 229
CGT. *See* General Confederation of Workers
Chamber of Mezcal Producers of Jalisco (Cámara de Mezcaleros de Jalisco), 68
Chamber of Owners (Cámara de Propietarios), 134
Chapa, Pedro, 173
Chapultepec conference, 181, 182, 186–87, 189
charrazo, 203, 204
Chibber, Vivek, 202, 202 n. 146
Chumacero, Blas, 158, 165–66
científicos, 8, 26, 27, 28
CIM. See Mexican Industrial Center
Clark, Colin, 115, 116
class
    collaboration in Jalisco, 11, 55
    collaboration in Monterrey, 207, 214, 215, 234, 239, 245
    collaboration of CTM and CANACINTRA, 23, 170–71, 185, 187, 190, 192
    fraternity, 54, 60, 63–64
    harmony, 212, 214, 215, 219, 236
class conflict
    and capitalism, 18, 29

CTM and CANACINTRA, 234
    managed by economic planning, 30
    Monterrey response to, 212, 214
    and regionalism, 20
    state management of, 10–11
classical economics, 7, 28, 46, 97, 116, 123, 188–89, 193
Clayton, William, 181
clientelism
    crony capitalism and, 15
    economic planning and, 113
    and Monterrey Group, 231
    and Porfirian bankers, 28
    in Puebla, 142, 146
    and state, 34, 44
    technocratic opposition to, 27, 44, 109, 112, 114
Coatsworth, John, 7, 247 n. 14
COJ. *See* Labor Confederation of Jalisco
Cold War
    impact on Mexican politics, 23, 168, 190–92, 206, 229, 231–33
    industrial protection during, 170, 247
    role in labor repression, 165
    U.S.-Mexican relations, 169
El Colegio de México, 98, 115
Colín, José R.
    on communism, 191
    conflict with conservative business, 174, 191
    on economic planning, 117–18, 126
    on industrial protectionism, 186
    and labor, 121
    split with CANACINTRA, 172–73, 204
collective contracts
    arbitration, 64
    efforts at renegotiation in 1940s, 10, 132, 151, 154, 154 n. 86, 156, 165–68, 244
    employer opposition to, 147, 217, 218, 238
    labor opposition to revision of, 158
    negotiation of in 1910s and 1920s, 38, 133, 135–39
Comisión Arbitral. *See* Arbitration Commission
Comisión de Fomento Industrial. *See* Commission for Industrial Promotion
Comisión de Importaciones y Exportaciones. *See* Import and Export Commission
Comisión Federal de Fomento Industrial. *See* Federal Commission for Industrial Promotion
Comisión Federal de Planificación Económica. *See* Federal Economic Planning Commission
Comisión General de Aranceles. *See* General Tariff Commission

INDEX | 279

Comisión Intersecretarial de Coordinación de Normas sobre Inversiones de Capital Extranjero. *See* Intersecretarial Commission on Foreign Capital Investment Rules
Comisión Mixta Especial de Modernización de la Industria Textil del Algodón y sus Mixturas. *See* Special Joint Commission on the Modernization of the Cotton and Cotton Blends Textile Industry
Comisión Nacional de Planeación Industrial. *See* National Industrial Planning Commission
Comisión Nacional de Planeación para la Paz. *See* National Commission for Peace Planning
Comité Mexico-Norteamericano de Hombres de Negocios. *See* Mexican-American Committee of Businessmen
Comité Pro-Economía del Occidente de la República. *See* Pro-Economy Committee of Western Mexico
Comité Pro-Industrialización, Progreso, Yucatán, 241
Commissariat Général du Plan, 15
Commission for Industrial Promotion (Comisión de Fomento Industrial), 91, 114
communism, 20
  anticommunism, 191, 203, 231
  influence on economic planning and policy, 32, 115, 130
  influence on labor, 59–61, 190–92, 206, 219–20, 236
  Mexican Communist Party, 231
  role in business community conflicts, 185, 190–92, 218–20, 229, 236
Compañía Comercial Azteca, 200
Compañía Exportadora e Importadora Mexicana, S.A. (CEIMSA), 201, 201 n. 144, 228
Compañía General de Aceptaciones, 220
Compañía Industrial de Atenquique, 84, 85–86, 88
Compañía Industrial de Guadalajara, 56
Compañía Industrial de Orizaba, 137
Compañía Industrial Manufacturera, 56
Compañía Industrial Veracruzana, 137
comparative advantage, 108, 176, 184, 187
  See also export-oriented growth
Compensated Exchange (*trueques*), 200
CONCAMIN. *See* Confederation of Industrial Chambers
CONCANACO. *See* Confederation of National Chambers of Commerce
CONCANACOMIN. *See* Confederation of National Chambers of Commerce and Industry

Confederación de Agrupaciones Obreras Libertarias de Jalisco. *See* Confederation of Libertarian Workers Groups of Jalisco
Confederación de Cámaras Industriales. *See* Confederation of Industrial Chambers
Confederación de Cámaras Nacionales de Comercio. *See* Confederation of National Chambers of Commerce
Confederación de Cámaras Nacionales de Comercio y de Industria. *See* Confederation of National Chambers of Commerce and Industry
Confederación de Trabajadores de México. *See* Confederation of Mexican Workers
Confederación Fabril Nacional Mexicana. *See* Mexican National Manufacturing Confederation
Confederación General de Trabajadores. *See* General Confederation of Workers
Confederación Nacional Campesina. *See* National Campesino Confederation
Confederación Nacional de Organizaciones Populares. *See* National Confederation of Popular Organizations
Confederación Nacional Proletaria. *See* National Proletarian Confederation
Confederación Obrera de Jalisco. *See* Labor Confederation of Jalisco
Confederación Patronal de la República Mexicana. *See* Mexican Employers Association
Confederación Regional Obrera Mexicana. *See* Regional Confederation of Mexican Workers
Confederation of Industrial Chambers (CONCAMIN; Confederación de Cámaras Industriales)
  clientelism in, 173
  conflict with CANACINTRA, 174, 185, 190, 191, 243
  defense of economic nationalism, 170, 193
  on industrial protectionism, 44, 170, 188, 196, 245
  and labor, 136, 216
  origins and internal function, 34, 172, 175
  political representation of, 42–43, 71, 200
  role in peso devaluation, 195, 228
  on state regulation, 189, 201, 246
Confederation of Libertarian Workers Groups of Jalisco (CAOLJ; Confederación de Agrupaciones Obreras Libertarias de Jalisco), 59–60
Confederation of Mexican Workers (CTM; Confederación de Trabajadores de México)
  alliance with CANACINTRA and ruling party, 4, 100, 171, 185–87, 191–92, 194, 204, 244

Confederation of Mexican Workers (*continued*)
  conflict with employers, 131, 158, 160–61, 166
  on industrial protectionism, 170
  labor factionalism and, 65, 66, 90, 143, 159, 190, 203
  in Labor Unity Pact, 102
  and Monterrey Group, 206, 214, 217–19, 233–34
Confederation of National Chambers of Commerce (CONCANACO; Confederación de Cámaras Nacionales de Comercio), 43, 191, 201, 216
Confederation of National Chambers of Commerce and Industry (CONCANACOMIN; Confederación de Cámaras Nacionales de Comercio y de Industria), 69, 71–73, 108
Consejo de Colaboración Municipal de Guadalajara. *See* Guadalajara Council on Municipal Collaboration
Consejo Nacional de Economía. *See* National Council of the Economy
Consejo Nacional de Empresarios de la Industrial Textil. *See* National Council of Textile Industry Entrepreneurs
Consejo Nacional Económico. *See* National Economic Council
Consejo Nacional Obrero. *See* National Labor Council
consumer goods
  durable, 59
  manufacturers of, 10–11, 54, 59, 95, 210, 225, 226
  non-durable, 59, 86–87
  protection for, 130, 198–99, 225
Contreras, Ariel José, 230
controls, trade, 5
  in economic planning, 16, 202
  export permits, 178, 200
  import permits, 22, 132, 165, 166, 244
  licensing, 181, 197, 199, 201–3, 239
  opposition to, 9, 23, 170, 181, 188, 206, 228, 233
  postwar implementation of, 181–82, 194–97, 199, 203, 226
  quotas, 78, 150, 169, 178, 199, 200, 203
  support for, 10, 23, 170, 186, 244
  trade barriers, 193–94, 203, 212, 247
  trade permits, 199, 202, 202 n. 148
  during World War II, 101
Convención Industrial y Obrera del Ramo Textil. *See* Industrial and Labor Convention for the Textile Sector
Convención Mixta Revisora de la Industria Textil del Algodón. *See* Joint Review Convention for the Cotton Textile Industry
COPARMEX. *See* Mexican Employers Association
corporatism, labor
  government support for, 10, 22, 100–104, 168, 244
  industrialist support for, 54, 56, 92
  opposition to, 9, 69, 133, 151, 163, 206–7, 213–14, 219, 229, 233, 239–40
  ruling party support for, 12, 22, 27, 52, 56, 59, 70, 168, 244–45, 248
Cosío Villegas, Daniel
  critique of ruling party, 248 n. 14
  on economic planning, 113
  on Mexico's wealth, 126
  on tariffs, 40, 44
  ties to technocrats, 30, 95, 98, 107, 115
cotton
  protection for, 42, 221
  subsidy for cotton textile industry, 37, 133, 138–39
  taxes on, 146, 147
CPN. *See* National Proletarian Confederation
Cremería La Danesa, 88
cristeros, 40, 57, 61, 61 n. 25, 81, 88
CROM. *See* Regional Confederation of Mexican Workers
cronyism, 27
  in Banco de México, 33
  crony capitalism, 15
  in Porfirian period, 25 n. 5, 35
  after Revolution, 25, 27, 51, 70, 95, 204
Cruz y Celis, José, 173–74
CTM. *See* Confederation of Mexican Workers
Cuauhtémoc group, 210, 220, 226, 229, 233, 237
CYDSA. *See* Celulosa y Derivados

Dean, Warren, 2 n. 4
de Antuñano, Esteban, 133
Decree No. 3564, Jalisco, 81, 82
de la Garza, Arturo, 205, 231–32
de la Huerta, Adolfo, 30–31, 141, 211
De la Huerta-Lamont Treaty, 30–32
de la Peña, Joaquín, 172–73, 185–86
Departamento (or Oficina) de Investigaciones Económicas. *See* Office of Economic Research
Department of Labor, 33, 36, 138
dependency
  critique of structuralism, 4 n. 11, 244
  dependent development, 17–18, 191–95, 246–47
  economic independence from U.S., 1–5, 28, 33, 75, 112, 182, 187, 189, 236, 241

INDEX | 281

impact on economic planning, 27, 170, 188, 190
impact on state intervention, 16, 108, 110, 116–17, 128, 243
and industrial protectionism, 42, 78–79, 182, 194, 203–4
and nationalism, 40–42
ties to comparative advantage, 169, 176, 184–85
dependency theorists. See *dependentistas*
dependentistas (dependency theorists), 14, 20 n. 61, 125 n. 131
desarrollismo (developmentalism), 6, 8, 12, 14, 15, 26, 52, 96
desarrollo hacia afuera. See export-oriented growth
developmentalism. See *desarrollismo*
developmentalist liberals, 26, 47
Díaz, Porfirio, 28, 211
Dirección General de Industrias. See Industrial Affairs Office
Dirección General de Industrias de Transformación. See Manufacturing Industries Affairs Office
Doria Paz, Francisco, 131–32
Duara, Prasenjit, 18

ECLA. See Economic Commission for Latin America
Economic Commission for Latin America (ECLA)
analysis of labor in textile industry, 156, 166
on structuralism, 4 n. 11, 6, 7, 14, 170
economic planning
in 1920s, 21, 26, 45–52
as attack on private enterprise, 117
CANACINTRA opinion of, 117–19
as counter to politics in economic decision-making, 15, 114–15, 119, 243–44
impact of World War II on, 112, 114, 129–30, 228
impact on regional development, 92–93, 125, 211, 241
labor opinion of, 95–96, 119, 122
limits to in Mexico, 15–16, 51–52, 114–15, 129–30
and market imperfections, 98 n. 8
Office of Industrial Research and, 22, 95, 114–17, 128–30, 243–44
opposition to, 201, 202
popular opinion of, 103, 109
and rationalization, 111–13
and regulation, 202
on tax exemption laws, 77, 195, 197

U.S. response to, 247 n. 14
See also rationalization; technocrats; industrial research; *and* Office of Industrial Research
ejido, 105–8
election, 1940 presidential
FROC participation in, 143
impact of, 71, 74–75, 91, 99, 230
Monterrey Group participation in, 229–31
National Action Party opposition, 70, 91, 98–99, 229–30
Equipos Camiones Monterrey, 225
Escamilla, Alberto, 223
Escuela Nacional de Economía. See National Economics School
Estado de México, 138, 149, 167, 210, 225
Esteve, Adrián, 127
Export-Import Bank, 173 n. 14, 182
export-oriented growth (*desarrollo hacia afuera*), 6, 25, 37, 96, 150, 185, 194, 247
See also comparative advantage
export pessimism, 6, 187

Fábrica de Cerillos La Regiomontana, 224
Fábrica de Fósforos y Cerillos El Fénix, 224
Fábrica de Ladrillos Industriales y Refractarios, 237
Fábrica La Trinidad, 131, 143
Faletto, Enzo, 14
Federación de Trabajadores de Jalisco. See Federation of Jaliscan Workers
Federación de Trabajadores de Nuevo León. See Federation of Workers of Nuevo León
Federación de Trabajadores de Puebla. See Federation of Pueblan Workers
Federación Regional de Obreros y Campesinos. See Regional Workers and Campesinos Federation
Federal Commission for Industrial Promotion (Comisión Federal de Fomento Industrial), 114
Federal Economic Planning Commission (Comisión Federal de Planificación Económica), 112, 114
Federal Labor Law (1931), 62–65, 140, 212, 216–17
Federation of Jaliscan Workers (Federación de Trabajadores de Jalisco), 66–67, 90
Federation of Pueblan Workers (Federación de Trabajadores de Puebla), 162
Federation of Workers of Nuevo León (Federación de Trabajadores de Nuevo León), 219
Ferrara, Vicente, 221
First National Banking Convention (Primera Convención Nacional Bancaria), 31
First National Congress of Industrialists. See National Congress of Industrialists

FitzGerald, E. V. K., 42, 194 n. 114
fomento, 111
Fomento Industrial y Mercantil, 84
Fondo de Cultura Económica, 98
Ford, Bacon, & Davis, 127
Fordism, 111 n. 69
Foreign Trade Council, 179, 246
Franco P., César, 145
free trade
　economic planning and, 45
　opposition to, 37, 185–87, 192–94, 194 n. 114
　during Porfiriato, 40
　support for, 45, 170, 184, 188, 192–94, 220
　tariffs, 43, 44
　U.S. pressure on Mexico to pursue, 23, 169, 176, 179–81, 186–87, 189, 247
　versus marxism, 115
　See also laissez-faire growth; individualism; property rights; private enterprise; *and* liberalism
Friedrich, Paul, 144 n. 44
FROC. *See* Regional Workers and Campesinos Federation
Fundidora de Hierro y Acero de Monterrey
　labor relations, 215, 233, 237
　political ties, 174, 229, 230
　origins and protection, 209, 209 n. 16, 210–11, 221
　during World War II, 22

García Barragán, Marcelino, 89–90, 89 n. 138
Garza Sada family, 207, 208, 210, 217, 220
　Garza Sada, Eugenio, 237
　Garza Sada, Luis, 215
　Garza Sada, Roberto, 173–74, 215, 224, 227
Gaxiola, Francisco Javier, 71, 102
General Agreement on Tariffs and Trade, 182, 185
General Confederation of Workers (CGT; Confederación General de Trabajadores), 61, 102, 218
General Tariff Commission (Comisión General de Aranceles), 200–201
The General Theory of Employment, Interest and Money, 116
　See also Keynes, John Maynard
Gerschenkron, Alexander, 8, 15, 17, 116–17
Gleason Álvarez, Miguel, 188
Gold Shirts (*Camisas Doradas*), 218, 219
Goldhamer, H. F., 223
Gómez Galvarriato, Aurora, 7, 139 n. 24, 167, 167 n. 143
Gómez Morin, Manuel
　and Banco de México, 33–34
　on foreign capital, 41
　founder of National Action Party, 70
　and Monterrey Group, 227, 229
　response to Sanford Mosk, 243
　role in economics field, 97–98
　technocrat, 29, 33, 34
　and textile industry 154
González, Porfirio G., 211
González, Roberto, 225
González Gallo, Jesús, 89, 90–91, 92
González Luna, Efraín, 70, 92
González Salinas, Felix, 205
Gonzalo Escobar, José, 61–62
Great Depression
　early onset in Mexico, 40, 45, 45 n. 87
　economic impact, 23, 48, 54, 215
　impact in Guadalajara, 57, 66, 81, 87
　impact in Monterrey, 226
　impact on consumption, 212–13
　impact on labor, 61, 141, 215
　impact on textile industry, 139, 141
　role in origins of ISI, 5–7, 107
　state economic intervention during, 212
　U.S.-Mexican relations during, 41
Guadalajara
　industrialist relations with federal government, 2, 8, 10–11, 22, 53–55, 90–93, 244–45
　1940 elections, 70–71, 99
　origins of industry, 56–57
　postrevolutionary industrial growth, 57–58, 58 n. 14, 125
　regional identity and alliances, 18, 20–21, 58–59, 74
　ruling party influence in, 91–92
　tax exemptions, 82, 89
　urbanization, 87–89, 171
Guadalajara Council on Municipal Collaboration (Consejo de Colaboración Municipal de Guadalajara), 91
Guerrero, Anacleto, 218–19
Gunder Frank, André, 14
Gutiérrez, Juan, 228–29

Haber, Stephen H., 7 n. 20, 15, 28, 45 n. 87
Halperín Donghi, Tulio, 19 n. 57
Hamilton, Nora, 17
Havana Charter, 188
Hayden Stone and Company, 247 n. 11
"Hecho en México," 1, 232
Heilbroner, Robert, 7
Henríquez Guzmán, Miguel, 90
Hernández Loza, Heliodoro, 64–65, 65 n. 90
Herrigel, Gary, 17
Higgins Industries, 127

Hirschman, Albert, 14, 103
Hojalata y Lámina, S.A. (HYLSA), 226, 227
Hudson, Pat, 17 n. 50
Huerta, Victoriano, 28, 210, 211
Hulera Monterrey, 235
HYLSA. *See* Hojalata y Lámina, S.A.

Import and Export Commission (Comisión de Importaciones y Exportaciones), 201
import substitution
  causes, 6, 40, 42
  easy phase, 198, 245
  impact of Great Depression on, 107
  impact of World War II on, 87
  policies, 202, 223, 232
  See also Import Substitution Industrialization
Import Substitution Industrialization (ISI)
  causes, 5, 6–7, 169, 171
  definition, 5 n. 13
  links to economic nationalism, 192, 204, 246
  role in economic "miracle," 246–48
  uniqueness in Mexico, 7, 7 n. 20
income tax
  business opposition to, 32, 32 n. 33, 49
  and creation of central bank, 32
  exemption from, 76
  source of state revenue, 40
Independent Unions of Nuevo León, 217
indicative planning, 15, 113
  See also Commissariat Général du Plan
individualism, 189
  attacks on, 32, 34, 36–37, 54, 220–21
  and business chambers, 69, 92
  in labor relations, 29, 54, 60, 62, 67, 159, 217
  in Monterrey identity, 9, 206, 220–21, 228, 239
  See also laissez-faire growth; free trade; liberalism; property rights; *and* private enterprise
Industrial Affairs Office (Dirección General de Industrias), 76, 79
Industrial and Labor Convention for the Textile Sector (Convención Industrial y Obrera del Ramo Textil), 137–38
industrial research, 35, 125–26, 164, 237
  to counter market inefficiencies, 98 n. 8
  during Porfiriato, 50
  regional focus of, 46
  technocrats pursuit of, 16, 97–98, 114, 126–28, 156
  U.S. loans and aid, 183
Industrial Revolution in Mexico, 242, 242–43
industrialism, 4, 8, 20–22, 94, 96–97, 168, 245, 248
  definition, 5

  See also statist industrialism *and* state economic intervention
Industrias Nuevas. *See* New Industries decree
Industry Protection Law, 1932 (Ley de Protección a la Industria, 1932), 81–82
Institute of Industrial Research, 237
Institutional Revolutionary Party (PRI; Partido Revolucionario Institucional)
  alliance with CANACINTRA and CTM, 4, 23, 171, 244
  authoritarianism of, 12, 14, 23, 246, 248, 248 n. 15
  on communism, 231
  crony capitalism and, 204
  and labor, 203, 229
  and Monterrey Group, 233, 239
  on nationalism, 3, 232
  on statist industrialism, 17, 204, 232, 248
Instituto Mexicano de Investigaciones Tecnológicas. *See* Mexican Institute for Technological Research
Instituto Tecnológico y de Estudios Superiores de Monterrey. *See* Monterrey Institute of Technology and Higher Education
intermediate goods, 39, 42
  protection for, 198, 223, 225, 226–27
  regional production of, 59, 226–27
internal colonialism, 14 n. 40, 125 n. 131
Internal Work Regulations (Reglamento Interior de Trabajo), 135
International Bank for Reconstruction and Development, 183
Intersecretarial Commission on Foreign Capital Investment Rules (Comisión Intersecretarial de Coordinación de Normas sobre Inversiones de Capital Extranjero), 183
ISI. *See* Import Substitution Industrialization

J. Cram y Compañía, 222
Jalisco
  class relations, 20, 54
  elites and planning, 49
  elites and state, 22, 55, 92, 244–45
  governors, 55, 66–67, 89–91
  industrial growth, 57–58, 87–88, 149
  labor relations, 10, 59–63, 66–67, 89
  regional business organizations, 67–75, 172
  regional identity, 59
  regional supplies and markets, 56–57
  small- and medium-sized production, 53–55, 65–66, 88
  tax exemptions, 81–84, 86
Jalisco Chamber of Commerce (Cámara de Comercio de Jalisco), 68
James, Daniel, 161 n. 120

JCCA. *See* Central Board of Conciliation and Arbitration
Jenkins, William O., 35–36, 143–44
Joint Review Convention for the Cotton Textile Industry (Convención Mixta Revisora de la Industria Textil del Algodón), 158–59
Junta Central de Conciliación y Arbitraje. *See* Central Board of Conciliation and Arbitration
Junta Regional Consultiva del Comercio y de la Industria. *See* Regional Consulting Board for Commerce and Industry

Keynes, John Maynard, 97, 115, 116, 120. *See also The General Theory of Employment, Interest and Money*
Knight, Alan, 12, 13, 27, 66 n. 47, 132, 144
Korean War, 148, 149, 197, 201

La Luz, 157
labor
  alliance with CANACINTRA and ruling party, 4, 23, 100–101, 130, 187, 190–92, 194–95, 204
  Central Board of Conciliation and Arbitration, 64, 67, 137–38, 218, 233
  economic planning and, 95–96, 109, 119–23
  on industrial protectionism, 37–38, 79, 186
  in Jalisco, 56, 59–61, 63–65, 89–92
  role in industrialism, 2, 4, 8
  Social Action, 54, 55–56, 89
  in textile industry, 133, 135–40
  See also corporatism; unions; class; class conflict; machinery, modern; labor laws; *and* labor conflicts
Labor Confederation of Jalisco (COJ; Confederación Obrera de Jalisco), 60, 62, 64, 65, 66
labor conflicts, 18
  during 1940s, 90, 94, 101–2, 187, 191, 237
  Central Board of Conciliation and Arbitration, 64, 67, 137–38, 218, 233
  impact on production, 122
  in Jalisco, 59, 60, 66
  in Monterrey, 215, 217–19, 233
  in Puebla, 131, 135–36, 138, 140–43, 165
labor laws
  federal, 62–65, 139–40, 212, 216–17
  role in industrial protectionism, 79
  state-level, 60, 137
Labor Unity Pact (Pacto de Unidad Obrera), 102
Laboratorio de Normas. *See* Standards Laboratory

laissez-faire growth, 7, 116, 117. *See also* free trade; liberalism; property rights; private enterprise; *and* individualism
Langton, John, 18 n. 56
Lavín, José Domingo
  on communism, 191
  conflicts with conservative business interests, 174, 191, 243
  on economic planning, 124, 126, 129
  and labor, 120–21
  response to Sanford Mosk, 243
Law on Chambers of Commerce, 1908 (Ley de Cámaras de Comercio, 1908), 68, 69
Law on Chambers of Commerce and Industry, 1936 (Ley de Cámaras de Comercio e Industria, 1936), 68–69, 145
Law on Chambers of Commerce and Industry, 1941 (Ley de las Cámaras de Comercio y de las de Industria, 1941), 67, 71–75
Law on Federal Executive Powers in Economic Matters (Ley sobre Atribuciones del Ejecutivo Federal en Materia Económica), 201
Law on Industrial Promotion, 1941, Jalisco (Ley de Fomento Industrial, 1941, Jalisco), 80–84
Law on Manufacturing Industries, 1941 (Ley de Industrias de Transformación, 1941), 75–79, 76 n. 85, 80–86, 195, 227
Law on the Promotion of Manufacturing Industries, 1946 (Ley de Fomento de Industrias de Transformación, 1946), 195
Legorreta, Agustín, 30, 32, 174
Legorreta, Luis, 173–74
Ley de Cámaras de Comercio, 1908. *See* Law on Chambers of Commerce, 1908
Ley de Cámaras de Comercio e Industria, 1936. *See* Law on Chambers of Commerce and Industry, 1936
Ley de Fomento de Industrias de Transformación, 1946. *See* Law on the Promotion of Manufacturing Industries, 1946
Ley de Fomento Industrial, 1941, Jalisco. *See* Law on Industrial Promotion, 1941, Jalisco
Ley de Industrias de Transformación, 1941. *See* Law on Manufacturing Industries, 1941
Ley de las Cámaras de Comercio y de las de Industria, 1941. *See* Law on Chambers of Commerce and Industry, 1941
Ley de Protección a la Industria, 1932. *See* Industry Protection Law, 1932
Ley sobre Atribuciones del Ejecutivo Federal en Materia Económica. *See* Law on Federal Executive Powers in Economic Matters
Ley Sobre Planeación General de la República. *See* National Law on General Planning

liberalism
  conflict with protectionism, 7, 23, 45, 96–97, 192–94, 220
  in mid-twentieth century, 23, 204
  Monterrey Group and COPARMEX opinion of, 35–37, 206, 224, 227
  and nationalism, 192–94, 239
  in nineteenth century, 4, 7, 26, 28
  and state economic intervention, 129, 206, 237
  technocrat opinion of, 26, 28, 36, 47
  See also laissez-faire growth; free trade; individualism; property rights; *and* private enterprise
Lobatón, Aurelio, 152
Lombardo Toledano, Vicente, 94, 113, 141, 190–91, 218, 234
Lomnitz-Adler, Claudio, 11 n. 27
Lyttelton, Adrian, 9, 13 n. 37, 207

machinery, modern
  to break collective contracts, 10, 22, 132, 155–57
  labor and, 158–61, 162, 168
  lack of, 139, 151–53, 152 n. 75, 166–67
  in Monterrey, 209, 225, 238
  state limits on imports of, 10, 132, 163–66, 168, 244
  tax exemptions for, 76, 81, 166
  textile industrialist pressure for, 153–54, 154 n. 86, 161–63, 167–68
  U.S. export controls on, 78, 129, 177–80
Madero, Francisco, 26, 28
Malinche complex, 1, 2 n. 3
manta, 150, 153, 164
Manufacturing Industries Affairs Office (Dirección General de Industrias de Transformación), 199
Márquez Colín, Graciela, 7, 40
Marshall Plan, 183–84, 187–88
Marxism
  and capitalism, 18
  intellectual influence on technocrats, 97, 115
  and interpretations of the state, 12, 14, 17
Maurer, Noel, 15, 16
El Mayorazgo, 152
McKinley tariff, 209
Messersmith, George, 181
Metepec, 133–34, 134 n. 5, 136, 152
Mexican-American Commission for Economic Cooperation, 177
Mexican-American Committee of Businessmen (Comité Mexico-Norteamericano de Hombres de Negocios), 246
Mexican-American Conference on Industrial Research, 173–74

Mexican Association of Catholic Youth, 92
Mexican Association of Roads (Asociación Mexicana de Caminos), 174
Mexican Communist Party (PCM; Partido Comunista Mexicano), 231, 234
Mexican Economic Planning Association (Asociación Mexicana de Planificación Económica), 113
Mexican Employers Association (COPARMEX; Confederación Patronal de la República Mexicana)
  conflict with CANACINTRA, 185, 190, 243
  on economic nationalism, 193
  on Federal Labor Law, 62, 216–17
  on industrial protectionism, 170, 188, 189
  and labor, 233, 238
  role in peso devaluation, 195, 228
  on state economic intervention, 112, 189, 201, 204, 220, 237
Mexican Industrial Center (CIM; Centro Industrial Mexicano), 134, 135, 137, 145
Mexican Institute for Technological Research (Instituto Mexicano de Investigaciones Tecnológicas), 127
Mexican National Manufacturing Confederation (Confederación Fabril Nacional Mexicana), 137
mexicanidad, 3–4, 17–18, 232, 241
Mexico City
  business chambers in, 67, 72–75, 100, 145, 170–75
  industrial concentration, 9, 58, 59, 85, 86, 99, 124–25, 198–99
  1940 election, 71, 99
  role in ruling party consolidation, 99, 99 n. 10, 170, 244, 245
  tax exemption legislation, 84, 225, 226
  urbanization, 108 n. 58, 94, 108–9, 108 n. 58
Mexico: The Struggle for Peace and Bread, 242
Meyer, Jean, 106 n. 45
mezclilla, 150, 153
migration, 19, 87
  foreign immigrants, 19, 56, 57–58, 65, 134, 208
  rural-to-urban, 5, 57, 65, 94, 108–9
Milberg, William, 7
Miner-Metalworkers Union, 217
"miracle," Mexican, 2, 170, 239, 242, 246
Miranda, Rafael, 146
MITI, 15
El Molino de Enmedio, 152
Monterrey
  alternative power center, 23, 207, 223–24, 232, 245

Monterrey (*continued*)
   industry, 88, 125, 210, 223, 226
   location, 207–9, 213
   "moral capital," 9, 207, 213, 239–40
   1940 election, 99
   urbanization, 171 n. 9
   See also Monterrey Group
Monterrey Group
   on class harmony, 214–15, 219, 236
   conflicts with CANACINTRA, 191, 233
   and COPARMEX, 216
   on Federal Labor Law, 62
   on industrial protection, 35, 36, 220–21
   and labor, 214, 217–18, 234, 236–37
   and National Action Party, 229–30
   and President Alemán, 231–33
   and President Cárdenas, 217–18
   regional identity of, 206, 213, 214
   role in National Prosperity Campaign, 212–13
   and ruling party, 9, 23, 205–6
   on state economic intervention, 212, 220, 228
Monterrey Institute of Technology and Higher Education (Instituto Tecnológico y de Estudios Superiores de Monterrey), 237
Montes de Oca, Luis, 174 n. 17
Montgomery, David, 160, 161
"moral capital," 9, 207, 239, 245
Morales Sánchez, Gregorio, 218–19
Morones, Luis N., 33, 61, 131, 141
Morones Prieto, Ignacio, 232
Mosk, Sanford, 242, 242–43
Myrdal, Gunnar, 103

Nacional Distribuidora y Reguladora, 102
Nacional Financiera, S.A. (NAFINSA), 16, 86, 98, 164, 173, 173 n. 14
Nacional Textil Manufacturera, 84
NAFINSA. *See* Nacional Financiera, S.A.
National Action Party (PAN; Partido Acción Nacional), 70, 91–99, 219, 229–30, 244
National Association of Textile Industry Entrepreneurs, 145
National Autonomous University of Mexico (UNAM; Universidad Nacional Autónoma de México), 97
National Campesino Confederation (Confederación Nacional Campesina), 104
National Chamber of Commerce, Industry, and Mining of Jalisco (Cámara Nacional de Comercio, Industria, y Minería de Jalisco), 68
National Chamber of Manufacturing Industry (CANACINTRA; Cámara Nacional de la Industria de Transformación)
   alliance with CTM and ruling party, 4, 96, 100, 103, 131, 170–71, 185–87, 191–92, 204, 244
   on bias against small industry, 173–74
   on communism, 191
   conflicts with conservative business, 184, 190–91, 233
   on consumption, 1–2, 123–26
   on economic nationalism, 170–71, 185–86, 190, 193–94, 196
   on economic planning, 128, 129
   on foreign loans and investment, 182, 183, 247
   on "Hecho en México," 1
   intellectual influences, 120
   internal divisions, 172–75
   jurisdiction, 74 n. 78, 172
   and labor, 96, 119, 120–22, 123
   in Mexico City, 99, 100, 171–72
   and national populism, 96
   origins, 73–74, 97, 100
   on state economic intervention, 22, 95, 110, 117–19, 170, 201, 244
National Commission for Peace Planning (Comisión Nacional de Planeación para la Paz), 177
National Confederation of Popular Organizations (Confederación Nacional de Organizaciones Populares), 91
National Congress of Industrialists
   First National Congress of Industrialists (Primer Congreso Nacional de Industriales), 34
   Second National Congress of Industrialists (Segundo Congreso Nacional de Industriales), 63
National Consumption Week (Semana del Consumo Nacional), 213
National Council of Textile Industry Entrepreneurs (Consejo Nacional de Empresarios de la Industrial Textil), 159
National Council of the Economy (Consejo Nacional de Economía), 48, 112
National Economic Council (Consejo Nacional Económico), 46, 48
National Economics School (Escuela Nacional de Economía), 98
National Federation of Independent Unions, 236–37
National Industrial Planning Commission (Comisión Nacional de Planeación Industrial), 118
National Labor Council (Consejo Nacional Obrero), 102, 103
National Law on General Planning (Ley Sobre Planeación General de la República), 48, 49

National Proletarian Confederation (CPN; Confederación Nacional Proletaria), 190
National Prosperity Campaign (Campaña de Prosperidad Nacional), 212–13, 232
National Revolutionary Party (PNR; Partido Nacional Revolucionario)
  callismo and CROM in, 104, 131
  creation of, 25, 46, 70
  in regions, 90, 211
National Union of Industry and Commerce of Guadalajara (Unión Nacional de Industria y Comercio de Guadalajara), 68
National Unity (Unidad Nacional), 94, 102, 103, 187
nationalism, 18
  anti-U.S., 41, 78, 169–70, 184–85, 247
  and class collaboration, 170–71, 190
  economic nationalism, 30, 41, 76, 86, 170, 177, 184, 223
  and industrial protectionism, 4, 23, 170, 192–94, 204, 220, 244, 246
  and *mexicanidad*, 3–4
  Monterrey Group promotion of, 206, 212–13, 223, 239
  and regionalism, 9, 20–21, 48
  ruling party adoption of, 12, 14, 18, 23, 103, 195
  and statist industrialism, 2, 4, 13, 21, 170, 204, 232, 242, 245, 248
Nationalist Civic Action (Acción Cívica Nacionalista), 219
neo-*científicos*, 27
Nestlé, S.A., 82, 88
new economic history, 14, 15 n. 43
New Industries decree (Industrias Nuevas), 39
Nolan, Mary, 111 n. 69
Novoa, Carlos, 124
Nuevo León
  industry, 58, 58 n. 14, 88, 210, 220, 226
  ruling party in, 206, 217, 219

Obregón, Álvaro
  crony capitalism under, 25
  on economic planning, 46
  on industrial protectionism, 42, 43
  and labor, 38
  pursuit of state fiscal autonomy, 27, 31
  relations with business elites, 36, 37, 211
  on state economic intervention, 36, 37, 43
  U.S.-Mexican relations under, 30–31, 40–41
Office of Economic Research (OIE; Departamento (or Oficina) de Investigaciones Económicas), 97, 98, 109
Office of Industrial Research (OII; Oficina de Investigaciones Industriales)
  on agrarian reform and social change, 103, 106–7, 109–10
  on basic industry and regional production, 124, 125
  conservative opposition to, 115
  developmentalist currents in, 96
  intellectual influences, 111, 113, 115–16
  and labor, 95, 119–20, 122–23
  origins, 97–98
  pursuit of industrial research, 127–28, 164
  on rationalization and economic planning, 16, 98, 110, 114, 128–30, 243
  on state economic intervention, 15, 22, 95, 114, 119
  on underdevelopment, 116–17
Oficina de Investigaciones Industriales. *See* Office of Industrial Research
OIE. *See* Office of Economic Research
OII. *See* Office of Industrial Research
oil
  Bucareli Accords, 31
  conflicts with U.S., 26, 29–31, 34, 38, 41, 42, 177, 192
  labor, 187, 203
  state support for, 38, 76
  taxes, 32
Orozco, Soledad, 90
Ortiz Rubio, Pascual, 40

Pacto de Unidad Obrera. *See* Labor Unity Pact
Pacto Obrero-Patronal. *See* Worker-Employer Pact
Palazuelos, Leopoldo, 71
PAN. *See* National Action Party
Pani, Alberto
  and creation of central bank, 30–33
  on industrial protectionism, 36, 43–44
  relationship with business, 34, 49
  on state economic intervention, 28–29, 34, 47
  on taxes, 32, 49, 51 n. 106
Parra Gutiérrez, Manuel Germán, 242
Partido Acción Nacional. *See* National Action Party
Partido Comunista Mexicano. *See* Mexican Communist Party
Partido de la Revolución Mexicana. *See* Party of the Mexican Revolution
Partido Nacional Revolucionario. *See* National Revolutionary Party
Partido Revolucionario Institucional. *See* Institutional Revolutionary Party
Party of the Mexican Revolution (PRM; Partido de la Revolución Mexicana)
  creation, 70

Party of the Mexican Revolution (*continued*)
    and labor, 101
    legitimacy, 71, 79, 99
    political moderation of, 91
    relations with industrialists, 71, 73, 74, 103, 205–6, 230–31
Passananti, Thomas, 25 n. 5
paternalism, 5, 60, 63, 122, 238 n. 135, 245
    of CANACINTRA toward labor, 121
    in Monterrey labor relations, 9, 23, 206, 207, 213–15, 219, 229, 233, 236–37
    of technocrats toward labor, 8, 29, 109
    in textile industry, 132, 135, 159, 163
patria chica 20, 66
patronage, 70, 96, 120, 132, 134, 144
PCM. *See* Mexican Communist Party
Pellón Mediavilla, José, 167
Plan sexenal, 105, 112
PNR. *See* National Revolutionary Party
Portes Gil, Emilio, 49, 98, 138–39, 216
positivism, 55
    and labor, 60, 120
    during Porfiriato, 24, 126
    and technocrats, 8, 27–29, 95, 105
poverty, 27, 187, 246
    and agrarianism, 4–5, 105–7, 109
    and developmental nationalism, 192–94
    and Federal Labor Law, 216
    and industrialization, 110, 122, 174
    in Mexico City, 94, 108 n. 58
    and Mexico's national riches, 126
Prebisch, Raúl, 115
PRI. *See* Institutional Revolutionary Party
Prieto, Adolfo, 211
primary materials
    economic planning as way to manage use of, 48, 50, 111, 124–27, 199
    foreign markets, 6, 41, 187–89, 195
    production, 43, 149, 157, 160, 162, 222, 223
    protection of, 34, 39, 76–78, 80, 81, 186
    raw material supplies, 209
    raw material tax exemptions, 41, 42
    raw materials and industry, 125
    U.S. pressure to produce, 169, 176, 177, 179, 180, 185
    World War II supplies of, 176, 178, 196
Primer Congreso Nacional de Industriales. *See* National Congress of Industrialists
Primera Convención Nacional Bancaria. *See* First National Banking Convention
private enterprise, 69, 116
    attacks on rights of, 23, 46, 67, 92, 117
    and economic nationalism, 184–85
    and economic planning and policy, 51, 117
    opposition to attacks on, 55, 170, 206, 216, 220, 233, 239
    See also laissez-faire growth; individualism; free trade; liberalism; *and* property rights
PRM. *See* Party of the Mexican Revolution
Productos Químicos de San Cristóbal, 78
Pro-Economy Committee of Western Mexico (Comité Pro-Economía del Occidente de la República), 50
property rights
    attacks on rights of, 9, 34, 36, 220–21, 229, 235, 245
    defense of, 91, 228
    and liberalism, 189, 223–24
    in 1920s, 60
    during Porfiriato, 52
    See also laissez-faire growth; free trade; individualism; liberalism; *and* private enterprise
protectionism, 26, 28
in 1920s, 34–45
    conflict with liberalism, 7, 23, 192–94
    foreign opposition to, 179, 246
    and ISI, 5 n. 13, 203–4, 246–48
    in Jalisco, 47, 56, 65, 80–81, 83–84, 86
    liberal reaction to, 7, 36
    Monterrey Group role in, 23, 36–37, 206, 220–21, 226–28
    and nationalism, 4–5
    postwar growth of, 169–70, 186, 196–98, 247
    postwar reaction to, 181, 184, 187–90, 243
    and regionalism, 21
    of textile industry, 138–40, 146, 150–53, 155 n. 90, 167, 244
    See also tax exemptions; tariffs; regulation; *and* controls
Puebla
    business organizations in, 59, 75, 134, 144–45
    regional identity, 18
    statist industrialism in, 10, 22, 132, 167–68, 244
    textile industry in, 58, 132–34, 147–51, 210, 226
Puebla and Tlaxcala Chamber of the Textile Industry (Cámara de la Industria Textil de Puebla y Tlaxcala), 145
Puebla Chamber of Commerce (Cámara de Comercio de Puebla), 134

Quiroga, Pablo, 215–16

Radványi, László, 125, 125 n. 132, 130
Ramírez, Margarito, 60, 62, 81
Rangel Frías, Raúl, 232

rationalization
    intellectual movement, 7, 95, 110–14, 111 n. 69, 116, 119
    and OII, 16, 95, 109–16, 119, 129–30, 243
    popular groups opinion of, 103, 122, 161, 161 n. 20, 162, 164, 238
    and private enterprise, 117, 206 n. 4
    religious, 105, 106, 106 n. 45
    See also economic planning
raw materials. See primary materials
Razo, Armando, 15, 16
Reciprocal Trade Agreement (1942)
    abrogation, 197
    description, 176
    efforts to modify, 180–81, 195, 196
    industrialist reaction to, 150, 180, 185–86, 188, 189
    limits on Mexican trade, 101–2
    U.S.-Mexican relations, 175–77, 180
regional identity and alliances, 8, 18–21, 243–45, 248
    in Guadalajara, 10, 22, 54–55, 59, 62, 65–67, 87, 90–93
    in Monterrey, 9, 206–9, 214, 215, 219, 222, 228, 234, 239, 245
    in Puebla, 132–33, 140, 144
    industrial projects emerging from, 2, 16–17, 47, 52
Regional Confederation of Mexican Workers (CROM; Confederación Regional Obrera Mexicana)
    cromistas, 141
    and employers, 131
    on industrial protectionism, 186
    Labor Unity Pact, 102
    and Maximino Ávila Camacho, 142, 143
    on modern machinery, 156
    role in labor factionalism, 60–61, 140–41, 159, 190
Regional Consulting Board for Commerce and Industry (Junta Regional Consultiva del Comercio y de la Industria), 50
Regional Workers and Campesinos Federation (FROC; Federación Regional de Obreros y Campesinos), 140, 143, 159
regionalism
    and capitalist modernization, 18–19, 47
    challenges to by the state, 9, 11–13, 11 n. 27, 20, 32, 74–76
    and dependency theory, 14
    studies of, 11–13
    See also regional identity and alliances
Reglamento Interior de Trabajo. See Internal Work Regulations
regulation, state, 9, 95, 102, 193
    of banking, 32
    in economic planning, 48, 117
    enforcement, 20
    goals, 5, 181, 232
    of industrialist organizations, 22, 54–55, 68–69, 74
    opposition to, 23, 49, 147, 184–85, 189, 206, 212, 220, 228, 239, 245
    and rationalization, 110–11
    of trade, 181–82, 194–96, 199, 201–3
Reichskuratorium für Wirtschaftlichkeit, 113–14, 114 n. 82
reverse contraband, 2 n. 4
Reyes, Bernardo, 208, 222
Río Blanco, 135
Rio conference (1947), 176–77, 182
Rivero Quijano, Jesús, 69, 145
Rivero Quijano, José, 155
Robles, Gonzalo
    on agrarian reform, 106–7
    critique of U.S. views on Mexican industrialization, 184
    on economic planning, 95, 103, 109, 113, 129
    on industrial research, 127
    and labor, 122, 123
    and technocrats, 30, 95, 115
Rocha, Joel, 173–74, 212
Ruiz, Ramón, 224
Ruiz Galindo, Antonio, 2 n. 3, 124, 174, 178, 196

Sáenz, Aarón, 33, 174, 211
Sáenz, Josué, 192–93
Salinas Leal, Bonifacio, 228–29
Sanderson, Steven, 176
Sarro, Enrique, 173–74
Schumpeter, Joseph, 17, 115
scientific management, 111, 161, 168, 206, 206 n. 4, 215. See also Taylorism
scientific politics, 27–30
Second National Congress of Industrialists. See National Congress of Industrialists
Secretaría de Economía. See Secretariat of the Economy
Secretaría de Hacienda y Crédito Público. See Secretariat of the Treasury and Public Credit
Secretaría de Industria, Comercio, y Trabajo. See Secretariat of Industry, Commerce, and Labor
Secretaría de la Economía Nacional. See Secretariat of the National Economy
Secretaría de la Presidencia. See Secretariat of the Presidency
Secretaría del Trabajo y Previsión Social. See Secretariat of Labor and Social Welfare

Secretariat of Industry, Commerce, and Labor (SICT; Secretaría de Industria, Comercio, y Trabajo), 33, 43, 44, 49, 217
Secretariat of Labor and Social Welfare (STPS; Secretaría del Trabajo y Previsión Social), 79, 159
Secretariat of the Economy (Secretaría de Economía), 127, 128, 172, 197, 200
Secretariat of the National Economy (SEN; Secretaría de la Economía Nacional)
  and business chambers, 72, 74, 145
  role in economic planning, 48, 51, 52, 98
  role in industrial protectionism, 76, 77, 79, 80
Secretariat of the Presidency (Secretaría de la Presidencia), 16, 129, 129 n. 147
Secretariat of the Treasury and Public Credit (SHCP; Secretaría de Hacienda y Crédito Público)
  relations with business, 42, 228 n. 94
  role in economic planning, 16, 98, 129 n. 147
  role in industrial protectionism, 181, 197, 200, 222
  and tax exemptions, 76 n. 85, 77, 79, 128
Seghers, Anna, 125 n. 132
Segundo Congreso Nacional de Industriales. *See* National Congress of Industrialists
Segundo plan sexenal, 1941–1946, 112
Semana del Consumo Nacional. *See* National Consumption Week
SEN. *See* Secretariat of the National Economy
Serrano, Gustavo, 124, 173
Shadlen, Kenneth, 100
SHCP. *See* Secretariat of the Treasury and Public Credit
SICT. *See* Secretariat of Industry, Commerce, and Labor
Sierra, Justo, 28
Siller, Jerónimo, 50–51, 211
Silva Herzog, Jesús, 97–98
Snodgrass, Michael, 215
Social Darwinism, 120
Social Security, 101, 120, 157, 162, 167
Spanish Chamber of Commerce of Puebla (Cámara Española de Comercio de Puebla), 134
Special Joint Commission on the Modernization of the Cotton and Cotton Blends Textile Industry (Comisión Mixta Especial de Modernización de la Industria Textil del Algodón y sus Mixturas), 158
stabilizing growth, 14
Standards Laboratory (Laboratorio de Normas), 127
state economic intervention
  business organization opinion of, 69, 74
  and economic planning, 110, 112–18, 129
  growth in, 5, 6
  in Guadalajara, 70, 86, 92
  and liberalism, 7, 10
  limits on, 15, 16, 50–51
  Monterrey Group opinion, 23, 36, 206–7, 213, 221, 228–29, 233, 239–40, 245
  opposition to, 2, 8–9, 10, 17, 35, 36, 147, 189–90
  and revolutionary goals, 28–29, 204, 232
  staged development, 14
  and state consolidation, 26, 29, 33, 46, 52, 144
  support for, 4, 22, 95, 170, 184, 194
  tariffs, 39
  See also statist industrialism
statist industrialism, 30, 147, 199
  definition, 4–5, 11–13, 21–22, 228, 241–45
  and economic planning, 15–16, 93
  industrialist role in, 2, 9, 21–23, 119, 170–71, 175, 186, 204
  legacy, 245–46, 248
  in Mexico City, 4, 22
  Monterrey Group reaction, 9, 206–7, 212, 220, 239
  in Puebla, 22, 132, 167
  and regions, 11, 244
  and revolutionary goals, 3–4, 17–18, 232, 241–43
  See also state economic intervention
statolaters, 12, 13
STPS. *See* Secretariat of Labor and Social Welfare
structuralism, 4, 14, 190, 193–94, 220
  definition, 4 n. 11
  links to economic nationalism, 170, 244
  in origins of ISI, 6–7
Suárez, Eduardo, 53, 124, 146, 174 n. 17, 177, 178, 181
Suárez, Mariano, 238

Tannenbaum, Frank, 242
Tapetes Luxor, 199–200
Tariff Code (1930), 40–42, 212
tariffs
  definition, 169
  growth after World War II, 130, 180, 185–86, 193–99, 203–4
  legacy, 245
  Monterrey Group opinion and use of, 209, 212, 220–22, 226, 228
  and nationalism, 5, 244
  opposition to, 188
  Reciprocal Trade Agreement (1942), 176, 180, 185

and regulation, 202, 202 n. 146, 228
support for, 7, 118, 170–71, 184, 188–89, 193, 220–22
Tariff Code (1930), 40–42, 212
tariff commissions, 35, 42–45, 200–201
for textile industry, 10, 37, 133, 139, 139 n. 24, 150, 153–54, 244
U.S. reaction and impact, 169, 193–99, 247
Tarrow, Sidney, 20 n. 61
tax exemptions
application process, 128
bias in, 11, 100, 173
Decree No. 3564, Jalisco, 81, 82
federal, 38–39, 41, 75–81, 84–86
Industry Protection Law, 1932 (Ley de Protección a la Industria, 1932), 81–82
Law on Industrial Promotion, 1941, Jalisco (Ley de Fomento Industrial, 1941, Jalisco), 80–84
Law on Manufacturing Industries, 1941, (Ley de Industrias de Transformación, 1941), 75–79, 76 n. 85, 80–86, 195, 227
Law on the Promotion of Manufacturing Industries, 1946 (Ley de Fomento de Industrias de Transformación, 1946), 195
in Monterrey, 209, 221–28, 230, 232
state-level, 80–85, 89–90, 89 n. 138
and statist industrialism, 22, 54, 87, 92, 169, 194–95, 199
for textile industry, 133, 150, 166
Taylorism, 111, 161, 215. *See also* scientific management
technocrats, 5, 7, 21, 22, 43, 92
on agrarian reform and social change, 106, 109
in Banco de México, 33
on dependency, 169, 176, 178, 180, 184
on economic planning, 50, 95, 103, 109–16, 118, 125, 128–29, 243–44
on industrial protectionism, 76–77, 80, 84
intellectual life, 8, 15–16, 26–30, 33–34, 45, 51–52
and labor, 119, 120, 122–24
and President Calles, 35, 45–47
and ruling party, 91
and textile industry, 147–51
See also industrial research; Office of Industrial Research; economic planning; *and* rationalization
Técnica Industrial, 237
Tecnotex, 165
textile industry (in Puebla), 58, 132–34, 147–51, 210, 226
Thorp, Rosemary, 6
Topete, Everardo, 66, 82, 87

Torón, Luis, 127
Torres, Martín, 160
Torres Bodet, Jaime, 187–88
Torres Gaitán, Ricardo, 193
Toyoda de México, 165
Treviño, Gregorio, 224
El trimestre económico, 98, 116
trueques. *See* Compensated Exchange

UNAM. *See* National Autonomous University of Mexico
underdevelopment, 4 n. 11, 126, 184, 188, 190, 192, 194
unemployment, 61, 61 n. 27, 108, 120, 121, 157, 216
Unidad Nacional. *See* National Unity
Unión de Azucareros de Occidente. *See* Western Sugar Producers Union
Unión Nacional de Industria y Comercio de Guadalajara. *See* National Union of Industry and Commerce of Guadalajara
unions
employers unions/*sindicatos blancos*, 67, 67 n. 50, 216, 219, 233, 236–37
on industrial protectionism, 38, 186
in Jalisco, 60–61, 63, 66–67, 89–90
on modern machinery, 132, 151, 152 n. 75, 155–63, 167, 168
in Monterrey, 206, 215–20, 233–38
on National Unity, 102
in Puebla, 31, 136, 139–43, 168
state-backed, 10, 89–90, 132–33, 136–39
See also labor *and* labor conflicts
United Glass Workers Union, 218
United States
conflicts over oil and loans in 1920s, 26, 29, 30–32, 36–38, 40–41
conflicts over loans and trade after World War II, 129, 169, 180–86, 188–89
diplomatic pressure on Mexico, 25
economic nationalism directed at, 185, 192–94, 196–97, 200, 220, 247 n. 11, 247 n. 14
and Great Depression, 41, 61
independence from, 5, 41, 169, 177–82, 192–94
influence on Mexican production in 1940s, 77–78, 99, 127, 139, 148, 153–54, 166, 166 n. 140, 178–80
Mexico's dependence on, 16, 169, 178, 192–94, 203, 246
opinion of ISI, 246–47
role in Monterrey, 36, 208, 209
See also Reciprocal Trade Agreement
Universidad Nacional Autónoma de México. *See* National Autonomous University of Mexico

urbanization, 8, 19, 242, 246
   foreign immigration and, 57–58
   in Guadalajara, 57–58, 84, 87–89, 88 n. 134, 91
   in Mexico City, 99, 107–9, 108 n. 58, 125, 171, 199
   in Monterrey, 210
   rural-to-urban migration and, 5, 65, 134, 208
   social change and, 5
   urban labor force growth, 26, 96
Urquidi, Víctor, 76, 111–12, 115, 179, 181, 184
U.S. Board of Economic Warfare, 178
U.S. Council of Foreign Relations, 179
U.S. Foreign Economic Administration, 127
U.S. Metals and Minerals Procurement program, 127

Valores Industriales, S.A. (VISA), 220
Van Young, Eric, 18
vecindades, 108
Velázquez, Fidel, 94, 158, 165–66, 187
Veracruz, 84, 134–35, 137–38, 145, 153
Vidaurri, Santiago, 207–8
Vidriera de Monterrey, 217, 218, 219, 220, 233
Villa Michel, Primo, 47–48
Villaseñor, Eduardo, 97–98, 115, 123, 173
VISA. *See* Valores Industriales, S.A.
von Humboldt, Alexander, 126

Walker, David, 19
Wasserman, Mark, 47 n. 91
Weber, Max, 110, 113
Welles, Sumner, 176–77
Western Regional Chamber of Oils, Soaps, Fats, and Similar Products (Cámara Regional de la Industria de Aceites, Jabones, Grasas, y Similares de Occidente), 86
Western Sugar Producers Union (Unión de Azucareros de Occidente), 68
Williamson, Jeffrey, 7
Worker-Employer Pact (Pacto Obrero-Patronal), 187, 190–92
World War II
   economic planning during, 112, 114, 129–30, 228
   impact on economy and production, 87, 99, 101, 225, 226
   impact on textile industry, 146–49, 152–53, 164–66, 244
   and industrial protectionism, 76–79, 82–83
   labor problems during, 90, 94, 97, 101–3, 120, 157–58, 187
   in origins of ISI, 5–6
   trade during, 127, 169, 175–80, 184

Zuazua, Fortunato, 218–19
Zuno Hernández, José Guadalupe, 59–60, 62

www.ingramcontent.com/pod-product-compliance
Lightning Source LLC
Chambersburg PA
CBHW021356290426
44108CB00010B/262